The
SARASOTA,
SANIBEL ISLAND
& NAPLES
Book
A Complete Guide

Karen T. Bartlett

THE SARASOTA, SANIBEL ISLAND & NAPLES BOOK

A Complete Guide

A Revision of
The Gulf Coast of Florida Book

Written by
CHELLE KOSTER WALTON

Photography by
KAREN T. BARTLETT

Berkshire House Publishers
Lee, Massachusetts

On the Cover and Frontispiece: Photographs by Karen T. Bartlett
Front Cover: *Palm trees on Sanibel Island.*
Frontispiece: *A view of the beach at Lowdermilk Park, Naples.*
Back Cover: *Fisherman and snowy egret near Naples; marine education at Delnor-Wiggins State Recreation Area; sea-kayaking in Tarpon Bay, Sanibel Island.*

The Sarasota, Sanibel Island & Naples Book: A Complete Guide
Copyright © 1993, 1998 by Berkshire House Publishers
Cover and interior photographs © 1993, 1998 by Karen T. Bartlett and other credited sources

Library of Congress Cataloging-in-Publication Data

Walton, Chelle Koster.
    The Sarasota, Sanibel Island & Naples book : a complete guide / Chelle Koster Walton.
        p.   cm. — (The great destinations series, ISSN 1056-7968)
    Rev. ed. of: The Gulf Coast of Florida book. c1993.
    Includes bibliographical references and indexes.
    ISBN 0-936399-98-8
    1. Gulf Coast (Fla.)—Guidebooks. 2. Sarasota Region (Fla.)—Guidebooks. 3. Sanibel Island (Fla.)—Guidebooks. 4. Naples Region (Fla.)—Guidebooks. 5. Charlotte Harbor Region (Fla.)—Guidebooks. I. Walton, Chelle Koster, 1954- Gulf Coast of Florida book. II. Title. III. Series
    F317.G8W36   1998
    917.59′6—dc21   98-6938
                                            CIP

ISBN: 0-936399-98-8
ISSN: 1056-7968 (series)

Editor: Elizabeth Tinsley. Managing Editor: Philip Rich. Text design and typography: Dianne Pinkowitz. Cover design and typography: Jane McWhorter. Maps: Matt Paul/ Yankee Doodles.

Berkshire House books are available at substantial discounts for bulk purchases by corporations and other organizations for promotions and premiums. Special personalized editions can also be produced in large quantities. For more information, contact:

Berkshire House Publishers
480 Pleasant St., Suite 5, Lee, MA 01238
800-321-8526
E-mail: info@berkshirehouse.com
Website: www.berkshirehouse.com

Manufactured in the United States of America

10 9 8 7 6 5 4 3 2

The GREAT DESTINATIONS™ Series

The Berkshire Book: A Complete Guide
The Santa Fe & Taos Book: A Complete Guide
The Napa & Sonoma Book: A Complete Guide
The Chesapeake Bay Book: A Complete Guide
The Coast of Maine Book: A Complete Guide
The Adirondack Book: A Complete Guide
The Aspen Book: A Complete Guide
The Charleston, Savannah & Coastal Islands Book:
   A Complete Guide
The Newport & Narragansett Bay Book: A Complete Guide
The Hamptons Book: A Complete Guide
Wineries of the Eastern States
The Texas Hill Country: A Complete Guide
The Nantucket Book: A Complete Guide
The Sarasota, Sanibel Island & Naples Book: A Complete Guide
The Monterey, Big Sur & Gold Coast Wine Country Book:
   A Complete Guide

The Great Destinations™ series features regions in the United States rich in natural beauty and culture. Each Great Destinations™ guidebook reviews an extensive selection of lodgings, restaurants, cultural events, historic sites, shops, and recreational opportunities, and outlines the region's natural and social history. Written by resident authors, the guides are a resource for visitor and resident alike. All volumes include maps, photographs, directions to and around the region, lists of helpful phone numbers and addresses, and indexes.

To Gene and Theresa Koster,
who first instilled in me
a love for the road

Contents

CHAPTER ONE
Mangroves, Man, & Magnates
HISTORY
1

CHAPTER TWO
Blazing the Trail
TRANSPORTATION
28

CHAPTER THREE
Seashore Sophisticate
SARASOTA BAY COAST
40

CHAPTER FOUR
Wild and Watery
CHARLOTTE HARBOR COAST
114

CHAPTER FIVE
Sand, Shells, & Serenity
SANIBEL ISLAND & THE ISLAND COAST
145

CHAPTER SIX
Precious Commodities
NAPLES & THE SOUTH COAST
216

CHAPTER SEVEN
Practical Matters
INFORMATION
270

Acknowledgments

I can't list all of the people whose patience and understanding I counted on to see me through this project. First dibs on my gratitude must go to my husband, Rob, for not divorcing me, and my son, Aaron, who helped particularly with my beach and "kids' stuff" research. Thanks to Ron and Mindy Koster, who visited during my most intense stretch of writing-under-deadline, and managed to enjoy the Gulf Coast without me and with — thankfully — Aaron.

Special thanks to Prudy Taylor Board, who checked up on my historical facts and who will no doubt cringe at the pirate legends I couldn't bring myself to omit. Thanks to Ginny Papanicolas, who spent days on the phone doing final fact-checking.

I owe a debt of gratitude to several who helped me with my research: Nancy Hamilton and Lee Rose at the Lee County Visitor & Convention Bureau, Larry J. Marthaler at the Sarasota Convention & Visitors Bureau, Alexandra Owen at the Manatee County Convention & Visitors Bureau, and Beth Preddy at Visit Naples; also Melissa Speir, Bob and Hannah Spencer, Alisa Sundstrom Bennett, and Amy Bressler Drake.

Then there are the friends and fellow devoted diners who assisted with reviews and suggestions, including Patty Kitchen, Ginny Papanicolas, Jani Stone, Rob Walton, Beth Preddy, Alisa Sundstrom Bennett, and Bob and Hannah Spencer.

Thanks to photographer Karen Bartlett, who devoted extraordinary energy to the project, and to my supportive editors at Berkshire House: Elizabeth Tinsley and Philip Rich. You all helped me to extract the inherent agony of guidebook detail work and to make this book a joyful undertaking.

Introduction

Morning dawns like a boater's dream. The sky is clear except for a trace of last night's moon: wispy, like a wadded-up cloud. The water looks like cellophane stretched tight between Sanibel and Pine Islands. It is a morning to wonder why one ever does anything else on days off but return to the sea. On cue, a family of three dolphins pierces the surface with their fins and their smiles. The show has begun.

In the course of our leisurely, two-hour cruise between Sanibel Island and Boca Grande, we are entertained by leaping stingrays, a school of mackerel, and the usual dive-bomb squadron of brown pelicans.

At lights-out call — after lunch in a marina-side fish house, beach time on an unbridged island, and a duck-the-afternoon-rains cocktail at a historic island inn — nature's revue reaches its spectacular finale. In the moonless dark, the wake behind our boat sparkles like a watery fireworks display. The gulf has thrown an electric breaker switch. Liquid lightning strikes all around us as our 21-foot Mako powerboat parts the seas. White caps puff like nuclear popcorn.

Scientists call the phenomena *dinoflagellates*. Lay folks call the glowing organisms phosphorescence. Jamaicans call them sea-blinkies. The Ancient Mariner called them death-fires. I call their unpredictable visits to our summer waters magic: a topsy-turvy, ethereal feeling that someone — without warning — has transformed the sea into a starry sky.

Such a perfect day isn't required in order to appreciate fully the Gulf Coast of Florida, but such days do help to remind me why I moved here from long-john land more than 15 years ago. Like so many who constitute our hodge-podge population, I escaped, I loved, I dug in. I stayed for the exotic, warm quality of tropical nature. I remain because of the miracles I discover — and watch my young son discover — every day.

Chelle Koster Walton
Sanibel Island, Florida

THE WAY THIS BOOK WORKS

ORGANIZATION

The area bounded on the north by the Braden River and on the south by Ten Thousand Islands is often lumped under the heading Southwest Florida. Sometimes the Bradenton-Sarasota area is omitted from the region this heading defines, and grouped otherwise with Tampa as Central West Florida. For the purpose of this guide, it is included. The book often refers to the region covered as Gulf Coast Florida, or West Coast Florida, although it, of course, does not cover the entire coast. It does cover in depth the cities, towns, and communities from Bradenton-Sarasota in the north to Naples-Marco Island and the Everglades in the south.

I have sliced this delectable pie into four geographical region chapters, north to south: Sarasota Bay Coast, Charlotte Harbor Coast, Island Coast, and South Coast. Within these chapters, I scan under separate headings each region's lodging, dining, culture, recreation, and shopping.

Other chapters deal with the coastline's history as a whole, transportation, and nitty-gritty information.

A series of indexes at the back of the book provides easy access to information. The first, a standard index, lists entries and subjects in alphabetical order. Next, hotels, inns, and resorts are categorized by price. Restaurants are organized in two separate indexes: one by price, one by type of cuisine.

LIST OF MAPS

The Gulf Coast of Florida
Gulf Coast Access Maps
Sarasota Bay Coast
Charlotte Harbor Coast
Island Coast
South Coast

PRICES

Rather than give specific prices, this guide rates dining and lodging options within a range.

Lodging prices normally are based on per person/double occupancy for hotel rooms; per unit for efficiencies, apartments, cottages, suites, and villas. Price ranges reflect the difference in off-season and high season. Generally, the colder the weather up north, the higher the cost of accommodations along the coast. Rates can double during the course of a year. Many resorts offer off-season packages at special rates.

Pricing does not include the 6 percent Florida sales tax. Many large resorts add gratuities or maid charges. Some counties impose a tourist tax as well, proceeds from which are applied to beach and environmental maintenance.

If rates seem high for rooms on the Gulf Coast, it's partially because many resorts cater to families by providing kitchen facilities. Take into consideration what this could save you on dining bills. A star after the pricing designation indicates that accommodations include at least continental breakfast with the cost of lodging; a few offer the American Plan of serving all meals, which is then explained within the description copy.

Dining costs are calculated upon a typical meal (at dinner, unless dinner is not served) that would include an appetizer or dessert, salad (if included with the meal), entrée, and coffee. To save money at the more expensive restaurants, look in this guide to see which ones offer "early bird specials." Restaurants at some large resorts add gratuities to the tab. This is also customary for large parties at most restaurants, so check your bill carefully before leaving a tip. Satisfied diners are expected to tip between 15 and 20 percent.

Heavy state taxes on liquor served in-house can mount up a drinking tab quickly. Paying as you drink is a wise measure to prevent sticker shock.

PRICE CODES

	Lodging	**Dining**
Inexpensive	Up to $50	Up to $15
Moderate	$50 to $110	$15 to $25
Expensive	$110 to $180	$25 to $35
Very Expensive	$180 and up	$35 or more

The following abbreviations are used for credit card information:

AE - American Express
CB - Carte Blanche
D - Discover Card

DC - Diners Card
MC - MasterCard
V - Visa

AREA CODE

One area code covers the entire realm of this book: 941. Numbers prefixed with 800 or 888 are toll free.

TOURIST INFORMATION

Local visitors' bureaus, tourism development councils, and chambers of commerce are adept at the dissemination of materials and information about their area. These are listed in Chapter Seven, *Information*.

For information on the entire region and other parts of Florida, contact Visit Florida, 661 E. Jefferson St., Suite 300, Tallahasee, FL 32301; 800-7FLA-USA; www.flausa.com.

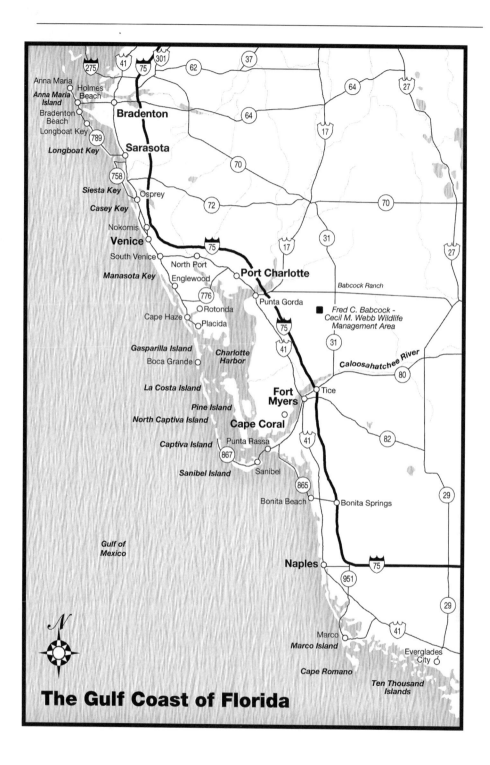

The Gulf Coast of Florida

CHAPTER ONE
Mangroves, Man, & Magnates
HISTORY

Once an Indian trading post, Smallwood's Store today serves as a museum in the secluded Everglades outpost of Chokoloskee Island.

The essence of Gulf Coast Florida seems to lie in a balance between polar extremes: the ultimate both in natural wilderness and in social civility. To understand the region and the richness of its heritage, culture, and environment, one must understand its roots, learn the names, and revel in the legends of its past — a past steeped in romance, adventure, and power.

The story begins with a single mangrove tree and evolves around man's need to conquer that tree's primeval world. Enter the characters: Ambition, Wealth, and Social Grace. How does the story end? Happily, we can hope, with the modern rediscovery of the coast's unique natural and historical heritage.

NATURAL HISTORY

FROM GRAINS OF SAND

"Each wave helps build a ridge of accumulating sand and shell that runs roughly parallel to the beach. Over a period of hundreds or thousands of years, a ridge may become a barrier island."

—Lynn Stone, Voyageurs Series, *Sanibel Island,* 1991

"On the floor is a straw mat. Under the mat is a layer of sand that has been tracked into the cottage and has sifted through the straw. I have thought some of taking the mat up and sweeping the sand into a pile and removing it, but have decided against it. This is the way keys form, apparently, and I have no particular reason to interfere."

—E. B. White, *On a Florida Key,* 1941

Billions of years ago, the Florida peninsula existed only as a scattering of volcanic keys, akin to the Caribbean islands. The passing years, silt, and the sea's power eventually buried all evidence of these volcanic origins. What is now Florida remained submerged until some 20 million years ago, when matter buildup brought land to the surface in the form of new islands.

Ice Age sea fluctuations molded Florida into solid land, and islands continued to grow along its fringes. From a single grain of sand or mangrove sprout they stabilized into masses of sand and forests composed of leggy roots and finger shoots. As shells and marine encrustations accumulated, islands fell into formation along the Gulf Coast, protecting it from the battering of a storm-driven sea. In the gaps between the islands, the gulf's waters scoured the shore to forge inlets, estuaries, bayous, creeks, and rivers. The sea chiseled a mottled, labyrinthian shoreline that kept the southern Gulf Coast a secret while the rest of the state was being tamed.

During its infancy, the region hosted a slow parade of ever-changing creatures. In prehistoric graveyards modern archaeologists have found mummified remains of rhinoceroses, crocodiles, llamas, camels, pygmy horses, saber-toothed tigers, mastodons, and great woolly mammoths — Florida's first winter visitors at the advent of the Ice Age. Another era brought giant armadillos, tapirs, and other South American creatures. Fauna and flora from these ancient eras survive today: cabbage palms (the state tree), saw palmettos, garfish, seahorses, horseshoe crabs, alligators, manatees, armadillos, and loggerhead sea turtles.

THE MIRACLE OF THE MANGROVE

The mangrove forest is both a fertile incubator and a marine graveyard, the home of an island construction crew and a vegetative ballet troupe. It is a self-sustaining world marked by vivid contrasts. The Mangrove Coast (as one local historian terms it) is fringed by red, black, and white species of the tree. Red mangroves strut along coastlines, canals, and island leesides on graceful prop roots. At least they look graceful until low tide reveals the oysters, barnacles, and tiny marine metropolises that weigh them down and keep them connected to the sea.

Farther inland, black and white mangroves create thick, impenetrable forests that buffer waves, filter pollutants, send out shoots, and always busily build. Encrustations of shellfish grab algae, silt, and sand, creating rich soil out of decaying material. Fish, crabs, and mollusks skitter among the roots, nibbling dinner, depositing eggs, and tending to their young. Birds rest and nest in the mangroves' scraggly branches, ready to dive for the fish on which they feed. Mother trees send their tubular offspring bobbing upon sea currents to find a foothold elsewhere and begin, perhaps, a new island.

The cycle is ancient and ongoing, threatened only by the chain saws of developers. A few decades ago these natural builders were leveled in favor of cement seawalls. Strict regulations prohibit mangrove destruction today. The crucial role of the mangrove in the survival of Florida's sea life finally has been realized. And cherished.

AN EARLY PICTURE

"In the bay of Juan Ponce De Leon, in the west side of the land, we meet with innumerable small islands, and several fresh streams: the land in general is drowned mangrove swamp.... From this place [Cape Romano, latitude 25:43] to latitude 26:30 are many inconsiderable inlets, all carefully laid down in the chart, here is Carlos Bay, and the Coloosa Hatchee, or Coloosa river, with the island San Ybell, where we find the southern entrance of Charlotte harbour...."

—Bernard Romans, 1775

One of the earliest recorders of Florida native life and topography, Bernard Romans is credited with naming Charlotte Harbor after the queen of England, his adopted homeland, and Cape Romano after himself. Native Americans and earlier Spanish explorers are responsible for other regional place names.

The harbor was already the center of west coast life when the first explorers discovered it. Its deep waters and barrier-island protection made it most suitable to early aborigines and their predecessors by creating a pocket of unusually mild climate.

Romans and his contemporaries found the Gulf Coast alive with wild turkeys, black bears, deer, golden panthers, bobcats, possums, raccoons, alligators, otters, lizards, and snakes. Wild boars and scrub cattle roamed freely, descendants of stock brought by Spanish missionaries. Birds and waterfowl of all varieties filled the skies and back bays, some permanent, some migratory. Majestic ospreys and bald eagles swooped; kites soared effortlessly; sandhill cranes dotted the coun-

Creatures of the sky, sea, and land first populated southwest Florida.

Karen T. Bartlett

tryside; wood storks nested; pelicans came in colors of brown and white; gulls, terns, and sandpipers patrolled seashores; cormorants, ducks, anhingas, ibises, egrets, roseate spoonbills, and herons fed among the mangroves.

Marine life flourished. Manatees cleared waterways, dolphins frolicked in the waves, and mullet burst from bay waters like cannonshot. Tarpon, rays, snapper, snook, flounder, ladyfish, and mackerel churned the otherwise calm backwaters. Grouper, triple tail, tuna, and shark lurked in deep waters offshore.

On land, a wide variety of vegetation abounded. Sea grapes, mahoes, sea oats, nickerbean, and railroad vine anchored sandy coasts. Thick, impenetrable jungle clogged inland areas. Cabbage palms and gumbo-limbo trees stood tall. Papayas, native to the region, flourished along with indigenous flowering shrubs. In hardwood forests, pines climbed skyward and live oaks wore their eerie veils of Spanish moss. Cedars fringed islands along the Sarasota Bay coast. Ferns and grasses carpeted the marshes. Swamplands were home to great cypress trees with bony knees and armfuls of parasitic plants: mistletoe, orchids, bromeliads, and epiphytes.

Primeval and teeming, Florida held an exotic and mysterious aura. The swamp nurtured all of life, from the Everglades upward along the lowlands of the Gulf Coast. It was a perfect ecosystem, designed by nature to withstand all forces — except man.

FACELIFTS AND IMPLANTS

With the arrival of the first settlers, the natural balance that existed along the Gulf Coast began to tilt. The Spanish brought citrus seedlings and livestock. Naturalists and growers introduced specimens from the north and south: mangoes, avocados, bougainvillea, hibiscus, frangipani, coconut palms, pineapples, sapodillas, tomatoes, and legumes. For the most part these exotics proved harmless to the fragile environment.

Three nonnative plants brought to the area in the past century have, however, harmed the ecosystem and changed the land's profile. The prolific *Melaleuca* tree (or cajeput), casuarina (Australian pine), and Brazilian pepper choke out the native vegetation upon which wildlife feed, and harm both man and property. Many communities are attempting to eradicate these noxious plants, especially the pepper tree.

The complexion of the west coast was further changed by dredging and plowing. In times when swampland was equated with slimy monsters and slick realtors, developers and governments thought nothing of filling it in to create more buildable land. This, too, threw the ecosystem off balance. Fortunately, such mistakes were realized before their effects became irreversible. Today government strives to preserve, and even restore, the delicate balance of the wetlands.

SOCIAL HISTORY

DATELINE: GULF COAST FLORIDA

The modern settlement of Florida's southwest coast can be traced like a dateline that begins on the shores of Sarasota Bay in 1841 and ends at Naples in 1887. At first glance this time frame makes the region look young, without the gracious patina of age and the wrinkles of an interesting past. Common is the belief, in fact, that the Gulf Coast has no history because it lacks Williamsburg's colonial homes or Philadelphia's monuments.

True, the Gulf Coast's early pioneers left no standing architecture. Termites, flimsy building styles, erosion, and tropical storms saw to that. But earlier settlers did leave other proof of their existence, artifacts that date as far back as 10,000 years. If that isn't history, what is?

CALUSA KINGDOM

Archaeologists of this century have discovered remnants of early architecture and lifeways in the shell mounds of the Calusa and Timucua tribes, who settled the coastlines more than 2,500 years ago. The Timucua inhabited the Sarasota Bay coast for many years and then migrated northward; the

Calusa later moved into the area around Sarasota and were centered around Charlotte Harbor.

Evidence of earlier civilizations has been found, placing Florida's first immigrants, possibly from Asia, in the upper coast regions circa 8200 B.C. Little is known about these early arrivals except that they used pointed spears.

Archaeological excavations and the writings of Spanish explorers give us a more complete picture of the Calusa and other tribes who built shell mounds to bury their dead and debris. Popular consensus brings the Calusa and the Timucua to southern Florida from the Caribbean islands; evidence of similar lifestyles and sustained contact suggests a connection to the peaceful Arawak Indians of the West Indies. Similarities have also been found between the Calusa and South American tribes, leading some historians to consider Florida's tribes to be wayward relatives of the Mayans or Aztecs, given evidence of their great engineering skills. Others trace the connections to trade rather than origin.

The name Calusa, or Caloosa, was used first by Spanish conquerors, who understood the name of the tribe's chief to be Calos. They were said to be heavyset people with hip-length hair, which men wore in a topknot. When clothed, men dressed in breeches of deerskin or woven palmetto fiber, and women fashioned garments out of Spanish moss. They cultivated corn, pumpkins, squash, and tobacco; fished for mullet and mackerel with harpoons and palmetto-fiber nets; hunted for turkey, deer, and bear with bow and arrow, deer-bone dirks, and Aztec-style weapons; and harvested wild sea grapes, fruit, yams, swamp cabbage (hearts of palm), and the coontie root, out of which they pounded flour for bread. Conchs and whelks were crafted into tools for cooking and raw materials for building. The natives spent leisure time wrestling, celebrating the corn harvest, and worshiping the sun god.

Great men of the sea, the Calusa built canoes and traveled in them to Caribbean islands and the Yucatán. A different style of pirogue took them along riverways and bay waters to visit villages of their own tribe and those of other Nations.

Much of our information about Calusa ways comes from the son of a Spanish official stationed in Cartagena, in what is now Colombia. The youngster, Hernando de Escalante Fontaneda, was shipwrecked along Calusa shores en route to Spain. He lived among the tribe for 17 years, learned its language, and, upon returning to Spain in 1574, recorded its customs.

Frank Hamilton Cushing explored Charlotte Harbor in 1895. He surmised that the Calusa's religious structures and palmetto homes on pilings had perched on shell mounds along riverbanks and coastlines. Terraces and steps bit into the towering mounds where gardens and courts had been built. Manmade canals up to 30 feet wide connected neighboring villages.

Excavations along the Gulf Coast continually provide new information about the region's native inhabitants and their symbiotic relationship with nature.

SPANISH IMPOSITION

Early Florida explorers encountered savage beauty on Gulf Coast shores.

Karen T. Bartlett

Greed and religious fervor eventually warped this idyllic picture, and peaceful fishermen became vicious warriors in order to preserve the life they knew. Juan Ponce de León first crashed the party in 1513, although it's possible that early slavers from the Caribbean were responsible for the Calusa hostility he encountered. Perhaps, however, the Amerindians' early hatred of the conquistadores was gained secondhand, from trading with island natives. Whatever the reason, Ponce was "blacklisted" by the Calusa shortly after he began his search, according to legend, for Bimini, a storied land of treasure and youth.

Ponce de León made his first landing on Florida's east coast. This celebrated Eastertime event went off without a hitch, and the conqueror named the land after the Spanish holiday *Pascua Florida*. However, his second landing, days later, was met by shell-tipped spears and bows and arrows. His three wounded sailors were the first Europeans known to shed blood in Florida. Ponce de León's ship continued to the west coast, where it stopped in the vicinity of Marco Island. Here one native astounded him by speaking to him in Spanish — learned, perhaps, from West Indies contacts. Impressed, Ponce de León allowed his party to be tricked by a marauding native army in canoes but escaped with the loss of only one man's life.

Live reenactments demonstrate the conquistadores' way of life at De Soto National Memorial Park.

Karen T. Bartlett

The next stop for the explorer was an island the Spaniards named Matanza ("slaughter") for the profusely bloody battles they fought there. Still treasureless and now middle-aged, Ponce de León returned to Puerto Rico to plot a new scheme. In 1521 he set out to establish a Gulf Coast colony as a base for treasure explorations. This time the party he crashed had been forewarned, perhaps by smoke signals. Calusa arrows pierced the heavy armor of the Spaniards, killing and wounding many, including the great seeker of youth himself. Returned to Havana for medical attention, Ponce de León died there at the age of 60.

Lust for gold overcame common sense as more explorers and invaders followed in Ponce de León's tragic footsteps. In 1539 Hernando de Soto sailed from Havana and headed up the Gulf Coast seeking, it would seem, a way to confuse future historians. Three different crew members described the expedition three different ways. The Smithsonian Institution has published a report some locals still dispute, which claims that de Soto landed first on Longboat Key and then, looking for fresh water, headed toward Tampa Bay. Others are convinced his first landfall was at Fort Myers Beach. De Soto set up his first mainland camp, according to the Smithsonian, at an abandoned native village at the mouth of the Manatee River, near modern-day Bradenton. Regardless of where the landing took place, we know that de Soto scoured the coast for gold, all the while torturing and killing native Americans who would not, or could not, lead him to it.

Sarasota and its environs embrace the Smithsonian study's findings. Some say the name of the town itself, initially written as "Sara Sota," comes from the conqueror. Others prefer a more romantic legend regarding his fictional daughter, Sara. Sarasota's first hotel, in any case, took its name from de Soto. Near Bradenton, a small national park marks the alleged spot of his first landing.

Legend has it that early conquistadores wrote letters and plotted maps on the leathery leaves of the native sea grape.

Karen T. Bartlett

In 1565 Pedro Menendez de Aviles came to the Gulf Coast, searching for a son lost to shipwreck and a group of Spaniards being held captive by the Calusa. With the aid of one of Chief Calos's Spanish captives he befriended Calos with flattery and gifts, then built a fort and a mission at a spot called San Anton, believed to have been on Pine Island. But Menendez insulted the great chieftain by rejecting his sister as a wife and allying himself with enemy tribes. Sensing Calos's anger, Menendez tricked the leader into captivity and had him beheaded. When Menendez later executed Calos's son and heir to the throne, along with 11 of his subchiefs, tribesmen burned their own villages, forcing the settlers to bail out in search of food.

The century that followed is considered the Golden Age of the Calusa. It was marked by freedom from European intrusion and great cultural advances, heightened by the input of Spanish captives who had refused to be saved by Menendez's rescue party and others who found Calusa ways preferable to "civilization."

Eventually, peaceful trading softened the hostility between Spanish settlers and the Calusa. Cuban immigrants began building a fishing industry around Charlotte Harbor.

The Calusa had won the war against Spanish invaders but were defenseless against the diseases the Europeans brought with them. By the turn of the 19th century, smallpox and other diseases had killed off most of them; the others were absorbed by inbreeding with the Cubans and newly arriving tribes. The most prominent of the latter were the Seminoles, a mixture of Georgian Creek, African, and Spanish bloodlines. The Calusa hold the distinction of being the last tribe to make peace with the U.S. government.

THE VARMINT ERA

"**A** haunt of the picaroons of all nations," wrote explorer James Grant Forbes in 1772. He spoke of Charlotte Harbor: layover, if not home, for every scoundrel who sailed its island-clotted waters. The Gulf Coast's maze of forbidding bayous and barely navigable waterways made it a favorite hideout for escaped criminals, bootleggers, government refugees, smugglers, and — that favorite of all local folk characters — the buccaneer.

Pirate legends color the pages of local history books in shades of blood red and doubloon gold. Besides willing to residents a certain cavalier spirit, these pirates have left, if one believes the tales, millions of dollars in buried treasure. "After researching the subject in 1950 . . . then State Attorney General Ralph E. Odum estimated that some $165 million is still buried beneath Florida's sands and waters," reports a 1978 issue of *Miami Herald's Florida Almanac*, "$30 million of it originally the property of Jose Gaspar."

Besides the mostly mythical Gaspar, other picaresque names resound along the Gulf Coast: Jean La Fitte, of New Orleans fame; Bru Baker, Gaspar's Pine Island cohort; and a dark soul named Black Caesar, who headed Gaspar's Sanibel Island contingent. Henry Castor supposedly buried treasure on Egmont Key in the mid-1700s. Local legend places the notorious Calico Jack Rackham and his pirate lover, Anne Bonny, on the shores of Fort Myers Beach for a playful honeymoon. Black Augustus lived and died a hermit on Mound Key, to the south. On Panther Key John Gomez, Gaspar's self-proclaimed cabin boy, lived to be 122 and sold maps leading to Gasparillan gold to many a gullible treasure hunter.

According to more reliable historical records, island pirate havens were replaced by, or coexisted with, crude Spanish fishing *ranchos*, which cropped up as early as the 1600s. The camps provided Cuban traders with salted mullet and roe to eat. They consisted of thatched shacks, some built on pilings in shallow waters, where families lived, according to customs inspector Henry B. Crews, "in a state of Savage Barbarism with no associate but the Seminole Indians and the lowest class of refugee Spaniards who from crime have most generally been compelled to abandon the haunts of civilized life."

Ice-making and railroads changed the direction of fish exportation from southern points to northern destinations. Punta Gorda, with the area's first railroad station, became the center for the shipment of fresh fish. Major fish-shipping companies built stilt houses for the more than 200 men who harvested their mullet crops. These structures straddled shallows from Charlotte Harbor to Ten Thousand Islands, providing homes for the fishermen and their families until the late 1930s, when modern roads and the burning of Punta Gorda's Long Dock brought the era to a close. Less than a dozen of the historic fish shacks have survived hurricanes, erosion, and the state's determination to tear them down as a public nuisance. They strut the shallows of Charlotte Harbor, in greatest concentration off the shore of Upper Captiva Island.

"It is highly important that no person should be permitted to settle on the Islands forming 'Charlotte Harbor'... which are of no value for the purpose of agriculture, being in general formed of sand and shells," advised Assistant Adjutant General Captain Lorenzo Thomas in 1844.

Nonetheless, out of this era of varmints sprouted a tradition of farming. Coconuts, citrus, tomatoes, and other crops were raised, despite hardship and heartbreak, as plucky pioneers trickled in to coax their livelihood from a hostile environment.

Kingdom of Gasparilla

Of all the rum-chugging and throat-slashing visitors to have set foot upon southwest Florida's tolerant shores, Jose Gaspar (known by the more properly pirate-sounding name "Gasparilla") is the one remembered most fondly. Gaspar set up headquarters, it is said, on Gasparilla Island, where Boca Grande now sits. In his time it was called High Town. He built a palmetto palace there and furnished it with the finest booty. Low Town he placed on a separate island, so as to distance himself from the crude lifestyles of his rowdy shipmates. On Cayo Costa stood Gasparilla's fort.

Legends say Gasparilla got his start as a pirate after some nasty business with the wife of a crown prince. He gave up his cushy position as admiral of the Spanish navy for the hardships of life at sea and in the jungles of late-19th-century Florida.

His address might have changed, but his love of beautiful women did not. He kidnapped the loveliest and wealthiest of them from captured ships and whisked them off to another Gulf Coast island named for its inhabitants — Captiva — until ransom money arrived.

Gasparilla took to High Town the most beautiful of his captives, to woo them with fine wines, jewels, and Spanish poetry. One object of his affection, a Mexican princess named Josefa, would have nothing to do with such a barbarian. Finally, driven to madness by her insults, Gasparilla beheaded his beloved. He carried her body to another key in his island fiefdom, where he buried her with remorse and sand. He named the island Josefa, which, through the years and the twistings of rum-swollen tongues, has been perverted to Useppa. And so the exclusive island is called today.

Nearby Sanibel Island, according to one legend, got its name from the abandoned lover of Gaspar's gunner. However, variations abound and improve with each telling. The legend began with the ramblings of old "Panther Key John" Gomez and was perpetuated by railroad press agents and optimistic treasure hunters.

Serious historians doubt the existence of a man named Gasparilla but agree that one of the many Gulf Coast pirates may have borrowed the island's name. Others hold tenaciously to the legend, plying coastal sands with shovels and dredges in search of his ill-gotten booty.

YEARS OF DISCONTENT

The bloody years of the Wars of Indian Removal began in 1821, when Andrew Jackson, then governor of the territory, decided to claim northern Florida from the Seminole tribes that were wreaking havoc on American settlers. By 1837 fighting had spread to the southern reaches of the peninsula, and two forts were built upriver from present-day Fort Myers. The following year the government reached an agreement with the Seminoles, restricting them to mainland areas along the Charlotte Harbor Coast, Caloosahatchee River, and southward.

News of imminent peace prompted Josiah Gates to build a hotel on the banks of the Manatee River, near modern-day Bradenton, in anticipation of the influx of settlers from Fort Brooke (Tampa) that the treaty would bring. A modest community rose up around this precursor of Gulf Coast resorts. Families of soldiers and wealthy southern planters settled in the area. The latter brought their slaves and built sugarcane plantations on vast expanses of land that they bought for $1.25 an acre.

Sarasota got its first permanent settler in 1842. William Whitaker, a fisherman, built his home on Yellow Bluffs, overlooking Sarasota Bay. He and his new wife, daughter of one of the Manatee planters, had 10 children and later went into cattle ranching and farming.

The story of Chief Billy Bowlegs finds an audience along Venice's main thoroughfare.

Karen T. Bartlett

The year after the peace treaty was signed, a tribe of Seminoles attacked a settlement across the river from their village, on the same site as present-day Fort Myers. The Harney Point Massacre rekindled the war. Fort Harvie was built near the site of the violent attack. Chief Billy Bowlegs led his people in evasive tactics through the wild and mysterious Everglades, but by 1842 the government had captured 230 of his people and shipped them west. Further pursuit was abandoned. Only Fort Harvie and one other fortification remained operational. A new agreement contained the Seminoles along the Caloosahatchee and barred them from the islands, to protect the fishermen and their families. The treaty made no mention of the swampland, probably because the government considered it useless; the Seminoles assumed the territory was theirs.

By 1848, three years after Florida's admission to the Union as the 27th state, there was a surge of interest in the wetlands. The government, envisioning drainage projects to create more land, offered the Seminoles $250 each to relocate in the West. When they refused, a systematic plan to conquer them went into effect.

The plan included the repair of Fort Harvie , which was renamed Fort Myers after a U.S. colonel who had served for many years in Florida and was engaged to the commanding general's daughter. Manpower was increased there, and the fort was reinforced and enlarged. Scouting parties stalked the Seminoles but usually found only the remains of abandoned and burned villages.

In December 1855, after soldiers destroyed Billy Bowlegs's prize banana patch, he and his people retaliated. Fort Myers became the center of war activity. The government placed a bounty on the head of any Seminole brought to the fort and offered $1,000 to each Seminole warrior ($100 to each woman and child) who agreed to leave the area. Finally, in 1858, after soldiers had captured his granddaughter and other women of the tribe, Billy Bowlegs capitulated, thus bringing an end to 37 years of killing and deception. Fort Myers was abandoned, and the remaining Seminoles dispersed deep into the Everglades. White farmers, planters, fishermen, and cattlemen continued peacefully in their trades, although government vigilance against alliances with the Seminoles forced some of the *ranchos* to close during the war's final years. Today the Seminoles live on reservations, earning an income from tourism, fishing, and a casino.

In the late 1850s, Virginia planter Captain James Evans bought Fort Myers on the auction block. He brought his slaves to work the crops he envisioned — tropical fruits, coconut palms, coffee, and other exotic plants. The Civil War interrupted this venture, sending him back to his home. Florida joined the Confederacy in 1861. West coast inhabitants generally remained uninvolved until a federal blockade at Key West cut off supplies, at which point they turned to the profitable business of blockade running.

CATTLE KINGS, CARPETBAGGERS, AND CRACKERS

Jacob Summerlin epitomized the Florida cattle king. He dressed in a cowboy hat, leather boots, a beard, and trail dust. Having established a steady trade between Florida and ports south before the Civil War, Summerlin was in a good position to provide the Confederate Army with contraband beef. Working with his blockade-running partner, James McKay, Sr., he drove his

The elements — not Yankee soldiers — reduced Braden Castle, the Tara of the Gulf Coast, to romantic ruins.

cattle from inland Florida to Punta Rassa, where the causeway from Sanibel Island makes landfall today. There he sold his scrub cattle, descendants of live-stock left by the early Spaniards. The U.S. Navy eventually learned of these illegal dealings and stationed boats at Sanibel and Punta Rassa. In spite of this attempt to interrupt their trade, however, Summerlin and McKay sold 25,000 steers to the Confederates between 1861 and 1865.

Jacob Summerlin lived by the seat of his pants, driving cattle to Punta Rassa and collecting big bags of Cuban gold, which he spent at the end of the line on drinking and gaming. In 1874 he built the Summerlin House at Punta Rassa, where he and his men could bunk and invest in frivolity the profits of the busi-ness.

The rough, free-and-easy lifestyle of the cow hunter attracted young post–Civil War drifters. In addition, Summerlin's success lured Civil War officers into the prosperous life of the cattle boss, including Captain F. A. Hendry, founder of a Fort Myers dynasty. Between 1870 and 1880 they sold 165,000 head of cattle at Punta Rassa for over $2 million. Into the 1900s, the cow hunters drove their herds through the streets of downtown Fort Myers, past the homes of wealthy investors and bankers.

Reconstruction brought other settlers to Florida's west coast. Judah P. Benjamin, one notable rebel refugee who served as secretary of state in the Confederacy, ducked indictment as a war criminal by hiding out in Florida.

His week-long refuge at the old Gamble plantation near Bradenton ensured the landmark's preservation by the United Daughters of the Confederacy.

The first visitors to Fort Myers were the vultures who picked the fort clean of coveted building materials. Then came men who remembered the old fort in its heyday and hoped to settle with their families in this land of plenty. The first settler, Captain Manuel A. Gonzalez, had run a provisions boat from Tampa during the Seminole War. He and his family moved from Key West with another family named Vivas. Other war officers and refugees settled in and around the ruins of the old fort, planting gardens, opening stores, and living a blissful existence unknown elsewhere in the devastated South.

Captain James Evans returned to Fort Myers from Virginia to find his land comfortably occupied. After struggling in the courts to keep the land out of government hands, he split it with the squatters in exchange for a share of his legal fees. In 1872 the first school in Fort Myers was built. County government was centered 270 miles away, in Key West.

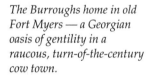

The Burroughs home in old Fort Myers — a Georgian oasis of gentility in a raucous, turn-of-the-century cow town.

Greg Wagner

Some historians credit the cow hunters with contributing the name "Cracker" to early Florida settlers. They say it derives from the cracking of the long whips men used to drive their herds. Others say it originated with the Georgia settlers who cracked corn for their hush puppies, corn pone, and fritters. Though less romantic, the latter theory is likely the more accurate. Georgians did, in fact, drift down to southwest Florida, most notably the Knight clan, which founded a settlement at Horse and Chaise, named by seamen to describe a landmark clump of trees. (The name was changed to Venice in 1888 by developer Frank Higel, who was reminded of the Italian city by the area's many bayous and creeks.)

The Homestead Act, passed in 1862, entitled each settler in Florida to 160 acres of land, provided they built a home and tended the land for five years. As it was meant to, the act brought a flood of intrepid settlers into the area from all over the eastern seaboard and the Deep South. They built rough palmetto huts, burned cow chips to ward off mosquitoes that carried yellow fever, ate raccoon purloo and turtle steaks, and traveled by foot or boat. They stubbornly endured the heat, hurricanes, and freezes that stymied a number of enterprises: sugar refining, fish oil production, and pineapple and citrus shipping.

Florida's cow hunters proved detrimental to the agriculturally based enterprises associated with the Crackers of the Sarasota Bay region. They allied themselves with greedy land speculators who dishonestly nullified the beneficial effects of the Homestead Act. By 1883 speculators had discovered a loophole in Florida's land development legislation, namely the Swamp Land Act. It allowed them to purchase flooded land at rock-bottom prices while overriding homestead claims. They succeeded in declaring arable property swampland and ultimately bought up a good 90 percent of present-day Manatee County, much of which had been worked for years by hardy pioneers. Together the speculators and the cattlemen fought farmers' protests against free ranging — the practice of letting herds roam and feed without restriction. A Sara Sota Vigilance Committee formed in opposition, and by the time the fighting ended, two men lay dead.

Fort Myers' thriving cattle-shipping business precipitated Sanibel Island's first permanent structure, a lighthouse built in 1884. Its caretaker's cottages represent prime examples of Cracker or so-called Old Florida style architecture.

Greg Wagner

As thatch homes gave way to wooden farmhouses — the tin-roofed, vernacular style today termed Cracker — Gulf Coast settlements entered a new era, an era that made "riffraff" out of Crackers, rich men out of schemers, and exclusive getaways out of crude frontier towns.

AT THE DROP OF A NAME

When your first guests are Juan Ponce de León and Hernando de Soto, whom do you invite next? The standard has been set, and it won't do to host just anybody. So began west coast Florida's tradition of larger-than-life visitors with impressive names and pedigrees, all of whom just as impressively influenced the region's development. Thomas Edison, Henry Ford, Harvey Firestone, John and Charles Ringling, Charles Lindbergh, Teddy Roosevelt, Henry Du Pont, Andrew Mellon, Rose Cleveland, and Shirley Temple were among the wide array of southwest Florida winterers. Their fame and following quickly elevated the status of the Gulf Coast from crude and backward to avant-garde and exclusive and attracted the cutting-edge elite. They set national trends by declaring new hot spots — fresh, wild, unspoiled places about which no one else knew, especially the paparazzi. It was they who balanced the very wild coast with a very civilized clientele. The area's natural endowments of fish, fowl, and game attracted adventurers, fishermen, and hunters with the means to make the long, slow journey.

The first and most influential name in any Gulf Coast retrospective is Thomas Edison. Disappointed by the cold winters of St. Augustine, the ailing inventor embarked on a scouting cruise along the Gulf Coast in 1885, the same year Fort Myers was incorporated. As Edison sailed along the Caloosahatchee River, he sighted a stand of bamboo trees. Then and there he decided to move to Fort Myers. And he wanted that property.

The bamboo worked well as filament in Edison's light bulb experiments, and the climate bolstered his failing health, helping to add another 46 years to his life. On the banks of the Caloosahatchee the inventor fashioned his ideal winter home, Seminole Lodge, complete with laboratory and tropical gardens. Holder of more than 1,000 patents, the genius experimented with rare plants in his quest to produce inexpensive rubber for his friend, tire mogul Harvey Firestone. So enamored with Fort Myers was Edison that he persuaded Firestone to spend his winters there. And he set up fellow visionary Henry Ford on an estate next to his. A self-styled botanist, Edison planted the frequently photographed row of royal palms lining the street that eventually ran past his home, McGregor Boulevard, thereby earning the town its nickname, City of Palms.

Meanwhile, the Florida Mortgage and Investment Company — connected with such Scottish notables as the archbishop of Canterbury and estate owner Sir John Gillespie — lured a colony of politically disgruntled Scotsmen to Sara Sota, a paradise of genteel estates, bountiful orange groves, and cheap land. Or so the brochures promised. But instead of the Garden of Eden and the ready-made manor houses they had read about, the colonists found shortages of food and building materials. Only through the kindness of the Whitakers and other pioneers did they survive their first month. Then the Gulf Coast's unpredictable winter weather dealt another cold blow, causing most of the colonists to return to their homeland. Those who stayed, however, brought life to the struggling village and sparked it with a determined spirit.

Most influential among the Scottish ranks was John Hamilton Gillespie, son of Sir John. He built the city's first hotel, the De Soto, became its first mayor in 1902, and introduced the game of golf to Florida. Gillespie transplanted the game from his homeland, first by building a two-hole links down Main Street in Sarasota, near his hotel. He later built the area's first real course and clubhouse nearby.

It was an American woman, however, who firmly and definitively upgraded Sarasota's image. At the turn of the century the name Mrs. Potter (Berthe) Palmer stood for social elitism — not only in her hometown, Chicago, but also in London and Paris, where she kept homes and hobnobbed with royalty. When the widowed socialite decided to visit Sarasota in 1910, hearts palpitated: She could make or break the new town. Enchanted by the area's beauty and the town's quaintness, Mrs. Palmer immediately bought 13 acres that eventually grew into 140,000. She built her home, The Oaks, and a cattle ranch in a community south of Sarasota called Osprey, and from there proceeded to spread the word.

Mrs. Palmer's much-publicized love affair with the Gulf Coast drew the attention of John and Charles Ringling, the youngest of the illustrious circus family's seven sons. The two brothers, in a contest of one-upmanship, began buying property around town. They became active in civic affairs, built bridges to Sarasota's islands, and stoked the economy by making the town the winter home for the Ringling Circus. John Ringling, especially, and his wife, Mabel, brought to Sarasota a new worldliness born of their extensive travels and love of European art.

The fate of the Charlotte Harbor coast lay mostly in the hands of one powerful man, Henry B. Plant. The west coast's counterpart to Henry Flagler — builder of the east coast's railroad and great hotels — Plant brought the railway to Tampa, where he built a fabulous resort of his own, always in competition with Flagler. At the same time, a different railway company extended its tracks to some unknown, unsettled spot in the wilderness of Charlotte Harbor's shores and erected the Punta Gorda Hotel. It reigned briefly as the latest posh outpost for wealthy sportsmen and adventurers, counting Andrew Mellon and W. K. Vanderbilt among its patrons. But in 1897, after Plant had acquired the railway to Punta Gorda, he decided the town's deepwater port and resort posed too much competition for his Tampa enterprises. So he choked the life out of a thriving commercial and resort town by severing the rails to Punta Gorda's Long Dock.

Deep ports, railroads, and fabulous hotels went hand in hand in those days: Developers had to provide transportation before they could attract visitors. In Boca Grande, where a railroad had been built in 1906, the deep waters of Boca Grande Pass attracted Rockefellers, Du Ponts, J. P. Morgan, and other industrialists, who used the port for transshipping phosphate from central Florida. To accommodate them, the graciously refined Gasparilla Inn was built in 1913.

Another man who was to influence the discovery and development of the Gulf Coast came to town in 1911. John M. Roach, Chicago streetcar magnate and owner of Useppa Island, introduced Barron Collier to the area. Collier eventually bought Useppa from his friend and there established the Useppa Inn and the Izaak Walton Club. Both attracted tarpon fishing enthusiasts the likes of Shirley Temple, Gloria Swanson, Mae West, Herbert Hoover, Zane Grey, and Mary Roberts Rinehart, who then bought nearby Cabbage Key.

Collier went on to infuse life into the south coast by underwriting the completion of Tamiami Trail, stalled on its route from Tampa to Miami. He acquired land throughout the county that today bears his name, after earlier attempts by Louisville publisher Walter Haldeman had failed to put Naples on the map.

Along the Gulf Coast of Florida Collier bought more than a million acres, much of it under the infamous Swamp Act. Although he dreamed of development on the scale of Flagler and Plant, anticorporation outcry, hurricanes, the Depression, and war brought him death before success. His sons inherited his kingdom, which they ruled with a heart for the unique environment their father so loved. Collier's influence led to the discovery of the Gulf Coast as a refuge for crowd-weary stars and illuminati. These islands still are popular with the rich and famous who seek anonymity.

Old fish houses around Charlotte Harbor survive from the 1930s, when fishermen's families lived in and worked out of the stilted structures.

Lee Island Coast Visitor & Convention Bureau

But what about the ordinary people — native Americans, fishermen, cattlemen, Crackers, pioneers, and common folk — who loved this land long before it became fashionable to do so? For the most part they lived side by side with this new brand of resident, called the "winterer" or "snowbird." (In Boca Grande they were termed "beachfronters" for their unusual — at the time — idiosyncrasy of building dangerously close to the shore.) The locals became their fishing guides, cooks, and innkeepers. In some cases their heads were turned by their brush with great wealth. In other instances heightened standards pulled the curtain on cruder lifestyles, especially that of the cow hunter, whose boisterousness and preference for free-running stock hurried his extinction.

Sometimes the common folk protested big-bucks development and were classified as riffraff. The "Cracker" label today, despite that group's enriching influence on architecture and cuisine, is considered an insult by some native Floridians.

BOOMS, BURSTS, AND OTHER EXPLOSIONS

The Gulf Coast's resort reputation came of age at the turn of the century. Sarasota's De Soto, the Punta Gorda Hotel, Boca Grande's Gasparilla Inn, the Useppa Inn, Fort Myers' Royal Palm Hotel, the Naples Hotel, and the Marco Inn pioneered in the hotel field, hosting visitors in styles ranging from bare bones to bend-over-backwards. They sparked an era touched with Gatsbian glamour, giddiness, and graciousness.

The Gulf Coast's halcyon days peaked in the early 1920s as the state entered a decade known as the Great Florida Land Boom. Growth came quickly to the young communities of Bradenton, Sarasota, Fort Myers, and Naples. Having struggled for so long to attract residents and commerce, the good people of the Gulf Coast grew dizzy with the whirl of growth and success.

According to the 1910 census, Sarasota's population was 840; before the 1920s drew to a close, almost 8,400 people called it home. In the meantime the city shaped itself with schools, sidewalks, streets, a newspaper, a pier, an airfield, and the establishment of its own county, having split from Bradenton's Manatee County. A bridge to Siesta Key added a whole new element to the town's personality by plugging it into the gulf and attracting a seaside resort trade.

World War I briefly interfered. Prohibition brought to the coast yet another roguish character: the rumrunner. Homes and hotels popped up like toadstools after a summer rain shower. Increased lodging options opened the Gulf Coast to a wider range of vacationers. The average traveler could now afford Florida's Gulf Coast, no longer a socialites' haven. A new class of winterer, known as the "tin can tourist," arrived in force, pulling mobile homes, trailers, and campers. Tourist camps sprang up overnight, and southwest Florida became Everyman's paradise. Real estate profits added to the lure of tourism, and many visitors decided to remain permanently.

The 1920s created Charlotte County along the Charlotte Harbor coast. A bridge was built across the Peace River, connecting the pioneer towns of Charlotte Harbor and Punta Gorda, spurring growth, and spawning subdivisions by the score.

Fort Myers became the seat of a new county named for Robert E. Lee. The population grew from 3,600 to 9,000 between 1920 and 1930, boosted by the completion of Tamiami Trail in 1928. Fort Myers grew from a raucous cattle town to a modern city with electricity, telephone lines, and a railroad. The Royal Palm Hotel treated guests to a regal departure from the cow trails that ran adjacent to the property. A country club put Fort Myers on the golfing map, and a bridge to Estero Island's beautiful beaches further boosted tourism. Real adventurers took the ferry to Sanibel Island, to be accommodated at Casa Ybel or the Palm Hotel.

South of Fort Myers, Survey, a farming community, was renamed Bonita Springs. In 1923 Naples (previously a well-kept secret among buyers from such faraway places as Kentucky and Ohio and distinguished vacationers from the upper echelons) became a city just in time to feel the effects of the tourism boom. The same year, Collier County seceded from Lee. Everglades City became the first county seat; later, growing, thriving Naples took the honors. The Naples Pier, which had served as a landing point for visitors and cargo since 1887, was replaced in importance by a railroad depot in 1927.

Gulf Coast skies had never been sunnier. Visitors spent lots of money. Residents prospered. Real estate prices soared. It seemed too good to be true. And indeed it was.

Along the Gulf Coast the Great Depression affected each community differently. A 1926 hurricane hit Fort Myers, worsening a condition of already deepening debt. In Sarasota, John Ringling suffered severe financial losses from which he never recovered. On the south coast, however, the national economy had little impact on the surge of interest sparked by the opening of Tamiami Trail.

The Depression blunted the momentum with which the Gulf Coast had developed during the 1920s but in many ways affected the region less drastically than it did other parts of the country. Since it most tragically affected the middle class, wealthy Gulf Coast residents were largely spared. Works Progress Administration (WPA) recovery projects built Fort Myers its waterfront park, yacht basin, and first hospital. And, despite serious financial problems, Ringling kept his promises to build bridges and an art museum. The WPA funded the building of Bayfront Park, a municipal auditorium, and the Lido Beach Casino along the Sarasota Bay coast.

By the beginning of World War II, southwest Florida had firmly joined the 20th century, with modern conveniences that made it popular among retirees. New golf courses accommodated active seniors, who participated in the civic affairs of their adopted communities, often more vigorously than they had in those of their hometowns. Professional golf tournaments were introduced, first in Naples and then along the coast, making the area golf's winter home. Spring baseball camps later brought another spectator sport to this land of year-round recreation.

Warmth seekers turned their attention to the Gulf Coast's islands and beach-

The Naples Pier and down-town Naples circa 1958.

fronts. Golfing communities and waterfront resorts swallowed up local farming and fishing industries. High-rise condominiums replaced Cracker houses, posh resorts toppled tourist fishing camps, and the Gulf Coast continued to grow — albeit not quite as loudly or erratically as in pre-Depression times.

Some areas learned to control their growth. Sanibel Island served as a model, taking control of its fate after a causeway connected it to the mainland in 1963. It incorporated and introduced measures to protect wilderness areas and to limit takeover by developers.

The southward expansion of Interstate 75 during the 1970s and 1980s changed the Gulf Coast from a series of towns connected by two-lane roads to communities keeping pace with the world. Communication and transportation systems improved. Commercial development spread to the freeway corridor, leaving downtown areas to fade in bygone glory. Light industry and winter-weary entrepreneurs relocated. Postsecondary schools worked to prepare local youth for the changing marketplace. The construction and tourism industries continued to prosper.

The Gulf Coast remained seemingly untouched by the fluctuations of the American economy. Urban blight was a distant reality. Northerners fled to the Gulf Coast to escape overcrowding, smog, and crime. In previous decades this had caused unnatural development in some of the metropolitan areas. The delicate balance of infrastructure, human services, nature, heritage preservation, and the arts went out of kilter. The coast lived very much in the present, deaf to the demands of residents, both human and otherwise.

The new trends of eco-tourism and social responsibility finally amplified the voices of the few who had screamed over the decades for preservation of the environment against tourism and cultural sterility. While Sarasota and Naples served as cultural prototypes, Sanibel and Gasparilla Islands provided environmental models. The 1990s saw the dawn of an awareness of the fragility of the west coast's islands, wetlands, and shorelines. At the same time, interest in the area's history grew, and movements were launched to preserve architectural treasures spared by the bulldozer. Finally, the dipping economic trends of the early 1990s affected the Gulf Coast. Construction slowed its racing pulse, and unemployment figures jumped as northerners continued to arrive, looking for nonexistent jobs in this legendary land of treasure and youth.

All of these factors have contributed to the current perspective on the Gulf Coast. Economic fluctuations give city planners occasion to pause and rethink. Future growth is being mapped out with more care than ever before. Dying downtown neighborhoods and abandoned Cracker homes are being revitalized, recognized as an important part of the area's heritage. Government is drawing into its blueprints the need for environmental preservation, cultural enrichment, and historic renovation. With economic recovery comes a more enlightened attitude that promises to return the sunshine to Gulf Coast skies, free of the recent past's dimming clouds. The grain of sand and the mangrove pod from which this land was wrought will once again play a role in its future.

COASTAL CULTURE

Seminole Henry John Billie crafts canoes the traditional way.

Karen T. Bartlett

One of southwest Florida's great contradictions is that it lies more to the north than to the south on the cultural map. To the north, or inland, you will find Deep South cookery, clog dancing, bluegrass music, and traditional southern arts. In southwest Florida, however, midwestern and eastern U.S.

influences are most noticeable. The only truly indigenous art forms have their origins in the Seminole Indian traditions of weaving, dancing, and festivals.

The arts have been heavily influenced through the years by the region's winter population. Many northern-based artists have relocated here, lured by the sea and the tropical Muses. Others bring their appetite for culture with them, sparking the finest in visual, performing, and culinary arts.

SOUTHWEST FLORIDA ARCHITECTURE

A Seminole trademark, chickee (cheek-ee) huts have dotted the Everglades landscape since the Seminole Wars forced the Indians into hostile swampland.

Karen T. Bartlett

Years of simmering together Seminole, Cracker, "Yankee," and Caribbean traditions have yielded a unique southwest Florida style, particularly in architecture and cuisine. But if one overall style were chosen to represent local architecture, it would have to be Mediterranean — specifically Italian and Spanish-mission versions. Cracker vernacular runs a close second.

Southern European and North African influences are found primarily in public and commercial buildings constructed during the boom years of the Roaring Twenties, when they were lumped together under the label "Mediterranean Revival." It reveals itself in stucco finish, mission arches, red barrel-tile roofing, bell towers, and rounded step façades. Re-revived, Mediterranean Post-Modern serves as a popular style for upscale housing developments and commercial enterprises. It's updated Mediterranean Revival blended with elements of tropical styles adopted from the Cracker era.

Pure Cracker style began as folk housing. From the vernacular, single-pen home — a wood-frame, one-room house featuring a shady veranda, tin roof, and clapboard siding — grew more sophisticated interpretations of the style. With Gothic touches, Victorian embellishments, Palladian accents, and New England influences, the humble Cracker house evolved into a trendy, modern-day version termed "Old Florida." Boxy and stilted, its most distinctive characteristics include a tin roof and wide, wraparound porch.

The latest influence on the Cracker house comes from the Caribbean and the Bahamas via the Keys. Since indigenous West Indian styles are greatly similar to Cracker, especially in their suitability to tropical weather, the convergence was inevitable. The result: sherbet colors and hand-carved fretwork — used as much for ventilation as for decoration — that add charm and whimsy to the basic unit.

Like the Cracker home, the Seminole Indian's chickee hut conformed to the tropical climate with its high-peaked roof, wide overhangs, and open sides. Today the thatched roofing that is the chickee's most distinctive feature has become an art form. Still a popular style of housing for the Seminoles and Miccosukees of the Everglades, the chickee has evolved as a trademark of the Gulf Coast watering-hole tradition known as chickee or tiki bars.

With the mid-1920s influx of "tin can tourists," the mobile home replaced the Cracker house on the low end of the architectural totem pole. Mobile home parks still provide low-cost housing, mostly to part-time winter residents. Singer Jimmy Buffett once sang, "They'd look a lot better as beer cans."

The concrete-block ranch, a popular residential style of the 1970s, was built to withstand hurricanes. The flood regulations of the 1980s raised these upon pilings; lattice and fretwork added interest. Art Deco returned later in the decade as Miami Beach's Art Deco District attracted attention.

Today's Gulf Coast towns are seasoned with period styles and spiced with contemporary looks that strive for compatibility with nature. Screened porches, windowed Florida rooms, and lots of sliding doors let the outside in, to take full advantage of our unique, enviable climate and environment.

COASTAL CUISINE

As for culinary *richesse,* southwest Florida has wowed hungry visitors since the first Europeans came ashore and discovered its abundantly stocked pantry. The seas were teeming with Neptune's bounty, and exotic fruits and vegetables flourished on land. In fact, some locals adhere to a theory that this was the original Paradise, and that it was a sweet, luscious mango, not an apple, that caused Eve's downfall. Hence the fruit's name: Man! Go!

Mangoes, as a matter of fact, are not native to southwest Florida but grow bountifully along with other naturalized tropical fruit: bananas, coconuts, pineapples, avocados, sapodillas, carambola (star fruit), and lychees. Citrus fruit, particularly oranges, is of course the region's most visible and profitable crop. Key lime trees grow in profusion as well. Practically year-round producers, they are a standard part of any good Florida cook's landscaping scheme. Here, as in the Florida Keys, where the tree got named and famed, key lime pie is a culinary paradigm, and each restaurant claims to make the best. In the finest restaurants with the most extravagant dessert menus, key lime pie inevitably outsells the rest. The classic recipe, created by Florida cooks before refrigeration, uses canned condensed and sweetened milk, and is elegant in its simplicity. The most important factor is the freshness of the limes — sometimes a problem for restaurants since the fruit does not lend itself to commercial farming. One sure sign of an inauthentic version is the color green. The key lime turns yellow when ripe and, unless the cook adds food coloring, should impart a buttery hue to the pie.

Historically, crop farming has provided coastal residents with economic sustenance. Weather conditions bless farmers with two growing seasons for most ground crops. As land becomes too valuable to farm, agriculture has been pushed inland. Bonita Springs, where vast acreage remains devoted to tomatoes, and Pine Island, known for its tropical fruits, are the region's final bastions of the agricultural tradition.

Fishing, an enduring way of life in southwest Florida.

Karen T. Bartlett

Seafood is most commonly associated with Gulf Coast cuisine, including some delicacies unique to Florida. The stone crab, our prize catch (Florida author Marjorie Kinnan Rawlings once described the taste: "almost as rare as nightingales' tongues"), was discovered as a food source in the Everglades. They are in season from October 15 through May 15. Restaurants serve them hot, with drawn butter, or cold, with tangy mustard sauce. Their aptly named shells are usually precracked to facilitate diners' enjoyment.

The gulf shrimp is an emblem of local cuisine. Its poorer cousin, the rock shrimp, gets less publicity because of its hard-to-peel shell. More economical and with a flavor and texture akin to lobster, it's certainly worth tasting.

Restaurants change their menus, or at least their daily specials, according to what's in season. Grouper, the most versatile food fish in the area, traditionally has been available year-round, but environmental pressure is limiting its availability. A large and meaty fish, its taste is so mild you hardly know it's fish. Winter months bring red and yellowtail snapper to diners' plates. Warmer weather means pompano, cobia, shark, and dolphinfish (also known as mahi mahi). Tuna and flounder are caught sporadically, but year-round. Some restaurants serve less well-known species, such as triggerfish and catfish, to offset spiraling costs caused by dwindling supplies of the more popular varieties. Fish farming also addresses these shortages. Catfish and a Brazilian fish called tilapia (which tastes similar to snapper) are cultivated most commonly. Fresh fish from around the nation supplement local bounty.

The best Gulf Coast restaurants buy their seafood directly from the docks of local commercial fishermen to ensure the utmost freshness. The traditional style of cooking seafood in Florida is deep frying. Although this constitutes a mortal sin in this age of gourmet standards and cholesterol awareness, it is a true art when properly executed. There's a vast difference between what you find in the frozen food department at the supermarket and what comes hand-breaded, crunchy, and flavor-sealed on your plate at the local fish house.

New Florida style, at the other extreme, has evolved from so-called California, new American, new world, and eclectic styles of cuisine. This style also depends on freshness — of all its ingredients. For this reason it uses local produce, prepared in global culinary styles. Regional cookery, sometimes termed Gulfshore or Floribbean cuisine, prefers tropical foodways and ingredients and is inspired by the cuisines of New Orleans, Mexico, Cuba, Puerto Rico, Haiti, the Bahamas, Jamaica, and Trinidad. Pacific Rim influences are often apparent, given today's obsession with lightness. Depending on the cook, Deep South traditions take their place at the table, too. The outcome at its tamest merely twists the familiar and, at its most adventurous, can treat your taste buds to a veritable bungee jump.

Between the two extremes of old and new Florida styles, continental cuisine survives in both classic and reinvented forms. Along with restaurants that serve the finest in French and Italian haute cuisine, you will find others that represent the Gulf Coast's melting pot, with authentic renditions or interpretations of a wide variety of cuisines: native American, Thai, Vietnamese, East Indian, German, Irish, Greek, Cuban, Jamaican, Amish, Jewish, Mexican, and Puerto Rican.

In its cuisine and cultural makeup, as well as its history, the map of Gulf Coast Florida resembles a patchwork quilt. It blankets its people in warmth, checkers its past with colorful and contrasting patterns, and layers its character with intriguing, international textures.

CHAPTER TWO
Blazing the Trail
TRANSPORTATION

Karen T. Bartlett

Art shows and community functions give new life to the old Naples Depot, where celebrities disembarked in the Roaring Twenties.

The Gulf of Mexico and its great rivers and intracoastal waterways comprise the region's oldest and lowest-maintenance transportation system. From the days when the Calusa traveled the bays and estuaries in dugout canoes, through the romantic steamboat era, and until 1927, when the railroad to Naples was completed, boat travel was the most popular means of getting around. Early homes lined the waterways and today still face the water and not the roads that accommodate modern-day traffic. Even today the Caloosahatchee River, which empties into the sea along the Island Coast and connects to the east coast via Lake Okeechobee, constitutes a major intercoastal water route.

The railroad first came to Charlotte County's deepwater port in 1886 and created the town of Punta Gorda, much to the chagrin of Fort Myers' leaders, who had tried for years to persuade company officials to extend their Florida Southern Railroad to the Caloosahatchee River. Instead, an unpopulated location was selected and a fabulous hotel built there, according to the custom of Florida's great railroad builders of the day. Besides transporting wealthy winterers to the nation's southernmost railroad stop, the trains hauled fresh fish, cattle, and produce.

A train nicknamed "Slow and Wobbly" ran between Bradenton and Sarasota from 1892 to 1894. The Seaboard Airline Railroad built a more reliable version to Bradenton in 1902. In 1911 it was extended beyond Venice and played musical chairs with town names. Infuriated residents of Venice changed the town's name to Nokomis, and the Venice of today sits where the new station was built. The Charlotte Harbor and Northern Railway laid track in 1906 to ship phosphate from inland mines to the deep waters of Boca Grande Pass, off Gasparilla Island. Another exclusive resort came with it.

Fort Myers finally got its first railroad station in 1904. In 1922 the trestles reached Bonita Springs and were later extended to Naples and Marco Island. Famous passengers such as Hedy Lamarr, Greta Garbo, and Gary Cooper rode the rails to vacation at the posh Naples Beach Hotel & Golf Club, one of Florida's first resorts to have golf greens on the property.

A stretch of Tamiami Trail remains close to its original state on old Highway 41 in Bonita Springs.

Karen T. Bartlett

The concept of Tamiami Trail made headway when, in 1923, a group called the Trail Blazers traveled the proposed route that would connect Tampa and Miami. Mules, oxen, and tractors were used to complete that first motorized crossing of the Everglades. Before the trail was paved, it had a sand surface. Summer rains caused flooding. Old-timers remember getting out of the car to catch fish in the road while their parents tried to get unstuck. Even after the rains subsided, jarring, muck-crusted ruts made the trip less than comfortable.

As the trail's west-coast leg inched toward its destination, it changed the lives of the communities it penetrated, opening them to commerce and tourism. Progress was slowed by dense jungles, forbidding swampland, devastating heat, and mosquitoes so thick that they covered exposed skin like a buzzing body glove. Builders lived at the work site, and a whole body of legend grew up around the monumental task. The project was hampered by war and depletion of funds. A special new dredge had to be invented to build the section across the Everglades.

Thirteen years in the building, the completion of Tamiami Trail in 1928 opened communities to land travel, trade, and tourism, and was met with euphoria. Today the trail, also known as Highway 41, strings together the region's oldest towns and cities, and newer communities have grown up around it.

Ed Frank (second from far right) invented the swamp buggy, an amphibious form of transportation engineered for travel in the Everglades. He poses here in 1947 with his brainchild and his hunting buddies.

Collier County Historical Society, Inc.

With the extension of parallel Interstate 75, Tamiami Trail has now lost its role as the sole intercoastal lifeline. Nonetheless, it remains the backbone of the lower west coast. Probing both metropolitan interiors and rural vistas, it provides glimpses of a cross-section of life — as it was and as it is — in southwest Florida.

For the most part, Highway 41 draws the eastern boundary of the area covered in this book. At the Gulf Coast's northern and southern extremes it edges close to the shoreline. In midsections it reaches inland to communities built along harbors and rivers.

I-75 glimpses, at top speed, Gulf Coast life as it enters the 21st century. Although convenient and free of traffic lights, it misses the character that the more leisurely pace of Tamiami Trail reveals. It extends the boundaries of Highway 41's family of communities and creates new ones. Occasionally this book will use it as a reference point, especially where attractions along its path merit mention.

GETTING TO THE COAST

BY CAR

Southwest Florida is plugged into Florida's more highly charged areas by both major conduits and small feeders. Tampa lies at the Sarasota Bay coast's back door, along Highway 41 or I-75. Tamiami Trail ends here, but Highway 41 continues on. The interstate continues northeast and connects to Orlando and the east coast via Interstate 4. Highway 19 takes up the coastal route in St. Petersburg, heading toward Georgia. Highway 70 cuts across the state above Lake Okeechobee, to connect the east coast to the Sarasota Bay coast at Bradenton, and at Sarasota and Punta Gorda via Routes 72 and 17 respectively. These roads meander into native American reservation territory, Arcadia's cowboy country, and the expansive Myakka River State Park. The route runs jaggedly between the Island Coast, the big lake, and West Palm Beach, following a series of lazy two- and four-lane roads, including Routes 80, 27, 441, and 98.

Alligator Alley (I-75) crosses the Everglades with a certain mystique. Once, upon this two-lane toll road, encounters with crossing gators and panthers were common. (Tragically, cars inevitably fared better in such encounters.) The state recently completed connections with I-75 on both ends and widened Alligator Alley to four lanes, with underpasses for wildlife. Certain times of the year, it continues to earn its name. That's when a sharp eye can spot hundreds of gators sunning on water banks. But it's still a toll road and still less than user-friendly. Gas up before you approach — only one fuel station/restaurant exit breaks up the two-hour drive. It reaches the east coast at Fort Lauderdale. Highway 41 takes you into Miami and branches off into Highway 1 to the Florida Keys.

Welcome to paradise: Southwest Florida International Airport in Fort Myers.

Southwest Florida International Airport

GULF COAST ACCESS

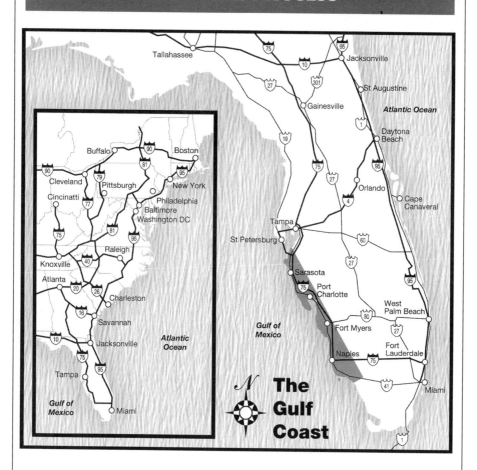

FROM FLORIDA CITIES

From	To Sarasota Bay	To Island Coast	To South Coast
Miami	212 mi./4.25 hr.	148 mi./2.5 hr.	110 mi./2 hr.
Orlando	132 mi./2.25 hr.	167 mi./3.5 hr.	187 mi./3.75 hr.
Daytona	185 mi./3.75 hr.	219 mi./4.25 hr.	241 mi./4.5 hr.
Jacksonville	239 mi./4.5 hr.	311 mi./6 hr.	325 mi./6.25 hr.

BY PLANE

Two major airports service the Gulf Coast: Sarasota-Bradenton International Airport (SRQ) and Southwest Florida International (RSW) in Fort Myers. The Sarasota-Bradenton facility gives the best introduction to the region, with shark tanks and tropical orchids from local attractions, a two-story waterfall, and works from its prolific artist community.

Smaller airports and fields service shuttle, charter, and private planes. The Charlotte County and Venice airports cater mainly to private crafts. North Captiva Island and Everglades City have their own landing strips for private planes, and seaplane service is available to some islands.

Sarasota-Bradenton International Airport (SRQ), 941-359-5200. American, Continental, Delta, Northwest, Trans-World Airlines, United, USAir.

Charlotte County Airport, 941-639-1101.

Southwest Florida International Airport (RSW), 941-768-1000. Air Canada, American, American TransAir, Continental, Delta, Northwest, Trans World Airlines, United, USAir.

Naples Municipal Airport (APF), 941-643-0733. American Eagle, Comm-Air, Delta, USAir.

Marco Island Airport, 941-394-3355.

BY BUS

Greyhound Bus Lines depots are found along the west coast at Sarasota (575 North Washington Boulevard; 941-955-5735), Fort Myers (2275 Cleveland Avenue; 941-334-1011), and Naples (2669 Davis Boulevard; 941-774-5660).

BY TRAIN

Amtrak (800-872-7245) stops at Bradenton's Manatee County Courthouse Bus Terminal (Manatee West at 12th Street West) and Sarasota's City Hall Bus Terminal (Lemon Avenue between First and Second Streets).

GETTING AROUND THE GULF COAST

BY CAR

BEST ROUTES

The Tamiami Trail (Highway 41) forms the heart of the Gulf Coast's major metropolitan areas and provides north-south passage within and between them.

Sarasota Bay Coast

In Bradenton and Sarasota, Highway 41 runs along bay shores and converges with Highway 301, another major trunk road. Principal through-streets for east-west traffic in this area generally are those with exits off I-75, north to south: Manatee Avenue (Route 64), Carter Road (Route 70), University Parkway, Fruitville Road, Bee Ridge Road, Clark Road (Route 72), and Venice Avenue. To reach the islands from I-75, follow Route 64 (exit 42) or 72 (exit 41).

Bradenton's 75th Street West (De Soto Memorial Highway) skims the town's western reaches close to the bay front. Streets hiccup through downtown Sarasota, starting and stopping without warning. Main Street runs north-south, crossed by Orange Avenue, one of the neighborhood's longest streets. Bayfront Drive arcs around the water and sees a lot of the town's water-sports action. Bahia Vista intersects Orange at its southern extreme and constitutes a major route. To cross town from north to south between Highway 41 and I-75, take Tuttle Avenue, Beneva Road, McIntosh Road, or Cattlemen Road. Take Venice Avenue off Interstate 75 to get to Venice's beaches and old, Mediterranean-influenced neighborhoods. Highway 41's business route splits from Tamiami Trail at Venice and takes you to the older part of town. Harbor Drive travels north-south along the beaches. The Esplanade and Tarpon Center Road reach into waterfront communities.

Charlotte Harbor Coast

Highway 41 heads inland, running within miles of I-75 at some points. In these parts getting to the gulf entails crossing several bodies of water. Most of the routes qualify as back roads and are listed under that heading.

Island Coast

Bonita Beach is touted as the closest sands to I-75 in this area. Highway 41 again distances itself from its modern counterpart to take you into downtown business districts and past upscale golfing communities. Pine Island Road, Route 78, diverges from the major arteries and crosses North Fort Myers and Cape Coral to reach Pine Island.

On the other side of the Caloosahatchee Bridge, Fort Myers' main east-west connectors are Martin Luther King, Jr. Boulevard, Colonial Boulevard (which feeds into the new Mid-Point Bridge to Cape Coral), College Parkway (which also crosses the river between Fort Myers and Cape Coral), and Daniels Parkway/Gladiolus Drive. Traveling roughly from north to south, historic and royal-palm-lined McGregor Boulevard (Route 867) follows the river past the old homes that line it. Summerlin Avenue (Route 869) and Metro Parkway run parallel, to the east. Tamiami Trail becomes Cleveland Avenue. Take McGregor or Summerlin west (they eventually merge) to get to Sanibel and Captiva Islands, lands of no traffic lights. There's a $3 toll for crossing the

Greg Wagner

Thomas Edison is credited with planting the royal palms flanking Fort Myers' prestigious McGregor Boulevard, thereby earning the city its nickname, "City of Palms."

bridge to Sanibel without a transponder gizmo. Periwinkle Way is the main drag and connects to Sanibel-Captiva Road via Tarpon Bay Road. Policemen with white gloves direct traffic at the main intersections during high-traffic hours. Sanibel-Captiva Road dead-ends at Captiva, with no return route to the mainland except by backtracking.

South Coast

Here, Highway 41 (also known as Ninth Street) closes in on the sea once again as it travels through Naples. At Bonita Springs, Old Highway 41 branches off toward the town's business district. Parallel to Highway 41 in Naples, major city dissectors include Goodlette-Frank Road (Route 851) and Airport-Pulling Road (Route 31). East-west trunks are the Naples-Immokalee Highway (Route 846) at the north edge of town, Pine Ridge Road (Route 896), Golden Gate Parkway (Route 886), Radio Road (Route 856), and Davis Boulevard (Route 84) in town, and Rattlesnake Hammock Road (Route 864) at the southern extreme.

ALTERNATE BACK ROADS & SCENIC ROUTES

Gassing up at the pink pump Boca Grande style.

Karen T. Bartlett

The Gulf Coast has many scenic back roads that bypass traffic and plunge the traveler into timeless scenes and unique neighborhoods. These routes are especially good to know when you tire of counting out-of-state license plates during rush hour in high season.

Sarasota Bay Coast

Follow the twisty road through a string of barrier islands, from Anna Maria in the north to Bird Key at the end. Route 789 adopts a different name on each island: Ocean Boulevard, Gulf of Mexico Drive, etc. Route 758, along Siesta Key, makes a short, beachy bypass between Siesta Drive and Stickney Point Road. The loop through lovely Casey Key begins between Sarasota and Venice at Blackburn Point Road, off Highway 41, then proceeds south through Nokomis Beach and back to the mainland.

Charlotte Harbor Coast

To reach Englewood from Venice, cross quiet, out-of-the-way Manasota Key along Route 776 through Englewood Beach. Then follow Routes 775 and 771 back to Route 776 for a scenic drive through the peninsula, separated from the mainland by Charlotte Harbor, or to get to Gasparilla Island. (It costs $3.20 to cross the causeway onto the island.) Keeping straight on 776 takes you more directly to Highway 41. To skirt Highway 41's chain-outlet anonymity in the Port Charlotte area, take Collingswood Boulevard off 776 to Edgewater Drive and back to 41.

Between Charlotte County and the Island Coast, Route 765, or Burnt Store Road, rambles through the county's Cracker era: scrub cattle, rusty tin roofs, and old fishermen bobbing cane poles. This connects to Highway 78, which leads to Pine Island when taken west, or Highway 41 and I-75 when followed east. To enter Cape Coral the back way, go east to Chiquita Boulevard and then south to Cape Coral Parkway.

Island Coast

The back roads along the Island Coast's shores plunge you briefly into the frenzied activity of Fort Myers Beach along Routes 968 and 865, then carry you along at a more mellow pace as you cross into Lover's Key and Big and Little Hickory Islands. The road returns you via Bonita Beach Road to Highway 41 at Bonita Springs.

South Coast

Gulfshore Boulevard, which stops and starts to make way for Naples' waterways, is the town's most scenic route, skirting beaches and beautiful homes.

South of Naples, Routes 951, 952, and 953 carry you to Isles of Capri, Marco Island, Goodland, and back to Highway 41 just before the Everglades.

CAR RENTALS

R ental agencies with airport offices or shuttle service are listed below:

Alamo: 800-327-9633 (SRQ, 359-5540; RSW, 768-2424)
Avis: 800-331-1212 (SRQ, 359-5240; RSW, 768-2121; APF, 643-0900)
Budget: 800-527-0700 (SRQ, 359-5353; RSW, 768-1500; APF, 643-0086)
Dollar: 800-800-4000 (SRQ, 355-2996; RSW, 768-2223)
Hertz: 800-654-3131 (RSW, 768-3100; APF, 643-1515)
National: 800-328-4567 (RSW, 768-2100; APF, 643-0200)
Thrifty: 800-367-2277 (RSW, 768-2322)

AIRPORT TAXIS/SHUTTLES

S ome hotels and resorts arrange pickup service to and from the airport. Taxi and limousine companies operate in most areas. To find which companies service the Bradenton-Sarasota airport, call 941-359-5225.

Boca Grande Limo (941-964-0455 or 800-771-7433) provides 24-hour connections to all Florida airports. For a more dramatic arrival or departure, call *Boca Grande Seaplane* (941-964-0234).

Pine Island Taxi and Limousine Service (941-283-7777) provides 24-hour service anywhere with advance notice.

Sanibel Island Taxi (941-472-4160) makes airport pickups and deliveries for

Sanibel and Captiva visitors. Or call **Sanibel Island Limousine** (941-472-8888).

In the South Coast area, call **Affordable Limousine Service** (941-455-6007 or 800-245-6007), **Naples Shuttle** (941-262-8982), or **Naples Taxi** (941-643-2148). **Admiralty Transportation** (941-394-4411) services Marco Island airport arrivals and departures.

BY BUS

The Sarasota Bay coast boasts dependable public transportation, with discounts for schoolchildren and seniors. Buses run every day but Sunday, 6 am to 6 pm. For route information, call **Sarasota County Area Transit** (SCAT) (941-951-5851) or **Manatee County Transit** (941-747-8621 or 941-749-7116).

On the Island Coast, city buses follow routes around Fort Myers, Cape Coral, and south Fort Myers. Call **Lee Tran** (941-275-8726) for schedules and information about trolley rides to and around Fort Myers Beach.

The trolley is a popular way to go for residents and sightseers alike.

Karen T. Bartlett

The **Naples Trolley and Blue Trolley Line** (941-262-7300) conducts sightseeing and shopping tours in the Naples area. The **Marco Island Trolley** (941-394-1600) visits 13 different historical sites.

BY CARRIAGE

Naples Horse and Carriage Company (941-649-1210) provides evening tours of Old Naples, the beaches, and the fishing pier in season.

BY TRAIN

The **Seminole Gulf Railway** (941-275-6060 or 800-SEM-GULF), stationed at Amtel Flea Market (Colonial Blvd. and Metro Pkwy.) in Fort Myers, and in

Bonita Springs at the loading platform off Pennsylvania Blvd., does dinner trips, Murder Mystery tours, and other excursions throughout the area.

BY WATER

Speedy, wetlands-efficient airboats travel the Everglades' watery trails. Some fear they are detrimental to local wildlife.

Marco Island & the Everglades
Convention and Visitors Bureau

Water no longer provides functional transportation routes. On the Gulf Coast today, boat travel is purely recreational (except for commercial fishing, of course). The region boasts two trademark water vessels. The noisy, power-driven airboat is designed especially for the shallow waters of the Everglades. The swamp buggy is an all-terrain vehicle, built to carry two to 20 passengers, and travels on fat tire treads. In addition, pontoon boats offer a more conventional way to explore the Everglades and coastal shallows.

Numerous sightseeing tours and charters originate at marinas and resorts daily. Some specialize in fishing, others in shelling or birding. Many include lunch at an exotic island restaurant, while a few serve meals on board. All cater to the sightseer. Most tour operators are knowledgeable about sights on local waterways. These are all listed in the "Recreation" section of each chapter. Included here are shuttles designed purely to carry passengers to one or more island destinations where "by water" is still the only means of arrival.

The *Miss Cortez* (941-794-1223), an excursion boat out of the fishing village of Cortez near Anna Maria Island, takes visitors to Egmont Key every Tuesday and Thursday afternoon.

Island Charters (941-283-1113) offers shuttles from Pine Island's Pineland Marina to North Captiva.

CHAPTER THREE
Seashore Sophisticate
SARASOTA BAY COAST

Classical European statuary heralds the Renaissance pleasures inside the John and Mabel Ringling Museum of Art.

Karen T. Bartlett

The cities of **Bradenton** and **Sarasota** dominate the Sarasota Bay coast, an expanse of metropolitan sprawl barricaded behind sybaritic, beach-centric islands. History and a heritage of high culture add dimension to this world of sand and city streets.

In Bradenton and the surrounding mainland communities, two pioneering influences dictated a low-key attitude and light development. The first, the wealthy plantation owners of the 1840s, made Manatee County the largest area in the state for sugar and molasses production. Sugar's aristocratic families set the social standards of the town until the Civil War turned the lucrative sugar industry sour.

Nineteenth-century land speculators who exploited Florida's Swamp Act had an opposite, stunting effect on the area's development. By having homestead property fraudulently declared wetlands, they prevented agricultural expansion and delayed its by-product, the building of railroads.

Most of Bradenton's modern growth has occurred since 1970, when tourism

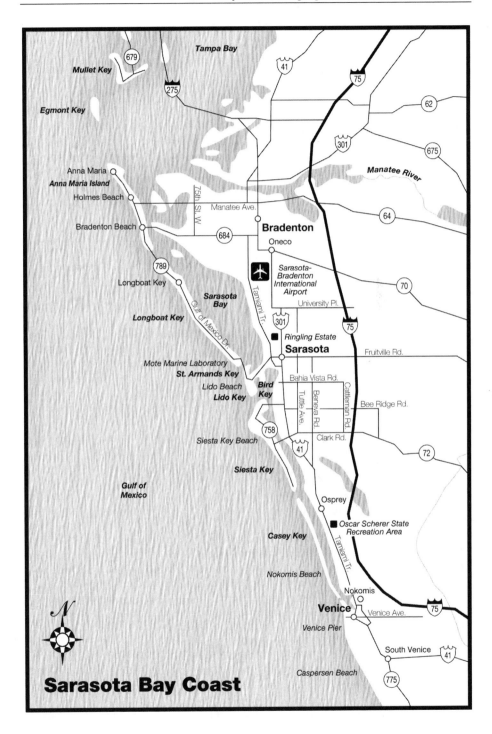

Sarasota Bay Coast

and shipping into deepwater Port Manatee became major sources of income. Today, preservation of the Gamble Plantation and original village sites, along with pier and waterfront restoration projects, make Bradenton a vital city textured with an interesting past.

Fishing, resorts, and heterogeneous neighborhoods mark the three incorporated towns of **Anna Maria Island**: **Anna Maria**, **Holmes Beach**, and **Bradenton Beach**. The first Anna Maria Island settlers of record were George Emerson Bean and his family, circa 1890. He developed the island in the early 1900s for tourists, who arrived by boat at the Anna Maria City pier. In 1921 the first bridge to the island was built from Cortez.

Longboat Key was mentioned often on the maps and journals of early Spanish explorers. It supposedly got its name from the longboats that

---

The Town the Circus Built

"The circus comes as close to being the world in microcosm as anything I know; in a way it puts all the rest of show business in the shade. Its magic is universal and complex."
— E. B. White, *Ring of Times*, March 22, 1956

Legend has it that Sarasota's barrier islands of **Bird Key** and **St. Armands Key** became John Ringling's possessions in a poker game. Tales of the circus master's influence on the area's development have grown to mythic proportions: elephants that built bridges, midgets who built fortunes, and an eccentric who built himself an Italian palace. However true the legends, during the 20 years after he came to Sarasota to house his circus here in winter, John Ringling demonstrated a three-ring influence over the city and its barrier islands.

After falling in love with the fledgling mainland village and purchasing real estate offshore, Ringling erected his lavish Cà D'Zan ("House of John" in Italian, modeled after a Venetian palazzo). He undertook the construction of a causeway to **Lido Key** by filling and dredging. He dreamed of a city park and a shoppers' haven on **St. Armands**. For **Longboat Key** he envisioned a world-class hotel. With unbridled fervor he set out during his worldwide travels to acquire a fine collection of Baroque art.

The dreams Ringling failed to realize before he died in 1936 were not abandoned. The causeway was completed and donated to the state. St. Armands Circle today is famed for its shops. The skeleton of what was to be the world's finest hotel sat rusting on Longboat Key for years until it was reborn as a modern resort. The John and Mabel Ringling Museum of Art encompasses acres of bayside estate. Its collection and grounds include Baroque statuary, original Rubens masterpieces, a rose garden, Cà D'Zan, a circus museum, and an antique Italian theater.

Aside from John Ringling's concrete legacy to Sarasota, he bequeathed an undying commitment to beauty, fantasy, art, and showmanship. The circus remains an important industry in Sarasota, with 18 companies and a clown school now headquartered in the vicinity. At the high school, circus is an extracurricular activity, like football. Theaters and galleries thrive, thanks to Ringling's patronage of the arts. Without his influence the entire coast might well have remained a cultural frontier.

Hernando de Soto's scouting party used to come ashore. Aside from one tucked-away village with a salty, local flavor, Longboat Key is known for its prim-and-proper-ness. It, along with Sarasota and its bracelet of other keys, proclaim John Ringling as godfather. He is responsible for putting the area on the cultural map. His arrival in 1911 sparked Sarasota's first land boom.

Remote **Siesta Key** resisted settlement until the turn of the century, when a hotel launched the island's reputation as a restful place. A bridge built in 1917 finally brought permanent residents. Siesta Key has historically attracted creative types. One of its best-known citizens was prolific writer John D. Macdonald, most famous for his Travis McGee detective novels. While living on Siesta Key he is believed to have written more than 70 novels. Pulitzer Prize–winning author MacKinlay Kantor settled on the island; abstractionist Syd Solomon and Pulitzer Prize–winning cartoonist Mike Peters live there today. Other cartoonists and artists, as well, have found the area conducive to creativity. Hagar the Horrible's Dik Browne and Garfield's Jim Davis live on Longboat Key. Surrealist Jimmy Ernst, son of Dada master Max Ernst, spent much time on Casey Key. Artist Thornton Utz still has a home in the area.

The Webb family first arrived in the Sarasota area in 1867 to plant the seed for a town they named **Osprey** 17 years later. Mrs. Palmer (Bertha) Potter, a Chicago socialite, settled here in 1910 and exerted an influence equal to Ringling's in attracting attention to the area around Sarasota Bay.

The original village of Venice sat where **Nokomis** does today. It moved south and seaward after the railroad bypassed it in 1922 toward a station in the middle of nowhere. Actually an island separated from the mainland by narrow waterways, it reflects the influence of Ringling and other aficionados of Italian art.

Casey Key was built on the principle that island real estate should be reserved for the well-to-do. This has kept it pristine and lightly developed, particularly at its north end. **Nokomis Beach**, at the southern end, contrasts as a beachy, fishing-oriented resort area.

LODGING

On Siesta Key you won't find a single chain hotel. You *will* find accommodations large and small by the score, however. Most vacationers on the Sarasota Bay coast gravitate toward the barrier islands. The others have their chains, but more mom-and-pops, B&Bs, inns, destination resorts, and privately owned places. On the mainland, especially around the airport, business travelers find no-nonsense franchise and small motels, plus a couple of luxury options. With downtown's renaissance, more and more vacationers are choosing mainland accommodations.

Privately owned second homes and condominiums provide another source of accommodations along the Sarasota Bay coast. Vacation brokers who match visitors with such properties are listed under "Home and Condo Rentals," at the end of this section.

I've listed here a well-rounded selection of Sarasota area accommodations, including a few of the better chain hotels. Toll-free 800 or 888 reservation numbers, where available, are listed after local numbers.

A star after the pricing designation indicates that the rate includes at least a continental breakfast in the cost of lodging.

Pricing codes are explained below. They are normally per person/double occupancy for hotel rooms and per unit for efficiencies, apartments, cottages, suites, and villas. The range spans low- and high-season rates. Many resorts offer off-season packages at special rates. Pricing does not include the 6 percent Florida sales tax. Some large resorts add service gratuities or maid surcharges. Sarasota County also imposes a 2 percent tourist tax.

Rate Categories

Inexpensive	Up to $50
Moderate	$50 to $110
Expensive	$110 to $180
Very Expensive	$180 and up

The following abbreviations are used for credit card information:

AE - American Express	DC - Diners Club
CB - Carte Blanche	MC - MasterCard
D - Discover Card	V - Visa

Anna Maria

ROD & REEL MOTEL
Managers: Todd and Janet Test.
941-778-2780.
877 North Shore Dr., Anna Maria Island 34216.
Price: Moderate.
Credit Cards: AE, D, MC, V.
Handicap Access: No.

This motel sits prettily on a narrow slab of bayfront beach with flowery landscaping, shuffleboard, picnic facilities, a sunning deck, and a tiki-roofed "Beach Yak Shack." Each of the 10 one-room efficiencies is fully furnished with a kitchenette (microwave, stovetop, and refrigerator), ironing board, couch, plastic dining room chairs, and spic-and-span housekeeping. The motel is next to the independently owned Rod & Reel Pier

Bradenton

HOLIDAY INN RIVERFRONT
General Manager: Peter Saloukas.
941-747-3727 or 800-HOLIDAY.

This is mainland Bradenton's loveliest property, perched riverside, pertly landscaped, and designed to mesh with Bradenton's Spanish colonial heritage. Heavy wood and wrought iron embellish the striking atrium lobby, off which lies a

100 Riverfront Dr. W.,
Bradenton 34205.
Price: Moderate.
Credit Cards: AE, CB, D,
DC, MC, V.

pleasant fountain courtyard dripping with hibiscus and oleander blossoms. Here you'll also find the pool and spa and the entrance to the hotel's various indoor and outdoor restaurants and bars. A few steps away spreads the Manatee River, edged by the new Bradenton Waterfront Park. Other amenities include a fitness center, complimentary morning coffee and newspaper, and a gift shop. All 153 rooms of the five-story hotel overlook the river or courtyard with private balconies, and are stocked with coffee makers, wet bars, refrigerators, and hair dryers.

Bradenton Beach

DUNCAN HOUSE B&B
Innkeepers: Joe and Becky
Garbus.
941-778-6858.
1703 Gulf Dr., Bradenton
Beach 34217.
Price: Moderate*.
Credit Cards: AE, MC, V.
Handicap Access: No.

Scrunched between a breakfast joint and some trailers, across the street from the beach, resides an oasis of whimsy in tropical purple, pink, and blue, with carved balusters and scalloped edging — a vision amongst ugliness. Built in the 1800s, this home was moved from downtown Bradenton in 1946 to its present location. Ask the innkeepers to see pictures of the original building, its ferry trip, and their renovation project, which turned a decrepit triplex into a charming, six-room facility. Public rooms are compact and lined with board-and-batten walls. The spacious accommodations include private baths and complete kitchen facilities and are dressed in extraordinary antique pieces, cheerful window treatments, and floral wallpaper. A separate entrance leads to each apartment. A gourmet breakfast, pool, and beach access add to this bed-and-breakfast's special qualities.

SEASIDE MOTEL
Owners: Kwan and Fawn
Ker.
941-778-5254 or
800-447-7124.
2200 Gulf Dr. N., Bradenton
Beach 34217-2236.
Price: Moderate to
Expensive.
Credit Cards: D, MC, V.
Handicap Access: No.

We stayed here once several years ago, when it was called El Bandito and we were looking for an inexpensive beach place for the family for the weekend. Wisely, they've changed the name. They've also completely renovated and lightened up the eight units — another wise decision. The studios and one efficiency (there's also one motel room) now have all-new kitchen counters, refrigerators, microwaves, and stovetops, plus remodeled bathrooms and all-white room interiors. Each room looks out on the gulf, and the motel has its own private beach, segregated behind an eyesore concrete wall. Here guests can use the round wooden picnic tables and chaise lounges or walk the steps down to the beach and water. It's a good bargain for beachside lodging with pleasant amenities.

Holmes Beach

BEACH INN
General Manager: Stephen
M. Hogan.
941-778-9597.
101 66th St., Holmes Beach
34217-1345.
Price: Moderate to
Expensive.
Credit Cards: CB, D, DC,
MC, V.
Handicap Access: No.

Along the shores of Anna Maria Island you'll find dozens of small motels with a mom-and-pop feel. Typical is Beach Inn, with 14 units, 10 of them beachfront and sharing a porch or balcony. Furnishings are modern and include that beach requisite, a mini-fridge. Efficiencies have full kitchens. Surroundings are pleasantly landscaped but small, confined by a white picket fence. In places such as this, vacationers come to commune with the beach, and this one is perfect, so what else matters? Across the dead-end side street is a bistro-bar for utter beach convenience.

One of Florida's few beachside B&Bs takes up residence in Roaring Twenties digs at Holmes Beach's Harrington House.

Karen T. Bartlett

**HARRINGTON HOUSE
B&B**
Innkeepers: Jo and Frank
Davis.
941-778-5444.
5626 Gulf Dr., Holmes
Beach 34217.
Price: Expensive to Very
Expensive*.
Credit Cards: MC, V.
Handicap Access: Living
area and one downstairs
room.

One of Florida's loveliest and best-maintained bed-and-breakfasts, Harrington adds to its homey, historic allure with a beach front. Built in 1925 of local coquina rock and pecky cypress, with Mediterranean flourishes, the home was refurbished with casual elegance and magical touches. Each of the seven rooms is labeled — Renaissance, Birdsong, Sunset, etc. — with a needlepoint door sign. Room sizes vary, from spacious with a king-sized bed to comfortably cozy. Each guestroom has its own bath-room, refrigerator, and TV. An eclectic collection of handpicked antique furniture enhances guests' com-fort. A dramatic cut-stone fireplace dominates the sitting room, where taped classical music is interrupted only by an occasional piano solo and homemade chocolate chip cookies are always on hand. Guests enjoy full home-cooked breakfasts at individual tables, amid Victorian pieces and filmy white curtains. Outdoor areas include sun decks, a pool, a wide beach, and charmingly colorful landscaping around picket fences and arched alcoves. Four more rooms occupy the Beach House, one door down. Bikes and kayaks are available for guests' use.

Lido Key

HALF MOON BEACH CLUB
General Manager: Shelley Lederman.
914-388-3694 or 800-358-3245.
2050 Ben Franklin Dr., Sarasota 34236.
Price: Moderate to Expensive.
Credit Cards: AE, D, DC, MC, V.

Half Moon's stretch of beach is so romantic that people come here to get married and shoot commercials. During the winter months, repeat business, comfortable social areas, and the sheer intimacy of the property lend it a community feeling. Two neo Art Deco buildings roughly form a half-moon and hold 86 guestrooms, efficiencies, and suites, all with refrigerators, coffee makers, and hair dryers. Contemporary light-wood, glass-cube, and Deco appointments grace the rooms and public areas, but the beach is the British-owned resort's best feature. Everything draws you outdoors, including an indoor restaurant that overlooks the pool, bike rentals, a beach sun deck with thatch cabanas, well-tended grounds, volleyball, a curiously wild-feeling dunes-edged beach, and dramatic sunsets.

RADISSON LIDO BEACH RESORT
General Manager: Tim Hunter.
941-388-2161 or 800-333-3333.
700 Ben Franklin Dr., Sarasota 34236.
Price: Moderate to Very Expensive.
Credit Cards: AE, D, MC, V.

Located next to Lido Key's public beach, the 116-unit Radisson provides attractive, pleasant accommodations and a full range of water sports in the thick of beach activity. The tiled pool sits on the shell-scattered beach and has its own beach bar. The color scheme indoors and out and in the alfresco restaurant is tropical greens and pinks. Modern, nicely furnished rooms come with or without full kitchens. Some have a small refrigerator and microwave instead; all have coffee makers.

Longboat Key

COLONY BEACH AND TENNIS RESORT
General Manager: Katherine Klauber Moulton.
941-383-6464 or 800-426-5669.
1620 Gulf of Mexico Dr., Longboat Key 34228.

The Colony ranks among Florida's finest resorts, a place where you could hide indefinitely behind security gates without ever having to face the real world. It stakes its reputation on top-notch tennis and dining. Its 21 courts are state-of-the-art soft surface, including 10 that use a revolutionary underground watering system known as Hydro-

Price: Very Expensive.
Credit Cards: AE, CB, D,
DC, MC, V.

Court. The Colony Restaurant, one of the property's four dining spots, consistently wins awards. The 18-acre resort occupies a stretch of private beach that was recently renourished. Complimentary kids' recreational programs take young guests to the courts, beach, pool, and off-property attractions. The Colony's 235 privately owned units range from a high-rise penthouse to tony beach houses, but most are one- or two-bedroom suites. All units contain modern kitchen facilities; designer lamps, art, and furnishings; and marble master baths. Guests have free use of tennis facilities as well as a spa and a health club with an aerobic studio. A golf-around program allows the sports-minded to sample the best of Sarasota's links.

HOLIDAY INN
General Manager: Gary
Dorschel.
941-383-3771 or
800-HOLIDAY.
4949 Gulf of Mexico Drive,
Longboat Key 34228.
Price: Moderate to Very
Expensive.
Credit Cards: AE, CB, DC,
D, MC, V.

There's less starch in the attitude of Longboat Key's northern end than in the southern. The Holiday Inn here is classier than the average hotel chain standard but is still more easygoing than the island's secured southern properties. The lobby makes an elegant introduction, with marble floors and potted plants. One of two swimming pools is contained inside the Holidome, an indoor, climate-controlled recreation center complete with whirlpool and exercise room. Other recreation possibilities center around a wide and luxurious beach with a cabana, sailboat rentals, and a beach bar and cafe. There's also an outdoor swimming pool, sauna, four lighted tennis courts, a bar, a restaurant, and a convenience food court. Rooms and suites — 146 in all, 23 of them kitchen suites — provide comfortable accommodations with above-standard furnishings and a view of either the indoor or outdoor pool. Thirteen of the rooms and two of the suites have recently been renovated as "kids' suites," perfectly structured for families, with a separate room within a room where kids have their own bunk beds, television, video games, and radio.

LONGBOAT KEY CLUB
General Manager: Russell
LeGrande.
941-383-8821 or
800-237-8821.
301 Gulf of Mexico Dr.,
P.O. Box 15000, Longboat
Key 34228.
Price: Expensive to Very
Expensive.
Credit Cards: AE, CB, DC,
MC, V.

Located where John Ringling built the foundation for his doomed Ritz-Carlton in the 1920s, a community resort today thrives on 400 acres of luscious gulf-front property. One 18-hole and three nine-hole courses attract serious golfers. Two tennis centers and a complete array of bicycles, rafts, sailboats, boogie boards, kayaks, and snorkeling gear provide plenty of activity options. In all there are 38 Har-Tru tennis courts, an Olympic-size swimming pool, a golf school, and a kids' club. Six dining rooms range in style from formal to poolside. Classy touches and a Sun Belt motif grace the open, recently renovated public areas as well as the 233 condominium suites and guestrooms, which occupy seven buildings with views of the gulf, golf course, or lagoon — all behind security gates. Special attention to detail, such as twice-daily cleanings, refrigerators, preferred seating at local entertainment centers, and complimentary use of exercise facilities, earns Longboat Key Club all its stars, diamonds, and accolades.

ROLLING WAVES COTTAGES

General Manager: Kathy Wikes.
941-383-1323.
6351 Gulf of Mexico Dr., Longboat Key 34228.
Price: Moderate to Expensive.
Credit Cards: MC, V.
Handicap Access: No.

What more could you ask of a beach vacation: a cute little 1940s cottage furnished modernly in bright colors, containing a remodeled full kitchen and bath and provided with picnic table, grill, sea grapes, huge pink hibiscus blossoms, and a quiet beach outside the door? Rolling Waves' eight cottages are kept meticulous and decorated with touches of character — white saltillo kitchen floor tiles, a rag rug over wood floors in a couple of the cottages, full-sized futons in the living room. Located in Longboat Key's old, historic section, it escapes the glitz and the throngs.

Nokomis Beach

A BEACH RETREAT

Owner: David Macrae.
941-485-8771 or 888-235-6161.
105 Casey Key Rd., Nokomis 34275.
Price: Moderate to Expensive.
Credit Cards: MC, V.
Handicap Access: Yes.

Having taken over the fishing-oriented Sea Grape, A Beach Retreat now has efficiencies and apartments on both the beach and the bay. The new owner has substantially fancied up the place with a jaunty yellow paint job and lattice trim. There's a swimming pool on the bay side, where six boat docks and five units accommodate guests and their vessels. The gulf rooms, mostly ground level, are steps from a lovely, natural beach, but because of the wonderful, tall sea oats, they have no view of the gulf. The 27 units all have their own look and layout — largely modern but with some imperfections that lend beach character. All but two have a full kitchen.

Sarasota

THE CYPRESS

Innkeepers: Vicki Hadley and Robert and Nina Belott.
941-955-4683.
621 Gulfstream, Sarasota 34236.

Details make a bed-and-breakfast inn, and the Cypress's attention to special touches, flourishes, and minutiae place it among the top in its genre. Notice the antique ice cream table with swivel-out stools in the sunny breakfast room, Robert's masterful photographs on the walls, the

Price: Expensive to Very Expensive*.
Credit Cards: AE, D, MC, V.
Handicap Access: No.

exquisite crown molding throughout, the vintage Edison phonograph in the Martha Rose room, the fresh flowers in every room, the multicourse gourmet breakfasts, the happy-hour hors d'oeuvres, the complimentary top-shelf cordials before bedtime, and the cookie-turndown service. The innkeepers, in short, spoil their guests. This young trio of talent took a 1940s home that the original owner's daughter refused to sell out to encroaching condos. That leaves the Cypress — named for its sturdy building material — a flower in the shadow of high-rises. Still, the location is quite enviable. From the front deck guests can watch the sun set over the masts of yachts in the marina across the way. Downtown's burgeoning Palm Avenue district of galleries, sidewalk cafes, and specialty shops, meanwhile, is a short stroll away.

HYATT SARASOTA
General Manager: John O'Hara.
941-366-9000 or 800-233-1234.
1000 Blvd. of the Arts, Sarasota 34236.
Price: Expensive to Very Expensive.
Credit Cards: AE, CB, D, DC, MC, V.

Inside the Hyatt, the pinnacle of mainland lodging in Sarasota, unfolds a world of modern decor, contemporary comfort, and bayside splendor. A soaring atrium makes way for a clubby lounge and formal dining room with windows overlooking the water. At the front desk, staff in crisp uniforms are efficient but cool. The lack of warmth carries throughout the property, I've noticed. Spaciousness and good taste characterize the 12-story hotel's 297 rooms and 12 suites, which are decorated plainly, in dark tones, and come complete with deluxe amenities. Boat slips, a marina, and a waterfront restaurant highlight the bay. A full fitness center, a swimming pool, and close proximity to the Sarasota Quay, Van Wezel Performing Arts Hall, and downtown attractions make this long-standing landmark a favorite with business travelers.

Siesta Key

BANANA BAY CLUB
Owners: Stephen and Linda Meylan.
941-346-0113 or 888-6BAN-BAY (888-622-6229).
8254 Midnight Pass Rd., Siesta Key 34242.
Price: Moderate to Expensive.
Credit Cards: AE, MC, V.
Handicap Access: No.

Banana Bay Club called to me as I drove by it. Among all the high-rise condos and beach clubs on Siesta Key, this one seemed to stand out. One thing different about this island property is that it occupies not a beach but the shoreline of a quiet, tidal lagoon, also a bird sanctuary, traveled only by canoes and rowboats. When the manager described the seven guest units as very Floridian, I prepared myself for yet another rattan-and-floral rubber-stamp job. But lo and behold, there was nothing ordinary about this interior scheme. Safari patterns, colored bed sheets, European-style kitchen cabinets, splashy boldness, and individual style marked the difference. "We use the word 'pizzazz' a lot," the manager told me, "and 'immaculate.'" Confirmed! Accommodations range from a studio apartment to a two-bedroom house, and include a small heated swimming pool. Bikes, boats, canoes, and a fishing dock are available free of charge. Units are stocked with more than just the necessities, and the staff provides those small, special services that comprise the forgotten art of gracious hosting. Small pets welcome.

CRESCENT HOUSE B&B
Innkeeper: Jack Liss.
941-346-0857.
459 Beach Road, Siesta Key 34242.
Price: Moderate*.
Credit Cards: No.

If you enjoy feeling as though you are a guest in a friend's home, this is your kind of place. Interesting antique pieces add to its charm. The house is vintage 1920s, which means lots of lovely latticework, shake siding outside, and a wonderful fireplace inside. It also means small rooms that show their age. An antique pump organ in the jalousied Florida room plays only when the humidity is high (which occurs fairly regularly in these parts), and a key lime tree out back provides a squeeze for your refreshments. An outdoor hot tub and sun deck add to the amenities. Each of the four guestrooms has a television and an air-conditioning unit; baths are shared. Breakfast is self-serve on a venerable, lace-covered dining room table.

SARASOTA SURF AND RACQUET CLUB
Manager: Rosie A. Turner.
941-349-2200 or 800-237-5671.
5900 Midnight Pass Rd., Sarasota 34242.
Price: Moderate to Expensive (one-week minimum).
Credit Cards: MC, V.

Siesta Key holds a lot of different small, personalized places to stay. For those who prefer anonymity and amenities, this is one fine choice. Its mid- and high-rises tower over Siesta's white sands, giving most of the 182 two-bedroom luxury condos a magnificent sea view. All are fully furnished and equipped with kitchens. Four tennis courts — two Har-Tru and two Lakold — justify the "racquet" in the name; plus there are two swimming pools and a small fitness room. Rentals are by the week, month, or season.

Venice

BANYAN HOUSE
Innkeepers: Chuck and Susan McCormick.
941-484-1385.
519 S. Harbor Dr., Venice 34285.
Price: Moderate to Expensive*.

In the mid-1920s architects designed Venice in accordance with its Italian name. Homes and buildings were modeled after northern Mediterranean styles. The town's first community swimming pool was located in the backyard of one of the original homes, next to a fledgling banyan tree.

Karen T. Bartlett

A touch of the Old World at Banyan House, a venerable bed-and-breakfast in Venice.

Credit Cards: MC, V.
Handicap Access: No.

Today that small pool, with its Greek-maiden fountain and now-sprawling tree, is still next to the same home, a red-tile-roofed bed-and-breakfast inn today known as the Banyan House. Classic statuary, fountains, multihued blossoms, a courtyard, and a hot tub share the property. Four rooms, each with a private bath, exert their individual personalities, but with less panache than the public rooms. The Palm Room has a fireplace, the Laurel Room country-style appointments, the Tree House a sunny sitting room overlooking the pool, the Sun Deck a separate entrance. Only the Laurel Room has no outdoor deck. All units contain at least a small refrigerator; three are efficiencies. Deluxe touches include bathrobes in the closet and Irish cream cordials on the dressing table. Continental breakfast is served in a solarium off the formal sitting room. The latter is furnished with an antique Italian fireplace and comfortable furnishings that invite guests to lounge and linger over a glass of chardonnay. Pecky cypress, wood beam ceilings, terra-cotta slate tiling, and wrought-iron banisters are all original. Free use of bicycles allows guests to explore old Venice's nearby shopping mecca and beach.

SANDBAR BEACH RESORT (BEST WESTERN)
General Manager: Elaine S. Nanos.
800-822-4853 or 941-488-2251.
811 The Esplanade N., Venice 34285.
Price: Moderate to Expensive.
Credit Cards: AE, CB, D, DC, MC, V.

Venice does not offer a great variety of short-term beach accommodations. The Sandbar, though simple, is among the best in that genre. It sits squarely on the beach, and its 45 low-rise units are all either newly built or renovated with a modern, tropical appeal. Most are full efficiencies; others have a microwave and mini-fridge but not the two-burner stove. Volleyball on the beach and a waterfront cafe add to the sense of sand-between-the-toes informality.

HOME & CONDO RENTALS

American Realty of Venice (941-484-8080; 1700 W. Venice Ave., Venice 34285)

Longboat Accommodations and Travel (941-383-9505 or 800-237-9505; 4030 Gulf of Mexico Dr., Longboat Key 34228) Handles more than 300 waterfront properties.

Michael Saunders & Company (941-951-6660 or 800-881-2222; 1801 Main St., Sarasota 34236) Condominiums and homes on the most prime properties of Sarasota and its islands.

Paradise Rental Management (941-778-4800 or 800-237-2252; Holmes Beach 34217) Rental condos and homes on Anna Maria Island.

RV RESORTS

Horseshoe Cove (941-758-5335; 5100 60th St. E., Bradenton 34203) A 60-acre oak-grove riverfront site, including a 12-acre island with a pavilion and nature and biking trails. Resort has a heated pool and spa, a postal facility, hookup to phone and cable, lighted fishing docks on the Braden River, shuffleboard courts, and other recreational facilities.

Sarasota Bay Travel Trailer Park (941-794-1200 or 800-247-8361; 10777 44th Ave. W., Bradenton 34210) Located on the bay with full hookups, a boat ramp and dock, fishing, horseshoes, exercise room, recreation hall, and entertainment.

Venice Campground (941-488-0850; 4085 E. Venice Ave., exit 34 off Interstate 75, Venice 34292) Full hookups and waterfront sites. Amenities include security gates, heated swimming pool, shuffleboard, horseshoe, nature trail, fishing, boat and canoe rentals, laundry room, and supply store.

DINING

For Sarasotans, eating out is as much a cultural event as attending the opera. It is often an inextricable part of an evening at the theater or a gallery opening. Sarasotans take dining out quite seriously and keep restaurants full, even off-season. Their enthusiasm for newness makes kitchens more innovative than those of their neighbors to the south. Sarasota slides along the cutting edge of new Florida cuisine while maintaining classic favorites that range from rickety oyster bars to French cafes.

The following listings span the diversity of Sarasota Bay coast cuisine in these price categories:

Inexpensive	Up to $15
Moderate	$15 to $25
Expensive	$25 to $35
Very Expensive	$35 or more

Cost is figured on a typical meal (at dinner, unless dinner is not served) that would include an appetizer or dessert, salad (if included with the meal), entrée, and coffee. Many restaurants offer early dining discounts, usually called "early bird specials." These rarely are listed on the regular menu and sometimes are not publicized by tip-conscious servers. I have noted restaurants that offer them. Certain restrictions apply, such as time constraints, a specific menu, or number of people first in the door. Call the restaurant and ask about its policy. Those restaurants listed with "Healthy Selections" usually mark such on their menu.

The following abbreviations are used for credit card information and meals:

AE - American Express	DC - Diners Club
CB - Carte Blanche	MC - MasterCard
D - Discover Card	V - Visa
B - Breakfast	D - Dinner
L - Lunch	SB - Sunday Brunch

Anna Maria

ROTTEN RALPH'S
941-778-3953.
Galati Yacht Basin, 902 Bay
  Blvd. S.
Price: Moderate.
Early Dining Menu: Yes.
Children's Menu: No (kid-
  suitable items on regular
  menu)
Cuisine: Old Florida.
Liquor: Full.
Serving: L, D.
Credit Cards: CB, DC, MC,
  V.
Handicap Access: Yes.
Reservations: No.
Special Features: Dock
  seating on the marina.

The atmosphere here is due entirely to the setting. It's a place that locals frequent, full of character and characters. The laminated placemat menu describes many finger food selections (steamed shellfish, Buffalo shrimp, escargots, chili, chicken wings, nachos), Old Florida fried seafood standards, steamed seafood pots, and other, more esoteric concessions such as shrimp linguine Alfredo, Danish baby back ribs, and Cajun shrimp. The blackened grouper in my sandwich obviously had been swimming not long ago, and was well seasoned. We've always found the food fresh and tasty, but truthfully enjoy the view more.

SANDBAR
941-778-0444.
100 Spring Ave.
Price: Moderate to
  Expensive.
Early Dining Menu: Yes.
Children's Menu: Yes.
Cuisine: Seafood.
Healthy Selections: No.
Liquor: Full.
Serving: L, D.

At the Sandbar you can dine alfresco or within a porchlike, wood-paneled dining room. Either way you enjoy a close-up view of the gulf and an eroding, boulder-shored beach. The view makes it a popular spot. It's one of those places where you can sit outdoors 'neath an umbrella or in a lean-to on patio furniture and order a good sandwich, salad, or entrée. Selections are extensive, including conch fritters, Szechuan snapper sandwich, blue

Credit Cards: AE, CB, D,
  DC, MC, V.
Handicap Access: Yes.
Reservations: Preferred
  seating available indoors
  only.
Special Features: Outdoor
  deck seating on the
  beach.

crab-cake sandwich, lobster club sandwich, grilled bistro steak salad, seafood penne pasta, poached salmon in pastry, and stuffed veggie potato. The same lunch menu is served indoors. At dinnertime the two menus go their separate ways. On the deck, selections are much the same as at lunch. Inside, the Sandbar turns gourmet with shrimp fra diavolo, roast duckling, sesame-crusted tuna, citrus-barbecued salmon, crawfish étoufée, and steak au poivre. I have always preferred the atmosphere and beach cuisine on the deck. It's a great place to people-watch, and I've had better service there.

Bradenton

THE PIER
941-748-8087.
Memorial Pier, 1200 First
  Ave. W., downtown.
Price: Moderate.
Early Dining Menu: No.
Children's Menu: Yes.
Cuisine: American/
  Continental.
Healthy Selections: No.
Liquor: Full.
Serving: L, D, SB.
Credit Cards: AE, DC, MC,
  V.
Handicap Access: Yes.
Reservations: Accepted.
Special Features: River
  view, luncheon buffet,
  patio dining.

A bank of large, semicircular windows peers out upon waters once traveled by mail boats from Tampa coming to the old pier. Built in the 1940s, the pier knew many lives, which its modern-day namesake restaurant recalls with historic maritime memorabilia. The Pier's many rooms sport a modern, nautical look of dark wood and ships' lanterns. At lunch it caters to downtown's mixed bag of retirees and businessfolk with a menu and buffet dedicated more to flavor than to health. I've enjoyed the alligator appetizer, fired Caribbean style with hot and sweet peppers, onions, and mushrooms and served in a cast-iron skillet. I'm somewhat of a crab cakes connoisseur, and I found the Pier's to be among the most nicely seasoned I've tried, lightly sautéed and served on a grainy bun but slightly heavy on crumb fillers. The lunch buffet includes soup, the day's hot special and hot dessert (cobbler last time I was there), a fresh pasta bar, salad, and a cold dessert table. The dinner menu specializes in prime rib, all-you-can-eat grouper fingers, and seafood. Service is swift and friendly: Although my server had a large party arriving, he took the time to afford me, a lone diner, care and answers to my many questions.

Bradenton Beach

GULF DRIVE CAFE
941-778-1919.
900 Gulf Dr.
Price: Inexpensive.
Early Dining Menu: No.

On a Saturday or Sunday morning, this is the hottest spot on Anna Maria Island. Folks line up for its Belgian waffles and three-egg breakfast specials, with a view of the beach and gulf from

Children's Menu: Yes.
Cuisine: American.
Healthy Selections: No.
Liquor: No.
Serving: B, L, D.
Credit Cards: D, MC, V.
Handicap Access: Yes, but
tight quarters.
Reservations: No.
Special Features: Patio on
the beach.

**HISTORIC BRIDGE
STREET CAFE**
941-779-1706.
200 Bridge St.
Price: Inexpensive.
Early Dining Menu: No.
Children's Menu: No.
Cuisine: American/
Seafood.
Healthy Selections: No.
Serving: B, L, D.
Credit Cards: AE, MC, V.
Handicap Access: Yes.
Reservations: No.
Special Features: Outdoor
seating at the city pier.

the small, close dining room or patio. Efficient waitresses serve coffee in huge mugs and platefuls of home-style food. Lunch burgers and dinner seafood specials at reasonable prices have contributed to keeping the restaurant a local favorite for years. The cuisine is all-American cafe style: hot roast turkey sandwich, breaded shrimp, grilled rib-eye steak, and fresh strawberries topped with brown sugar and sour cream.

Wake up to the slosh of bay waters against pier pilings and the hum of early morning traffic crossing the Cortez Bridge. Breakfast is an event here. Not a grand event, but one steeped in local color and history; nothing fancier than French toast and patio furniture. The servers have a soft southern accent and a no-nonsense friendliness and sense of humor. The humble, shacklike cafe straddles the city pier, a truncated former bridge. You can take one of the few tables inside, but you'd be foolish to pass up the outdoor view in any weather short of a downpour. Lunch and dinner demonstrate classic Old Florida fish-house style with seafood selections from the deep fryer plunked into a basket: oysters, grouper, shrimp, crab cakes. For a sampler, order one of the two seafood platters. The cafe also serves great burgers, the signature one being the Pier Burger, with onions, mushrooms, and Swiss cheese.

Lido Key

OLD SALTY DOG
941-388-4311.
1601 Ken Thompson Pkwy.,
City Island.
Price: Inexpensive.
Early Dining Menu: No.
Children's Menu: No.
Cuisine: Seafood/British.
Healthy Selections: No.
Liquor: Beer, wine.
Serving: L, D.
Credit Cards: V, MC.
Handicap Access: Yes.
Reservations: No.
Special Features: Outdoor,
waterfront seating.

A spin-off of the Siesta Key original, this one has a more properly salty setting: a grizzled sort of shack tucked into a marina in the shadow of the Longboat Key bridge. If you sit outside on the patios, you'll be entertained by boaters, waverunners, and water skiers. But before 4 pm you'll have to wait on yourself and order at the counter inside. The menu, painted on signs over the boat-shaped outside bar and over the counter inside, lists fine casual eats, such as City Island wings, New England clam chowder, deep-fried clams with fries, peel-and-eat shrimp, burgers, fish 'n chips, and the trademark Salty Dog. I ordered the grouper sand-

You're in ship shape at the bar of Old Salty Dog, overlooking the waters between Longboat Key and City Island.

Karen T. Bartlett

wich special, blackened, and was pleased to have a choice of hot, medium, or mild. (Too many places assume palate sensitivity and water down the heat of a properly executed blackening.) I ordered hot and got it just right, not so fiery as to overpower the full-flavored freshness of the fish. This is a great place to stop after a visit to Mote Marine and its nearby attractions. We liked the wide selection of beers it offers on tap. My son liked that we didn't have to wait long for our food.

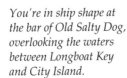

Longboat Key

THE COLONY DINING ROOM
941-383-5558.
Colony Beach and Tennis Resort, 1620 Gulf of Mexico Dr.
Price: Very Expensive.
Healthy Selections: No.
Children's Menu: Yes.
Cuisine: Continental.
Liquor: Full.
Serving: B, L, D, SB.
Credit Cards: AE, CB, D, DC, MC, V.
Handicap Access: Yes.
Reservations: Required for dinner.
Special Features: Gulf view, stellar wine list.

The Colony Restaurant set standards for the region when it opened in the 1970s. Since then it's stolen just about every award the food and wine world has to offer. The restaurant exudes perfection without being overly pretentious; the imposing gulf view seems to soften the starch. Servers are attentive but not snobbish or overbearing. The dining room juxtaposes touches of neoclassicism against the playful beach. The menu, which changes bimonthly, relies on traditional continental style sprinkled with nouvelle wizardry. Grill-seared tuna, for example, comes with yellow tomato salsa, chipolte butter, and a blue corn stick; the crispy fried lobster tail, with sweet potato fries, wildflower honey, Dijon sauce, and bitter greens. The chef is as creative with meats: roast Colorado rack of lamb (a signature selection) with couscous croquette and Moroccan tomato jam; grilled Texas ostrich with smoked cheddar grits, huckleberry conserve, and caramel jus. Sunday brunch is an event attended by resort guests and community alike. Lunch is equally elegant. Pickled ginger and cucumber salad accompany the crab cake, onion rings have a beer batter, and roasted red and yellow bell pepper coulis accents the grilled vegetable strudel.

EUPHEMIA HAYE
941-383-3633.
5540 Gulf of Mexico Dr.
Price: Very Expensive.
Early Dining Menu: No.
Children's Menu: No.
Cuisine: Continental.
Healthy Selections: No.
Liquor: Full.
Serving: D.
Credit Cards: MC, V, CB, DC, D.
Handicap Access: Yes.
Reservations: Yes.
Special Features: Dessert parlor; entertainment nightly.

Across between a dollhouse and an art gallery, Euphemia Haye exudes the sort of whimsy and distinction at which its unusual name hints. The name actually comes from the founder's grandmother. Nothing grandmotherly about the concept and cuisine, however. Dishes get their inspiration from around the world: a beef empanada appetizer from Argentina, lamb shank from Greece, Chicken San Pedro from Mexico, Shrimp Taj Mahal from India, planked salmon from the Pacific Northwest, and so on. The Warm Weather Salad is a masterpiece of tender greens, homemade mozzarella, sweet tomatoes, peppers, and Greek olives. With the creamy roasted garlic dressing I ordered, it could have served as a meal.

My prime peppered steak was caked with crushed black peppercorns and served with a dark hot and sweet orange brandy sauce that superbly complemented the bite and burn. The tuna special of the day came with ginger and chili slaw — a fine example of the perfected details that make a meal at Euphemia Haye surpass mere meal status. To top off the experience, a trip upstairs to the Haye Loft for dessert is de rigueur. The selection is mind-boggling (not to mention diet-blowing, but let that thought go in this atmosphere). Besides sinful desserts, you can order coffee and after-dinner drinks. The peanut butter mousse was much heavier than its name suggests, enough to go around a table of four; the coconut cream pie, extraordinary.

MAR-VISTA DOCKSIDE RESTAURANT & PUB
941-383-2391.
The Village, 760 Broadway St.
Price: Moderate.
Early Dining Menu: No.
Children's Menu: Yes.
Cuisine: Seafood.
Liquor: Full.
Serving: L, D.
Credit Cards: AE, Honors, MC, V.
Handicap Access: Restaurant yes, rest rooms no.

Locals refer to it simply as The Pub. Casual at its best, it has that lovely, lived-in, borderline ramshackle look on the outside, crowned by an appropriately rusting tin roof. Inside, tables don't match, mounted fish adorn the wall, boaters hoist beers at the bar, and a view of the harbor dominates the decorator's scheme. There's also seating on the patio, on plastic chairs. Seafood is fresh, and prepared with a tropical twist: oysters Longboat for an appetizer (topped with crabmeat, horseradish, and hazelnut dressing), grilled grouper reuben, Cajun-fried oysters, and blackened catfish sandwich for lunch; Longbeach Bouillabaise, sesame tuna, and

Reservations: Preferred seating.
Special Features: Boat access.

changing pasta selections for dinner. Steamer pots in two sizes brim with shellfish and vegetables, large enough to be shared by two. We've enjoyed the cuisine and casual atmosphere here many times. On a recent visit we stopped in for munchies and a couple of beers from their large selection of microbrews and drafts. We enjoyed the thick and chunky clam chowder, a spinach salad with a nice, light, apple-based dressing, a subtly flavored portabella wild-rice salad, and an Ybor Gold beer, brewed in nearby Tampa.

MOORE'S STONE CRAB RESTAURANT
941-383-1748.
The Village, 800 Broadway St.
Price: Moderate.
Early Dining Menu: No.
Children's Menu: Yes.
Cuisine: Old Florida/Seafood.
Liquor: Full.
Serving: L, D.
Credit Cards: D, MC, V.
Handicap Access: Yes.
Reservations: No.

Exemplifying an era of Florida dining marked by rough wood paneling, lodge-style openness, and a magnificent view of the bay, Moore's has been a Longboat tradition since the 1960s. Its reputation is built upon fresh crab, brought in by the restaurant's own fleet during stone crab season, mid-October through mid-May. The rest of the menu is devoted to Florida seafood — everything from fried frog legs to seafood primavera. Things are done simply here. The salad is plain old iceberg lettuce, and squeeze bottles of cocktail and tartar sauce decorate the tables. I took a chance on the grilled shrimp. I typically steer clear of grilled shellfish, which tends to be dry. This, however, was juicy and excellent. For a roundup of what Moore's does best, order a combination platter. Hush puppies come with all the dishes.

Nokomis

PELICAN ALLEY
941-485-1893.
1009 W. Albee Rd.
Price: Moderate.
Early Dining Menu: No.
Children's Menu: Yes.
Cuisine: Old Florida/Seafood.
Healthy Selections: No.
Liquor: Full.
Serving: L, D.
Credit Cards: AE, D, DC, MC, V.
Handicap Access: Yes.
Reservations: No.
Special Features: Waterfront view.

Simplicity is the key word here. Pelican Alley is housed in a funky little waterside shack with seating indoors and out, both overlooking the Intracoastal Waterway and the bridge to Nokomis Beach. Nothing fancy. The menu leans toward batter-fried fish and steamed shellfish, with a few modern concoctions such as the seafood white-cheese pizza on focaccia bread; black beans and rice; baked grouper with shrimp, crab, mushrooms, asparagus, and lobster sauce; pork chops provençal with Asiago cheese; seafood salad melt on basil bread with melted provolone; and oyster sandwich with prosciutto. Sandwiches and entrées are offered on both the lunch and dinner menu. The key lime pie is a gooey, frozen rendition we liked. The service is a little slow, just like the pace of life here.

St. Armands Circle

DAVID MICHAEL'S
941-388-4429.
328 John Ringling Blvd.
Price: Expensive to Very
   Expensive.
Early Dining Menu: No.
Children's Menu: No.
Cuisine: New American.
Healthy Selections: No.
Liquor: Beer and wine.
Serving: L, D.
Closed: Lunch Sun. and
   Mon. between Easter and
   Christmas.
Credit Cards: AE, D, DC,
   MC, V.
Handicap Access: Yes.
Reservations: Yes.

David Michael Sprowles has always been one of our favorite chefs. We were disappointed when he sold historic little Carmichael's downtown to open his new, smaller, more generic eatery. We were far from disappointed, however, with the quality of the food. Sprowles excels at wild game and mushrooms, and fresh seafood and vegetables, an inspired style he terms "harvest cuisine." The dinner menu changes regularly according to availability of products. We selected a duck pâté appetizer and a tuna dish, and a special of wild boar loin in Asian barbecue sauce. We began humming our *mmmm*'s with the first bite and didn't stop until we'd quaffed our last drop of St.-Emilion Grand Cru. The pâté, riddled with truffles, Amagnac, and lingonberry sauce, was smooth as butter. Warm toast points and condiments of lemongrass, fennel slices, rosemary sprigs, and red pepper crescents elevated to divine the enjoyment of the prettily presented dish. I love to eat this way, experimenting with the contents of the dish for different taste sensations. Our entrées arrived as works of art, stacked layer upon layer with intrigue. The ahi tuna, sushi quality, was cooked to a perfect, fork-tender medium rare, crusted with porcini mushrooms and toasted Szechuan peppercorns. It reposed on a bed of Oriental noodles, crispy vegetables, and Asian barbecue sauce, a foundation that could have stood alone as an entrée. The boar was lean, pleasantly tender at the center, and underpinned with mashed potatoes. Filet mignon of beefalo, the house specialty, was offered that evening with wild mushrooms and a bushberry-merlot reduction. On the lunch menu, the lean hybrid meat is hand ground and char-grilled for a healthy version of hamburger. The salad selection, however, is the lunch menu's strength, with masterpieces of greens, fine cheeses, fruits, and Latin fire. As we toasted with our finals sips of Burgundy, reflecting on the food and excellent service, we agreed that this was the best dining experience we had enjoyed in a long time.

Sarasota

BIJOU CAFE
941-366-8111.
1287 First St.

Seated in the midst of the Theater and Arts District, the Bijou is the pick of the pre- and post-theater crowd and the upper-echelon business

Price: Very Expensive.
Early Dining Menu: No.
Children's Menu: No.
Cuisine: New American.
Healthy Selections: Yes.
Liquor: Full.
Serving: L, D.
Credit Cards: AE, CB, DC, MC, V.
Handicap Access: Yes.
Reservations: Recommended.

community of Sarasota. Small and simply decorated, only lacy curtains on the French doors, some heavily framed paintings, and a few stylish vases (here you'd pronounce that "vazzes") embellish. Linen and fresh flowers dress the tables, even at lunch, when the clientele is equally dressed up. The eclectic menu offers choices from continental, New Orleans, and American cuisine, from fruit soup to duck. I sampled the cold soup of the day (there's also a hot soup daily), chilled orange and pineapple puree with yogurt, a perfect meld of sweet and tart. Try the Shrimp Piri Piri. A classic example of how chef/owner Jean-Pierre Knaggs perfectly balances flavors to create entirely fresh taste sensations, it is mildly spicy with citrusy tones. It appears on both the lunch and dinner menus. Other dinner specialties include roast duckling, potato-encrusted salmon with Dijon crème fraîche and dill sauce, veal Louisville breaded with crusted pecans and served with bourbon-pear sauce, and lamb shank basted with ginger-soy barbecue sauce. The pommes gratinées Dauphinoise is a signature side dish, available à la carte. Desserts, made in-house, have an excellent reputation. My service was prompt but a bit snobbish and selectively deaf (having been out on a day of field research, my mode of dress fell a bit short of the Bijou standard, I take it).

CAFE BACI
941-921-4848.
4001 S. Tamiami Trail.
Price: Moderate to Expensive.
Early Dining Menu: Yes.
Children's Menu: No.
Cuisine: Northern Italian.
Healthy Selections: No.
Liquor: Full.
Serving: L, D.
Closed: Lunch Sat. and Sun.
Credit Cards: AE, CB, D, DC, MC, V.
Handicap Access: Yes, but not in rest room.
Reservations: For dinner.

I describe this place as " affordably dressy." It has, after all, a porte cochere out front and linen on the tables (even at lunch) inside. Its business clientele and older crowd wear nice clothes. The northern Italian specialties dwell in the realm of fine cuisine. Yet its location on plebeian South Tamiami Trail, away from Sarasota's centers of chichi, allows it to price its menu reasonably. Lunch is especially popular with locals, who squeeze the parking lot full to capacity. I enjoy lunch there, too; it imparts a bit of affordable elegance in the middle of a hectic day alongside a road-rage street. Many of the dinner entrées are available in smaller portions and prices. I recently ordered, for example, the ravioli di funghi, an exquisite plate of homemade half-moon pasta pockets filled with delicately creamed wild mushrooms and topped with a buttery tomato cream sauce. It cost only $6.25 and was, with its rich sauce, the most I could eat for lunch — thanks also to the bread basket, which was filled with marvelous focaccia squares baked with onions, garlic, sun-dried tomatoes, and parmesan cheese. Both lunch and dinner menus touch on the four major Italian food groups: pasta, veal, chicken, and seafood. These and the salads and soups beforehand are tended with a creative hand. Here's a taste: corkscrew pasta with mushrooms, peas, prosciutto, and cream; lasagna verde (made with spinach noodles); breast of chicken sautéed with porcini mushrooms and artichokes in light tomato gravy; breaded veal scaloppine with arugula, onion, and basil; pan-seared salmon with white wine, leeks, pinenuts, and sun-dried-tomato sauce; and polenta-crusted sea bass. The dinner menu also features broiled meats and the fresh catch of the day. The extensive wine list has received the *Wine Spectator* Award of Excellence.

MICHAEL'S SEAFOOD GRILLE

941-951-2467.
214 Sarasota Quay,
  Tamiami Trail &
  Fruitville Rd.
Price: Expensive to Very
  Expensive.
Early Dining Menu: Sunset
  Dining Special (one
  entrée free with purchase
  of another).
Children's Menu: Yes.
Cuisine: Seafood/New
  American.
Liquor: Full.
Serving: D.
Credit Cards: AE, CB, D,
  DC, MC, V.
Handicap Access: Limited.
Reservations:
  Recommended.
Special Features: Jazz bar
  downstairs; disco
  Thurs.–Sat. at 10:30 pm.

Michael Klauber is a well-respected name in Sarasota culinary circles. He learned successful restaurateuring early in life as a member of Longboat Key's Colony Beach Resort family and is responsible for Sarasota's annual wine festival. Upon the success of his Michael's on East, he has created, with partners, a new restaurant where imagination and freshness take the menu to Sarasota culinary ascendancy. His place at The Quay adds a sweeping semicircular view of the bay to the appeal of kitchen renderings. As is to be expected, his wine list is select though extensive, including choices by the glass. To accompany my fruity 1995 Wild Horse Pinot Noir (in places such as this, I often choose my entrée to go with my wine instead of vice versa), I selected a salad of greens, hot-spiced walnuts, strawberries, and Gorgonzola, followed by pepper-crusted tuna. A perfect match. For the salad I chose a balsamic vinaigrette, which was yogurt-based, applied judiciously, not overpowering the inspired medley of tastes and textures. The last of the Gorgonzola I dabbed up with the crusty peasant-style bread. The pan-seared tuna, billed as medium rare, was more on the rare side, but that's not a problem for me. The pepper crusting was coarse enough to make a statement without being intrusive. The tuna was topped with a sassy mango and red pepper salsa. Roasted-garlic mashed potatoes and a selection of snow peas and other lightly sautéed vegetables rounded out a meal of which I could finish only half. The menu concentrates on seafood with the likes of crispy softshell crab with cilantro-horseradish sauce, cherrystone clams on the half shell, smoked Atlantic salmon, grilled fish, pasta-seafood combinations, and specialties such as sautéed pompano with hazelnut beurre blanc and Cajun-spiced mahi mahi. Menus change from summer to winter, but mostly by sauces. Meat is also represented in fine form.

COASTERS AT THE SOUTHBRIDGE

941-925-0300.
Sarasota Boatyard, 1500
Stickney Point Rd.,
before the bridge to
Siesta Key.
Price: Moderate to
Expensive.
Early Dining Menu: No.
Children's Menu: Yes.
Cuisine: Seafood.
Healthy Selections: No.
Liquor: Full.
Serving: L, D.
Credit Cards: AE, CB, D,
DC, MC, V.
Handicap Access: Yes.
Reservations: Accepted.
Special Features: Outdoor
seating, view of
Intracoastal Waterway.

Coasters has always been one of my favorite Sarasota dining locations. Part of a New England-style shopping complex, it has a nautical personality with a modern twist. Among its many dining areas are two outdoor decks that overlook waterway traffic and contribute greatly to its popularity. Through the years the food had somewhat declined, but now there's good news. My favorite Siesta Key restaurant, Summerhouse, has taken over and added its magic to the menu. Now it's my favorite location and favorite food combined! The new management has kept the Florida/New England seafood focus, specializing in such greats as the Maryland lump crab cakes with jalapeño remoulade, and lemon pepper salmon with vodka sauce and fresh snow peas over bowtie pasta. Appetizers, soups, salads, and sandwiches offer an extensive selection of above-the-ordinary lighter fare. The "oyster cargot" appetizer combines elements of oysters Rockefeller and escargots, topped with buffalo mozzarella; artichoke bottoms are filled with crab, spinach, and feta atop roasted-shallot oregano beurre blanc. Fresh yellowfin tuna salad is tossed with baby field greens, marinated cucumbers, and wasabi soy vinaigrette. Gorgonzola and smoked onions dress up the blackened chicken breast tucked into a sourdough roll. Just reading the menu is fun. Wait 'til you taste the food.

A boathouse motif and great seafood make Phillippi Creek Sarasota's hot spot for casual dining.

Karen T. Bartlett

PHILLIPPI CREEK VILLAGE OYSTER BAR

941-925-4444.

In Sarasota they call their fish houses "oyster bars," and Phillippi Creek sets the gold standard. Combo pots for two are the specialty of the house:

5353 S. Tamiami Trail.
Price: Moderate.
Early Dining Menu: No.
Children's Menu: Yes.
Cuisine: Seafood/Old
    Florida.
Healthy Selections: Yes.
Liquor: Full.
Serving: L, D.
Credit Cards: AE, MC, V.
Handicap Access: Yes.
Reservations: No.
Special Features: Patio and
    floating dock seating
    creekside.

pans full of steamed oysters, shrimp, corn on the cob, and a selection of specialty items (clams, lobster, snow crab, or scallops). The seafood is so fresh it ought to be slapped. We've eaten here on several occasions; it's my husband's first choice when we're in town. They've made a few changes recently: new, modern bathrooms, a healthy section on the menu, and a general perk-up. I typically pick the blackened grouper sandwich, but last time I bravely broke tradition and tasted the day's special. Also grouper, this was char-grilled, then topped with a fresh tomato and shrimp provençal sauce. The mushrooms had a canned quality, but the rest was flavorful and everything I've come to expect from Phillippi. You have your choice of settings here, either indoors, in a boathouse motif at picnic tables covered with blue oilcloth, or out in the breeze on dry dock. Either way you get a blue-water view and the kind of service that puts you at ease.

SUGAR & SPICE
941-342-1649.
4000 Cattlemen Rd.
Price: Inexpensive.
Early Dining Menu: No.
Children's Menu: Yes.
Cuisine: Mennonite/
    Home-Style.
Healthy Selections: Yes,
    vegetarian.
Liquor: No.
Serving: L, D.
Closed: Sun.
Credit Cards: D, MC, V.
Handicap Access: Yes.
Reservations: No.
Special Features: Folk art —
    quilts, country-style
    wood items, etc. —
    decorate the restaurant
    and are for sale, along
    with books on the
    Mennonite faith.

A happy outgrowth of the Amish/Mennonite community on Sarasota's outskirts is the home cooking found in family restaurants throughout the area. These folks principally are farmers, so you can expect homegrown freshness at their table. Most of their eateries occupy large dining rooms with all the ambiance of a fast-food chain. This one displays some nice home touches, such as frilly curtains and homemade quilts. Daily specials showcase typical old-fashioned goodness: baked chicken, beef and noodles, Swiss steak, and barbecued pork ribs. Under the "Just Downright Good Eat'n'" heading you can choose from meat loaf, fried ham, roast beef, breaded chopped veal, turkey and dressing — good old midwestern comfort foods, all enhanced by home-baked bread and your choice of side dishes. There are also sandwiches, salads, and vegetarian items on the menu. Don't dare forget to leave room for the famous Amish forte — pie. "Sugar & Spice" tempts you with close to two dozen desserts, including cakes. I reveled in my rhubarb pie, crusted with sugar and topped with rich, ivory-colored vanilla ice cream. The specialty is shoofly pie, with a cakelike texture, wet bottom, and molasses flavor.

Siesta Key

THE BROKEN EGG
941-346-2750.
210 Avenida Madera.
Price: Inexpensive.
Children's Menu: No.
Cuisine: American.
Healthy Selections: No.
Liquor: Beer and wine.
Serving: B, L daily; D
Thurs.–Sat. only.
Credit Cards: AE, CB, D,
DC, MC, V.
Handicap Access:
Restaurant yes, rest
rooms no.
Reservations: No.
Special Features: Outdoor
seating, attached deli and
bakery.

If you're wondering where all the islanders are at breakfast time, turn the corner at Coldwell Banker on Beach Avenue and take a seat indoors or out at the Broken Egg. I was warned that this was cholesterol overload, and it's true: How could a restaurant with egg in its name not be? Besides breakfast omelets, pancakes, blintzes, muffins, coffee cake, and other fresh bakery items, the cafe serves lunch, which consists of soup, salad, and sandwiches. Brad's Fave is a grilled, seasoned chicken breast with onion, tomatoes, cheddar, and pineapple pepper jelly between slices of sourdough bread. Dottie's Own is a grilled turkey, jalapeño jelly, and cheddar sandwich. If you do feel the compulsion to offset the richness of the menu, do as I did: Order a carrot-apple-juice cocktail. *Then* ask for dessert.

THE SUMMERHOUSE
941-349-1100.
6101 Midnight Pass Rd.
Price: Very Expensive.
Early Dining Menu: No.
Children's Menu: No.
Cuisine: Continental.
Healthy Selections: Yes.
Liquor: Full.
Serving: D.
Credit Cards: AE, CB, DC,
D, MC, V.
Handicap Access: Yes.
Reservations: Yes.
Special Features: Glass
walls surrounded by
gardens; piano and other
live entertainment.

Summerhouse: It connotes an upscale informality. I love the name, always have. And I love the setting. The Summerhouse is acclaimed for its design. A prime example of the so-called Sarasota School of Architecture, it brings the outdoors inside via walls of glass and jungled grounds. You feel like you're dining in a garden, surrounded by bamboo, palms, and wild coffee plants. It's a totally pleasant experience. The servers are unpretentious; mine went out of his way to make my meal all that it could be. The menu is a study in continental gone off on a nouvelle tangent. The accent is more on flavor than lightness. Take my Tournedos Rossini. Fork-tender beef medallions were prepared exactly as I ordered (I have a difficult time making chefs believe I really want my meat rare) and topped with seared foie gras and the most elegant port and sage sauce. Mashed potatoes, roasted fresh corn, and broccoli rabe accompanied, all fresh and nicely seasoned. Entrées favor meat over seafood: pork tenderloin medallions, roast duckling, veal Oscar, seared venison tenderloin, grouper piccata, and lightly pan-blackened yellowfin tuna, as a sampling. I recommend the heart salad (artichoke hearts, hearts of palm, asparagus, and juicy tomato slices with balsamic vinaigrette) to start and the crème brûlée for the perfect finish. The latter had the most delicate custard I've tasted 'neath an ever-so-thin caramel veneer. Classical music in the background, a satisfying glass of pinot noir, and sunset on the nearby soft, white beach afterward — all accounted for an evening nearly impossible to top.

Venice

THE CROW'S NEST
941-484-9551.
1968 Tarpon Center Dr. on the South Jetty.
Price: Moderate to Expensive.
Early Dining Menu: No.
Children's Menu: Yes.
Cuisine: Seafood/Florida.
Healthy Selections: No.
Liquor: Full.
Serving: L, D.
Credit Cards: AE, D, MC, V.
Handicap Access: Limited to downstairs pub, where full menu is available to persons unable to get to the upstairs restaurant.
Reservations: No.
Special Features: Marina view.

Perched in the second story over a marina, the Crow's Nest also earns its name from a tastefully seaworthy ambiance. No, not tons of dusty fish netting and tired trappings — this is yacht-class stuff. Tall windows look down upon spiring masts. Brass, mounted fish, and navy-blue trim decorate wood walls and the garret ceiling. The menu relies on a variety of styles to stay interesting and multidimensional. Appetizers and burgers are served in the tavern downstairs all day. Upstairs at lunchtime you'll find a well-designed selection: baked Brie, seafood bisque, smoked peppered mackerel (large, tasty, and nicely presented), char-broiled mahi mahi sandwich, classic reuben, and seafood platter. Dinner entrées change nightly and concentrate on seafood in both traditional and inventive guises: hand-breaded butterfly shrimp, oysters tossed in cracker meal, saffron-seasoned bouillabaisse over linguine, roasted Bahamian lobster tail, grouper Key Largo (with crab, shrimp, scallops, and hollandaise), pan-seared scallops with spinach and forest mushrooms over linguine with peppered garlic cream, orange roughy with Florida citrus sauce. Good bets: the sun-dried tomato rolls, crab cakes with red pepper mayonnaise, key lime pie, and Chocolate Lovin' Spoonful (dense cake with blackberry coulis).

SNOOK HAVEN
941-485-7221.
5000 E. Venice Ave., exit 34 off Interstate 75.
Price: Inexpensive.
Early Dining Menu: No.
Children's Menu: No, but kid-appropriate items on regular menu.
Cuisine: American/Barbecue.
Healthy Selections: No.
Liquor: Beer and wine.
Serving: L, D.
Closed: Tues., June–Sept.
Credit Cards: MC, V.

For a poignant taste of rural Old Florida close to the freeway, visit Snook Haven on a Sunday for live bluegrass and barbecue. Make a day of it and go for a boat or canoe ride. Hear the legend of the killer turtles (a leftover from the 1940s on-site filming of Tarzan's Revenge of the Killer Turtles). Or visit any day and enjoy ultracasual dining — burgers, fried fish, chicken gizzards, barbecue specialties, etc. — on the banks of the wild and scenic Myakka River. The baked beans are among the best I've ever tasted, liberally flavored with bacon and cooked a long, long time. Sit at the stretch tables and plastic chairs inside or at a picnic table on the

Karen T. Bartlett

It may look relaxing, but watch out for "killer turtles" at Snook Haven, where legend and Florida rural style persist.

Handicap Access: Yes (rest rooms not accessible).
Reservations: No.
Special Features: Barbecue bashes Sundays, live music nightly, view of the Myakka River with canoeing available.

screened porch or riverside deck. Afterward, work off your meal with a leisurely canoe paddle down the lazy river. It's truly a "y'all come" kind of place.

FOOD PURVEYORS

BAKERIES

Berliner Backstube German Bakery & Coffee (941-778-7344; 117 Bridge St., Bradenton Beach)

Caribbean Pie Co. (941-925-9069; 5773 Beneva Rd. S. at Clark, Sarasota) Freshly baked desserts. Key lime and Caribbean cream pies, whole or by the slice, and ice cream.

Pastry Art Bakery (941-795-1719; 6753 Manatee Ave. W., Bradenton) Cakes, desserts, European pastries, breads, rolls, and espresso bar.

CANDY & ICE CREAM

Bresler's Ice Cream & Yogurt (941-488-0332; 249 W. Venice Ave., Venice) Old-fashioned parlor with full fountain service and ice cream specialties.

Kilwin's Chocolates & Ice Cream (941-388-3200; 312 John Ringling Blvd., St. Armands Circle) Homemade ice cream, specialty sundaes, Mackinac Island fudge, and handmade chocolates.

Joe's Eats & Sweets (941-778-0007; 219 Gulf Dr. S., Bradenton Beach) 40 gourmet brands of ice cream made on the premises, including sugar-free flavors, fat-free and low-fat yogurt. Sodas, sundaes, shakes, espresso, and cappuccino.

Martha's Candy & Clutter (941-485-4904; 237 W. Venice Ave., Venice) Homemade bonbons, chocolates in all shapes and foils, old-fashioned hard candies.

COFFEE

Joffrey's Coffee & Tea Co. (941-388-5282; St. Armands Circle) Espresso, baked goods, and desserts.

Venice Wine & Coffee (941-484-3667; 121 Venice Ave. W., Venice) Buy gourmet coffee by the bag or cup at the espresso bar. Also wine, international beers, chocolates, and cookies.

DELI & SPECIALTY FOODS

Centre Market (941-383-2887; Centre Shops, 5370 Gulf of Mexico Dr., Longboat Key) European-style market with fresh produce, seafood, meats, prepared food, baked goods, wine, specialty grocery items, and German newspapers.

Geier's Sausage Kitchen (941-923-3004; 7447 Tamiami Trail, Sarasota) European-style sausage and smoked meats, prime fresh meats.

The Gourmet Market (941-953-9101; 1469 Main St., Sarasota) Pastas, oils, vinegars, coffees, and sauces.

Islanders' Market (941-778-1925; 9807 Gulf Dr., Anna Maria) Deli items, produce, and meat market.

Siesta Key Market (941-349-1474; 205 Canal Rd., Siesta Key Village) Deli, bakery, and grocery.

The Tomato Patch (941-448-0828; 125 W. Venice Ave., Venice) Eat-in and take-out pocket and other style sandwiches. Specializes in Middle Eastern health food. Watch fudge being made or buy some chocolate Shark Bites in the Shark Tooth Capital of the World.

FRUIT & VEGETABLE STANDS

Bradenton Farmers' Market (941-748-7949; Bradenton City Hall Parking Lot, 500 15th St. W., Bradenton) Runs 8 to noon Saturday, October through April. Fresh local produce, plants, flowers, and baked goods.

Mixon Fruit Farms (941-748-5829 or 800-608-2525; 2712 26th Ave. E., Bradenton) Large, old, family-owned business specializing in citrus. Tours of the grove and processing plant, free samples, shipping, and a gift shop.

Sarasota Farmers' Market (941-951-2656; Lemon Ave. and Main St., downtown Sarasota) Florida fruits, vegetables, flowers, plants, and honey. Every Saturday 7 to noon.

NATURAL FOODS

Here's to Your Health (941-778-4322; 5340 Gulf Dr., Holmes Beach) Juice bar, teas, produce, vitamins, homeopathic treatments, organic beer and wine. Delivery available.

PIZZA & TAKEOUT

Crusty Louie's Pizza (941-366-3100; Paradise Plaza, 3800 Tamiami Trail S., Sarasota) Stuffed, pan, Chicago-style, or thin-crust pizza made with whole-wheat crust and low-fat, low-salt cheeses.

Portobello (941-927-9600; Boatyard Shopping Village, 1538 Stickney Point Rd., near Siesta Key south bridge) Highly touted pizza, pasta, soup, salads, and sandwiches.

Steve's Super Subs & Sandwiches (941-484-7151; 339 W. Venice Ave., Venice) Deli and veggie sandwiches.

SEAFOOD

Siesta Fish Market (941-349-2602; 221 Garden Ln., Siesta Key) A long-standing family operation whose fresh and prepared products have become an island institution. Specializes in smoked fish and stone crab. This rustic little piece of Siesta history also serves prepared food for lunch and dinner.

CULTURE

Culture arrived on the Sarasota Bay coast with the early settlers of wealth and means. Eager at first to escape metropolitan ways for the simplicity of life on the beach, they eventually craved access to serious theater and fine arts, and so ensured their existence.

Sarasota benefited most from the generous cultural endowment of the Ringling brothers. Not only did the Ringlings bring circus magic to a quiet frontier town, but they also exposed the pioneers to the wonders of European art and architecture. In their wake they left a spirit still palpable and entirely unique to the Gulf Coast. Art schools and theater groups in Sarasota breed a freshness, vitality, daring, and avant-garde spirit unusual for a town its size. Siesta Key, especially, has an atmosphere that has attracted writers, artists, actors, and cartoonists since folks began settling there.

For information on visual and performing art happenings, see the monthly *Sarasota Arts Review*, available free throughout the area.

ARCHITECTURE

In the Bradenton area, the Greek Revival style of plantation house has left its mark. The best example of it survives grandly at Gamble Plantation. Pioneer styles are preserved at the Manatee Historical Village, including a Cracker Gothic farmhouse and an early brick store. In downtown Bradenton you'll find primo Mediterranean influence at the pink Riverpark Residence Hotel (rumored to have hosted Al Capone in a former life), the later-generation Pier Restaurant, and the Old Florida-Victorian homes in neighborhoods around downtown.

On Longboat Key resorts and mansions are modern and ostentatious. In the village once known as Longbeach one finds a return to comfortable, older styles, with a bit of New England charm.

Sarasota's downtown and bay areas hold a smorgasbord of old European styles, from the lavish Italian-inspired Cà D'Zan at the Ringling Estate to the Spanish Opera House. John Ringling Towers, Gothic medieval with Mediterranean flourishes, is one of the town's finest examples of boom-time architecture. It's undergoing rehabilitation and, rumor has it, is destined to become a Ritz-Carlton (wouldn't John Ringling be proud?). Fine examples of old residential architecture are found on the fringes of the downtown area.

Sarasota's old downtown neighborhoods see new life, brightened at the hands of artists.

Karen T. Bartlett

In the 1950s Sarasota revolutionized local architecture by developing a contemporary style suitable to the environment. Examples of the "Sarasota School of Architecture" are spread throughout the area, notably at Summerhouse Restaurant on Siesta Key.

Often overlooked, Venice houses many architectural treasures created in the 1920s, when the Brotherhood of Locomotive Engineers selected it as a retirement center and subsequently built a model city in northern Italian style. Two shining examples are the Park Place Nursing Home at Tampa Avenue and Nassau Street — originally the Hotel Venice — and the nearby Venice Centre Mall, once the San Marco Hotel, later the Kentucky Military Institute. The length of West Venice Avenue reveals stunning homes in the prevailing Mediterranean Revival style.

CINEMA

FILM

Project Black Cinema (941-953-6424; 1359 Fruitville Rd., Sarasota) Sponsors an international African film festival each year (see "Calendar of Events" at the end of this chapter).

Sarasota Film Society (941-364-8662, box office 955-FILM; Burns Court Cinema, 506 Burns Ln., downtown Sarasota) Group devoted to screening quality international films year-round, both first-run and classic. Sponsors the Cine-World Film Festival (see "Calendar of Events" at the end of this chapter).

MOVIE THEATERS

Bradenton Cinema 8 (941-379-6684; 7150 Cortez Rd. W., Bradenton)

Burns Court Cinema (941-346-8662; 506 Burns Ln., Sarasota) Bright pink movie theater showing art and other out-of-the-mainstream films.

Hollywood 20 (941-379-6684; 1993 Main St., downtown Sarasota) New, state-of-the-art theaters with stadium seating and surround-sound stereo.

Venetian 6 Theatres (941-493-0522; Venetian Plaza, 1733 Tamiami Trail S., Venice)

AMC 12 Theatres at Sarasota Square Mall (941-922-9600; Tamiami Trail S. and Beneva Rd., Sarasota)

DANCE

American International Dance Centre (941-955-8363; 556 S. Pineapple Ave., Sarasota) Ballroom dancing instruction and competition for adults and children.

Babiak Dance Ensemble (941-966-1847; Sarasota) Folkloric, costumed dance performances: German, Latin, Italian, Irish, Greek, Middle Eastern, Slavic, Portuguese, and American ethnic dances for festivals and special occasions.

Grapevine Folk Dance Group (941-351-6281; Adult Recreation Center, 801 Tamiami Trail, Sarasota) Authentic international folk dances.

Sarasota Ballet (941-359-0771; Asolo/Florida State University Center, 5555 N. Tamiami Trail, Sarasota) Classic and interpretative dance performances are staged by professionals at the Asolo Center, Sarasota Opera House, and Van Wezel Performing Arts Center, from September through April.

Sarasota Contra Dance (941-366-8569; The Ballroom, 5660 Swift Rd., Sarasota) Beginning instruction and performance.

Sarasota Scottish Country Dancers (941-485-7488 or 755-6212; Sarasota) Evidence of the town's Scottish heritage, the group meets regularly and participates at special events.

Town and Country Ballroom (941-954-8696; Town & Country Shopping Center, 501 N. Beneva Rd., Suite 620, Sarasota) Participatory ballroom dancing.

GARDENS

HISTORIC SPANISH POINT
941-966-5214.
337 N. Tamiami Trail, Osprey.
Open: 9–5 Mon.–Sat.; 12–5 Sun.
Admission: $5 adults, $3 children 6–12.

This multi-era historic attraction (see "Historic Homes & Sites," below) features the ornamental and native gardens built by Sarasota matriarch Bertha Matilde Palmer in the 1910s. The Duchene Lawn, the most dramatic, is lined with towering palms and holds a Greek-column portal that once framed a view of the sea. To create the lovely jungle walk, Mrs. Palmer built a miniature aqueduct system. A sunken garden, fern walk, and ornamental pond also provide oases of lush respite along the path at this 30-acre site.

MARIE SELBY BOTANICAL GARDENS
941-366-5731.
811 S. Palm Ave., Sarasota.
Admission: $8 adults, $4 children ages 6–11, free for children 5 and under.

This 1920s residence on Sarasota Bay occupies 10 acres planted in gardens that wow plant lovers with plots of palm, bamboo, award-winning hibiscus, tropical food plants, herbs, and other exotic flora. Selby is world-renowned for its collection of more than 6,000 orchids in a lush rainforest setting. Best times to visit are the Christmas season, when poinsettias and greenery festoon the grounds and the historic home, and in April, when blooming orchids inspire a festival.

RINGLING ESTATE ROSE GARDEN AND GROUNDS
941-359-5725.
Ringling Estate, 5401 Bay Shore Rd., Sarasota.
Open: Daily 10–5:30.
Admission: Free.

Mammoth banyan trees, a showy poinciana, statuesque royal palms, and a rose garden planted in 1913 are the centerpieces of the lovely, bayfront Ringling Estate. Family graves are situated in the Secret Garden near Cà D'Zan, and the Dwarf Garden lies between the art museum and Asolo Theater. A free tram takes you around the grounds with commentary on the different species.

SARASOTA JUNGLE GARDENS
941-355-5305.
3701 Bayshore Rd., Sarasota.
Open: Daily 9–5.
Admission: $9 adults; $5 children 3–12.

Although this is largely a kiddie attraction, plant lovers will enjoy the botanical gardens and cool, tropical jungle. Winding paved paths lead easily through the grounds' 16 acres, 100 varieties of palms, and countless species of indigenous and exotic flora, all identified. Private nooks and bubbling brooks make this a lovely spot for quiet reflection, especially in the early morning before the throngs arrive. Exotic birds and other attractions are gravy for the connoisseur of nature. (See "Kids' Stuff" in this section.) Snack bar and gift shop.

HISTORIC HOMES & SITES

ASOLO THEATRE
941-355-5101.
Ringling Estate, 5401 Bay
  Shore Rd. off Tamiami
  Trail, Sarasota.
Open: Daily 10–5:30.
Closed: Holidays.
Admission: Free.

Built in 1798 in the castle of the Italian queen, the elaborately baroque theater was moved to the Ringling Estate in the 1940s, just as it was to be torn down. Here it was reassembled and served as the home for the Asolo Theatre Company until the troupe outgrew the ornate, gilded playhouse. The new Asolo was then built on the property, but the old Italian theater remains open for touring. It also hosts art films, lectures, and other programs.

BRADEN CASTLE RUINS
27th St. E. and Rte. 64,
  Bradenton.
Open: Sunrise to sunset.

At the juncture of the Manatee and Braden Rivers, antebellum memories crumble gracefully in a setting recognized by the National Register of Historic Sites. Just short of spectacular, the plantation house ruins are chain-linked and posted with "Keep Out Danger" signs. They hide at the center of a retirement trailer community in a riverside park that's not easy to find. A marker tells the story of Dr. Joseph Addison Braden from Virginia and his ill-fated Braden Plantation.

Cà D'Zan, a salute to Gilded Age prosperity on the Ringling Estate.

Karen T. Bartlett

CÀ D'ZAN
941-359-7500.
Ringling Estate, 5401 Bay
  Shore Rd., Sarasota.
Open: Daily 10–5:30.
Closed: Major holidays.
Admission: $9 adults,

Using the Doges Palace in Venice as a model, circus king John Ringling spared no expense building a monument to success and overindulgence in the 1920s. He imported styles, materials, and pieces from Italy, France, and around the world to embellish his so-called (in Italian) "House of John." Baroque, Gothic, and Renaissance ele-

$8 seniors 55 and over; covers entry to all Ringling attractions. Children 12 and under accompanied by an adult, free; Florida students and teachers free with proper ID.

ments contribute to a breathtaking and ornate look of Gilded Age opulence in the 30-room, $1.5 million mansion on the bay at the John and Mabel Ringling Museum of Art (see "Visual Arts Centers & Resources," below).

CORTEZ VILLAGE
Cortez Rd. and 123rd St., Bradenton.

Remnants of an 1880s fishing village include old tin-roofed fish houses, boat works, and a waterfront store. Exhibits throughout the ramshackle district describe local culture and environmental practices.

Walking in history's footsteps at De Soto National Memorial Park in Bradenton.

Karen T. Bartlett

DE SOTO NATIONAL MEMORIAL PARK
941-792-0458.
75th St. NW, Bradenton.
Open: 8–5:30 daily

Somewhat off the beaten path, this is a place where you can imagine yourself back in the 16th century among conquistadores in heavy armor trying to survive among irate native Americans, mosquitoes, and sweltering heat. Engraved plaques, a re-created Amerindian village, and a half-mile-long trail tell the story of Hernando de Soto's life and adventures here, where supposedly he first breached the shores of the Florida mainland to begin his heroic trek to the Mississippi River. A visitors' center holds artifacts and shells, and a 22-minute video presentation is available. In the winter, rangers dress and play the part of 16th-century inhabitants, demonstrating weaponry and methods of food preparation.

**DOWNTOWN
BRADENTON**
9th Street and Route 64.

Old Main Street and the city yacht basin are the historic downtown district's backbone. It includes some interesting architecture, a great museum, and a few yuppie bars for business and government workers. Locals are trying hard to pump new life into a river town that died with the advent of the automobile. A walking plaza is in the works. Visit the antique shops on Main Street and have lunch at the Pier, then stroll around nearby Point Pleasant for a taste of Bradenton's oak-dotted homeyness and heritage.

Karen T. Bartlett

Sugar built the antebellum plantations along Bradenton's Manatee River, perhaps literally in some cases. It is rumored that molasses was mixed into the Gamble Mansion columns' tabby (seashell) mortar.

**GAMBLE PLANTATION
STATE HISTORICAL
SITE**
941-723-4536.
Route 301 near I-75 in
Ellenton.

Major Robert Gamble, originally from Scotland, learned about sugar planting in Virginia and Tallahassee before he moved to the Manatee River. He eventually cleared 1,500 acres of jungle using slave labor and built a home in

Open: Visitors' Center 8–5 (closed 11:45–12:45); tours depart at 9:30, 10, 1, 2, 3, and 4.
Closed: Tues., Weds.
Admission: Mansion tour, $3 adults, $1.50 children 6–12. Free admission to visitors' center museum.

Greek Revival style. The mansion's crowning touch — 18 Greek columns — he constructed with a mortar known as "tabby," made of crushed and burned seashells. The spacious — by local standards — palace was inhabited by bachelor Gamble alone but served as the area's social hub until the major was forced to sell it in 1856 because of hurricane, frosts, and market losses. In 1925 the United Daughters of the Confederacy rescued the mansion from decades of neglect. The site was declared a Confederate shrine for its role in sheltering Confederate Secretary of State Judah P. Benjamin when he fled for his life after the Civil War. The United Daughters donated the monument to the state a couple of years later. Visitors can see the inside of the home by tour only, which takes less than an hour. The two floors contain period furnishings and housewares, which the ranger explains in lively, interesting dialogue. You'll learn, for example, how such expressions as "hush puppy," "sleep tight," and "pop goes the weasel" came to be, and about the lives of 19th-century plantation owners and slaves. The museum in the visitors' center tells the plantation's story through the eras.

HISTORIC SPANISH POINT
941-966-5214.
337 N. Tamiami Trail, Osprey.
Open: 9–5 Mon.–Sat.; 12–5 Sun.
Admission: $5 adults, $3 children 6–12.

This historic site spans multiple eras of the region's past — 2150 B.C. through 1918. Its importance lies not only in its historical aspects but also in its environmental and archaeological significance. Assembled on the 30-acre Little Sarasota Bay estate, once owned by socialite Mrs. Bertha Palmer, are prehistoric Indian burial grounds, a cutaway of a shell midden mound, the relocated homestead and family chapel of the pioneering Webb dynasty, Mrs. Palmer's restored gardens, a late Victorian pioneer home, and lovely gardens (see "Gardens" in this section). Local actors give living-history performances Sundays during the winter season. Guided tours and tram rides are available on some days; you must reserve ahead for tram rides. Another tip: Bring mosquito repellent in warm weather.

MANATEE VILLAGE HISTORICAL PARK
941-741-4075.
Manatee Ave. & 15th St. E., Bradenton.
Open: 9–4:30 weekdays, 1:30–4:30 Sun.

Several buildings with local historical significance have been restored and moved to a pleasant, oak-shaded park strongly representative of Bradenton's wooded and winding neighborhoods. The County Courthouse is the oldest of the structures, completed in 1860. Others include a circa-1889 church, a Cracker farmhouse, a one-room schoolhouse, a smokehouse, and a general store

Closed: Sat. year-round and also Sun. July–Aug.
Admission: Free.

from the early 19th century. A museum of artifacts, photographs, and hands-on exhibits for children is located in the general store. The Stephens House is stocked with preserves, period kitchen items, furniture, and farm implements. Fogarty Boat Works reflects Bradenton's boat-building heritage. The staff wears historically accurate dress. Across the street the Manatee Burying Ground, which dates from 1850, is appropriately eerie, with strands of Spanish moss straggling from craggy oaks. All in all the park is a romantic site, grossly underrated and lightly visited.

KIDS' STUFF

BISHOP PLANETARIUM
941-746-4131.
201 10th St. W., Bradenton.

Changing Saturday morning family programs for students K-3, including star show and hands-on program in adjacent South Florida Museum. In summer the facility hosts the Junior Space Camp.

GULF COAST WONDER & IMAGINATION ZONE
941-359-9975.
8251 15th St. E., behind the airport on Old Hwy. 301, in the Airport Mall.
Open: Tues.–Sat. 10–5, Sun. 1–5.
Admission: $3 adults, $1.50 children 2–18.

A homey, unintimidating, hands-on museum with a fossil dig, laser harp, live animals (snakes, tarantulas, gopher tortoises, hedgehogs, and more), stuffed game safari, whisper dishes, computer games, native garden, and gift shop.

MANATEE COUNTY CENTRAL LIBRARY
941-748-5555.
1301 Barcarrotta Blvd. W., Bradenton.

Family story time for all ages Monday evenings at 7; regular story time year-round, at various times but usually Thursdays at 10 am, for toddlers and preschool children.

SARASOTA JUNGLE GARDENS
941-355-5305.
3701 Bayshore Rd., Sarasota.
Admission: $9 adults, $5 children 3–12.
Open: Daily 9–5.

Exotic bird and reptile shows, free-strolling peacocks and other feathered friends, a playground with a jungle theme, a bird posing area, black leopards, monkeys, flamingos, swans, wallabies, and other live animals make this the area's favorite children's attraction. Highlight of the bird show is Elvis, a macaw that can paint. Peaceful, jungly gardens appeal to others. (See "Gardens" in this section.)

**VAN WEZEL SATURDAY
   MORNINGS FOR KIDS**
941-953-3366.
777 N. Tamiami Trail,
   Sarasota.

*C*inderella, Wind in the Willows, other kiddie clas-sics, ballet, and fun concerts take the stage one Saturday morning each month at 10:30, October through May.

Venice Little Theatre runs its season during the winter months and children's theater in summer.

Karen T. Bartlett

**VENICE LITTLE
   THEATRE FOR
   YOUNG PEOPLE**
941-488-1115.
140 W. Tampa Ave., Venice.

*O*ne of the most successful nonprofit commu-nity theaters in the U.S., the Little Theatre hosts off-season summer theatrical instruction and performances for youngsters.

MUSEUMS

**ANNA MARIA ISLAND
   HISTORICAL MUSEUM**
941-778-0492.
402 Pine Ave., Anna Maria.
Open: 10–4 Nov.–Apr.,
   10–1 other months.
Closed: Mon., Fri., Sun.
Admission: Donations
   accepted.

*A*homey little museum inside an icehouse of the 1920s holds photos, maps, records, books, a shell collection, a turtle display, and vintage movies on video. Next door sits the old jail, its humorous graffiti worth a chuckle.

**BELLM CARS & MUSIC
   OF YESTERDAY**
941-355-6228.
5500 N. Tamiami Trail,
   Sarasota.

*D*isplays of nearly 50 antique cars and 1,200 musical instruments combine under one roof. A half-hour tour explains the history of the player piano, phonographs, music boxes, hurdy-gurdies, and record albums. Browse among 75 classic and antique cars — from a 1905 horseless carriage to a

Open: 9–6 daily.
Admission: $9 adults; $5 children 6–12.

1971 fire-engine-red Maserati — on your own or by tour. The collection includes four of John Ringling's Rolls Royces and Pierce Arrows. While waiting for the tour, you can spend nickels, dimes, and quarters in the vintage game arcade. Make Peppy the Musical Clown dance, get your fortune told by the Great Swami, and motor cross-country on the Drive Mobile. It's lots more fun than modern-day arcades.

RINGLING MUSEUM OF THE CIRCUS
941-355-5101.
Ringling Estate, 5401 Bay Shore Rd., Sarasota.
Open: Daily 10–5:30.
Closed: Holidays.
Admission: $9 adults, $8 seniors 55 and over; covers admission to all Ringling attractions. Children under 12 free. Florida students and teachers free with proper ID.

The Circus Museum was Florida's way of saying thank you back in 1948. Its re-creation of Big Top magic paid tribute to a man many believed invented the circus, a man who bequeathed to the city — along with the giddy world of the Big Top — a legacy of exotica, sophistication, and art appreciation. In 1989 the museum underwent a half-million-dollar renovation with world-class museum designers at the reins. The new Circus Museum reflects Ringling's seemingly contradictory interests. Fine-arts displays counterbalance high-wire exhibits. Black-and-white photography is juxtaposed with gilded fantasy. Tasteful cloth mannequins model plumed and sequined costumes. Dutch prints depict bareback riders, striking a perfect equilibrium between circus raucousness and the art of form. A favorite display is a recently opened addition from the old museum: a scale model of the circus grounds and a narrated behind-the-scenes look at circus lifestyles. The museum is located on the grounds of the John and Mabel Ringling Museum of Art (see "Visual Arts Centers & Resources," below).

SOUTH FLORIDA MUSEUM
941-746-4131.
201 10th St. W., Bradenton.
Open: 10–5 Mon.–Sat., 12–5 Sun.
Closed: Mon. May–Dec. (except July).
Admission: $7.50 adults, $6 seniors, $3.50 children 5–12.

This two-story museum scans Florida history with a focus on native American life and Civil War days. The star of the museum is Snooty, the oldest manatee born in captivity (1948) in the United States. You can watch him and his new playmate, Newton, underwater from aquarium windows or from above at the Parker Aquarium, where interactive exhibits explain the plight of the endangered manatee. The museum walks you through the region's historical eras with realistic, life-size native American dioramas, replicated early Spanish buildings, a log cabin, Victorian furniture, and a host of other displays. The Bishop Planetarium adjoins the facility with a 50-foot hemispherical dome, laser shows, and other special effects.

MUSIC & NIGHTLIFE

Sarasota dances with action throughout the week and especially on weekends. Besides local bands, both well-known and up-and-coming stars appear in theaters, cabarets, and nightclubs. Cores of activity include downtown, the neon-bright Sarasota Quay, and posh St. Armands Circle. Check the *Sarasota Herald-Tribune's Ticket* and *Bradenton Herald's Weekend* every Friday to learn what's happening in the clubs throughout the area.

Sarasota

Club Bandstand (941-955-5221; 300 Sarasota Quay, Fruitville Road at Tamiami Trail) The setting is pure discotheque with a nostalgia theme. Live bands perform some nights.

Down Under Jazz Club (941-951-2467; 214 Sarasota Quay, Fruitville Road at Tamiami Trail) The Gulf Coast's top jazz performers, cigars, and casual dockside meals.

Euphemia Haye's Haye Loft (941-383-3633; 5540 Gulf of Mexico Dr., Longboat Key) Try to resist the temptations of the Loft's dessert menu as you listen to nightly live entertainment — guitar music, jazz, vocalists, or keyboards.

Florida West Coast Symphony (941-953-4252; 709 Tamiami Trail N., Sarasota) Besides classical symphony concerts, this group sponsors various related ensembles, including a string quartet, wind quintet, brass quintet, new artists' quartet, youth orchestra, and pops series.

The Gator Club (941-366-5969; 1490 Main St., downtown Sarasota) One of the hottest places downtown, with pool tables and live music weekends.

In Extremis (941-954-2008; Sarasota Quay, Sarasota) It parties with laser, light, sound, video, and live shows.

Jazz Club of Sarasota (941-366-1552; 290 Coconut Ave., Bldg. 3) This organization dedicates itself to the perpetuation and encouragement of jazz performance by presenting various monthly and annual events, Saturday jazz jams, clinics, workshops, and youth programs, with a musical instrument lending library. It sponsors a four-day Jazz Festival in April, featuring top musicians (see "Calendar of Events" at the end of this chapter).

Sarasota Concert Band (941-955-6660; 1345 Main St., Sarasota) This ensemble's 50-some members perform at Van Wezel Performing Arts Hall from October through May and at outdoor concerts throughout the Sarasota Bay coast.

Sarasota Friends of Folk Music (941-377-9256; Sarasota) Musical group specializing in Florida folk music performs free monthly concerts on City Island at the Sarasota Sailing Squadron.

Sarasota Pops (941-383-0734; Sarasota) Presents four concerts each year at Van Wezel Performing Arts Center.

Venice Symphony (941-488-1010) Classical and pops concerts November through May.

Siesta Key

Beach Club (941-349-6311; 5151 Ocean Blvd.) Amid the atmosphere of a rowdy college bar, it hosts local rock, jazz, and reggae groups nightly.

St. Armands Key

ChaCha Coconuts (941-388-3300; 417 St. Armands Circle) Contemporary music and dancing nightly.

The Patio (941-388-3987; Columbia Restaurant, 441 St. Armands Circle) Spirited, with youthful dance energy and popular music nightly.

Venice

Crow's Nest (941-484-9551; 1968 Tarpon Center Dr.) Features live jazz musicians and singers on a changing calendar.

SPECIALTY LIBRARIES

Arthur Vining Davis Library (941-388-4441; Mote Marine Laboratory, 1600 Ken Thompson Pkwy., City Island) Gathers research for lab scientists. Open to the public for reference, preferably by advance appointment.

Family Heritage House (941-792-7411; 1707 15th St. E., Bradenton) Part of Florida's Black Heritage Trail, it contains children's books, videotapes, audiotapes, books, magazines, and other materials relevant to black heritage, arts, and culture.

Historical Records Library (941-741-4070; 1405 Fourth Ave. W., Bradenton) Manatee County's early records and governmental documents.

John and Mable Ringling Museum of Art Research Library (941-359-5743; 5401 Bay Shore Rd., Sarasota) Specializes in 17th-century Dutch, Flemish, and Italian paintings.

Manatee County Central Library (941-748-5555; 1301 Barcarrotta Blvd. W., Bradenton) The Eaton Room contains a collection of Florida and county historical photographs, newspapers, books, census records, and articles.

Selby Public Library (941-316-1181; 1001 Blvd. of the Arts, Sarasota) The region's central library, it schedules cultural events throughout the year.

Verman Kimbrough Memorial Library (941-359-7587; Ringling School of Art and Design, 2700 N. Tamiami Trail, Sarasota) Art history and instruction.

THEATER

Anna Maria Island Players (941-778-5755; Pine and Gulf Dr., Anna Maria) Year-round community theater in an Old Florida-style building.

Asolo Center for the Performing Arts/Florida State University Acting Conservatory (Box office 941-351-8000 or business office 351-9010; 5555 N.

Tamiami Trail, Sarasota) The Asolo tradition began in Italy in 1798, in a theater built in the queen's castle. It ended up on the Ringling Estate in the 1940s, where it was reconstructed and, in 1965, designated State Theater of Florida. In the early 1980s a new center was built, incorporating into the interior of one of its theaters another dismantled, historic European theater — a Scottish opera house circa 1900. Carved box fronts, friezes, and ornate cornice work from the old theater decorate the new. Opened in 1989, the 500-seat Harold E. and Esther M. Mertz Theatre hosts the **Asolo Theatre Company** and is open for free touring when it's not being used for rehearsals. The season is December through June. A separate, more intimate, 161-seat theater called the Conservatory Theatre is the home of Florida State University's graduate actor training program.

Florida Studio Theatre and Cabaret Club (941-366-9000; 1241 N. Palm Ave., downtown Sarasota) A major testing ground for budding playwrights and new works, Florida Studio Theatre's professional troupe presents seven productions during its December–May season and a summertime Florida Playwrights Festival at its intimate mainstage (see "Calendar of Events" at the end of this chapter). Cabaret shows December through May in the new Cabaret Club, with full-service dining.

Golden Apple Dinner Theatre (941-366-5454; 25 N. Pineapple Ave., downtown Sarasota) Year-round Broadway dinner entertainment.

Manatee Players Riverfront Theater (941-748-5875; 102 Old Main St., Bradenton) Community theater in a historic setting.

Players of Sarasota (941-365-2494; 838 N. Tamiami Trail, Sarasota) Community theater that stages musicals, live music, and other programs.

Sarasota Opera House (941-953-7030; 61 N. Pineapple Ave., downtown Sarasota) Don't even try to park or dine downtown on opera opening nights during the February-March season. Southwest Florida's only opera company's opening galas are popular events that require ticket purchase months in advance. In operation for more than 30 years, the Sarasota Opera Association stages all the classics. Its beautifully restored Spanish-mission-style structure in the Theater and Arts District was built in 1926. In summer the theater hosts **Clown College** (800-755-9637), which puts on regular performances. You can tour the facility (and see the chandelier from the set of *Gone With the Wind*) for $2. Advance arrangements required.

Theatre Works (941-952-9170; 1247 First St., downtown Sarasota) Professional, experimental drama October through May in the historic, intimate setting of the **Palm Tree Playhouse**.

Van Wezel Performing Arts Hall (941-953-3366; 777 N. Tamiami Trail, Sarasota) It's that purple eye-catcher that radiates outward like a scallop shell on the shores of Sarasota Bay, designed by the Frank Lloyd Wright Foundation. If it's worth seeing, it's at the Van Wezel. Tickets should be purchased at least a month in advance. The Van Wezel hosts name comedians, musicians, and dance groups; Broadway shows; major orchestras; ethnic

The sculpture Applause *greets visitors to the Van Wezel Performing Arts Center.*

Karen T. Bartlett

music and dance groups; chamber and choral music; and Saturday children's shows.

Venice Golden Apple Dinner Theater (941-484-7711; Holiday Inn, 447 Hwy. 41 Bypass, Venice) Broadway dinner theater June through September, cabaret dining entertainment the rest of the year.

Venice Little Theatre (941-488-2419; 140 W. Tampa Ave., downtown Sarasota) A community theater company performs seven mainstage shows in a Mediterranean Revival structure, September through June.

VISUAL ARTS CENTERS & RESOURCES

The canvas of Sarasota Bay arts reveals a complex masterpiece, layered with the diverse patterns and local color of its many communities. With its backdrop of artistic types dating back to avid collector John Ringling, Sarasota leads the region to avant-garde heights.

The following entries introduce you to opportunities for experiencing art as either an appreciator or a practicing artist. A listing of commercial galleries is included under "Shopping" in this chapter. Read the *Sarasota Arts Review* for openings and changing exhibitions.

Artists Guild Gallery of Anna Maria Island (941-778-6694; 5414 Marina Dr., Holmes Beach) Features changing exhibitions in various media by Gulf Coast artists.

Art League of Manatee County (941-746-2862; 209 Ninth St. W., Bradenton) Classes and demonstrations in all media for all ages; sales gallery.

The Fine Arts Society of Sarasota (941-953-3366; Van Wezel Performing Arts Hall, 777 N. Tamiami Trail, Sarasota) Van Wezel houses a permanent collection of Florida artists' works on loan from the Society, which conducts tours weekdays November through April.

Galleries on Main Street (941-746-1754; 302 Main St., downtown Bradenton)
The work of regional artists — paintings, sculpture, pottery, and furniture.
Also serves latte. Suggested donation: $2 per person.

The John and Mabel Ringling Museum of Art, one of the circus's most enduring legacies to Florida.

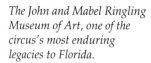

Karen T. Bartlett

The John and Mable Ringling Museum of Art (941-359-5700; 5401 Bay Shore
Rd., Sarasota) Sarasota's pride and joy, this is not only an art museum but
also the nucleus of tourism activity and the heart of the local art community.
It shares its 66-acre bayfront estate with Ringling's extravagant Cà D'Zan
Palace, the antique Italian Asolo Theatre (see "Historic Homes & Sites" in this
section), a circus museum (see "Museums"), a rose garden (see "Gardens"),
and a Big Top-shaped restaurant. Designated the State Art Museum of
Florida, the collection specializes in late medieval and Renaissance Italian
works, covering 500 years of European art, most of which was purchased by
Ringling. The Old Masters collection contains five original Rubens tapestries
as well as Spanish Baroque, French, Dutch, and northern European works,
mostly of a religious nature. A kids' gallery provides huge art pads for creative scribbling, word blocks, and the "Dream Machine," where you can
watch your golden wishes fly. The museum continually adds to its collection
of American and contemporary works. The lushly landscaped courtyards
feature reproduction classic statues and Italian decorative columns, which
Ringling originally purchased for the hotel he hoped to build on Longboat
Key. Admission is charged every day but Saturday and covers all property
attractions: $9 for adults, $8 for seniors, and free for children 12 and under
and Florida students and teachers with ID.

Longboat Key Art Center (941-383-2345; 6860 Longboat Dr. S., Longboat Key)
Hidden from mainstream traffic, here is a find for the buyer and would-be
artisan. A gallery sells works mostly by Florida artists. Changing exhibits
feature local, emerging, and experimental artists. A crafts shop sells wares

made at the center's surrounding workshops, where classes are taught in basketry, watercolor, jewelry making, metal craft, pottery, and more.

Manatee Community College Fine Art Gallery (941-755-1511 ext. 4251; 5840 26th St. W., Bradenton) Features works of major artists.

Sarasota Visual Arts Center (941-365-2032; 707 N. Tamiami Trail, Sarasota) Exhibition and sales galleries feature the paintings, jewelry, sculpture, pottery, and enamelware of local and national artists. Art instruction and demonstrations are available. The gallery features an outdoor sculpture garden.

Sarasota County Arts Council (941-365-5118; 1351 Fruitville Rd., Sarasota) The Council supports local artists and organizations through grants, marketing, advocacy, and educational programs.

Selby Gallery (941-359-7563; Ringling School of Art and Design, 2700 N. Tamiami Trail, Sarasota) Exhibits the works of contemporary local, national, and international artists and designers.

Towles Court Art Association (1945 Morrill St., Sarasota) A charming, blossomy district of restored and brightly painted tin-roofed bungalows turned art colony. Art schools, showings, studios, and galleries. Third Friday "Stroll at Towles" gallery walks, 6–10 pm.

Venice Art Center (941-485-7136; 390 S. Nokomis Ave., Venice)

RECREATION

Known both for its superlative white sand beaches and as the birthplace of Florida golfing, Sarasota and its environs draw outdoors lovers to its year-round playgrounds.

BEACHES

Hitting the waves off Anna Maria Island.

Karen T. Bartlett

The Sarasota area claims more than 35 miles of sandy seashore. Island beaches are, for the most part, highly developed, with lots of facilities and concessions. Recent years have seen a concession of another sort — to nature — as boardwalks and sea oat plantings restore the dunes. On the upper islands, erosion takes its toll and beaches must be periodically renourished. This stretch of the Gulf Coast boasts some of the whitest beaches this side of the Florida Panhandle. Parking is free at all area beaches.

ANNA MARIA BAYFRONT PARK
Northeast end of Anna Maria Island.
Facilities: Picnic areas, rest rooms, showers, playground, recreational facilities, fishing pier.

One of the region's more secluded beach parks, this one is narrower than the rest of the island's beaches. You get a magnificent view of St. Petersburg's Sunshine Skyway Bridge from the bay. A historical marker tells about the islands' early settlers. Heed danger signs that mark where heavy tidal currents make swimming perilous.

BROHARD BEACH
941-316-1172.
Harbor Dr., Venice.
Facilities: Picnic areas, rest rooms, showers, fitness trail, fishing pier, restaurant.

This narrow, dark-sand beach threads under the Venice Fishing Pier and around picnic tables. Folks come here to fish, hang out at the pier tiki bar, and hunt for sharks' teeth.

CASPERSEN BEACH
941-316-1172.
South end of Harbor Dr., Venice.
Facilities: Picnic areas, rest rooms, showers.

For secluded sunning, head south where the beach widens at Venice's south end. The sand is pebbly and dark, and not as good for shark-toothing. From here you can walk to Manasota Key Beach, to the south.

COQUINA BEACH
Southern end of Gulf Dr., Bradenton Beach, Anna Maria Island.
Facilities: Picnic areas, rest rooms, showers, lifeguard, cafe, concessions, boat ramps.

Recently renourished, this large and popular park boasts plump wide sands edged in Australian pines. Waters at the south end provide good snorkeling. The park continues on the bay, where swimming should be avoided because of currents and boat traffic. The Coquina BayWalk takes you to environmentally restored Leffis Key, with its towering mound and newly replaced mangrove habitat, a $321 million restoration project.

CORTEZ BEACH
North end of Gulf Dr., Bradenton Beach, Anna Maria Island.

Here's a long stretch of revamped sands that meets up with Coquina, its more popular cousin. Surfers like it here. It's convenient for the heavily laden beacher because you park right along the sand's edge.

LIDO BEACH
941-346-3310.
400 Benjamin Franklin Dr.,
    Lido Key.
Facilities: Picnic areas, rest
    rooms, showers,
    lifeguards, swimming
    pool, snack bar, swings,
    volleyball.

This is the main beach on the island, heavily developed and popular. Canvas cabanas and stylish, umbrella-shaded lounge chairs may be rented along the stretch of shelly sand. Shellers look for best finds among the piles of boulders and sea rubble. It's a great beach for tiki-bar-hopping along the hotel strip. South of the pavilion you'll find water-sports equipment rentals.

LONGBOAT KEY
Public accesses at
    Broadway St. on the
    north end of island.

Longboat Key has beautiful beaches, mostly enjoyed by resort guests and waterfront residents. Public accesses are marked subtly and have no facilities or lifeguards. Parking is limited. The beach stretches wide as well as long, with fluffy white sand and dramatic sunset views.

Pull up a stretch of sand and give it a test lounge at Holmes Beach on Anna Maria Island.

Karen T. Bartlett

MANATEE COUNTY
    PARK
Gulf Blvd., Holmes Beach.
Facilities: Picnic area, rest
    rooms, showers,
    lifeguard, playground,
    restaurant, beach rentals,
    volleyball.

The hot spot of Anna Maria Island beaching, this park appeals to families because of its full complement of facilities. The beach is wide enough to accommodate rows and rows of beach towels. Australian pines shade picnic areas.

NOKOMIS BEACH/
    NORTH JETTY
914-316-1172.
South end Casey Key Rd.,
    Casey Key.

Remote and exclusive Casey Key gives way to beachy abandon at its south end. The town of Nokomis Beach is a fisherman's haven, and North Jetty, at its south end, lures anglers. A bait shop

Facilities: Picnic area, rest rooms, showers, lifeguards, concessions.

keeps them supplied. The beach's wide sands, festooned with Australian pines and sea grape trees, are well loved by serious local beachers, too.

NORTH LIDO BEACH
941-316-1172.
North end of Ben Franklin Dr., Lido Key.

The beach less traveled on Lido, this one extends from the main beach up to New Pass. Lack of facilities and limited parking keep the throngs away. Wide with fine, spic-and-span sand.

PALMA SOLA CAUSEWAY BEACH
Anna Maria Bridge, Route 64.
Facilities: Picnic area, rest rooms, restaurant, watersports rentals.

Fairly narrow sands edge the causeway between the mainland and Anna Maria Island. They gain some character from Australian pines and are popular with windsurfers and jet skiers. Most beachers congregate around the restaurant and rental concession at the causeway's west end.

POINT OF ROCKS BEACH
941-316-1172.
Access #12, south of Siesta Public Beach on Midnight Pass Rd. near Stickney Point Rd. intersection, Siesta Key.

Part of Crescent Beach, named for its shape, this beach is popular with snorkelers and fishermen because of an accumulation of rocks that attract marine life. Like the main public beach (see below) it boasts sands whiter than white but has neither the facilities nor the ease of parking.

SIESTA KEY COUNTY BEACH
941-346-3310.
Midnight Pass Rd. at Beach Way Dr., Siesta Key.
Facilities: Picnic areas, rest rooms, showers, lifeguard, snack bar, playground, volleyball courts, tennis courts, ball fields, soccer field, fitness trail, sun decks.

Siesta Key's Crescent Beach sand was once judged "the finest, whitest beach in the world" by the Woods Hole Oceanographic Institute. (Anna Maria Island's placed third.) The blinding whiteness comes from its quartz origins; the fineness, from Mother Nature's efficient pulverizer, the sea. Unfortunately, these facts have not been kept secret. The park averages nearly 20,000 visitors a day. Arrive early to find a parking space. Condos and motels line the edge of the wide beach. Swimming is wonderful, with gradually sloping sands and usually clear waters. Public accesses along Beach Road to the north provide more seclusion, but parking is on the street and limited.

SOUTH JETTY
941-316-1172.
End of Tarpon Center Dr., Venice

Also known as Humphris Park, the jetty — a favorite of fishing types — is shored with huge boulders. Past them stretches a span of condo-lined beach that's popular with surfers and sailboarders.

SOUTH LIDO BEACH
941-316-1172.
South end of Benjamin
  Franklin Dr., Lido Key.
Facilities: Picnic areas, rest
  rooms, showers,
  playground, volleyball,
  ball fields, soccer field,
  fitness trail, nature trail,
  sun decks.

A wide sugar beach wraps around the tip of the island from the gulf to the bay, facing Siesta Key. Picnic areas are overhung with Australian pines and carpeted by their needles. Within its 130 acres several brands of Florida ecology thrive on different waterfronts. Squirrels are the most evident wildlife throughout the park. Hiking trails lead you to an observation tower and along the mangrove worlds of Little Grassy and Big Grassy lagoons. Brushy Bayou is a good place to canoe.

TURTLE BEACH
941-346-3310.
South end of Blind Pass
  Rd., Siesta Key.
Facilities: Picnic areas, rest
  rooms, showers,
  playground, volleyball,
  boat ramp, horseshoes;
  restaurants and bars
  across the street.

The sands become coarser and more shell-studded at Siesta's lower extremes as the high-rise buildings become scarcer. Along here and Midnight Pass Road reside the island's upper echelon behind iron gates. Less crowded than the other Siesta beaches, it's sports- and family-oriented, but without lifeguards.

Toothsome finds on Venice Beach, hailed as the Shark's Tooth Capital of the World.

Karen T. Bartlett

VENICE BEACH
941-316-1172.
100 The Esplanade, Venice.
Facilities: Picnic area, rest
  rooms, showers,
  concessions, lifeguards.

Known for its prehistoric shark-tooth fossils, this beach even rents sand-sifters. You are bound to find some specimens because of the area's ancient offshore "shark graveyard." This beach feels cramped to me compared to the spaciousness of Venice's south-end beaches.

BICYCLING

S arasota's best bikeways lie on barrier islands, in parks, and in rural areas to the east. Most biking elsewhere is on the sides of roads or sidewalks.

By state law, bicyclists must conduct themselves as pedestrians when using sidewalks. Where they share the road with other vehicles, they must follow all the rules of the road. Children under 16 must wear a helmet.

BEST BIKING

Longboat Key's 12 miles of lanes parallel Gulf of Mexico Drive's vista of good taste and wealth on both sides of the road. Bike paths travel through parts of Lido Key and Siesta Key. The Oscar Scherer State Recreation Area provides a lovely venue for biking in the wilderness.

RENTAL SHOPS

Resorts and parks often rent bikes or provide free use of them.

Bicycle Center (941-377-4505; 4084 Bee Ridge Rd., Sarasota) Offers pickup and delivery on mountain bike and beach cruiser rentals.

Mr. CB's (941-349-4400; 1249 Stickney Point Rd., Siesta Key) Rents one-speed beach cruiser bikes.

Siesta Sports Rentals (941-346-1797; 6551 Midnight Pass Rd., Southbridge Mall, Siesta Key) Has beach cruisers, kid bikes, tandems, surreys, jogger strollers, and in-line skates.

BOATS & BOATING

CANOEING & KAYAKING

In addition to the outlets listed below, many resorts and parks rent canoes.

Florida Sports Outlet (941-778-5883; Captain's Marina, 5501 Marina Dr., Holmes Beach) Rents solo and tandem kayaks.

Oscar Scherer State Recreation Area (941-483-5956; 1843 S. Tamiami Trail, Osprey) Canoe rentals and tidal creek canoeing along scrubby and pine flatwoods. River otters and alligators inhabit the waters; scrub jays, bobcats, and bald eagles, the land.

Silent Sports (941-922-4042; Southpointe Mall Marina, 7660 S. Tamiami Trail, Sarasota) Rents kayaks and canoes and leads three-hour tours.

Snook Haven (941-485-7221; 5000 E. Venice Ave., Venice) Canoe rentals and trips on the Myakka River.

Sweetwater Kayaks (941-346-1179; 5263 Ocean Blvd., Siesta Key) Geared toward instruction, it offers introductory and advanced lessons, rentals, and extended instructional trips and tours.

DINING CRUISES

LeBarge Tropical Cruises (941-366-6116; Marina Jack's, Bayfront Park, Sarasota) Island-style crooning, an aquarium bar, and live on-board coconut palms put the tropical in this excursion, which departs two times daily (food service including a cookout). Saturday night dance cruise.

Marina Jack II (941-366-9255; Marina Jack's Restaurant, Bayfront Park, Sarasota) Lunch cruises during season, dinner cruises all year.

Seafood Shack Showboat Dinner Cruise (941-794-5048; 4110 127th St. W., Cortez) Afternoon scenic tours enlivened by entertainment and a cocktail bar. Does not run on Saturday.

MARINE SUPPLIES

Boat Surplus (941-755-7797; 1124 58th Ave. W., Bradenton)

Boat/US Marine Center (941-925-7361; 4229 Tamiami Trail S., Sarasota) All boating, yachting, and fishing needs. Memberships available for discounts and emergency service.

Gulfwind Marine (941-485-3388; 1485 Tamiami Trail S., Venice)

PERSONAL WATERCRAFT RENTALS/TOURS

Cortez Watercraft Rentals (941-792-5263; at the Cortez bridge) Jet ski rentals.

Don & Mike's Boat Rental (941-966-4000 or 800-550-2007; Casey Key Marina, 520 Blackburn Point Rd., Casey Key) Rents jet skis and waverunners.

Palma Sola Boat Rentals (941-778-4083; on Anna Maria Island causeway at 9915 Manatee Ave. W., Bradenton) Half-hour to full-day rentals. Pickup and delivery available.

POWERBOAT RENTALS

Cannons Marina (941-383-1311; 6040 Gulf of Mexico Dr., Longboat Key) Rentals by half-day, day, and week; runabouts, deck boats, and open skiffs. Also tackle and water skis.

Club Nautico International Powerboat Rentals (941-951-0550; Marina Jack's, Bayfront Park, Sarasota) Rentals for two to 12 passengers; also skis, kneeboards, and fishing rods.

Don & Mike's Boat Ski Rental (941-966-4000 or 800-550-2007; Casey Key Marina, 520 Blackburn Point Rd., Casey Key) Power- and sailboats, pontoons, and waterskiing equipment.

Mr. CB's (941-349-4400; 1249 Stickney Point Rd., Siesta Key) Runabouts, center console boats, pontoons, and deck boats, also rod and reel rentals and fishing licenses.

Palma Sola Boat Rentals (941-778-4083; on Anna Maria Island causeway at 9915 Manatee Ave. W., Bradenton) Bowriders, center console boats, and pontoon rentals.

PUBLIC BOAT RAMPS

City Island (Ken Thompson Pkwy.) Three ramps.

Coquina Beach Bayside Park (Gulf Blvd., Bradenton Beach) Picnic and recreational facilities; rest rooms nearby.

Higel Park (Tarpon Center Dr., Venice Beach, Venice Inlet)

Kingfish Ramp (Hwy. 64 on causeway to Anna Maria Island) Picnic facilities.

Marina Boat Ramp Park (215 E. Venice Ave., Venice)

Nokomis Beach (Venice Inlet)

Palma Sola Causeway (Palma Sola Bay and Route 64) Rest rooms and a picnic area.

Turtle Beach (Blind Pass Rd., Siesta Key) Two ramps.

SAILBOAT CHARTERS

The Enterprise Sailing Charters (941-951-1833; Marina Jack's, Bayfront Park, Sarasota) Morning, afternoon, sunset, and full moon sails on a Morgan 41-footer.

Key Sailing (941-346-7245 or 888-539-7245; Siesta Key) Sail-away adventures that last one, two, or however many days you decide, aboard a 41-foot Morgan Classic.

Spice Sailing Charters (941-778-3240; Galati Yacht Basin, Anna Maria) Sails to Egmont Key and for sunset aboard a 27-foot vessel. Sailing lessons available.

Spindrift Yacht Services (941-383-7781; 410 Gulf of Mexico Dr., Longboat Key) Sailing ventures for up to six.

SAILBOAT RENTALS & INSTRUCTION

Many resorts have concessions that rent Hobie Cats and other small sailboats. Instruction is often available with the rental. For something more sophisticated, try these.

Bradenton Beach Sailboat Rentals (941-778-4969; 1325 Gulf Dr., Bradenton Beach) Free sailing lessons with G-Cat rentals.

Don & Mike's Boat Rental (941-966-4000 or 800-550-2007; Casey Key Marina, 520 Blackburn Point Rd., Casey Key) Rental and instruction.

O'Leary's Sarasota Sailing School (941-953-7505; Marina Jack's, Bayfront Park, Sarasota) Rents sailing crafts 14 to 50 feet long; rates for two hours, half-days, full days, and weekly. Instruction and captained boats available.

SIGHTSEEING & ENTERTAINMENT CRUISES

Bay Lady (941-485-6366; Osprey Marine Center, 480 Blackburn Point Rd., Osprey) Two-hour cruises along the Intracoastal Waterway to see bird sanctuaries, manatees, and the lovely homes of Sarasota and Venice.

Ko Ko Kai Charter Boat Service (941-474-2141; 5040 N. Beach Rd., Ko Ko Kai Resort, Englewood Beach) Island-hopping trips to Gasparilla, Palm, Cayo

Costa, Cabbage Key, Upper Captiva, and Captiva islands, plus shelling excursions.

LeBarge Tropical Cruises (941-366-6116; Marina Jack's, Bayfront Park, Sarasota) Sightseeing, nature, and live-entertainment party cruises depart four times daily.

FISHING

Catch of the day on Venice Pier.

Karen T. Bartlett

Nonresidents age 16 and over must obtain a license unless fishing from a vessel or pier covered by its own license. You can buy inexpensive, temporary nonresident licenses at county tax collectors' offices and most Kmarts and bait shops.

Bradenton waters are known to avid fishermen and divers as "Jewfish Country" for the profusion of the gigantic sea creatures. Other fine catches include mangrove snapper, sheepshead, and pompano in backwaters, and grouper, amberjack, and mackerel in deep seas. Check local regulations for season, size, and catch restrictions.

DEEP-SEA PARTY BOATS

Flying Fish Fleet (941-366-3373; Marina Jack's, Bayfront Park, Sarasota) Half-day, six-hour, and all-day trips.

Miss Cortez Fleet (941-794-1223; 4330 127th St. W., Cortez) Charters out of the region's fishing hub, lasting four hours to a day.

Spindrift Yacht Services (941-383-7781; 410 Gulf of Mexico Dr., Longboat Key) Half-day offshore fishing excursions.

Fishing Charters/Outfitters

To find fishing guides, check with major marinas, such as Marina Jack's in downtown Sarasota. Capacity is smaller and prices higher than for party boat excursions.

Big Catch (941-366-3373; Marina Jack's, Bayfront Park, Sarasota) Four- to eight-hour charters.

Gypsy Guide Service (941-923-6095; Sarasota) Light tackle and fly fishing, bay and backwater fishing, half- or full-day trips, and summer night fishing.

Mr. CB's (941-349-4400; 1249 Stickney Point Rd., Siesta Key) Light tackle and fly-fishing charters in Sarasota Bay for up to six people.

Fishing Piers

Anna Maria City Pier (Anna Maria Island) Unrailed and low to the water, it juts 700 feet into Anna Maria Sound at the south end of Bayshore Park.

Bradenton Beach City Pier (Bridge St., Bradenton Beach) Juts into intracoastal waters; it was part of the first bridge from the island to the mainland. Restaurant and bait concession. Admission for fishing.

Ken Thompson Pier (941-316-1172; 1700 Ken Thompson Pkwy., City Island) Three small piers into New Pass.

Nokomis Beach North Jetty (941-316-1172; south end Casey Key Rd., Nokomis Beach) Manmade rock projection into the gulf, with beach and picnic area.

Osprey Fishing Pier (west end of Main St., Osprey)

Rod & Reel Pier (875 North Shore Dr., Anna Maria) A privately owned fishermen's complex with cafe and bait shop. Admission.

Tony Saprito Fishing Pier (941-316-1172; Hart's Landing, Ringling Causeway Park on way to St. Armands Key) Bait store across the road.

Turtle Beach's pier (941-346-3310; south end Blind Pass Rd., Siesta Key) Recreational facilities and boat ramps available.

Venice Fishing Pier (Brohard Park, Harbor Dr., Venice) 750 feet long, complete with rest rooms, showers, bait shop, and restaurant. Admission.

Venice's South Jetty (941-316-1172; Tarpon Center Dr.) A stretch of boulder buffer with a paved walkway at Venice's north end.

GOLF

In 1902 Sarasota's founder and first mayor, a Scotsman, built a two-hole golf course in the middle of town. This is believed to have been Florida's first golf course. The sport has grown in Sarasota through the years. Today there are more courses than you can swing a club at, the majority of which are private or semiprivate. Many large resorts have their own greens or arrange golf-around programs at local links.

PUBLIC GOLF COURSES

Bobby Jones Golf Complex (941-365-4653; 1000 Azinger Way, off Circus Blvd., Sarasota) Sarasota's only municipal course, it has 36 holes plus a nine-hole executive course. Restaurant and lounge.

Heather Hills Club (941-755-8888; 101 Cortez Rd. W., Bradenton) Public executive course with 18 holes, par 61. Snack bar.

Palma Sola Golf Club (941-792-7476; 3807 75th St. W., Bradenton) 18 holes, par 72. Snack bar.

Sarasota Golf Club (941-371-2431; 7280 N. Leewynn Dr., Sarasota) Public course with 18 holes, par 72. Restaurant and bar.

GOLF CENTERS

David Leadbetter Junior Golf Academy (941-753-0177; Bollettieri Tennis & Sports Academy, 1414 69th Ave. W., Bradenton) A highly respected full-time boarding school that also offers summer and week-long lesson programs.

Evie's Eagle Golf Center (941-377-2399; 4735 Bee Ridge Rd., Sarasota) Practice sand traps, chipping and putting greens, lessons with PGA pros, miniature golf.

HEALTH & FITNESS CLUBS

Arlington Park & Aquatic Complex (941-316-1346; 2650 Waldemere St., Sarasota) City-owned, county-operated facility.

Sarasota Family YMCA (941-366-6778; 1819 Main St., Sarasota) Weight machines, sauna and steam room, classes, lap pool, Jacuzzis, racquet sports, day care.

Southside Athletic Club (941-921-4400; 8383 S. Tamiami Trail, Sarasota) Exercise equipment, sauna, steam, whirlpool, lap pool, suntanning, child care.

HIKING

Oscar Scherer State Recreation Area (941-483-5956; 1843 S. Tamiami Trail, Osprey) More than five miles of nature trails, including a trail for disabled persons.

Sarasota Bay Walk (941-361-6133; 1550 Ken Thompson Pkwy., City Island, next to Mote Marine) Self-guided nature hike.

South Lido Park (941-316-1172; south end of Benjamin Franklin Dr., Lido Key) Nature trails into the wetlands of Brushy Bayou.

HUNTING

Knight Trail Park (941-486-2350; 3445 Rustic Road, east of Interstate 75 at exit 35A, Laurel Rd.) Public facility maintained by the Sarasota Parks and Recreation Department. Trap and skeet, pistol and rifle range, picnic areas, shooting supplies.

ICE SKATING

Ice Pavilion (941-484-0080; 1266 Hwy. 41 Bypass S., Venice) Yes, ice skating in Florida. For those suffering frostbite nostalgia, don blades and get over it. Admission $5.50. Rentals available for $2 each. Open for two sessions Monday through Thursday and an extra session Friday through Sunday.

KIDS' STUFF

Pirates Cove (941-755-4608; 5410 14th St. W., Bradenton) Baseball/softball cages, go-carts for all ages, bumper boats, kiddie rides, laser tag, game rooms, and snack bar. Admission is free; charges per activity.

Smuggler's Cove Adventure Golf (941-756-0043; 2000 Cortez Rd. W., Bradenton) 18 holes with an island motif. Admission is per player per game.

RACQUET SPORTS

Anna Maria Youth Center (Magnolia Ave., Anna Maria) Two lighted courts.

Gillespie Park (941-316-1172; 710 N. Osprey Ave., Sarasota) Three courts.

Glazier Gates Park (Manatee Ave. E., Bradenton) Two unlighted, cement, public tennis courts.

G. T. Bray Recreation Center (5502 33rd Ave. Dr. W., Bradenton) Eight each of cement, clay, and racquetball courts.

Hecksher Park (941-316-1172; 450 W. Venice Ave., Venice) Six courts with lights.

Holmes Beach Courts (near City Hall, Holmes Beach) Three lighted courts.

Jessie P. Miller (9th Ave. and 43rd St. W., Bradenton) Four lighted cement courts and one handball court.

Nick Bollettieri Tennis & Sports Academy (941-755-1000 or 800-872-6425; 5500 34th St. W., Bradenton) Training camp for adults and juniors, with state-of-the-art tennis, golf, soccer, and other sports facilities. Andre Agassi and other pros have trained here.

Siesta Key County Beach (941-346-3310; Midnight Pass Rd. at Beach Way Dr., Siesta Key) Four courts with lights.

SHELLING

Not comparable to the coast's southern beaches for shelling, the islands of Bradenton and Sarasota do yield some unusual finds. Venice Beach, for instance, is known for its sharks' teeth, which come in all sizes and various shades, from black to rare white. Manasota Beach also boasts toothy waters, but Venice's northern beaches have better pickings.

Sharks continually shed teeth and grow new ones. Most of what you find is prehistoric. The white ones are recent sheddings. Teeth range in size from one-eighth of an inch to a rare three inches. You can rent official sifters at Venice Beach. Or bring a colander. Some resorts provide "Florida snow shovels" — screen baskets fastened to broomsticks. You can also buy them in local hardware stores. Digging for specimens is taboo.

SPAS

Warm Mineral Springs (941-426-1692; San Servando Ave., Warm Mineral Springs, south of Venice) Water of a rare quality attracts health seekers to a 2.5-acre lake. If you know your spas, you will appreciate the springs' chemical analysis of 17,439 parts per million, way above that of the world's most renowned mineral waters. The lake, which maintains a year-round temperature of 87 degrees, has soothing and, some believe, healing powers. Folks bathe at a roped-off beach area. Opened in 1940, the facilities show their age with a less-than-modern look and attitude. Organic mud, laxative water, whirlpools, saunas, massage therapy, and staff doctors comprise the available services. Historical significance adds to the allure. Archaeologists have discovered artifacts suggesting that native Americans came here for a bit of mineral-washed R&R 10,000 years ago. Owners claim this was the Fountain of Youth they told Ponce de León about. An on-property cyclorama chronicles the history of the area, with dioramas and a 20-minute narration. There are apartments for rent for the real enthusiast. For the casual visitor, I suggest staying in one of the area's resorts instead. The odor of sulfur water would get to me after a while. Admission is $7.00. Visitors can rent beachwear, chairs, and towels.

SPECTATOR SPORTS

PRO BASEBALL

Ed Smith Stadium (941-954-SOXX; 2700 12th St., Sarasota) Spring training home of the Chicago White Sox (March and early April) and off-season home of the Sarasota Red Sox (941-365-4460).

McKechnie Field (941-748-4610 or 941-747-3031; Ninth St. and 17th Ave. W., Bradenton) Site of the Pittsburgh Pirates' exhibition games during March and into April.

Pirate City (941-747-3031; 1701 27th St. E., Bradenton) Spring practice field for the Pittsburgh Pirates. Catch them during spring season working out from 10 am to 1:30 pm.

POLO

Sarasota Polo Club (941-907-0000; 8201 Polo Club Ln., Sarasota) Watch from the grandstands or bring a tailgate picnic. Game time is 1 pm every Sunday, December through March. Admission.

RACING

Sarasota Kennel Club (941-355-7744; 5400 Bradenton Rd., Sarasota) Greyhound racing, pari-mutuel betting, matinee and evening shows year-round. Simulcasts thoroughbred horse racing from Miami year-round. Admission. Closed Sunday.

WATERSKIING

Sarasota Ski-A-Rees Show (941-388-1666; City Island, behind Mote Marine, Sarasota) Free amateur performances in the bay every Sunday at 2 pm.

WATER SPORTS

PARASAILING & WATERSKIING

Don & Mike's Boat & Ski Rental (941-966-4000; Casey Key Marina, 520 Blackburn Point Rd., Nokomis Beach) Ski rides and lessons.

Longboat Pass Parasail (941-792-1900; 4110-A 127th St. W., Cortez) Beach adventures from an offshore racing boat. Rides up to 1,200 feet.

Palma Sola Boat Rentals (941-778-4083; Anna Maria Island Causeway, 9915 Manatee Ave. W., Bradenton) Offers waterski captaining and instruction by appointment. Equipment rental available.

Siesta Key Parasail (941-349-1900; Mr. CB's, 1249 Stickney Point Rd., Siesta Key) Rides up to 800 feet.

SAILBOARDING & SURFING

Gulf Coast waters generally are too tame to inspire awe in surfers, except in inclement weather. Sailboarders, however, find perfect conditions all along the coast. Look in the "Beaches" section for surfing and windsurfing venues. Listed below are resources for lessons and rentals.

Palma Sola Causeway Beach (941-778-4083; Route 64 to Anna Maria Island) Good windsurfing and rentals.

Siesta Sports Rentals (941-346-1797; 6551 Midnight Pass Rd., Southbridge Mall, Siesta Key) Rents windsurfers at per-hour to per-week rates.

Surfing World (941-794-1233; 11904 Cortez Rd. W., Bradenton) Sells and rents surfboards and sailboards; lessons available.

SNORKELING & SCUBA

Of all the southern Gulf Coast, this region generally boasts the best visibility, especially in spring. Manmade reefs make up for the lack of natural reefs on Florida's west coast.

DIVE SHOPS & CHARTERS

Dolphin Dive Center (941-924-2785; 6018 S. Tamiami Trail, Sarasota) Local charters, instruction, rentals.

SeaTrek Divers (941-779-1506; 105 Seventh St. N., Bradenton Beach) Two-tank, offshore dives and snorkel trips to Egmont Key. Scuba certification courses.

SHORE SNORKELING & DIVING

Bradenton Beach (Anna Maria Island) An old sugar barge sank here many years ago and houses various forms of marine life.

Point of Rocks (Siesta Key) South of Crescent Beach at the island's central zone; rocks, underwater caves, and coral formations make good submerged sightseeing.

WILDERNESS CAMPING

Oscar Scherer State Recreation Area (941-483-5956; 1843 S. Tamiami Trail, Osprey) Nearly 1,400 acres in size, this natural oasis provides full facilities for the camper in a wooded, waterside setting of palmettos, pines, and venerable, moss-draped oaks. The threatened Florida scrub jay seeks refuge here, along with bald eagles, bobcats, river otters, gopher tortoises, and alligators. There's swimming in a freshwater lake, plus a bird walk, nature and canoe trails, picnicking, and fishing.

WILDLIFE SPOTTING

BIRDS

The Sarasota coast is the least natural of the Gulf Coast's four regions. Determined bird-spotters can find feathered friends at parks and refuges such

A great blue heron bird-eyes the beauty of Sarasota Bay.

Karen T. Bartlett

as the Passage Key sanctuary, north of Anna Maria Island (bring binoculars — landing ashore is forbidden); Rookery Islands, north of Siesta Key (approachable by boat only); and Oscar Scherer State Recreation Area in Osprey, home of the endangered scrub jay. Look for the wild peacocks that roam the streets of the village on Longboat Key and, I'm told, Holmes Beach.

DOLPHINS

Dolphins often follow in the wake of tour boats, but they're unpredictable. You can't plan on them; you can only be thrilled and charmed when they do appear. If you learn their feeding schedules you have a better chance of catching their act.

Holy Sea Cows!

We know them today as Florida manatees: 1,300-pound blimps with skin like burlap and a face only a nature buff could love. They also go by the name sea cow, although they are more closely related to the elephant. In days of yore, many a sea-weary sailor mistook them for mermaids.

Well, Ariel they're not, but bewitching they can be. Gentle and herbivorous — consuming up to 100 pounds of aquatic plants daily — they make no enemies and have only one stumbling block to survival: man. As mammals, manatees must surface for air, like whales and dolphins. Their girth makes them a prime target for boaters speeding through their habitat. Warning signs designate popular manatee areas. Instead of zipping through these waters and further threatening the seriously endangered manatee population, boaters can better benefit by trying to spot the reclusive creatures as they take a breath. It requires a sharp eye, patience, and experience. Watch channels during low tides, when the manatees take to deeper water. Concentric circles, known as "manatee footprints," signal surfacing animals. They usually travel in a line and appear as drifting coconuts or fronds.

If you happen to spot an injured sea cow, please report it to the Manatee Hot Line at 800-342-1821.

MANATEES

Named after the lovable creatures, Bradenton's Manatee County has erected "Manatee Watch" signs at manatee-frequented areas — on the bridges and city pier of the Manatee River, on the Palma Sola Causeway, and on Anna Maria Island at Bayfront Park, Coquina Beach and boat ramp, and Kingfish Boat Ramp.

NATURE PRESERVES & ECO-ATTRACTIONS

The Wyland Wall at Mote Marine Aquarium is one of a series of life-size outdoor marine walls artist Wyland has painted across the nation.

Karen T. Bartlett

MOTE MARINE LABORATORY AND AQUARIUM
941-388-2451 or 800-691-MOTE.
1600 Ken Thompson Pkwy., City Island, northeast of Lido Key.
Open: 10–5 daily.
Admission: $8 adults, $6 children 4–17.

Mote Marine is known around the world for its research on sharks, marine mammals, and environmental pollutants. Its visitors' center educates the public on projects and marine life. A 135,000-gallon shark tank centerpieces the original facility and is kept stocked with sharks and fish typical of the area: grouper, snook, jewfish, pompano, and snapper. Twenty-two smaller aquariums, one touch tank, and one no-touch tank hold more than 200 varieties of common and unusual species: starfish, octopus, seahorses, skates, and scorpion fish. Another huge glass-sided tank holds manatees Hugh and Buffett, the newest, most lovable additions, at the Marine Mammal Visitors Center, which was built a few years ago just down the street from the original facility. It also features a marine mammal rehabilitation tank and a sea turtle exhibit. In 1999, Mote doubled in size with more marine life exhibits and viewable research libraries.

OSCAR SCHERER STATE RECREATION AREA
941-483-5956.
1843 S. Tamiami Trail, Osprey.
Admission: $3.25 per car, $1 per pedestrian or cyclist.

Home of the threatened Florida scrub jay, plus bald eagles, bobcats, river otters, gopher tortoises, and alligators.

Birds find a haven at the Pelican Man's Bird Sanctuary on City Island in Sarasota.

Karen T. Bartlett

PELICAN MAN'S BIRD SANCTUARY
941-388-4444.
1708 Ken Thompson Pkwy., City Island, next to Mote Marine.
Admission: Free; donations accepted.

The work of one man, Dale Shields, laid the foundation for this refuge for injured pelicans and other birds. It's a must if you're visiting Mote Marine, and also for nature lovers. Don't expect exotic birds, just on-the-mend, local varieties.

SARASOTA BAY WALK
941-361-6133 (fax).
1550 Ken Thompson Pkwy., City Island, next to Mote Marine.
Admission: Free.

Take a quiet, self-guided walk along the bay, estuaries, lagoons, and uplands to learn more about coastland ecology. Boardwalk and shell paths take you past mangroves, old fishing boats bobbing on the bay, egrets, and illustrated signs detailing nature's wonders.

WILDLIFE TOURS & CHARTERS

Sarasota Bay Explorers (941-388-4200; Mote Marine Aquarium, 1600 Ken Thompson Pkwy., City Island) A pontoon tour of intracoastal waters between City Island and Siesta Key. Features include trawl net toss, binocular study of rookery islands, and naturalist narration.

SHOPPING

In season you may well be tempted, like everyone else, to save shopping and sightseeing for rainy, cold, off-beach days. Don't. You'll lose your diligently attained good beach attitude by the time you've found your first parking spot. Go in the morning for best results and the most relaxing experience. Otherwise you may find that the wear-and-tear outweighs the pleasure of window-shopping or the joys associated with the discovery of the perfect, one-of-a-kind gift or souvenir.

Folks shop till they dine in the blossomy setting of St. Armands Circle.

Karen T. Bartlett

Sarasota's St. Armands Circle is known far and wide for its arena of posh shops, galleries, and restaurants. Downtown Sarasota is steadily improving its shopping outlook, especially for art and antique lovers. On the islands you'll find fun shops and beach boutiques that blend with the sand and sun.

ANTIQUES & COLLECTIBLES

Antique shops are plentiful and easy to find in and around Sarasota. You'll find a row of them on Pineapple Street, downtown. Many specialize in fine art and rare, high-end pieces. Pick up a copy of the "Sarasota Antique Guide & Locator Map" from the Sarasota Visitors' Center.

Apple & Carpenter Antique Gallery (941-951-2314; 60-64 S. Palm Ave., downtown Sarasota) American and European paintings of the 19th and 20th centuries, as well as bronze and marble sculptures, fine furniture, clocks, French cameo glass, silver, bronze, porcelain, art glass.

Time Warp (941-483-3005; 101 W. Venice Ave., Venice) Baby-boomer and pop culture records and other collectibles, such as a Beatles ruler, a Flash Gordon belt, and a Dukes of Hazzard comic book.

Yellow Bird Antiques (941-388-1823; 640 S. Washington Blvd., Suite 230, Sarasota) An "antique boutique" specializing in decorative items.

BOOKS

Main Bookshop (941-366-7653; 1962 Main St., downtown Sarasota) A landmark store with four floors full of discounted and used books on all subjects.

Bookshop (941-488-1307; 241 W. Venice Ave., Venice) Small but complete store with several books on sharks and other local nature.

Sarasota News & Books (941-365-6332; 1341 Main St., downtown Sarasota) The old Charlie's News has gone the way of Barnes & Nobles et al. Beyond books and periodicals, it sells cards, gifts, coffee, and lunch. Specializes in art, architecture, and interior design.

Venice Newsstand (941-488-6969; 329 W. Venice Ave., Venice) Old-fashioned newsstand selling cigars, greeting cards, magazines, newspapers, and paperbacks.

CLOTHING

Cravats' (941-366-7780; 222 Sarasota Quay, Sarasota) Custom shirts and fine clothing for men.

Dream Weaver (941-388-1974; 364 St. Armands Circle) Fine woven wear that crosses the line to fabric art, in silk, suede, and other extravagant materials.

Global Navigator (941-388-4515; 357 St. Armands Circle) Men's explorer fashions.

Kepp's (941-388-5041; 301 John Ringling Blvd., St. Armands Circle) Carries distinctive designer labels and British name-brand men's clothing.

LaCheape Boutique (941-488-6388; 530 Highway 41 Bypass S., Venice) Liquidated stock from expensive boutiques sold at greatly reduced cost.

Nana's (941-488-4108; 223 W. Venice Ave., Venice) Quality kids' clothes and toys.

Peggy's (941-365-4485; 218 Sarasota Quay, Sarasota) Ladies' formal and evening wear.

Sun Bug (941-485-7946; 141 W. Venice Ave., Venice) The most fun in women's fashions, from dressy to casual: great cotton styles, swimsuits, and unusual, comfortable dresses.

Tropics (941-346-2950; 5251 Ocean Blvd., Siesta Key Village) Cool, tropical fashions and T-shirts for women and kids.

CONSIGNMENT

In Sarasota it's not the embarrassment it is in some places to buy second-hand. Because of the wealth and transient nature of its residents, the area offers the possibility of great discoveries in its consignment shops. In Sarasota especially, recycled apparel is the "in" thing among the young and artistic.

Designer Consigner (941-953-5995; 3639 Bahia Vista St., Sarasota) Wedding gowns, evening wear, sports and career fashions.

Kids Care-O-Sell Consignments (941-761-8405; 6600 Manatee Ave., W. Bradenton) Maternity wear, kids' clothes, and furniture.

Woman's Exchange (941-955-7859; 539 S. Orange Ave., downtown Sarasota) Furniture, family clothing, antiques, housewares, and china. Profits support local arts.

FACTORY OUTLET CENTERS

Gulf Coast Factory Shops (941-723-1150; I-75 exit 43, Ellenton) Nearly 100 shops, a food court, and a children's playground in a Caribbean setting.

Sarasota Outlet Center (941-359-2050; I-75 exit 40 at University Parkway, Sarasota) More than 40 factory outlets and discount stores.

FLEA MARKETS & BAZAARS

Bradenton Farmers' Market (941-748-7949; Bradenton City Hall Parking Lot, 500 15th St. W., Bradenton) Runs 8 to noon every Saturday, October through April. Fresh local produce, baked goods, and crafts.

The Dome (941-493-6773; 5115 Rte. 775, Venice) A small indoor market open Saturday and Sunday year-round; also on Friday, October through May.

Red Barn Flea Market (941-747-3794; 1707 First St. E., Bradenton) More than 700 stores and booths selling baseball cards to car parts. Open 8 to 4 Wednesday, Saturday, and Sunday.

Sarasota Farmers Market (941-951-2656; Lemon Ave. and Main St., downtown Sarasota) Fresh fruits, vegetables, baked goods, plants, arts and crafts. Open 7–12 Saturday, year-round.

GALLERIES

The Artful Dodger (941-925-8266; Boatyard Shopping Village, 1522 Stickney Point Rd., near Siesta Key) Eclectic collection of pottery, glass, jewelry, and whimsy from more than 80 artists nationwide.

Chasen Galleries (941-366-4278; 16 S. Palm Ave., downtown Sarasota) Contemporary sculpture, figures, paintings, and glass.

Exit Art Gallery (941-383-4099; Centre Shops, 5380 Gulf of Mexico Dr., Longboat Key) Mosaic tables, painted metal sculpture, pop art, posters, license-plate bags, unusual jewelry, and select clothes.

The Parrish Connection (941-484-4141; 201 W. Venice Ave., Venice) Fine investment-quality art by noted masters such as Maxfield Parrish, Edna Hibel, and Thornton Utz.

Downtown Sarasota's Towles Court, a working artists' colony, colorfully took over an old bungalow neighborhood.

Karen T. Bartlett

Towles Court Artist Colony (1945 Morrill St. off Hwy. 301, Sarasota) A charming district of restored and brightly painted bungalows turned art colony, featuring the galleries and working art studios of artists in all media. Third Friday "Stroll at Towles" gallery walks, 6 to 10 pm.

Wyland Galleries (941-388-5331; 465 John Ringling Blvd., St. Armands Circle) The work of artist Wyland (of cross-country Whale Walls fame) as well as other renowned marine and wildlife artists.

Ziegenfuss Gallery of Fine Art (941-365-3266; 76 S. Palm Ave., downtown Sarasota) Cow and bull art, tasteful Sarasota-theme and Miami South Beach paintings, pop art, sculptures by Jack Dowd, and the work of other local artists.

GIFTS

Some of the best gifts and souvenirs are found in attraction gift shops, especially those at the Ringling museums, Sarasota Jungle Gardens, Gulf Coast Museum of Science, and South Florida Museum.

Hurricane Rita's (941-346-7712; 5212 Ocean Blvd., Siesta Key Village. Also 941-388-2766; 319 John Ringling Blvd., St. Armands Circle) Unique and colorful home decorations, crafts for kids, and imported clothing.

Ivory Coast (941-388-1999; 15 N. Blvd. of Presidents, St. Armands Circle) Outstanding imported tribal masks, statues, gifts, decorative items, women's fashions, and jewelry inspired by Africa.

Rusticala (941-383-0787; Centre Shops, 5360 Gulf of Mexico Dr., Longboat Key) Pottery, antique and new jewelry, napkins, note cards, and a few of a lot of unusual things.

Sea Chantey (941-349-6171; 5150 Ocean Blvd., Siesta Key) Among the riffraff of pink flamingos, T-shirts, and shell jewelry at Siesta Key Village, this shop stands out with unusual objets d'art, boutique women's and children's clothes, jewelry, and imports.

Special Things at St. Armands (941-388-5003; 465C John Ringling Blvd., St. Armands Circle) Hand-painted and personalized furniture, gifts, and decorative items for children.

JEWELRY

Fawn Custom Jewelers (941-349-2748; 5221 Ocean Blvd., Siesta Key) Specializing in Florida seashore-motif pieces.

Heitel Jewelers (941-488-2720; 347 W. Venice Ave., Venice) New and estate jewelry and fine gifts.

Jess Jewelers (941-756-5019; 409 Cortez Rd. W., Bradenton) Estate diamonds, beach-theme pieces, master goldsmiths.

Thayer Jewelers (941-388-5200; 464 John Ringling Blvd., St. Armands Circle) Diamonds, precious gems, contemporary and estate jewelry and objets d'art. European-trained master jeweler/designer on staff.

KITCHENWARE & HOME DECOR

Basketville (941-493-0007; 4411 S. Tamiami Trail, Venice) Region's widest selection of basketry, wicker furniture, silk flowers, woodenware, and other items.

The Lofty Lion (941-485-2588; 203 W. Venice Ave., Venice) A select collection of whimsical home decor items: indoor fountains, cat lovers' dishware, and other country-style delights.

Longboat Interiors (941-383-2491; 12 Avenue of Flowers, Longboat Key) Rich Victorian parlor theme: heavy silver frames, silk flowers, antique pine, frilly and floral soft furnishings.

Pandora's Box (941-365-8700; 49 S. Palm Ave., downtown Sarasota) Framed, signed Hagar and Garfield cartoon art, Oriental bronze, frames, shells, and other functional home accessories.

Rolling Pin Kitchen Emporium (941-925-2434; Sarasota Square Mall, 8201 S. Tamiami Trail, Sarasota) German cutlery and fine kitchenware.

Rosemary Rabbit Home Collection (941-388-1833; 20 S. Blvd. of Presidents, St. Armands Circle) Hand-painted and country-style furnishings and accessories.

SHELL SHOPS

Sea Pleasures and Treasures (941-488-3510; 255 Venice Ave. W., Venice) Quantity, not necessarily quality: sea-theme gifts, shells, and shell craft supplies.

SHOPPING CENTERS & MALLS

De Soto Square (941-747-5868; Tamiami Trail at Cortez Rd., Bradenton) 700,000 feet of shop-till-you-drop: over 100 stores including Sears, Burdines, and Dillards.

Downtown Sarasota One of the Gulf Coast's most successful downtown restoration projects has returned Sarasota's vitality to Main Street and environs. The area is also known as the Sarasota Theater and Arts District. Rumors abound that Main Street may be converted into a walking mall, but for the time being it encompasses approximately a 1.5-mile area, centered at Five Points, where Main Street intersects with four other streets. Old, renovated buildings house galleries (particularly along South Palm Avenue), bookstores, clothing boutiques, antique shops, restaurants, sidewalk cafes, cabarets, clubs, and gift shops. Palm Avenue Association hosts gallery walks the first Friday of each month, with music, refreshments, and gallery openings, beginning at 6 pm. At Burns Court (Pineapple and Palm Avenues) lies a unique shopping enclave of historic bungalows and unusual finds.

Longboat Key You'll find a smattering of interesting shops at The Center Shops (5370 Gulf of Mexico Dr.) and Avenue of Flowers (off Gulf of Mexico Dr.).

St. Armands Circle (941-388-1554; St. Armands Key) John Ringling envisioned a world-class shopping center on one of the Sarasota barrier islands he owned, complete with park-lined walkways and baroque statuary. He would be gratified by St. Armands Circle. On a scale with Beverly Hills' Rodeo Drive and Palm Beach's Worth Avenue, it is named for developer Charles St. Amand [sic]. Its spin-off formation is suited geographically to the pancake shape of the island. Four sections arc off the circular center drive. "The Circle," as it is known in local shorthand, encompasses shops of the most upscale nature, galleries, restaurants, clubs, ice cream shops, and specialty boutiques. International style is well represented. The Circle is a hub of activity for the entire region. Horse-drawn carriages offer sunset rides. The Circus Ring of Fame honors distinguished Big Top entertainers. People dress in finery just to shop here, but don't feel obligated. Parking is free on the street and in the garage nearby.

Palm trees and paved courtyards add to the pleasure of spending money at St. Armands Circle.

Karen T. Bartlett

Southgate Plaza (941-951-0412; Siesta Rd. and S. Tamiami Trail, Sarasota) A major shopping mall, this one houses Burdines, Dillards, and Saks Fifth Avenue.

Venice Avenue (Venice Ave. W. and Tamiami Trail, Venice) Down a Mediterranean, date-palm-lined boulevard, you'll find shops and restaurants of every style, to fit every budget.

Venice Centre Mall (226 Tampa Ave. W., Venice) Occupying the erstwhile winter quarters of the Kentucky Military Institute, the mall is listed on the National Register of Historic Buildings. It includes shops that specialize in unique gifts and clothing and fall into formation along a spit-and-polish hall.

The Village at Siesta Key (Ocean Blvd., Siesta Key) Refreshingly barefoot in style, this area mixes beach bawdiness with an artistic temperament not quite as intense as that of downtown Sarasota.

SPORTS STORES

<u>Note:</u> This listing includes general sports outlets only. For supplies and equipment for specific sports, please refer to "Recreation" in this chapter.

Cook's Sportland (941-493-0025; 235 W. Venice Ave., Venice) Equipment for archery, golf, camping, and fishing; also fishing licenses, tackle repair, sportswear, shoes, and western clothing.

Mr. CB's Saltwater Outfitters (941-349-4400; 1249 Stickney Point Rd., Siesta Key) Fishing and snorkeling gear and sportswear.

CALENDAR OF EVENTS

JANUARY

Arts Day Festival (941-365-5118; downtown Sarasota) A gala confluence of Sarasota's visual and performing arts that spills from the galleries and theaters onto outdoor stages and sidewalks.

FEBRUARY

Cortez Commercial Fishing Festival (941-795-4637; village of Cortez) Food vendors, music, net-mending demonstrations, arts and crafts, and educational exhibits describing the community of Cortez's 100-year-old fishing industry. One weekend late in the month.

Festival of the Arts (941-951-2656; downtown Sarasota) Not your average open-air collection of mediocre and semitacky crafts, but a classy gathering of top-notch artisans from around the world for two days midmonth.

Florida Fishing College (941-748-0411; Manatee Convention and Civic Center, 1 Haben Blvd., Palmetto) Gear and guidance for beginners to professionals.

Greek Festival (941-355-2616; Sarasota) Greek food, dancing, arts, and crafts for one weekend near Valentine's Day.

Scottish Highland Games & Heritage Festival (941-953-6707; Sarasota Fair Grounds, Fruitville Ave.)

Sun Run (941-365-1277; Siesta Beach Pavilion, Siesta Key) 5K race.

MARCH

Anna Maria Island Springfest (941-778-2099) A celebration of island arts: artist and crafts booths, local entertainment, and food concessions. Two days early in the month.

Manatee Heritage Days (941-741-4070) An entire week at the end of the month is devoted to the celebration of local history and traditions throughout Bradenton and Manatee County. Special tours are arranged by local attractions, and demonstrators weave, quilt, and make baskets and doilies.

Medieval Fair (941-351-8497; Ringling Museum of Arts grounds, Sarasota) *The* event of the year, this fair is the culmination of Sarasota's love for art, theater, food, and circus, all within the atmosphere of a 15th-century flashback. Four days at the turn of March.

Sailor Circus (941-361-6350; 2075 Bahia Vista, Sarasota) Proof that the circus is still in the blood of many Sarasota families. Students from grades three to 12 perform professional circus feats during a two-week season.

APRIL

Florida Heritage Festival (941-747-1998; Bradenton) Commemorates Hernando de Soto's discovery of the region. A reenactment of the 1539 landing highlights the schedule of month-long events.

Florida Winefest and Auction (941-952-1109; The Resort at Longboat Key Club, Longboat Key) A prestigious event featuring food and wine seminars, tastes from the area's finest restaurants, top entertainment, black-tie dinner, and fine wine auction. Four days.

La Musica International Chamber Music Festival (941-364-8802; Sarasota Opera House, downtown Sarasota) Concerts at the Sarasota Opera House during two weekends.

Longboat Key Islandfest (941-383-2466; Longboat Key) A taste of the food and arts of the island, with live entertainment and children's activities.

Sarasota Jazz Festival (941-366-1552; Van Wezel Performing Arts Hall, 777 N. Tamiami Trail, Sarasota) Big-name jazz players lead a slate of big bands and jazz combos. Four days.

Siesta Fiesta (Siesta Key) A weekend of crafts shows, food fest, live musical and kids' entertainment.

MAY

Florida Playwrights Festival (941-366-9017; Florida Studio Theatre, 1241 N. Palm Ave., downtown Sarasota) Premieres the works of emerging playwrights from Florida and around the nation, launching mainstage productions for three weekends.

The National Circus School of Performing Arts (941-924-7054; Ringling Museum of the Circus, Ringling Estate, 5401 Bay Shore Rd., Sarasota) More than two weeks of rehearsal and performance in circus arts: acrobatics, gymnastics, trapeze, comedy, clowning, juggling, wire walking, trampoline, makeup, costuming, lighting, sound, and more.

JUNE

PrideFest Film Festival (941-346-8662; Burns Court Cinema, 506 Burns Ln., Sarasota) This week-long event features outstanding artistic films from around the world.

Sarasota Music Festival (941-953-4252; Florida West Coast Symphony, 709 N. Tamiami Trail, Sarasota) Presents classical and chamber music by promising young musicians from around the world. Sponsored by the Florida West Coast Symphony, the program includes lectures for participants. The public is welcome at the performances. Three weeks.

JULY

Suncoast Offshore Grand Prix (941-751-1644; Sarasota's islands) A national attraction, with powerboat racers from around the world. Fourth of July weekend.

AUGUST

Sharks' Tooth and Seafood Festival (941-488-2236 or 800-940-7427; Venice) A bacchanal of seafood bounty, the festival gets its name also from its reputation among shark-tooth collectors. One weekend.

SEPTEMBER

Project Black Cinema Film Festival (941-953-6424; Burns Court Cinema, 506 Burns Ln., Sarasota) African and African Diaspora films.

OCTOBER

St. Armands Art Festival (St. Armands Circle) Features 200 national artists.

Stone Crab, Seafood & Wine Festival (941-383-6464 or 800-4-COLONY; Colony Beach & Tennis Resort, Longboat Key) Celebrates the opening of stone crab season with dinners, cooking demonstrations, and wine tastings.

A Taste of Sarasota (941-379-2086; City Island Park, Sarasota) The best from Sarasota restaurants, plus live entertainment and a kids' park and petting zoo. Midmonth.

Renaissance art adorns Venice streets.

Karen T. Bartlett

Venice Sun Fiesta (941-484-9715; Venice) A celebration of food, folks, and fun. One weekend midmonth.

NOVEMBER

Blues Fest (941-377-3279; Sarasota Fairgrounds) Blues musicians of world renown. One day early in the month.

Cine-World Film Festival (941-955-FILM; Burns Court Cinema, 506 Burns Ln., downtown Sarasota) Screens 20 to 30 films from around the world for one week early in the month.

Discover the Past Festival (941-966-5214; Historic Spanish Point, Osprey) Living-history vignettes, historical crafts demonstrations, horse-and-buggy rides, canoe trips, food, and entertainment for two days late in the month.

Sarasota Comedy Festival (941-366-2686; various locations in Sarasota) A result of Sarasota's large population of cartoonists, the festival takes place for a week midmonth and includes a comedy film festival, comedy dinner shows with name comedians, a "cartoon walk," a mainstage show, golf events, and gala dinners.

Sarasota French Film Festival (941-351-9010; Sarasota) Weekend event that showcases French feature films and their stars and directors.

Taste of Manatee (941-729-7777; Barcarrota Blvd., Bradenton) Restaurant samplings one day early in the month.

DECEMBER

International Circus Festival and Parade (941-351-8888; Sarasota County Fairgrounds and downtown Sarasota) Circus acts, clown shows, exhibits, kiddie rides, and carnival. One week at the end of the month.

CHAPTER FOUR
Wild and Watery
CHARLOTTE HARBOR COAST

Angler's silver: a hooked tarpon fights for freedom in Boca Grande Pass.

Lee Island Coast Visitor and Convention Bureau

A s one of Florida's largest bays, Charlotte Harbor provides a huge gulp of nature and a place to play on many waterfronts. The region has remained the most isolated and undeveloped of any in southwest Florida, primarily because its beaches are so far removed from main highways. The Charlotte coast retains a quiet, natural temperament and still holds on to fishing as a way of life and livelihood.

This chapter begins where the last left off, on twisty, out-of-the-way **Manasota Key,** a refuge for wealthy isolationists at its north end and the site of the humble, underappreciated resort community of **Englewood Beach** at its south.

On the mainland peninsula bounded by the Myakka River and Charlotte Harbor, small residential communities such as **Englewood, Grove City, Cape Haze, Placida,** and **Rotonda West** hold Amerindian mounds, fishermen,

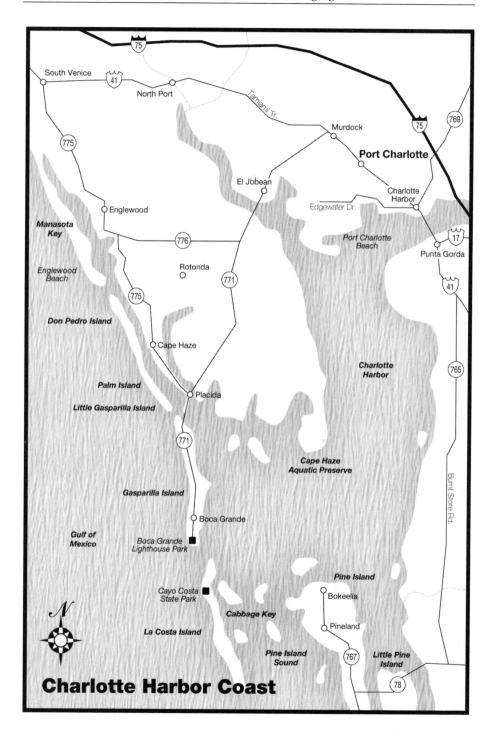

Charlotte Harbor Coast

retirees, and families. Placida is the jump-off point for **Gasparilla Island**, which has built its reputation and character on one fish in particular: the tarpon. Phosphate shipping and legends of bygone buccaneers first attracted attention to the area. Later the Silver King, prize of the fishing world, drew millionaires to the island community of **Boca Grande**. Privately owned **Little Gasparilla** and **Palm Islands** and mostly state-owned **Don Pedro Island** have run together with the shifts of tides and time. They remain three of Florida's most pristine barrier islands.

Inland, across the harbor, **Port Charlotte** is a new city that was built around Tamiami Trail, principally as a retirement community. The spring training grounds of the Texas Rangers baseball club are in nearby **Murdock**.

The town of **Charlotte Harbor** was settled shortly after the Civil War by farmers and cattle ranchers. Facing it across the Peace River's widest point, **Punta Gorda** boasts a past as deeply rooted. The southernmost station for the Florida Southern Railroad in 1886, the deepwater port town enjoyed a bustling era of commerce and tourism before railroad builder Henry Plant decided to shut it down in favor of further developing Tampa Bay. Ice making, turpentine stilling, pineapple growing, and especially commercial fishing continued for some time to earn local citizens a living. Today Punta Gorda is working to recover its past glories through downtown and riverfront restoration. Home of Ponce de León Park, it hosts subdivisions of modern-day youth-seekers.

LODGING

Accommodations along the Charlotte Harbor coast tend to exude personality. Sure, you have your Days Inn and Econo Lodge, but the remainder are either old-money polished, new-money luxurious, or money's-not-the-issue sporting. From beach cottages to the grand old Gasparilla Inn, the Charlotte Harbor coast promises something special in the way of lodging.

During high season, which begins shortly before Christmas and ends after Easter, rates may rise anywhere from 10 to 100 percent above those charged during the off-season. Some resorts schedule their rates based on as many as six different seasons, with the highest rates applying from mid-February through Easter. Reservations are suggested during these months. Some resorts and rental services require a minimum stay, especially during the peak season.

The following selection includes some of the coast's greatest lodging characters. Toll-free 800- or 888- reservation numbers, where available, are listed after local numbers. A star after the pricing designation indicates that the rate includes at least continental breakfast in the cost of lodging; a few follow the American Plan, pricing all meals into the rate charged.

Pricing codes are explained below. They are normally per person/double occupancy for hotel rooms and per unit for efficiencies, apartments, and cottages. Many resorts offer off-season packages at special rates. Pricing does not include the 6 percent Florida sales tax. Charlotte County also charges a 4 percent bed tax. Many large resorts add service gratuities or maid charges.

Rate Categories

Inexpensive	Up to $50
Moderate	$50 to $110
Expensive	$110 to $180
Very Expensive	$180 and up

The following abbreviations are used for credit card information:

AE - American Express	DC - Diners Club
CB - Carte Blanche	MC - MasterCard
D - Discover Card	V - Visa

Federal law mandates that properties with 50 rooms or more provide accommodations for physically handicapped persons. I have indicated only those small places that do not make such allowances.

Boca Grande

The Gasparilla Inn, doyenne of the Gulf Coast.

Karen T. Bartlett

GASPARILLA INN
General Manager: Steve
Seidensticker.
941-964-2201.
5th St. & Palm St., Boca
Grande 33921.
Closed: Mid-June to mid-Dec.
Price: Expensive to Very
Expensive*.
Credit Cards: No.

With subtle grandeur the Gasparilla Inn sits upon her throne of lush greenery. Dressed in pale yellow clapboard with white columns, Georgian porticos, and Victorian sensibilities, it has been a town anchor and social emblem since 1912. The region's oldest surviving resort, it first opened its doors as a retreat for families such as the Vanderbilts and Du Ponts, whose descendants still winter there. If you try to reserve a room during the "social season" (December through April) and you aren't "the right kind of people," you could be turned away even if rooms are available. Not that accommodations are ultraelegant. The 140 rooms and cottages reflect the era of their construction, with understated furnishings. A more elegant wood-and-wicker dining room, a beauty salon, an 18-hole golf course, a croquet lawn, tennis courts, and a beach club with fitness facilities and two pools provide amenities. It's said that the Gasparilla Inn, in quiet Boca Grande, was where Palm Beach socialites used to come to escape charity balls and the perpetual fashion show of their glittery hometown.

THE INNLET
General Manager: Jan
  Tatum.
941-964-2294.
11th St. and East Ave., P.O.
  Box 248, Boca Grande
  33921.
Price: Moderate to
  Expensive.
Credit Cards: AE, MC, V.

Little stepsister to the Gasparilla Inn, the Innlet has been yellowed to fit in with the family. Fancy lattice touches and new renovations pretty up a motel remake. The name is a double entendre on its sub-inn status and its bayou location, handy for boating and fishing types. Since the Inn took it over, it has added a nice little pool and coffee shop and redone the 32 rooms and efficiencies in modern attire.

Cape Haze

PALM ISLAND RESORT
President: Dean L.
  Beckstead.
941-697-4800, 800-824-5412
  (U.S.), 800-282-6142
  (Florida only).
7092 Placida Rd., Cape
  Haze 33946.
Price: Expensive to Very
  Expensive.
Credit Cards: AE, MC, V.

A true island getaway in grand style, Palm Island is a slab of sand above Gasparilla Island devoted mostly to a private resort with villa lodging. One must boat in; there's an hourly ferry from the resort's mainland marina and its two-level suite accommodations. On Palm Island, Old Florida-style villas front a wide, isolated apron of beach and come with fully equipped kitchens, laundries, one to three bedrooms, exquisite appointments, and screened porches overlooking more than two miles of deserted beach. The 160-unit (counting the mainland accommodations) property has five pools and 11 tennis courts, plus a restaurant and bar, island store, full-service marina, boat rentals, charter service, nature trail, bicycle and water-sports equipment rentals — all the makings for an I'm-never-leaving-this-island vacation. What it doesn't have is roads, cars, stress, and rigorous time schedules.

Englewood Beach

WESTON'S RESORT
Owner: Deborah L. Weston.
941-474-3431.
985 Gulf Blvd., Englewood
  34223.

Taking up a good block at Englewood Beach's southern end, Weston spreads from bay to beach to please both fishermen and sand-loving types. For the former it rents boats, motors, and

Price: Inexpensive to
   Moderate.
Credit Cards: D, MC, V.

paraphernalia and provides boat slips, fishing docks, and freezer storage. Free for the use of all guests are two swimming pools, tennis courts, barbecue grills, and shuffleboard. Accommodations on the 83-unit property range from studio efficiencies to three-bedroom apartments, all modernly outfitted. In some rooms the beds, Murphy-style, flip up into closets for more room. Kitchens are large and modern. The rooms are clean and well kept, with the exception of some carpeting that looked as though it needed replacing. Beach rooms look out on sea-walled sand and eroding beach beyond that. One pool sits in the middle of an asphalt parking lot. There's nothing luxurious about the resort, but its reasonable rates and beach location at the quiet end of the island make it a good choice for people who love water and water sports.

Manasota Key

MANASOTA BEACH CLUB
Owners: Robert and
   Sydney Buffum.
Managers: Jim and Dee Dee
   Buffum.
941-474-2614.
7660 Manasota Key Rd.,
   Englewood 34223.
Closed: Mid-May through
   mid-Nov.
Price: Very Expensive*.
Credit Cards: No.
Handicap Access: Yes.

A tiny, low-impact sign whispers "Manasota Beach Club." And although it occupies 22 acres of Manasota Key, the resort itself is just as unobtrusive. The unadvertised property preserves the island's natural attributes with a low-key attitude, wooded paths, and a deserted beach. I saw a pileated woodpecker while there, and guests have reported seeing 92 other species about the grounds. Fifteen cottages, from rustic to designer in style, the dining room, the bottle club (no alchohol is sold on the premises), and a library display Old Florida charm. The resort appeals to the "sink into oblivion" type of vacationer who wishes to hide out amongst natural, gnarly vegetation. (There are no televisions in the units, unless requested.) The property, which has a summer-camp feel to it, also appeals to the sportsperson, with three tennis courts, a swimming pool, bocci ball, shuffleboard, basketball, horseshoes, croquet, bicycling, sailing, windsurfing, and charter fishing. A private 18-hole golf course nearby is available to guests. During social season (January through mid-April), cottage room guests receive three meals a day on the American Plan. During November, December, and late April, the resort rents out entire cottages with kitchens and provides no meals.

Punta Gorda

FISHERMEN'S VILLAGE VILLAS
Manager: Diane Place.
941-639-8721 or
   800-639-0020.

One of the Gulf Coast's best lodging bargains, these spacious time-share units each contain a big, full kitchen with counter bar and stools, two bedrooms, one bath, a loft, and a living area, all

1200 W. Retta Esplanade #58, Punta Gorda 33950.
Price: Moderate.
Credit Cards: D, MC, V.
Handicap Access: Yes.

decorated in modern taste and all with a view of the water. The only bad news is that they're situated above the shops, restaurants, and courtyard action of Fishermen's Village, but the rooms are well soundproofed. Guests have free use of a swimming pool, clay tennis courts, and bicycles. They are close to all the action there is to find in Punta Gorda, on land and on water. Convenient for boat-in guests, the Village fronts a yacht harbor and a 98-slip full-service marina.

Gilchrist B&B has turned an early 20th-century home into a quiet corner of hospitality.

Karen T. Bartlett

GILCHRIST BED & BREAKFAST
Innkeepers: Betty and Johnny Surles.
941-575-4129.
115 Gilchrist St., Punta Gorda 33950.
Price: Moderate.
Credit Cards: MC, V.
Handicap Access: No.

In a charming old neighborhood lined with royal palms and Cuban laurels, and within walking distance of Punta Gorda's historic district and waterfront Gilchrist Park, this B&B fits right in. Green shake siding, a tin roof, lattice trim, flowery grounds, and a serene, fountained backyard give the small historic home (circa 1914) classic character. The Surles rent out two suites in season, plus a self-sufficient apartment in summer. The two suites each have their own porch entryway, bath, and nonworking fireplace. Original glossy pine floors and white bead-and-board are enhanced by a marble mantel in one room, the original brick mantel in another, and Virginia colonial antiques and Victorian bric-a-brac. A common area between the two suites provides a television, microwave, and mini-fridge. The apartment occupies the old carriage house and feels like a sanctuary for the soul. Breakfast is served either on the screened porch (which also holds a hot tub) or in the Surles' dining room, depending upon the weather.

HOME & CONDO RENTALS

Boca Grande Real Estate (941-964-0338 or 800-881-2622; 430 W. Fourth St., Boca Grande 33921) Large selection of vacation and seasonal accommodations.

Grande Island Vacations (941-964-2080 or 800-962-3314; 6020 Boca Grande Causeway, Boca Grande 33921) Homes and condominiums on Boca Grande.

Manasota Key Realty (941-474-9536 or 800-881-9534; 1927 Beach Rd., Engle-wood 34223) Grand mansions, beachside cottages, and bayside homes.

RV RESORTS

Punta Gorda KOA (941-637-1188 or 800-KOA-4786; 6800 Golf Course Blvd., Punta Gorda 33982) Full hookups, canoe rentals, fishing lake, game room, and convenience store.

Yogi Bear's Jellystone Park (941-993-2111 or 800-795-9733; 9770 SW Route 769/Kings Highway, Arcadia) Overnight, monthly, and seasonal rates for tents and RVs. Two heated pools, recreation center, canoe rentals, and spa.

DINING

Local cuisine smacks of midwestern influence, but in recent years Caribbean and Floribbean flavors have livened things up. My favorite places to eat are in Boca Grande and Englewood, where chefs get a bit more creative than in the mainland towns. Fishing crews bring just-hooked seafood to the table, but that doesn't mean some restaurants won't try to pawn off frozen products. Here I've tried to include a few that believe in freshness and fanfare at the dining table.

The following listings sample all the variety of Charlotte Coast feasting in these price categories:

Inexpensive	Up to $15
Moderate	$15 to $25
Expensive	$25 to $35
Very Expensive	$35 or more

Cost is figured on a typical meal (at dinner, unless dinner is not served) that would include an appetizer or dessert, salad (if included with the meal), entrée, and coffee.

The following abbreviations are used for credit card information and meals:

AE - American Express	DC - Diners Club
CB - Carte Blanche	MC - MasterCard
D - Discover Card	V - Visa

B - Breakfast   D - Dinner
L - Lunch   SB - Sunday Brunch

Boca Grande

HARPER'S
941-964-0232.
Miller's Marina, Harbor Dr.
Price: Moderate to
  Expensive.
Children's Menu: Yes.
Cuisine: Seafood/Florida.
Healthy Selections: No.
Liquor: Full.
Serving: L, D.
Credit Cards: D, MC, V.
Handicap Access: No.
Reservations: Suggested for
  dinner.
Special Features: View of
  harbor.

Formerly Lighthouse Hole, a super-casual favorite among boaters, tarpon fishermen, and locals, Harper's has been renovated to a classier level that some bemoan and others love. The porch still lets you peer longingly down at the million-dollar yachts parked at the marina. And the attitude is still best described by the names of its neighborhood streets: Damficare, Damfiwill, and Damfino (i.e., service can be a bit slow). But things are less rowdy and raw than they used to be. Wood lattice lines the ceiling, chair railing trims the walls, and an impressive mahogany bar graces the inner dining room, with its extra-long booths. Mounted fish and rods remind you you're in the fishing mecca of Boca Grande. A display case of pepper sauces lets you buy and self-fire whatever you order from the Creole-slanted menu. Many buy a bottle and leave it at the bar for others to dab on. We used a banana pepper sauce on our red beans and rice, which were seasoned with sausage and crunchy-fresh vegetables. We sampled the round, fritterlike romano hush puppies and Boca Onion Petals, a deflowered "blooming onion" that avoids the typical mushiness at the base of the "flower." Both appetizers came ungreasy, crisp, and served with tasty Cajun and dill dipping sauces. My marinated shrimp club was a triumph of tropical flavors. The shrimp were herb-infused and slightly tart, served on a beautiful bun stacked with apple-smoked bacon, mozzarella, alfalfa sprouts, and mango cocktail sauce. On the side, a creamy cucumber and red onion salad typified the freshness and creativity that go into each aspect of a meal at Harper's. The oyster po' boy, blackened grouper Cuban, and Portabelly Sandwich won rave reviews around the table. We got a chuckle from the potato chip sandwich, market price, depending upon Idaho's weather. Next time I go, it will be for dinner. Not sure what I'll order yet — perhaps the Oysters Mexifeller (in tequila salsa) and garlic shrimp, or jambalaya, or Artichicken, or . . .

Englewood Beach

MAD SAM'S
941-475-9505.
1375 Beach Rd.
Price: Moderate.
Children's Menu: Yes.

People all the way up in Venice told me about Mad Sam's. The name alone made me like it. They said I couldn't miss it. With a bright, grimacing, skeletal fish crashing through the entryway

A grumpy fish crashes through the entryway ceiling at Mad Sam's, Englewood's newest culinary sensation.

Karen T. Bartlett

Cuisine: American/
 Regional.
Liquor: Full.
Serving: L, D.
Credit Cards: AE, D, MC, V.
Handicap Access: Yes.
Reservations: No.
Special Features:
 Waterfront view and
 outdoor dining.

roof, it does defy nonchalance. The restaurant looks as though it sits upon its own cement island at the edge of the intracoastal waterway. This is what Florida restaurants should be — new ones, anyway (I'm still partial to the old, rickety kind). Mad Sam's is all bright, airy, tropical, and many-windowed. The food is as fresh as the setting, but not too daring for this part of back-roads Florida. My server revealed that the yogurt dressing I requested for my salad was bitter and not very well liked. Turns out it was flavored with curry, a favorite seasoning of mine. The chefs smartly add subtle touches of inspiration, such as with my pork chops, which were rum soaked and served with a side of sweet (not hot) pineapple salsa. Other lunch and dinner offerings include gator bites, sweet Florida onion rings, grilled chicken mango salad, pasta sandwich, oyster sandwich (topped with prosciutto, cole slaw, and provolone!), rack of lamb with tangerine sauce, grilled key lime grouper with roasted garlic cream sauce, and filet mignon. The desserts posed more temptation, and I yielded to the chocolate cake, layered with something gooey and wonderful.

Punta Gorda

CAPTAIN'S TABLE
941-637-1177.
Fishermen's Village, 1200
 W. Retta Esplanade.
Price: Moderate.
Cuisine: Continental/
 Seafood.

Sleek luxury yachts — some the size of small cruise ships — provide the view from this multi-windowed perch. In a plush, formal setting fraught with heavy pewter, shiny brass, and beautifully etched mirrors, a mood of high class prevails, as it should at the captain's table. In equal contention

Serving: L, D.
Credit Cards: AE, D, DC, MC, V.
Handicap Access: Yes.
Reservations: Accepted.
Special Features: Marina and harbor view.

with the view and motif, the dishes are prepared with the freshest of fish and a minimum of canned and frozen products. At lunch the buffet is a popular choice, featuring sliced roasted round of beef and hot entrées that change daily. The New York Beef Salad is a sure bet, prepared with grilled New York strip, greens, and Gorgonzola cheese dressing. The grouper primavera presented an intriguing tangle of angel hair pasta and al dente vegetables, but oddly its "fresh grouper sauté" component was first breaded and turned out rather mushy. The dinner menu is ambitious, with meat and seafood selections such as crab cakes (unfortunately made with fake crab) and Cajun mayo, salmon with dill sauce, blackened mahi mahi, Long Island duckling in raspberry sauce, chicken piccata, and twin lobster tails. The cuisine suits the local population with dependable homemade goodness that doesn't aspire to gourmet wizardry.

LEGAL CAFE
941-637-0700.
210 Taylor St.
Price: Inexpensive.
Early Dining Menu: No.
Children's Menu: No.
Cuisine: American.
Liquor: No.
Serving: B, L.
Closed: Sat., Sun.
Credit Cards: No.
Handicap Access: Yes.
Reservations: No.

This tidy little cafe gets its theme from the courthouse across the street. It is loved by the local business community for its wholesome sandwiches and other homemade goods. The menu, with clever court-related descriptions, comes on yellow legal paper clipped in a file folder. The staff is friendly and accommodating; the dining rooms are cheerful and bright with washed rattan chairs; the food is unpretentiously good. For breakfast ("First Appearance") there are homemade muffins, omelets, and Belgian waffles. Lunch ("Noon Recess") sandwiches with typical fillings (hamburger, frankfurter, grilled cheese, fried clams, and so on) surpass the ordinary by dint of fresh-baked rolls. Crispy salads and homemade chili and "soup-poena" complete the simple but well-executed (they're not the only ones who can make bad courtroom jokes!) menu.

FOOD PURVEYORS

BAKERIES

Belgian Bakery (941-625-1252; 4040 N. Tamiami Trail, Port Charlotte) Belgian breads from Old World recipes using no sugar, preservatives, milk, or eggs; Belgian-French pastries, Belgian cookies, meringues.

CANDY & ICE CREAM

Flamingo Yogurt (941-639-5515; Fishermen's Village, 1200 W. Retta Esplanade,

The Loose Caboose in Boca Grande's Railroad Plaza carries a cargo of highly acclaimed homemade ice cream.

Greg Wagner

Punta Gorda) Premium yogurt, granita, cold cappuccino, frozen fruit drinks, ice cream, and candy.

The Loose Caboose (941-964-0440; Railroad Plaza, Boca Grande) Katharine Hepburn, among scores of others, once left her compliments on the bulletin board at this restaurant known for its homemade ice cream.

DELI & SPECIALTY FOODS

Grapevine (941-964-0614; Theater Mall, Boca Grande) Specialty wines, imported cheese, fish market, gourmet foods, and baked goods daily.

Hudson's Grocery (941-964-2621; Park Ave., Boca Grande) Look for the hot pink (nonfunctional) gas pump out front. Cheeses, wines, deli products, and meat cut to order. Free delivery to boats, homes, and condos, with a minimum $25 order.

COFFEE

Coffee à la Carte (941-575-4344; Fishermen's Village, 1200 W. Retta Esplanade, Punta Gorda) Gourmet coffee, espresso, cappuccino, iced and frozen drinks, pastries, and bagels.

FRUIT & VEGETABLE STANDS

DeSoto Groves (941-575-6565; Burnt Store Square, Punta Gorda. Also 941-625-2737; Tamiami Trail, Murdock) Just-picked Florida citrus fruit.

PIZZA & TAKEOUT

Angelo's Pizza (941-474-2477; 2611 Placida Rd., Englewood) Pizza and Italian specialties. Takeout and delivery.

SEAFOOD

Village Fish Market (941-639-7959; Fishermen's Village, 1200 W. Retta Esplanade, Punta Gorda) New England and Florida seafood.

CULTURE

The Charlotte Harbor coast is small-town, even in its larger, urban-sprawl-infected communities. In 1996 *Money* magazine named the region "Best Small Place to Live in America." Long considered a refuge for the retired, the region is not known for its vibrant arts scene or cultural diversity. Overall, it has a midwestern flavor in coastal areas but is definitely Old Florida in inland rural parts. Awareness of the arts has developed slowly and on a part-time, hobby level. To reach the 24-hour ARTSLINE, call (941) 764-8101.

ARCHITECTURE

In the smaller towns around Charlotte Harbor, single examples of historic character appear serendipitously in the midst of concrete block homes. Downtown Englewood, a destination off the beaten path of Tamiami Trail, holds a few such treasures. One, a quaint clapboard church of stark, Puritan style, houses the Lemon Bay Historical Society. The community's first church, it was built in 1926 to accommodate the Methodist circuit preacher who traveled from Nokomis.

Punta Gorda sprinkles its architectural prizes along Marion Avenue, Olympia Avenue, Retta Esplanade, and their side streets. On the Esplanade, the Lewis Residence, circa 1883, and Hinkley House, circa 1887, are the jewels of the old riverfront district. In and around the town's historic section, an eclectic array of architecture ranges from old shotgun cigar workers' homes and tin-roofed Cracker shacks to Victorian mansions and a neoclassical city hall. For a guide to Punta Gorda's treasures, pick up a copy of "Punta Gorda Historic Walking Tour" at the chamber of commerce.

Boca Grande's most noteworthy examples of architecture, aside from grande dame Gasparilla Inn, are four historic churches, each with its own style, located in a four-block area downtown. The Catholic church takes its inspiration from Spanish missions. The others occupy early-century, wood-frame buildings and serve Episcopal, Baptist, and Methodist congregations.

A few blocks away, on Tarpon Avenue, old Cracker homes slump comfortably in a district sometimes called Whitewash Alley. For a taste of wealthy eccentricity, check out the Johann Fust Library on Gasparilla Road. It was built of native coquina, cypress, and pink stucco.

CINEMA

MOVIE THEATERS

Cinema Center 8 (941-624-3334; 19190 Toledo Blade Blvd., Port Charlotte)

Englewood Movie Cafe (941-475-8005; 200 S. Indiana Ave., Englewood) Dine and drink while you watch the show.

Promenades Cinema (941-627-3700; 3280-9 Tamiami Trail, Port Charlotte) Second-run, discounted shows.

DANCE

Country Line Dance Lessons (941-639-8721; Fishermen's Village, 1200 W. Retta Esplanade, Punta Gorda) Every Wednesday night, 7 to 9, by Lone Star Country Dance Association. $3 per person for lessons.

Starline Ballroom (941-627-9997; Sorrentino Plaza, 3109 Tamiami Trail, Port Charlotte) Country and ballroom dancing shows and classes.

HISTORIC HOMES & SITES

The A.C. Freeman House survives from Punta Gorda's early days of prosperity.

Charlotte County Visitors Bureau

THE A. C. FREEMAN HOUSE
941-637-0077.
639 E. Hargreaves Ave., Punta Gorda.
Open: Hourly winter tours Dec.–Apr., Fri. and Sat. 11–3.
Admission: Donations welcome.

Home of the Charlotte County Foundation today, it once was occupied by Punta Gorda's turn-of-the-century mayor and mortician. Narrowly escaping the wrecking ball in 1985, the lovely clapboard Queen Anne mansion was saved and restored by the people of Punta Gorda as a memento of gracious pioneer lifestyles.

**PONCE DE LEÓN
HISTORICAL PARK**
End of Marion Ave., Punta
Gorda.

A shrine commemorates Ponce de León's supposed 1513 landing here and his subsequent death during an Indian attack. The park is a wildlife and recreational area on the harbor, with boat ramp, picnic facilities, small beach, and native trail into the mangroves.

The Boca Grande Lighthouse is one of the state's most picturesque.

Lee Island Coast Visitor and Convention Bureau

**BOCA GRANDE
LIGHTHOUSE**
941-964-0375.
Gasparilla Island State
Recreation Area, Gulf
Blvd., Boca Grande.
Open: Self-guided tours
10–4 last Sat. of each
month, and by prior
arrangement for groups.

This 1890 structure was renovated in Old Florida style and put back into service in 1986 after 20 years of abandonment. It is the most photographed and painted landmark on the island.

MUSEUMS

**FLORIDA ADVENTURE
MUSEUM OF
CHARLOTTE COUNTY**
941-639-3777.
260 W. Retta Esplanade,
Punta Gorda.
Open: 8–5 Mon.–Fri.; 10–3
Sat.
Closed: Sun.
Admission: $1 per person.

The small facility features changing historical exhibits with a Florida focus, and a roomful of stuffed wildcats. Kids enjoy the crawl-through maze and historical dress-up costumes.

MUSIC & NIGHTLIFE

Boca Grande

South Beach (941-964-0765; 777 Gulf Blvd.) Live contemporary bands play weekend nights. Sunset plays (almost) every evening. Full dining menu.

Englewood

Englewood Performing Arts Series (941-473-2787) Fine cultural entertainment from around the nation, mid-November through mid-April.

Port Charlotte

Charlotte County Jazz Society (941-766-9422; 282 Goiana St.) Sponsors 10 jazz concerts each year, plus open jam sessions for local and visiting jazz musicians the third Sunday of every month.

Charlotte Symphony Orchestra (941-625-5996) Usually performs at the Port Charlotte Cultural Center Theater (see "Theater," below).

Gatorz Bar & Grill (941-625-5000; 3816 Tamiami Trail) Live music throughout the week: jazz and Top 40.

Punta Gorda

Charlotte County Memorial Auditorium (941-639-5833 or 800-329-9988; 75 Taylor St.) Waterfront host to Broadway plays, big band and swing orchestras, and national stars.

Gilchrist Park, overlooking the mouth of the Peace River, is the site of Thursday night jam sessions.

Karen T. Bartlett

Gilchrist Park (Retta Esplanade) On Thursday nights local musicians gather for impromptu jamming, to which the public is invited.

THEATER

Lemon Bay Playhouse (941-475-6756; 263 W. Dearborn St., Englewood) Home of the **Lemon Bay Players** community theater group.

Port Charlotte Cultural Center (941-625-4175; 2280 Aaron St., Port Charlotte)
Home of the **Charlotte Players** community theater group and the Charlotte
Symphony Orchestra (see "Music and Nightlife," above).

Royal Palm Players (941-964-2670; Boca Grande) A community theater group
sponsoring plays, readings, and other events November through May.

VISUAL ART CENTERS

A listing for commercial galleries is included in the "Shopping" section of this chapter.

Arts & Humanities Council (941-764-8100; LaPlaya Plaza, 2811 N. Tamiami
Trail, Port Charlotte) Hosts art displays and events.

Boca Grande Art Alliance (941-964-0177; 421 Park Ave., Boca Grande)
Sponsors art shows and encourages Art Sharks (children).

Englewood Art Guild (941-474-5548; 370 Dearborn St., Englewood)

Visual Arts Center (941-639-8810; 210 Maude St., Punta Gorda) Home of the
Charlotte County Art Guild. Exhibit halls, gift shops, library, darkroom,
and classes.

RECREATION

More behind-the-scenes than the touted playgrounds of its flanking neighbors, the Charlotte Harbor coast's greatest claim to recreational fame is its fishing, particularly for that king of all sports fish, the tarpon.

BEACHES

You must drive way off the beaten path to find the beaches of Charlotte County. That keeps them more natural, less trodden.

CHADWICK PARK BEACH
941-475-6606.
Route 776, south end of Manasota Key at Englewood Beach.
Facilities: Picnic areas, rest rooms, showers, volleyball, basketball, food and beach rental concessions.

Many refer to this simply as Englewood Beach. A popular hangout for the local youth, it is, nonetheless, a well-maintained and policed area — no alcohol, dogs, glass, surfboards, or motor vehicles are allowed. You can rent inner tubes, snorkel masks, bikes, and other beach toys across the street. Several resorts, shops, and restaurants huddle around the area, which keeps activity levels high.

DON PEDRO ISLAND STATE RECREATION AREA

Secluded beach at a 129-acre island getaway. Once separated from Palm Island and Little Gasparilla, Don Pedro Island is now connected to

941-964-0375.
South of Palm Island,
  accessible only by boat.
Facilities: Picnic area, rest
  rooms.

LIGHTHOUSE BEACH/ GASPARILLA ISLAND STATE RECREATION AREA
941-964-0375.
Along Gulf Blvd., Boca
  Grande, Gasparilla Island.
Facilities: Picnic tables,
  showers, rest rooms.
Parking: $2 per car.

MANASOTA BEACH
941-316-1172.
North end of Route 776,
  Manasota Key.
Facilities: Picnic area, rest
  rooms, showers,
  lifeguard, historical
  marker, boat ramps.

MIDDLE (BLIND PASS) BEACH
941-316-1172.
Route 776, midisland on
  Manasota Key.
Facilities: Rest rooms,
  showers.

PORT CHARLOTTE BEACH
941-627-1628.
Southeast end of Harbor
  Blvd., Port Charlotte.
Facilities: Picnic areas, rest
  rooms, showers,
  concessions, volleyball,
  basketball, tennis courts,
  playground, horseshoes,
  boat ramps, fishing pier,
  swimming pool.

PORT CHARLOTTE STATE RECREATION AREA
South end of Gulf Blvd.,
  Englewood Beach on
  Manasota Key.

the two to form one long, lightly developed barrier island. Don Pedro, the most natural component, is toward the southern end.

Marked by a historic lighthouse, the park edges the deepwater tarpon grounds of Boca Grande Pass. Its plush, deep sands encompass 135 acres. The view of oil tanks tends to intrude upon the otherwise uninterrupted feeling of awayness. Swimming is not recommended because of strong currents through the pass. In some parts the beach gets quite narrow.

A relatively peaceful sunning and shelling venue connected to Venice's Caspersen Beach about $1^1/2$ miles to the north. It also has a reputation — but not as pointed as Venice's — for sharks' teeth.

Sixty-three acres of lightly developed shoreline attract those drawn more to seclusion than to the sports and activities of Manasota Key's other beaches.

A highly developed recreational center that sits on Charlotte Harbor along a manmade beach, this is a good place to go if you (or the children) like to keep busy at the beach.

This beach has only its lovely, unspoiled seclusion to offer. It has a few parking spots, and that's it. (Many visitors drop off their gear and family, park at Chadwick Park, and walk down.) It spreads all the way to Stump Pass in a skinny strip of black-specked sand.

BICYCLING

The Charlotte Coast region, with its abundance of back roads and wide open spaces, gives cyclists an opportunity to pedal in peace. Many of its favored bikeways are on-road or designated bike lanes, which are separated from motor traffic only by a white line. According to state law, bicyclists who share the road with other vehicles must heed all the rules of the road. Children under 16 are required to wear a helmet.

BEST BIKING

About a mile after Gasparilla Island's causeway (which can be crossed by bicycle for $1), the Boca Grande bike path starts. Here you pedal along old railroad routes. Seven miles of pathway travel the island from tip to tip along Railroad Avenue and Gulf Boulevard. Highway 776 through Englewood and Englewood Beach is shouldered with a bike lane that ends at the Sarasota County line. In Punta Gorda, Gilchrist Park's bike path runs along a cliff overlooking the Peace River on Retta Esplanade.

RENTALS/SALES

Bicycle and Cycle Center (941-627-6600; 3755 Tamiami Trail, Port Charlotte) All types of bikes, including tandems, children's, and adult tricycles. Free pickup and delivery on weekly rentals within a 10-mile radius.

Bike 'n Beach (941-964-0711; 333 Park Ave., Boca Grande) Rentals and sales.

Bikes and Boards (941-474-2019; 966 S. McCall Rd., Englewood Beach) Bike rentals, sales, and service.

Ralph's Bicycle Shop (941-639-3029; 258 W. Marion Ave., downtown Punta Gorda) Bikes, trikes, BMX.

BOATS & BOATING

Charlotte Harbor Coast offers many waterfronts for adventure — the gulf, harbor, Peace River, Myakka River, and Lemon Bay Aquatic Preserve.

Wilderness canoeing is at its best along Charlotte Harbor's bayous and estuaries.

Charlotte County Visitors Bureau

MARINE SUPPLIES

Millers Marina (941-964-2283; Harbor Dr., Boca Grande) Tackle and marine supplies, bait, groceries.

PERSONAL WATERCRAFT RENTALS/TOURS

Island Hoppers Rentals (941-468-2932; Boca Grande) Free delivery.

POWERBOAT RENTALS

Bay Breeze Boat Rentals (941-475-0733; 1450 Beach Rd., Englewood Beach) Rents pontoon, fishing, and bowrider boats.

The Beach Place (941-474-1022 or 800-314-4838; 1863 Gulf Blvd., Englewood Beach) 16- to 21-foot skiffs or pontoons.

Capt. Russ' Boat Rentals (941-964-0708; Whidden's Marina, First and Harbor Streets, Boca Grande) 15- to 23-foot boats available for half or full days, or by the week.

Holidaze Boat Rental (941-505-8888; Fishermen's Village, 1200 W. Retta Esplanade, Punta Gorda) 17- to 20-foot boats and pontoons rented hourly and by the half or full day.

PUBLIC BOAT RAMPS

Indian Mound Park (941-474-8919; Winson Ave., downtown Englewood) On Lemon Bay. Access to Stump Pass, picnic pavilion, rest rooms, nature trails.

Laishley Park City Marina (Marion Ave. and Nesbit St., Punta Gorda)

Manasota Beach (Manasota Beach Rd., Manasota Key)

Placida (Causeway Blvd.)

Ponce de León Park (west end of Marion Ave., Punta Gorda)

Port Charlotte Beach (southeast end of Harbor Blvd., Port Charlotte) Beach recreational area, access to Charlotte Harbor.

SAILBOAT CHARTERS

Captain Lynda Suzanne (941-964-2027; First St., Boca Grande) Half- and full-day sails into Charlotte Harbor. Sailing instruction available.

International Sailing School and Charlotte Sailing (941-639-7492 or 766-1060; Fishermen's Village, 1200 W. Retta Esplanade, Punta Gorda) Instruction, including couples classes and certification courses; rentals and club memberships.

SIGHTSEEING & ENTERTAINMENT CRUISES

Grande Tours (941-697-8825 or 941-964-0000 from Boca Grande; 11 Fishery Rd., Placida) Tours: eco, shelling, bird watching, sunset, kid fishing, and narrated sightseeing. Kayak nature tours and rentals and water taxi service.

Island Charters (941-964-1100; Pass Marina at South Dock, Boca Grande) A ferryboat departs daily for Cayo Costa and Cabbage Key.

King Fisher Cruise Lines (941-639-0969; Fishermen's Village Marina, 1200 W. Retta Esplanade, Punta Gorda) Excursions to Cayo Costa and Cabbage Key aboard a 35-foot boat. Also sunset and sightseeing cruises.

River Boat Tours (941-627-3474 or 800-308-7506; Deep Creek Marina, Punta Gorda) Sunset, historic, and nature tours on the Peace River.

FISHING

Tarpon reigns as the king of southwest Florida fish — the "Silver King," to be exact, named for its silver-dollar-like scales. Boca Grande Pass is one of the most celebrated spots in the world for catching the feisty fighter.

Nonresidents age 16 and over who wish to fish must obtain a license unless fishing from a vessel or pier covered by its own license. You can buy inexpensive, temporary nonresident licenses at county tax collectors' offices and most Kmarts and bait shops. Check local regulations for season, size, and catch restrictions.

DEEP-SEA PARTY BOATS

King Fisher Fleet (941-639-0969; Fishermen's Village Marina, 1200 W. Retta Esplanade, Punta Gorda) Deep-sea fishing aboard a 35-foot boat.

FISHING CHARTERS/OUTFITTERS

Boca Grande Fishing Guides Association (941-964-2266; Boca Grande) Organization of qualified charter guides especially knowledgeable about tarpon.

Fishing Unlimited (941-964-0907 or 800-4-TARPON; 370 E. Railroad Ave., Boca Grande) Outfitters, fly shop, guides and charters, Orvis authorized dealer.

King Fisher Fleet (941-639-0969; Fishermen's Village Marina, 1200 W. Retta Esplanade, Punta Gorda) Back-bay fishing charters.

Silver Dollar Charters (941-475-0512; 1961 Beach Rd., Englewood Beach)

Striker I Charters (941-475-9476; 1450 Beach Rd., Englewood Beach) Deep-sea fishing.

Tarpon Hunter II (941-743-6622; Port Charlotte) Charters in Charlotte Harbor and backwaters. Specialties include fly and light tackle fishing.

FISHING PIERS

Charlotte Harbor Pier (Bayshore Dr., Charlotte Harbor) At the mouth of the Peace River.

Englewood Beach piers (along Beach Rd. east of the drawbridge)

Gasparilla Island old railroad bridge (near Courtyard Plaza, north end of Gasparilla Rd., Gasparilla Island)

Gilchrist Park (Retta Esplanade, Punta Gorda)

Port Charlotte Beach (southeast end of Harbor Blvd., Port Charlotte) Pier with bait and tackle concession, part of a beach and pool recreational center.

South Dock (south end of Gasparilla Island) Old phosphate shipping docks.

GOLF

PUBLIC GOLF COURSES

Deep Creek Golf Club (941-625-6911; 1260 San Cristobal Ave., Port Charlotte) Semiprivate, 18 holes, par 70. Snack bar.

Lemon Bay Golf Club (941-697-4190; 9600 Eagle Preserve Dr., Englewood) Semiprivate, 18 holes, restaurant.

Punta Gorda Country Club (941-639-1494; 6100 Duncan Rd., Punta Gorda) Semiprivate, 18 holes, snack bar.

HEALTH & FITNESS CLUBS

Charlotte County Family YMCA (941-629-2220; 22425 Edgewater Dr., Charlotte Harbor) Aerobics, trimnastics, body shaping, yoga, volleyball, basketball, golf tournaments, youth sports competition, and kiddie facilities.

Charlotte Racquet & Health & Fitness (941-629-2223; 3250 Loveland Blvd., Port Charlotte) Racquetball, squash, tennis, stairclimbers, bikes, treadmill, universal weights, ballet, karate.

HIKING

Charlotte Harbor Environmental Center (941-575-5435; 10941 Burnt Store Rd.) Four miles of nature trails.

Kiwanis Park (Donora St. at Victoria Ave., Port Charlotte) Self-guided nature trail and a lakeside Audubon trail.

HUNTING

Given southwest Florida's heightened environmental consciousness, most shooting of wildlife is done with a camera. But the Charlotte Harbor coast's wilderness does provide opportunities for hunting various species. The most popular game includes wild hogs, deer, doves, snipe, quail, turkey, duck, and coot.

To hunt in Florida preserves, you must obtain a state license plus a Wildlife Management Area stamp. Early-season hunters need a quota permit, which is awarded randomly in a drawing in June from applications submitted to the Game and Fresh Water Fish Commission. Special permits are also required for muzzleloading guns, archery, and turkey, migratory bird, or waterfowl hunting. Daily use permit fees are levied.

For more information about hunting seasons and bag limits, pick up a copy of the *Florida Hunting Handbook & Regulations Summary* when you buy your license.

Fred C. Babcock–Cecil M. Webb Wildlife Management Area (941-575-5768; 29200 Tucker Grade, Port Charlotte) 65,000 acres, one of Florida's 62 designated hunting preserves. Advance permission is required. There is a public shooting range on the property, accessible from Tucker Grade via Rifle Range Rd. The range opens daily during daylight hours, but closes the fourth Saturday of each month until 2 pm for hunter education training.

KIDS' STUFF

Charlotte BMX (941-637-1676; 2505 Carmalita St., Punta Gorda) Practice and racing events for BMX riders.

Fish Cove Adventure Golf (941-627-5393; 4949 Tamiami Trail, Port Charlotte) Two 18-hole putt-putt golf courses. Open daily 10 am to 11 pm. Admission for 18 holes of golf is $5.75.

KidSpace (Maracaibo and Avocado Streets, Port Charlotte) A county park created expressly for kids, with a cool playground, baseball, and picnicking.

Pelican Pete's Playland (941-475-2008; 3101 McCall Rd. S., Englewood) Miniature golf, go-carts for various age levels, batting cages, game room, and snack bar. A popular place that could use some renovating. Open daily; hours change according to season. Fees are charged per activity.

RACQUET SPORTS

Boca Grande Community Center (941-964-2564; 131 First St. W., Boca Grande) Two lighted courts.

Charlotte Racquet & Health & Fitness (941-629-2223, 3250 Loveland Blvd., Port Charlotte) Racquetball, squash, tennis, stairclimbers, bikes, treadmill, universal weights, ballet, karate.

McGuire Park (Elkcam Blvd., Port Charlotte) Four lighted, hard-surface courts.

Port Charlotte Junior High (941-625-5554; 23000 Midway Blvd., Port Charlotte) Three hard courts and two racquetball courts.

Punta Gorda Junior High (941-575-5485; 825 Carmalita St., Punta Gorda) Three hard courts and two racquetball courts.

SHELLING

Collecting live shells in state and national parks is prohibited in Florida. The definition of a live shell is one with a creature still inside, whether or not you believe that creature has died. Shellers who find live shells washed up on the beach — which most commonly occurs after a storm — are urged to gently (without flinging) return the shells to deep water.

You'll find some shells on the beaches along the Charlotte Harbor coast, but if you're serious, you'll head south to the Island Coast.

SHELLING CHARTERS

Ko Ko Kai Charter Boat Service (941-474-2141; Ko Ko Kai Resort, 5040 N. Beach Rd., Englewood Beach) Shelling excursions on and around the islands of Gasparilla, Palm, Cayo Costa, Cabbage Key, Upper Captiva, and Captiva.

SPECTATOR SPORTS

PRO BASEBALL

Charlotte County Stadium (941-624-2211; Route 776, Port Charlotte) Spring training grounds of the Texas Rangers during March and early April. Semiprofessional and amateur leagues compete here in the summer.

RACING

Charlotte County Speedway (941-575-2422; 8655 Piper Rd., Punta Gorda) Year-round weekend car racing. Admission.

WATER SPORTS

SAILBOARDING & SURFING

Bikes & Boards (941-474-2019; 966 S. McCall Rd., Englewood) Rents, sells, and services surfboards, sailboards, skimboards, and bodyboards.

SNORKELING & SCUBA

The best underwater sightseeing lies offshore some distance, where divers find a few wrecks and other manmade structures.

DIVE SHOPS & CHARTERS

Ko Ko Kai Charter Boat Service (941-474-2141; Ko Ko Kai Resort, 5040 N. Beach Rd., Englewood Beach) Diving charters.

The Beach Place (941-474-1022 or 800-314-4838; 1863 Gulf Blvd., Englewood Beach) Diving and snorkeling equipment sales and rentals.

WILDLIFE SPOTTING

The Charlotte Harbor coast is a haven for many of Florida's threatened and endangered species, including Florida panthers (this relative of the mountain lion is yellow, not black), bobcats, manatees, brown pelicans, wood storks,

Charlotte County Visitors Bureau

The shy panther is rarely seen in the wilds of southwest Florida, where it makes its home.

and black skimmers. White pelicans migrate to the region in winter. Look for them on sandbars and small mangrove islands in the bays and estuaries. They congregate in flocks and feed cooperatively by herding fish.

At Babcock Ranch, a massive preserve east of Punta Gorda, four rare whooping cranes recently moved in from a refuge to the north. Conservationists are watching them closely in hopes that they'll start families and boost their seriously endangered population. American bison have been reintroduced at Babcock as well.

On Gasparilla Island you may spot an iguana in the wild. They're not native but have established a colony along the bike path south of Boca Grande.

Nature Preserves & Eco-Attractions

CEDAR POINT ENVIRONMENTAL PARK
941-505-8243.
Off Route 775, Englewood.
Admission: Free.

Bald eagles, marsh rabbits, bobcats, gopher tortoises, and great horned owls are the stars of this 88-acre preserve, where free guided nature walks are offered on weekends and other days by appointment. It borders the Lemon Bay Aquatic Preserve.

CHARLOTTE HARBOR ENVIRONMENTAL CENTER
941-575-5435.
10941 Burnt Store Rd.
Admission: Free.

Conducts guided tours (in season) around four miles of nature trails through pine and palmetto flatlands, hammocks, and marshes, where alligators and bobcats live. Educational exhibits about local wildlife.

PEACE RIVER WILDLIFE CENTER
941-637-3830.
Ponce de León Park, Punta Gorda.
Admission: Donations requested.

A rescue and rehabilitation facility that conducts tours among cages of baby possums, taped-together gopher tortoises, and other rescued and recovering animals.

WILDLIFE TOURS & CHARTERS

This rustic shed was buit at Babcock Wilderness Adventures for the filming of Sean Connery's Just Cause.

Karen T. Bartlett

BABCOCK WILDERNESS ADVENTURES
941-489-3911 or 800-500-5583.
Route 31, Punta Gorda.
Hours: Tours 9–3 Nov.–Apr.; mornings only May–Oct.
Admission: $17.95 adults, $9.95 kids 3–12 (plus tax). Advance reservations required.

On a 90-minute swamp-buggy-bus ride through 90,000-acre Crescent B Ranch and Telegraph Cypress Swamp you will spot Old Florida wildlife, including white-tailed deer, relocated bison, fenced-in Florida panthers, wild turkeys, sandhill cranes, squirrels, and alligators. The driver gives an onboard demonstration with a live baby gator and leads a boardwalk hike through a cypress swamp to see the panthers. The adventure takes place on an actual ranch that dates back to the cow-hunting era. Cattle are still raised here, as well as alligators. A restaurant, live snake display, gift shop, and the stage set from Sean Connery's *Just Cause* (filmed partly on-site) provide other activities and accommodations. This is one of Charlotte Harbor coast's finest attractions.

GRANDE TOURS
941-697-8825 or 941-964-0000 from Boca Grande.
11 Fishery Rd., Placida.

Deck boat and kayaking tours of Myakka River and Charlotte Harbor Aquatic Preserve, led by naturalist. The "Sea Life Excursion" features seine net pulling to collect and study marine life. The "Back Country Adventure" combines boat and kayak touring.

SHOPPING

ANTIQUES & COLLECTIBLES

Corner Collectables, Antiques, Etc. (941-637-1545; 306 W. Marion Ave., downtown Punta Gorda)

Harbour Inn Antique Mall (941-625-6126; 5000 Tamiami Trail, Charlotte Harbor) More than 50 dealers selling antique furniture, dolls, china, books, and art. Antique fair held the second Saturday of every month.

Just Clowning Around (941-575-7009; Fishermen's Village, Punta Gorda) Colorful novelty clocks, carousels, and other circus collectibles, jewelry, glass water balls.

BOOKS

All Books (941-505-0345; 111 W. Marion Ave., downtown Punta Gorda) Used, rare, and hard-to-find volumes, local authors, and current books.

Ruhamas (941-964-0777; Railroad Plaza, Boca Grande) Books, cards, needlepoint, and gifts.

CLOTHING

Beaux et Belles (941-964-2899; Railroad Plaza, Boca Grande) Children's clothing, educational toys, and books.

Captain's Landing (941-637-6000; Fishermen's Village, Punta Gorda) Men's casual clothing with a nautical flair.

Giuditta (941-639-8701; Fishermen's Village, Punta Gorda) Exotic patterns and finely tailored styles for the sophisticated woman; mostly formal and dressy fashions.

The Island Bummer (941-964-2636; Railroad Plaza, Boca Grande) Casual, cotton, loose-fitting sportswear perfect for Florida climes.

Osprey Boutique & Gift Shop (941-964-0538; Millers Marina, Boca Grande) T-shirts; men's, women's, and kids' Florida wear.

CONSIGNMENT

Classy Consignments (941-743-2099; 3527 Tamiami Trail, Port Charlotte) Women's clothing and accessories, antiques, and collectibles.

Clotheshorse Consignment Shoppe (941-697-7722; 3031 Placida Rd., Englewood) Women's fashions.

Precious Children's Consignment (941-743-9200; 4485 Tamiami Trail, Charlotte Harbor) Children's clothes and baby gear.

FLEA MARKETS & BAZAARS

Rainbow Flea Market (941-629-1223; 4628 Tamiami Trail, Charlotte Harbor) Browsing in air-conditioned comfort Friday through Sunday.

GALLERIES

Paradise (941-964-0774; 340 Park Ave., Boca Grande) Works by island artists and artisans and emerging Florida artists. Sculptures by Sarasota's Jack Dowd.

Sea Grape Art Gallery (941-575-1718; 117 W. Marion Ave., downtown Punta Gorda) Displays and sells the paintings, silver jewelry, and fiber art of co-op members.

Serendipity Gallery (941-964-2166; Theatre Mall, Park Ave., Boca Grande) Local works in fiber, glass, sculpture, paint, and prints.

Smart Studio & Art Gallery (941-964-0519; 370 Park Ave., Boca Grande) Shows and sells works of artist Wini Smart. Closed in off-season.

GENERAL STORES

Gill's Grocery & Deli (941-964-2506; The Courtyard, 5800 Gasparilla Rd., Boca Grande) Beach needs, clothes, gifts, deli items.

GIFTS

Pirate's Ketch (941-637-0299; Fishermen's Village, Punta Gorda) Nautical clocks and lamps, weather vanes, seashell kitsch, framed sea charts, original art and prints.

Sand Pebble (941-639-6344; Fishermen's Village, Punta Gorda) A glass artist at work creates glass jewelry and collectibles.

Works by Hand (941-575-8512; Fishermen's Village, Punta Gorda) Pottery, wood, glass, jewelry, baskets, clocks, candles, prints, sculptures, and oil lamps.

JEWELRY

Serendipity Gallery (941-964-2166; Theater Mall, Boca Grande) Designer, estate, and island-themed pieces.

KITCHENWARE & HOME DECOR

The Caged Parrot (941-637-8949; Fishermen's Village, Punta Gorda) Garden accessories, wood block models of Punta Gorda buildings, fanciful wall hangings, bird and butterfly houses, and wind chimes.

The Galleria (941-964-1113; 410 E. Railroad Ave., Boca Grande) Exclusive decorative items, including antiques, handcrafted bamboo and teak furniture, bronze sculptures, fine art, Thai ceramic tableware, and garden accessories.

SHELL SHOPS

Earth & Sea (941-637-2625; Fishermen's Village, Punta Gorda) Shells, coral, nautical and lighthouse gifts, and other souvenirs and gifts.

SHOPPING CENTERS & MALLS

Downtown Punta Gorda Centered around Marion Ave. and Olympia, both one-way streets, between Nesbit St. and Tamiami Trail S., you'll find a quaint historic downtown that's undergone a renaissance. The shops are simple and neighborly. Streetscaping includes nifty old-fashioned street-lamps, alley arcades, and park benches.

Fishermen's Village gives a nautical spin to shopping.

Charlotte County Visitors Bureau

Fishermen's Village (941-639-8721; 1200 W. Retta Esplanade, Punta Gorda) More than 40 shops and restaurants occupy a transformed marina. This is Punta Gorda's most hyper center of activity, the site of festivals and social events. There's docking, lodging, charter boats, and fishing from the docks, besides shopping and dining, geared generally toward seniors. A preponderance of nautical clothing and gifts are reflective of the motif.

Port Charlotte Town Center (1441 Tamiami Trail, Port Charlotte) An indoor megamall with more than 100 commercial enterprises, including Burdines, Sears, and other chain outlets and specialty shops, such as Bombay Company and Victoria's Secret.

Railroad Plaza (Park Ave., Boca Grande) Despite the millionaires and power brokers who make Boca Grande their winter home, shopping here is low-key and affordable, with shades of historic quaintness. The restored railroad depot houses gift and apparel boutiques. Across the street you'll find an eccentric general store and a department store that's been there forever, both of which set a somewhat funky tone.

SPORTS STORES

Note: This listing includes general sports outlets only. For supplies and equipment for specific sports, please refer to "Recreation" in this chapter.

Champs Sports (941-627-5556; Port Charlotte Town Center) Clothes, shoes, and equipment for tennis, aerobics, weight training, and all ball sports.

CALENDAR OF EVENTS

APRIL

Ponce de León/Conquistador Landing (941-764-8100; Laishley Park, Punta Gorda) A staging of the conqueror's first landing on the Gulf Coast. One day.

Punta Gorda Block Party (Punta Gorda) Community celebration with music, food, crafts, and a variety of events. Early in the month.

Tarpon, snook, sheepshead, and snapper tantalize the casting crowd.

Karen T. Bartlett

MAY

Boca Grande Chamber of Commerce Ladies' Tarpon Tournament (941-964-0568) All-women, all-release competition early in the month.

Charlotte Harbor-Florida Fishing Tournament (941-625-0804) Thousands of dollars in prizes; includes a Kids' Day and barbecue. Entire month.

Florida Frontier Days (several locations in Charlotte County)

Miller's Marina Tarpon Tide Tournaments (941-964-2232; Miller's Marina, Boca Grande) Mid-May to early July.

JULY

Fourth of July Freedom Swim (941-639-8721; Seahorse Marina, Charlotte Harbor, and Fishermen's Village, Punta Gorda) More than 200 participants swim the half-mile stretch across the mouth of the Peace River from Charlotte Harbor to Fishermen's Village, accompanied by boaters. Entertainment and fireworks follow at Fishermen's Village.

Kids' Fishing Tournament (941-639-0969; King Fisher Fleet, Fishermen's Village, 1200 W. Retta Esplanade, Punta Gorda) One Saturday.

World's Richest Tarpon Tournament (941-694-0568; Boca Grande) Up to $100,000 top prize. Two days.

OCTOBER

Punta Gorda Waterfront Foods-Arts-Jazz Festival (941-639-3720; Gilchrist Park, Punta Gorda) Water activities, alligator wrestling, children's art fair, music, and crafts.

Salute to the Arts (throughout Charlotte County) Showcases performing and visual arts. One week late in the month.

Southwest Florida Boat Show (941-639-8721; Fishermen's Village, 1200 W. Retta Esplanade, Punta Gorda) Boats on display in the harbor and on trailers, in conjunction with a one-day seafood festival. Four days early in the month.

Southwest Florida Seafood Festival (941-639-8721; Fishermen's Village, 1200 W. Retta Esplanade, Punta Gorda) In conjunction with four-day boat show. One day early in the month.

NOVEMBER

International Fall Festival and Yankee Peddler Fair (941-627-2568; Bon Secours-St. Joseph Hospital grounds, 2500 Harbor Blvd., Port Charlotte) Ethnic crafts and foods, with children's carnival. One day.

DECEMBER

Christmas Peace River Lighted Boat Parade (941-639-3720) A procession of vessels in holiday attire. Sunday evening midmonth.

CHAPTER FIVE
Sand, Shells, and Serenity
SANIBEL ISLAND & THE ISLAND COAST

Cabbage Key harkens back to the days when the rich but rugged made their way to the Island Coast.

Karen T. Bartlett

A dreamy, tropical land necklaced with islands, this slab of coastland resembles more than any of its neighboring regions the laid-back islands of the Keys, the Bahamas, and the Caribbean. Tourism pundits term it the Lee Island Coast, a double entendre on the county's name and the island's reality-sheltered demeanor. More developed than its Charlotte Harbor neighbors and more relaxed than what lies to the south and at the Sarasota end of things, the Island Coast gives us the leafy greenery for the southwest Florida sandwich. It is considered one of Florida's most ecology-minded resort areas. How it balances its dual roles as wildlife preserver and tourism mecca has served as a model for state eco-tourism.

At their northern extreme, the islands are mired in an Old Florida time frame. **Cabbage Key, Useppa Island, Cayo Costa,** and **Pine Island** gave birth to the Gulf Coast's legacy of fishing lifestyles, back when the Calusa lived off the sea. On Pine Island, fishing, crabbing, and shrimping are still a way of life and survival, despite new net-ban laws that make it less and less profitable. Many have turned to charter captaining in the wake of the new legislation. Protected from rampant resort development by its lack of beaches, Pine Island clings to an older way of life like an oyster to a mangrove prop. Cayo Costa and **Upper Captiva,** both largely state-owned, remain the uncut jewels in the Island Coast necklace. Useppa and Cabbage Key preserve another era of island bygones, days graced by celebrity sporting types in search of escape, adventure, and tarpon.

Out in San Carlos Bay, to the south, the islands of **Sanibel** and **Captiva** developed quietly but steadily through the years. At various times in the past the islands have supported a lighthouse reservation, citrus and tomato farms, communities of fishermen, and a coconut plantation. From 1910 through 1940, wealthy notables made their way to the islands, intent on the relative anonymity that the wilds afforded them. Teddy Roosevelt discovered Captiva Island in 1914. Charles Lindbergh and his wife visited often; Anne was inspired to pen her well-loved seashell analogies in *Gift from the Sea*. Pulitzer Prize–winning cartoonist and conservationist Jay N. "Ding" Darling gained national attention for Captiva and Sanibel islands by fighting for the preservation of their natural attributes during his winter visits. It was largely through his efforts that the Island Coast's environmental conscience began to develop.

Fort Myers Beach on **Estero Island** is synonymous with gulf shrimp, beach bustle, and spring breakers. South of it, the trickle of islands ending with **Bonita Beach** is reminiscent of the coast's earliest times, with primeval estuaries, intact shell mounds, whispers of buried pirate treasure, and fishing lifestyles.

Lee Island Coast Visitor and Convention Bureau

The tropical gardens at Thomas Edison's historic winter estate in Fort Myers add color and dimension to any visit.

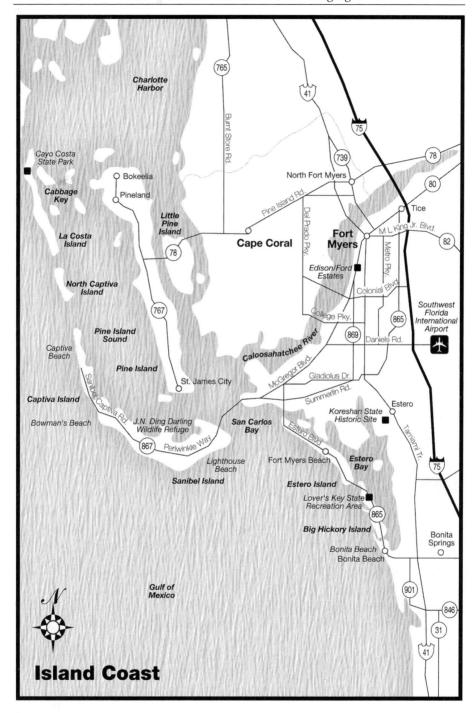

Charlotte Harbor

765

41

75

Burnt Store Rd.

739

78

North Fort Myers

80

Cayo Costa State Park

Bokeelia

Tice

Cabbage Key

Pineland

Pine Island Rd.

Del Prado Pkwy.

M L King Jr. Blvd.

Little Pine Island

Cape Coral

Fort Myers

Metro Pkwy.

82

La Costa Island

78

Edison/Ford Estates

Colonial Blvd.

Southwest Florida International Airport

North Captiva Island

767

College Pky.

865

Pine Island Sound

Caloosahatchee River

869

Daniels Rd.

Captiva Beach

Pine Island

McGregor Blvd.

Gladiolus Dr.

St. James City

Summerlin Rd.

Captiva Island

Sanibel Captiva Rd.

Estero

Bowman's Beach

J.N. Ding Darling Wildlife Refuge

San Carlos Bay

Koreshan State Historic Site

867

Periwinkle Way

Estero Blvd.

75

Lighthouse Beach

Fort Myers Beach

Estero Bay

Sanibel Island

Estero Island

Lover's Key State Recreation Area

865

Big Hickory Island

Bonita Springs

Bonita Beach
Bonita Beach

N

Gulf of Mexico

901

846

31

41

Island Coast

On the mainland, **Cape Coral** once was largely a hunting refuge for steel magnate Ogden Phipps, who vacationed in Naples. The second largest city in Florida in area, it was something of a developer's folly. The young city was cleared, canalled, and platted in 1970 and is slowly growing into itself, bordered on the east by **North Fort Myers** and on the south by the Caloosahatchee River.

Across the river from North Fort Myers and Cape Coral, **Fort Myers** has grown from its fort status of wartime into the hub of communications and transportation for the Gulf Coast. Cattle barons gave the community its early wild temperament; Thomas Edison and his class of successful entrepreneurs elevated it above its cow-trail streets.

The small community along Tamiami Trail named **Estero**, south of Fort Myers, was created by most unusual circumstances. The 19th-century religious cult that called itself the Koreshan Unity first settled there, led by Cyrus Teed. The Koreshans believed that the earth clings to the inside of a hollow globe like coconut meat to its shell. Members practiced celibacy and communal living. They experimented with tropical gardening, bringing to southwest Florida the mango and the avocado. The site of their brief stay has been preserved by the state, together with their buildings and the natural Florida they discovered there.

LODGING

Maine may boast its bed-and-breakfasts, Vermont its historic inns, and Colorado its ski lodges. But when vacationers envision Florida, it's the beachside resorts that flash first through the mental slide projector. The Island Coast has perfected this image of sun-and-sand abandon. Megaresorts are designed to keep guests (and their disposable income) on-property. Not only can you eat lunch, rent a bike, and get a tennis lesson — you can hire a masseur, charter a boat for a sunset sail, play 18 holes of golf, and enroll your child in Sandcastle Building 101. These destination resorts are in business to fulfill fantasies, and they spare no effort to achieve that goal.

You'll also find, side-by-side with the resorts, homey little cottages that have held their ground against buyouts and takeovers. In between the two extremes exists a wide variety of high-rise condos, funky hotels, retirement resorts, mom-and-pop motels, fishing lodges, and inns.

Privately owned second homes and condominiums provide another source of upscale accommodations along the Island Coast. Vacation brokers who match visitors with such properties are listed under "Home & Condo Rentals" at the end of this section.

The highlights of Island Coast hospitality listed here — alphabetically by town — include the best and freshest in the local industry. While spanning the range of endless possibilities, this list concentrates on those properties that break out of the skyscraping, wicker-and-floral mold. Toll-free 800 or 888 reservation numbers, where available, are listed after local numbers.

A star after the pricing designation indicates that the rate includes at least a continental breakfast in the cost of lodging; a few offer the American Plan, including all meals in the rate charged, or Modified American Plan, offering breakfast and dinner.

Pricing codes are explained below. They are normally per person/double occupancy for hotel rooms and per unit for efficiencies, apartments, cottages, suites, and villas. The range spans low- and high-season rates. Many resorts offer off-season packages at special rates. Pricing does not include the 6 percent Florida sales tax. Some large resorts add service gratuities or maid charges. Lee County imposes a tourist tax as well, which is applied to beach and environmental maintenance.

Rate Categories

Inexpensive	Up to $50
Moderate	$50 to $110
Expensive	$110 to $180
Very Expensive	$180 and up

The following abbreviations are used for credit card information:

AE - American Express	DC - Diners Club
CB - Carte Blanche	MC - MasterCard
D - Discover Card	V - Visa

Bonita Beach

THE BEACH & TENNIS CLUB
General Manager: Betty Brown.
941-992-1121 or 800-237-4934.
5700 Bonita Beach Rd. SW, Suite 3103, Bonita Springs 34134.
Price: Moderate (three-day minimum).
Credit Cards: No.

A string of five high-rise buildings and a complex of 10 Har-Tru tennis courts make up this property across the street from the bleached-blond sands of Bonita Beach. Each of the 360 one-bedroom, privately owned apartments has a balcony with a view of either the gulf or the backwaters. They are modernly equipped with full kitchens, sleeper sofas, and dining and living rooms. Two heated swimming pools, a children's pool, a beauty salon, a restaurant, shuffleboard courts, a tennis pro shop, and a laundry complete the amenities.

BONITA BEACH RESORT MOTEL
General Manager: Eric Mohlenhoff.
941-992-2137.

Bonita Beach has a reputation for recreational fishing. Its earliest lodging accommodated intrepid sportsmen, and the island still boasts a lion's share of motels designed around marinas

26395 Hickory Blvd., Bonita Springs 34134.
Price: Moderate.
Credit Cards: AE, MC, V.

and back-bay locations. Bonita Beach Resort is one of the few close to the gulf. It spreads its 20 units between the main drag and the bay, with lots of room for its dock, boat ramp, pontoon rentals, and playground. There's nothing plush or fancy about the rooms. They are clean, air-conditioned, and completely adequate for someone whose mind is set on finding the prime fishing hole. Some have kitchens, some water views.

Cabbage Key

Thousands of dollars wallpaper Cabbage Key Inn.

Karen T. Bartlett

CABBAGE KEY INN
Innkeepers: Rob & Phyllis Wells.
941-283-2278.
PO Box 200, Pineland 33945.
Price: Moderate to Expensive.
Credit Cards: MC, V.

Cabbage Key appeals to vacationers seeking an authentic Old Florida experience. Built on an unbridged island atop an ancient shell mound, the inn and its guest accommodations are reminiscent of the 1930s, when novelist Mary Roberts Rinehart used native cypress and pine to construct a home for her son and his bride. Six unpretentious guestrooms, five historically significant cottages, and a four-bedroom home accommodate overnighters. Four of the cottages have kitchens. The restaurant and currency-papered bar attract boaters and water tours for lunch, but the island shuts down to a whisper come sundown.

Cape Coral

CAPE CORAL GOLF & TENNIS RESORT

For Florida vacationers more concerned about sun "strokes" than suntans, Cape Coral's prime

General Manager: Todd Strane.
941-542-3191 or 800-648-1475.
4003 Palm Tree Blvd., Cape Coral 33904.
Price: Moderate to Expensive.
Credit Cards: AE, CB, D, DC, MC, V.

resort offers the best value. The newly renovated 18-hole course, with its Audubon sanctuary and putting, chipping, and driving practice areas, is the resort's focus. Its eight soft-surface courts contribute to the overall sports orientation. Lessons and clinics are offered for both golf and tennis. The resort also got a recent makeover in its main building, home to three restaurants (one outdoors on the course) and two bars. Its 100 rooms look typically motel-like; some have terraces overlooking the greens. Situated in the middle of Cape Coral, the resort is central to, but less than an hour away from, Fort Myers' historical attractions, Pine Island, and the beaches of Sanibel Island and Fort Myers Beach.

Captiva Island

JENSEN'S TWIN PALM COTTAGES & MARINA
Owners: David, John, and Jimmy Jensen.
941-472-5800.
P.O. Box 191, Captiva Island 33924.
Price: Moderate to Expensive.
Credit Cards: MC, V.

One of Captiva's most affordable lodging options, it's also one of its homier places. You get an immediate sense of neighborliness on the grounds. Perhaps it has to do with its partiality to fisherfolk — its bayside docks, fishing charters, boat rentals, and bait supplies. I expected to find the accommodations in that same vein, where what's out in the water matters more than what's indoors. The 14 units looked plain enough from the outside: white stucco cottages with tin roofs and a splash of blue trim. Each screened-in porch holds a plain picnic table. Inside, the one- and two-bedroom cottages are entirely cheery with their immaculate white tongue-and-groove walls, stylish curtains, and simple, sturdy wood furniture. The full kitchens are modern and spotless. Nothing fishy about 'em. Just charming old island style dressed up comfortable.

SOUTH SEAS PLANTATION
General Manager: Fred L. Hawkins.
941-472-5111 or 800-227-8482.
P.O. Box 194, Captiva Island 33924.
Price: Expensive to Very Expensive.
Credit Cards: CB, D, DC, MC, V.

South Seas is one of the great destination resorts of Florida, where it ranks as a standard for top-quality accommodations and service. It's one of those places where you can enter through the security gates and leave one week later without ever having gone off-property. Celebrities crave its privacy and discretion. South Seas offers any type of getaway dwelling you could imagine, from tennis villas to beach cottages to harborside hotel rooms — nine different types of accommodations in all. The plantation monopolizes a third of the island with 600 guest units, both privately owned and otherwise, six restaurants (most of which are closed to the public), lounges, shops, a nine-hole golf course, a fitness center, a yacht harbor, 18 swimming pools, 18 tennis courts, water-sports equipment rentals and lessons, excursion cruises, organized activities for children and teenagers, and two and a half miles of augmented beach. A free trolley takes guests wherever they want to go around the 300-acre property. Rooms are furnished with stylish, high-quality pieces and appointments. Everything is carried off with a South Pacific theme, and attention is detailed.

'TWEEN WATERS INN
General Manager: Jeff Shuff.
941-472-5161 or 800-223-5865.
Captiva Island 33924.
Price: Expensive to Very Expensive.
Credit Cards: AE, D, MC, V.

'Tween Waters spans the gap between beach cottage lodging and modern super-resort. Built early in the decade, when wildlife patron "Ding" Darling kept a cottage there, the property shows its age, with glints of Old Florida architecture (some of it rather unglamorous) and easygoing attitudes. Compact but complete, it holds 137 rooms (20 of which opened in 1998), cottages, efficiencies, and apartments, as well as restaurants, a marina, tennis courts, and a swimming pool. Named for its location between two shores at Captiva's narrowest span, it lies across the road from a length of beach that is usually lightly populated because it lacks public parking facilities. Its marina, one of its best features, is the island's top water sports center, with charters, tours, boat and canoe rentals, and the Canoe Club restaurant, whose lounge provides the island's nightlife.

Fort Myers

AMTEL MARINA HOTEL & SUITES
General Manager: Udo Jaritz.
941-337-0300 or 800-833-1620.
2500 Edwards Dr., Fort Myers 33901.
Price: Moderate to Very Expensive.
Credit Cards: AE, CB, D, DC, MC, V.

The tropical theme that dominates the hotel's decor is touched with Gatsbian elegance. The marble-pillared atrium lobby overlooks the city yacht basin, as do the majority of its 416 rooms and suites. The units continue the revived Art Deco motif with a tropical floral interpretation, stylized lamps, and comfortable armchairs. One of the resorts' two swimming pools is wrapped around a tiki bar and surrounded by a marine-life mural and cascading waters. A small fitness center, a hot tub, an outdoor pool, a restaurant and lounge, and a gift shop fill the creature-comfort bill at this high-rise hotel.

HOLIDAY INN SUNSPREE RESORT
General Manager: Mary Johnson.
941-334-3434.
2220 W. First St., Fort Myers 33901.

As downtown Fort Myers' future brightens, this tropical riverside gem attracts much-deserved notice. The marble-floored lobby introduces a Florida theme with coral rock block walls, jungle greenery, and a caged tropical bird at the entrance. The 170 rooms and suites are lavishly furnished,

Price: Moderate to
Expensive.

some with private whirlpools. The lushly landscaped courtyard holds a pool, a playground, a
beauty salon, and a popular waterside restaurant
and tiki bar, from which boat charters depart.

All that's missing from Sanibel Harbour Resort's Gatsbian setting and Old Florida demeanor is the bootleg gin.

Sanibel Harbour Resort

**SANIBEL HARBOUR
RESORT & SPA**
General Manager: Brian
Holly.
941-466-4000 or
800-767-7777.
17260 Harbour Pointe Dr.,
Fort Myers 33908.
Price: Expensive to Very
Expensive.
Credit Cards: AE, D, DC,
MC, V.

Stunningly beautiful for a property this size, the
public areas at Sanibel Harbour capitalize on
Florida style and a spectacular location. Not really
on Sanibel Island as the name suggests, the resort's
240 rooms, 80 condos, three restaurants, two outdoor swimming pools, high-tech tennis courts, spa
facilities, and beach are located on a chin of land
across the bay from the island, a bay known as
Sanibel Harbour. Ninety-five percent of the units
have water views of either the bay or nearby estuaries. One of the bars has a 280-degree view of the
sea, with a lovely, breezy cocktail patio. The
Promenade Cafe, which serves spa and regular
lunches, is set on a porch atop a waterside pool that brings to mind exotic
Roman baths. The world-class spa and fitness center, racquetball courts,
canoe/kayak trail, sun sports charters and rentals, and Sanibel Harbour
Princess dinner cruises provide guests a well-rounded menu of fitness and
recreation options. Rooms, suites, and condos, in their light-wood and tropical
motif, instill the sea's sense of space, lots of space. Kids Klub takes youngsters
on nature hikes and provides them with a variety of other activities.

Fort Myers Beach

THE GRANDVIEW
General Manager: Deana
  Turner.
941-765-4422 or
  800-325-2525.
8701 Estero Blvd., Fort
  Myers Beach 33931.
Price: Moderate to
  Expensive.
Credit Cards: AE, D, MC, V.

Newly remodeled and renamed in 1997, this skyscraping suite resort stands like a bookmark that separates the high-rise development of Fort Myers Beach from the natural world of Lover's Key. It overlooks the estuarine waters of Big Carlos Pass and Estero Bay, renowned for their dolphin populations. The small, unspectacular patch of sandy beach is offset by the many varieties of water-sports equipment available. The 104 rooms (only 78 available for general public rental) come with kitchens, balconies, and water views — the hotel's best asset. Rooms and the lobby have been redecorated in contemporary style, with tropical tinges. Modern kitchens are fully equipped. On the bay, a paved and nicely landscaped patio leads to a grill area and pool.

THE OUTRIGGER
  BEACH RESORT
General Manager: Dianne
  F. Major.
941-463-3131 or
  800-749-3131.
6200 Estero Blvd., Fort
  Myers Beach 33931.
Price: Moderate to Very
  Expensive.
Credit Cards: D, MC, V.

The Outrigger Beach Resort occupies the quiet south end of Fort Myers Beach, where the sand flares wide and gorgeous. The 30-year-old, 144-room resort boasts a casual, unstructured vacationing style that works well for families. Activity centers around its chain-link-fenced pool and tiki bar boardwalk area, where guests can sun, mingle, or rent water-sports equipment. Rooms are compact and modern, furnished inexpensively à la roadside motel. Five types of rooms range from the traditional to efficiencies with full kitchens. Prices depend also upon what floor they're on and the quality of the view. Shuffleboard, a putting green, a little cafe, and live weekend entertainment keep the place lively and fun.

PINK SHELL BEACH &
  BAY RESORT
General Manager: John
  Naylor.
941-463-6181 or
  800-237-5786.
275 Estero Blvd., Fort
  Myers Beach 33931.
Price: Moderate to Very
  Expensive.
Credit Cards: AE, D, MC, V.

Every sort of lodging imaginable is available at Fort Myers Beach. There are chains and small mom-and-pop places; upscale accommodations congregate in tall condo buildings or time-share villages. The range is wide, to fit all budgets. One single resort pretty well covers that range all within its own 12 acres. The nicest thing about Pink Shell is that it occupies — practically monopolizes — Estero Island's north end, where traffic slows to a trickle and the sugary sands span wide. Something of an island landmark since the 1950s, it has been completely renovated in a way that maintains its old island character. Forty-six of the 208 units are housed in endearing stilt cottages, with up to three bedrooms and less-than-cutting-edge accoutrements. Yet they are appealing in the way they willfully remain one step behind the times. Multistoried buildings contain modern efficiencies and suites with kitchen facilities and terraces. Guests, many of whom have been coming here for years, have access to three swimming pools, a wading pool, two lighted tennis courts, a fishing pier and bait shop, beach volleyball, a restaurant, a beach bar-and-grill, a deli-grocery, a kids' program, and wide-ranging recreational opportunities and programs on both waterfronts, including water taxis and tours. The Pink Shell is a world of its own. Guests meet at weekly cocktail parties and catch up on fellow vacationers via a newsletter.

North Captiva

NORTH CAPTIVA ISLAND CLUB
General Managers: Bryan and Bud Brillhart.
941-395-1001 or 800-576-7343.
P.O. Box 1000, Pineland 33945.
Price: Moderate to Very Expensive (three-day minimum).
Credit Cards: AE, D, DC, MC, V.

No roads. No cars. No bridges. Perhaps Upper (North) Captiva is best described by what it isn't. A favorite offshore hideaway for connoisseurs of unspoiled places, the North Captiva Island Club offers accommodations from a diverse menu of privately owned homes. All are designed for minimal intrusion upon nature but are furnished fashionably and with all the necessities. Guests enjoy a swimming pool, soft-surface tennis courts, a fitness room and spa, dockage, and golf cart and ferry privileges. Water-sports rentals, fishing charters, and restaurants are also available. The island truly provides the ultimate in natural tranquility and relaxation. The focus is the beach, the sea, fishing, and boating.

Sanibel Island

THE CASTAWAYS
General Manager: Tami Thompson.
941-472-1252 or 800-375-0152.
6460 Sanibel-Captiva Rd., Sanibel Island 33957.
Price: Moderate to Very Expensive.
Credit Cards: AE, D, MC, V.

The Santiva area that lies before the bridge to Captiva Island is unique to Sanibel. It's less demanding than the island's more exclusive beaches and their properties. Here, a barefoot and ultracarefree attitude prevails. With its marina and cottage style, The Castaways embodies my vision of what a Florida beach vacation should be. For those who shun the traffic of nearby Turner's Beach, which some of the cottages border, other accommodations hide bayside, where the preoccupation is fishing. The 37 units are spread out between the two waterfronts with lots of room in between. The weathered, blue-gray, one- to three-bedroom cottages provide clean, comfortable, and ample — if somewhat dated — accommodations. A small swimming pool (slightly shabby) and water-sports equipment and bicycle rental concession complement an ideal location.

Lodging on Sanibel Island ranges from elegant luxury to casual beach style, as at the Castaways.

Karen T. Bartlett

ISLAND INN
General Manager: Pegge
  Ford.
941-472-1561 or
  800-851-5088.
P.O. Box 659, 3111 W. Gulf
  Dr., Sanibel Island 33957.
Price: Expensive*.
Credit Cards: AE, D, MC, V.

Sanibel's only historic lodging — over 100 years old — displays all the refinement of Florida's great old inns and hotels, but without the snobbery. It has the same congenial and relaxed atmosphere Granny Matthews, a Sanibel matriarch of renown, created at the turn of the century when she entertained the whole island — including guests from other resorts — at Saturday night barbecues. She also initiated the Sanibel Shell Fair as a way to keep guests busy, and hosted it in the lobby, where white wicker, French doors, a lattice-edged dining room, and shell displays now give an immediate impression of immaculate spaciousness and island graciousness. During the winter season (November 15 to May 1) it's a Modified American Plan resort, including breakfast and dinner in its rates. Cottages and lodges house 57 units, all with a view of gentle gulf waves lapping at a shelly beach. Cottages have one or two bedrooms; lodges contain hotel rooms, with either full kitchens or refrigerators only. They can be combined into suites. The resort doesn't pretend to furnish extravagantly; all is done in uncontrived old island style. That does not translate into shoddiness, however. The Island Inn is owned by shareholders who reinvest profits for constant upgrading. Decor is cheerful, comfortable, and impeccably maintained. Outside each lodge room door sits a wooden table where guests display their shell finds for others to peruse and admire. It's an Island Inn tradition. The atmosphere is saturated with conviviality. Dinner, a coat-and-tie affair, is announced by the blowing of a conch shell. Outdoors, native vegetation is landscaped around tin-roofed structures. A butterfly garden frames a croquet court, a swimming pool sits squarely on the beach, and tennis and shuffleboard provide recreation.

SANIBEL'S SEASIDE INN
General Manager: Jack
Reed.
941-472-1400 or
800-831-7384.
541 E. Gulf Dr., Sanibel
Island 33957.
Price: Moderate to Very
Expensive.*
Credit Cards: AE, CB, DC,
D, MC, V.

I always recommend this place to visitors looking for intimacy on the beach without great extravagance. A measure of Key West blends with Seaside Inn's old island charm. Formerly The Gallery, the resort underwent a $1 million facelift in 1995. As one of Sanibel's oldest resorts, it lent itself nicely to an old Key West scheme of banana-yellow tints, tin roofs, and gingerbread-trimmed balconies. It's still the kind of place where you kick off your shoes the first day and don't find them again until you're packed to leave. Renovations have kept the character and added conveniences that make a vacation as breezy as the sea. Kitchen facilities and video cassette players come in every studio, beach cottage, and one-, two-, and three-bedroom suite, of which there are 32 in all. A swimming pool, complimentary continental breakfast (delivered to your door, if you so desire), a video and book lending library, and tropical appointments complete the picture of seaside coziness. Use of facilities and amenities at Seaside Inn's sister resorts, including Sundial Beach Resort and Sanibel Inn, is available free of charge to guests, and an interresort trolley provides transportation.

SONG OF THE SEA
General Manager: Linda
Logan.
941-472-2220 or
800-831-7384.
863 E. Gulf Dr., Sanibel
Island 33957.
Price: Very Expensive.*
Credit Cards: AE, CB, DC,
D, MC, V.

From the minute you walk along the sand-dollar stepping stones, open the door, and find a bottle of wine and fresh-cut blossoms awaiting you, the mood of romance and European innkeeping takes over. With only 30 studios and suites, Song of the Sea is inherently intimate. European touches include French country furnishings, Institute Swiss toiletries, bottled spring water, alfresco continental breakfast in the courtyard, individualized service, and down-filled comforters and pillows for building a cozy love nest. Each room is also supplied with a refrigerator. The sea lies across a green expanse of lawn outside each screened patio or balcony. An on-property Mediterranean-style pool and whirlpool, along with beach rentals, tennis courts, and other amenities of nearby Sundial Beach Resort, are available to guests.

**SUNDIAL BEACH
RESORT**
General Manager: Earl
Raven.
941-472-4151 or
800-237-4184.

Sundial promises the perfection of a worry-free vacation. Sanibel's fine shelling beach is the focus of the 20-acre resort, which takes its name from a species of shell. The resort provides recreation with 12 tennis courts, five heated swimming pools, bike and beach rental concessions, a fitness

1451 Middle Gulf Dr.,
  Sanibel Island 33957.
Price: Expensive to Very
  Expensive.
Credit Cards: AE, D, DC,
  MC, V.

center, game rooms, children's and family programs, and an eco-center complete with touch
tank. The lavish main building houses four restaurants — two overlooking the gulf, another serving
Japanese food, and one casual and poolside. Less
stylish, low-rise condo buildings are camouflaged
by well-maintained vegetation and hold 270 fully
equipped units decorated in coral pink, sea-foam
green, and natural wicker. They take advantage of gulf or garden views. Given
its high level of service, the Sundial is one of the area's least pretentious, most
comfortable properties, especially for families.

HOME & CONDO RENTALS

1-800-SANIBEL (941-472-1800 or 800-726-1800; 1715 Periwinkle Way, Sanibel
  Island 33957) Condo, home, and cottage rentals in Sanibel and Captiva.
Sanibel Accommodations (941-472-3191; 800-237-6004; 2341 Palm Ridge Rd.,,
  Sanibel Island 33957)

RV RESORTS

Fort Myers-Pine Island KOA (941-283-2415 or 800-992-7202; 5120 Stringfellow
  Rd., St. James City 33956) 371 sites, pool, saunas, hot tub, exercise room, ten-
  nis court, shuffleboard, horseshoes, and lake fishing.
Groves Campground (941-466-5909; 16175 John Morris Rd., Fort Myers 33908)
  Close to Sanibel Island, with full accommodations and swimming pool.
Red Coconut RV Resort (941-463-7200; 3001 Estero Blvd., Fort Myers Beach
  33931) Right on the beach, but packed in a bit tightly; 250 full hookup sites,
  on-site trailer rentals, laundry, shuffleboard, cable TV, and car rentals.

DINING

The Island Coast is home to two of the nation's shellfish capitals. Shrimp —
that monarch of edible crustaceans — reigns in Fort Myers Beach, where
more than 150 shrimp boats are headquartered and an annual festival pays
homage to America's favorite seafood. The sweet, pink gulf shrimp is the
trademark culinary delight of the town and its environs.

The fish markets of Pine Island, an important commercial fishing and transshipment center, sell all sorts of fresh seafood — oysters, shrimp, scallops,
mullet, snapper, catfish — but the signature seafood is the blue crab that
comes from local bay waters.

The following listings cover the variety of Island Coast feasting in these price categories:

Inexpensive	Up to $15
Moderate	$15 to $25
Expensive	$25 to $35
Very Expensive	$35 or more

Cost is figured on a typical meal (at dinner, unless dinner is not served) that would include an appetizer or dessert, salad (if included with the meal), entree, and coffee. Many restaurants offer early dining discounts, usually called "early bird specials." These are rarely listed on the regular menu and sometimes are not publicized by tip-conscious servers. I have noted restaurants that offer them. Certain restrictions apply, such as time constraints, a specific menu, or number of people first in the door. Call the restaurant and ask about its policy. Those restaurants listed with "Healthy Selections" usually mark such on their menu.

The following abbreviations are used for credit card information and meals:

AE - American Express	DC - Diners Club
CB - Carte Blanche	MC - MasterCard
D - Discover Card	V - Visa

B - Breakfast	D - Dinner
L - Lunch	SB - Sunday Brunch

Sizing Up a Shrimp

Gulf shrimp are graded by size and assigned all sorts of vague measurements: jumbo, large, medium-sized, boat grade, etc. The surest way to know what size shrimp you are ordering is to ask for the count-per-pound designation. This will be something like "21–25s," meaning there are 21 to 25 shrimp per pound. "Boat grade" normally designates a mixture of sizes, usually on the small side.

Bonita Beach

BIG HICKORY FISHING NOOK RESTAURANT
941-992-3916.
26107 Hickory Blvd. SW.
Price: Moderate to
　Expensive.
Children's Menu: Yes.
Cuisine: Seafood/Florida.

Big Hickory has always been a favorite of mine because it's how restaurants first were around here — bare-bones places where character came from the owners and the water view, and what was on the plate was swimming only hours ago. Recently the old marina fish house came under new management, which appears to have maintained the atmosphere while adding more character

Liquor: Beer, wine, and limited premixed cocktails.
Serving: B (Sat. and Sun. only), L, D.
Credit Cards: AE, CB, D, DC, MC, V.
Handicap Access: Yes.
Reservations: No.
Special Features: Old Florida marina atmosphere; dining dockside and in a screened porch.

and dependability to the menu. I prefer sitting outdoors in the classic old marina setting, watching boats and shorebirds come and go. On my last visit, under the faded awning, I dipped hearty conch chowder with a tinge of fire from a clear plastic clamshell bowl and watched pelicans feeding on a sandbar. My red snapper arrived practically flopping fresh, pan-bronzed (with blackening seasoning, without the blackening) and ringed on its Fiestaware plate with a delightful medley of side dishes: fresh fruit salad, a creamy scalloped carrot dish, sweet-sour red cabbage, and flavorful rice. All the sauces, dressings, and desserts are homemade at Big Hickory and taste it. Six varieties of fresh fish come in daily and can be prepared any number of ways, from fish-house flour-fried to grilled. Pan-seared Everglades alligator appetizer, Florida crab cakes, baked Caribbean pork loin, seafood pasta, fried grouper sandwich, and live whole Maine lobster are a few of the tempting offerings on the ambitious menu. Indoors, the small dining room features a lovely wood sculpture and a saltillo-paved floor. There's also seating on the screened porch. The service staff cheerfully accommodates in a way that takes you back to another time.

Cape Coral

IGUANA MIA
941-945-7755.
1027 Cape Coral Pkwy.
Price: Inexpensive to Moderate.
Early Dining Menu: No.
Children's Menu: Yes.
Cuisine: Mexican-American.
Healthy Selections: No.
Liquor: Full.
Serving: L, D.
Credit Cards: AE, D, MC, V.
Handicap Access: Yes.
Reservations: No.

This, the original Iguana Mia, spawned another in Fort Myers (see below), but we like this one better, even if it means we have to cross the Cape Coral bridge and pay the toll to get there. It's the more down-to-earth of the two. Sure, just as flashy, with its electric-green exterior paint job and nicely rendered interior Mexican murals; but it still retains some of the unpretentious lunchroom ambiance it started out with. Stacked cases of Mexican beer still count as decor elements. And most importantly, the food is flat-out better. Things seem more rushed at the newer place; here it's *mañana*-paced. My husband invariably orders the sour cream chicken chimichanga, a specialty. I — usually already half-full from shoveling in huge gobs of the salsa I can't resist with warm, crunchy tortilla chips — like their veggie burrito, nachos, or quesadilla. You're bound to find something you like on the menu — it's huge and lets you do some of your own meal engineering.

Captiva Island

Karen T. Bartlett

Captiva Island's Bubble Room effervesces fun and whimsy.

THE BUBBLE ROOM
941-472-5558.
15001 Andy Rosse Lane.
Price: Expensive.
Children's Menu: Yes.
Cuisine: American.
Liquor: Full.
Serving: L, D.
Credit Cards: AE, CB, D,
    DC, MC, V.
Handicap Access: Limited.
Reservations: No.
Special Features:
    Museumlike displays of
    '30s and '40s
    memorabilia.

The Bubble Room is something you have to experience once. It's especially fun to take kids there. The fun begins outside, where bubbles bedeck the kitsch-cottage structure and lawn gnomes greet you. Inside, the tables are glass-topped showcases filled with jacks, Monopoly money, comic books, dominoes, and assorted toys from the past. A Christmas elves scene, circus plaques, Betty Boop, Christmas cards, celebrity photos, a plaster hippo's mouth, and other nostalgic memorabilia fill every wall, phone booth, bathroom door, nook, and cranny. A toy train runs under the ceiling, and servers — Bubble Scouts — wear pins and badges on their uniforms and fun stuff on their hats. One waiter had a whole scene from Star Wars on his, rigged with lights, no less. So that's the atmosphere — you've gotta see it for yourself. The menu continues the frivolity. On the lunch menu, Al Jolson in Full Concert consists of sausage, black beans, and rice; Mae's West is a charbroiled chicken breast sandwich. Dinner's Duck Ellington is a tasty rendition of roasted duck with orange and banana sauce. My Dem Bones Dem Bones — a T-bone steak — arrived too well done, but the problem was quickly resolved. Service is exceptional, considering the tight quarters and the volume of business. Other things for which the Bubble Room is known is its basket of bubble bread (yum! cream cheesy) and sticky buns, its she-crab soup and Three Coins in a Fountain appetizer (shrimp, langostino, artichoke hearts, spinach, and mushrooms in a sherry sauce), and its fabulous desserts. You must leave room for red velvet cake or one of the many other tempting selections.

CHADWICK'S

941-472-5111.
South Seas Plantation
  Resort, 5400 Captiva Rd.
Price: Moderate to
  Expensive.
Early Dining Menu: No.
Children's Menu: Yes.
Cuisine: Tropical.
Healthy Selections: Yes.
Liquor: Full.
Serving: B, L, D, SB.
Credit Cards: AE, D, DC,
  MC, V.
Handicap Access: Yes.
Reservations: Yes.
Special Features: Daily
  luncheon and themed
  dinner buffets.

Chadwick's has perfected the buffet line. Theirs is sinfully sumptuous and the restaurant's best value. This is grazing at its finest, with beautifully displayed arrangements, ice sculptures, and tons of hot and cold food. Sunday champagne brunch is the most popular, with a dessert table divine. Throughout the week, dinner themes focus on seafood, Caribbean, Key West, New Orleans, or Captiva. The luncheon buffet is offered Monday through Saturday. Plan on a nap afterwards. The regular menus pale somewhat when compared to the lavishness of the buffets. Tropically inclined dishes often lack that true island "punch." At lunch there's black bean soup with rice and plantain chips, lobster burrito (a bit of a disappointment), vegetarian muffaletta, Cuban-style sandwich, and pasta Matlacha, which we found to be a nice dish with shrimp, scallops, sun-dried tomatoes, and kalamata olives. Dinner selections include grouper macadamia (pan-fried with orange-ginger sauce), portabella chicken breast, and shrimp Barbados (prepared similarly to the luncheon pasta Matlacha). White lattice detailing and tropical prints give the setting a plantation feel, in keeping with the restaurant's namesake, who once operated a coconut and key lime plantation here.

THE GREEN FLASH

941-472-3337.
15183 Captiva Dr.
Price: Moderate to
  Expensive.
Children's Menu: Yes.
Cuisine: Seafood.
Liquor: Full.
Serving: L, D.
Credit Cards: AE, D, DC,
  MC, V.
Handicap Access: Yes.
Reservations: Dinner only.
Special Features: Bay view.

Don't be fooled by this building's plain concrete streetside exterior. Its focus is what's at sea. From the water it's pretty and inviting, and that's how many patrons arrive. The name refers to a sunset phenomenon, but you can't see the sunset from this side of the island. You do have an elevated view of placid bay waters, and the menu is equally water-focused. If you go for lunch, I highly recommend the Green Flash sandwich. Served on grilled focaccia, you can have it with either smoked turkey or vegetables and cheese, which is my favorite. The barbecued shrimp and bacon is a winner on both the lunch and dinner menus. The house specialty, Grouper Cafe de Paris, wears a rich, well-seasoned butter cream sauce. Grilled tuna, broiled mahi mahi, filet mignon, veal Zurich, pork tenderloin Wellington, and a medley of other dishes provide an interesting and varied selection.

Fort Myers

BISTRO 41
941-466-4141.
Bell Tower Mall, Daniels
   Pkwy. and Cleveland Ave.
Price: Moderate to
   Expensive.
Early Dining Menu: No.
Children's Menu: No.
Cuisine: New American.
Healthy Selections: No.
Liquor: Full.
Serving: L, D.
Credit Cards: AE, MC, V.
Handicap Access: Yes.
Reservations: Yes.
Special Features: Outdoor
   seating.

Fort Myers celebrates this recently opened eatery for its sophisticated atmosphere and fare. Whether you choose a sidewalk table looking out at Saks Fifth Avenue or an indoor booth between mustard-colored walls, it feels festive and chic. Divine dishes come out of the oak-grill kitchen, visible through a showcase window overshadowed by a giant fork hanging on the wall above it. The regular lunch and dinner menus highlight grilled specialties such as Yucatan Pork Hogie (with caramelized onions and grilled pineapple chutney), rotisserie chicken, and oak-grilled salmon with Mediterranean vinaigrette. Other eclectic offerings include Tuscan veggie sandwich, seafood paella, meatloaf and roasted-garlic mashed potatoes with veal gravy, chicken pot pie, and wild mushroom pasta. To further complicate decision-making, a tableau of specials comprise a whole separate menu. On our visit we ordered from the specials menu the tomato and onion soup (sweet-sour, borschtlike, and excellent), sweet-potato bourbon soup (with just the perfect quota of bourbon), pan-seared filet mignon wrapped in apple bacon and served on a Gorgonzola potato pancake, and pan-seared snapper with lobster cream and a black bean/corn salsa. We ended with a delightful Heath bar cookie sundae. The potato pancake was a rare treat. The beans, corn, and baby zucchini that topped my snapper made my taste buds dance to the crescendo of fresh tastes and crunchy textures. The only thing we could find the least bit wrong with the whole experience was a bit of oversalting in my dish.

CASA CABANA
941-278-5533.
Toys "R" Us Plaza, 2158
   Colonial Blvd.
Price: Inexpensive.
Children's Menu: Yes.
Cuisine: Cuban/Mexican/
   Spanish.
Liquor: Full.
Serving: L, D.
Credit Cards: AE, V, MC.
Handicap Access: Partial.
Reservations: No.

The general rule for finding authentic Cuban home cooking is to look for the least amount of atmosphere. Not true at this recent newcomer, which took over a former restaurant done in a jungle theme, with wildlife wall murals, silk banana trees, waterfalls, and thatched cabanas. Thus the name. The menu, which lists three pages of specialties in English with Spanish subtitles, has a few misspellings (abocado salad) and tells you it takes 10 to 20 minutes to receive your meal. That, to me, spells character and care. If it spells frustration for you, don't go. If you do, you'll find the typical assortment of Cuban dishes — Cuban sandwich, arroz con pollo, ropa vieja — and then some. The *sancocho* stew offers a taste of Puerto Rico, the fajitas a taste of Tex-Mex, the shrimp Mexican style authentic south-of-the-border flavors, and the rolled steak with ham and Swiss an unusual melange of foodways. This is not, however, trendy Floribbean or Cuban-American cooking. The way you'll know this is the real stuff is by all the people from the local Hispanic community who dine here.

GARDEN GREENS
941-936-1888.
4329 Cleveland Ave.
Price: Inexpensive.
Children's Menu: Kids'
  pricing on salad bar.
Cuisine: Salad/American.
Healthy Selections: Yes.
Liquor: Beer and wine.
Serving: L, D.
Credit Cards: AE, MC, V.
Handicap Access: Yes.
Reservations: No.
Special Features: Deluxe
  all-you-can-eat salad,
  soup, pasta, bread, and
  potato bar.

Garden Greens takes America's love for the salad bar to an obsession. Don't think iceberg-lettuce-and-chocolate-pudding salad bar, although Garden Greens does contain those elements. This one is done with more creativity, flavor, nutrition, and variety than most because it's the main thing, its raison d'être. There is a menu, for those who prefer being served. The salad bar, which includes fresh pasta items, baked potatoes with all the fixings, fresh-baked breads, four kinds of soup, fresh fruit, and stir-fry veggies, has something for just about everyone, including the health-conscious, who know that most salad bars aren't necessarily that good for you. Garden Greens offers a variety of tasty low-fat dressings (including its delicious toasted sesame), sugar-free soft-serve sorbet, cream soups made with low-fat milk, and vegetarian black bean soup. Selections change on the food bar. Some favorites, such as the black bean salad (I'm still trying to figure out how they make it taste so good), couscous salad, and basil black beans and rice are uncommonly good. On the menu you'll find a smattering of grilled items with creative sauces — grilled tuna Caesar, stuffed potato with grilled chicken, grilled salmon with Dijon sauce, New York strip, and so on. Stop here for an alternative to a fast-food, fat-laden lunch or dinner. You'll feel better for it.

IGUANA MIA
941-939-5247.
4329 Cleveland Ave. near
  Edison Mall.
Price: Inexpensive.
Children's Menu: Yes.
Cuisine: Mexican-American.
Liquor: Full.
Serving: L, D.
Credit Cards: AE, CB, D,
  DC, MC, V.
Handicap Access: Yes.
Reservations: No.

Don't worry about missing this place. Drive to the Edison Mall and the lime-green edifice will jump out at you like a tree frog. You'll probably notice people waiting outside for dinner; it's a popular place. Inside, murals and trompe l'oeil paintings create a tropical jungle motif, accented with the ubiquitous Mexican blankets, cases of Dos Equis, and cantina background music. Menu selections range from the typical to some signature creations, such as sour cream chicken and West Coast quesadilla, made with yellowfin tuna. There's a lot to choose from, so ask for a menu to peruse if you have to wait. (Better yet, sidle up to the S-shaped bar and order one of its excellent margaritas while you're perusing.) You're given a variety of create-your-own and other customizing options. The salsa and guacamole are freshly made and good. The bar, like the entire place, is fun and convivial.

Karen T. Bartlett

Fort Myers' most popular Mexican restaurant is decorated in faux and trompe l'oeil kitsch.

**SHOOTERS WATER-
FRONT CAFE U.S.A.**
941-334-2727.
Behind Holiday Inn Sun-
    Spree Resort, 2220 W. 1st
    St.
Price: Moderate.
Early Dining Menu: No.
Children's Menu: Yes.
Cuisine: New American.
Healthy Selections: No.
Liquor: Full.
Serving: B, L, D, SB.
Credit Cards: AE, D, MC, V.
Handicap Access: Yes.
Reservations: No.
Special Features: Riverside
    view, outdoor seating,
    lively bar, party/dining
    cruises, complimentary
    valet parking.

This is a good-time place to eat. You can sit riverside, where there's usually a nice breeze and always lots of action (sometimes to the point of noisy, like the fast boat with loud bass music that drowned out all conversation at a recent meal we had there), or indoors, where quiet and air-conditioning appeal. The casual, creative menu, served lunch and dinner, covers soup, salad, pizza, pasta, sandwiches/burgers, seafood, meat, and other specialties. I have enjoyed the seared tuna salad; the chicken portabella mushroom on penne, which had a light, nicely flavored wine sauce; and the roasted pork loin with shallot mashed potatoes. Our shrimp and crab cakes appetizer was meaty and nicely seasoned, though a tad on the greasy side. The service was somewhat disappointing: We sat unattended for too long without so much as a greeting, and the courses were rushed. Nice selection of wines by the glass. Bring sunglasses if you dine around sunset.

THE VERANDA
941-332-2065.
2122 Second St.
Price: Expensive to Very
    Expensive.
Children's Menu: No.
Cuisine: Florida/Southern.
Liquor: Full.
Serving: L, D.

My husband and I had our first "big" dinner date at the Veranda, so it will always be one of my favorites, and not solely for sentimental reasons, either. Victorian trappings and southern charm create an atmosphere of romance in a historic home setting. Occupying two turn-of-the-century houses, the Veranda is elegantly furnished. The dining room huddles around a two-sided redbrick fireplace. A

Closed: Sat. lunch, Sun.
lunch and dinner.
Credit Cards: AE, CB, MC,
V.
Handicap Access: Yes.
Reservations: Recommended.
Special Features:
Garden/courtyard
dining, piano bar.

white picket fence separates the cobblestone garden courtyard from traffic. Historic Fort Myers photos and well-stocked wine cases line the dark-wood bar. Start with something unusual from the Veranda's appetizer board — perhaps escargots in puff pastry with Stilton cheese (a sublime rendition), artichoke fritters with blue crab and bearnaise sauce, or southern grit cakes with pepper jack cheese and grilled andouille sausage. The multidimensional house salad is served with fresh honey-glazed wheat bread (worth the trip in itself), corn muffins, and the Veranda's signature southern pepper jelly. Entrées wax traditional, but exceed the ordinary. Medallions of filet are dressed southern style, in smoky sour-mash whiskey sauce. Rosemary merlot sauce complements the rack of New Zealand lamb. Grilled grouper is mated with blue crab and black caper vinaigrette. Daily specials typically include fresh seafood catches, and the menu changes to reflect the seasons. Lunches span the spectrum from creative sandwiches, such as the Carpetbagger — roast beef, turkey, bacon, and tomatoes on freshly baked bread — to Florida-accented salads, including fried green tomato salad. At a recent luncheon I sampled the baked tomato pasta, a huge flavorful serving that fell short of perfection by dint of overcooked linguine. Desserts wilt willpower with temptations such as chocolate pâté, peanut butter fudge pie, and southern fruit cobblers.

Fort Myers Beach

Locals go to Fort Myers Beach expecting fresh seafood and reasonable prices. It's known more for fun dining and waterfront views than for culinary innovation.

ANTHONY'S ON THE GULF
941-463-2600.
3040 Estero Blvd.
Price: Moderate.
Early Dining Menu: No.
Children's Menu: Yes.
Cuisine: Italian/Seafood.
Healthy Selections: No.
Liquor: Full.
Serving: L, D.
Credit Cards: AE, D, MC, V.
Handicap Access: Yes.
Reservations: No.
Special Features: Outdoor
deck overlooking the
beach.

You can't get much more tropical than this. Silk jungle plants, stuffed toy monkeys and exotic birds, high-peaked ceilings, light wood, bamboo trim, and a stunning view of the beach set a Jimmy Buffett kind of mood. We find it better for lunch than for dinner; the menu for the latter fails to excite us. It contains all the standard Italian restaurant dishes: manicotti, lasagna, spaghetti, eggplant parmigiana, veal francese, mussels fra diavolo, and so on. They're done well but not spectacularly. I love lunch, sitting out on the open-air deck, sipping something frothy, munching the toasted ravioli and Buffalo shrimp. Many of the dinner items are available more inexpensively on the lunch menu.

Anthony's on the Gulf, the ultimate in tropical beach casual.

SNUG HARBOR
941-463-4343.
645 San Carlos Blvd.
Price: Moderate to
    Expensive.
Cuisine: Seafood/
    American.
Children's Menu: Yes.
Liquor: Full.
Serving: L, D.
Credit Cards: AE, D, MC, V.
Handicap Access: Yes.
Reservations: No.
Special Features: Waterside
    view, open-air dining.

A perennial favorite, Snug Harbor has been sold and remodeled in the past few years. The new look is much cleaner, with a distinct island feel — a thatched roof over part of the dining room, Haitian oil drum art on the walls, and outdoor dockside dining. Two different menus serve Snug's two different areas. The main dining room is lined with windows that look out upon boat traffic, shrimpers, and mangroves. The menu concentrates on seafood, prepared freshly and simply. Grouper Popeye is a holdover from the old Snug, featuring spinach, of course, and a lemon-butter sauce. Baked garlic shrimp is another Snug classic, as is Buffalo shrimp, an appetizer we order every time. Oysters, shrimp, seafood cakes (a bit bready), and lobster tails come fried or broiled. The vegetarian pasta is an ample and tasty serving. The menu also offers fine cuts of meat. Salad lovers will be pleased with the variety of selections on both the lunch and dinner menus: spinach, steak and bleu cheese Caesar, margarita Caesar, and shrimp and rainbow pasta salads, to mention a few. In The Cafe, which includes the bar and dock seating, the menu is more sandwich and munchies oriented. The only problem with dock seating is that the *SeaKruz* , a cruise ship, docks there when in port, quite ruining the view.

Pine Island

DOUBLE NICHOL PUB
941-283-5555.

This is a local-yokel place where islanders come to watch the game around the bar and boaters

3051 Stringfellow Rd., St.
  James City.
Price: Inexpensive.
Children's Menu: No.
Cuisine: Sandwiches.
Liquor: Beer and wine.
Serving: L, D.
Credit Cards: D, MC, V.
Handicap Access: Yes.
Reservations: No.
Special Features: Outdoor
  canalside seating.

float in for a bite to eat. The sandwiches are mostly deli-style, with a couple of hot selections — meatball sub, reuben, baked cod. On weekends you'll often find the barbecue cooker serving up great pork sandwiches. This is pure Pine Island — fun, unfancy, and good eating.

**WATERFRONT
  RESTAURANT**
941-283-0592.
2131 Oleander St., St. James
  City.
Price: Inexpensive to
  Moderate.
Children's Menu: Yes.
Cuisine: Seafood.
Liquor: Full.
Serving: L, D.
Credit Cards: AE, D, MC, V.
Handicap Access: Limited.
Reservations: No.
Special Features: Canalside
  seating.

Where schoolchildren once learned their three Rs, modern-day seafarers and islanders relax and revel in fresh seafood prepared in the traditional style, with a few fancifications. When there's stone crab to be had, have it. This is about the most reasonably priced you'll find it in these parts. Our son automatically equates the foot-long Waterdoggie with a boat trip to Waterfront. We usually choose from the fish specials, after whetting our appetites with gator tail, spicy shrimp, or jalapeño peppers. For the hearty appetite, there's the mariner platter and seafood combo, piled with gifts from the sea, baked or fried. The kitchen is extremely compliant, so order your seafood exactly the way you like it. Indoors, you can play hangman on the butcher paper tablecloths (way ahead of the bistros that now affect the notion). Outdoors, watch boaters trying to gracefully dock their vessels under the scrutiny of an audience. The key lime pie is good, but skip the "famous" waterfront (fruit) bakes.

Sanibel Island

HUNGRY HERON
941-395-2300.
Palm Ridge Plaza, 2330
  Palm Ridge Rd.
Price: Moderate.
Early Dining Menu: No.
Children's Menu: Yes.
Cuisine: American.
Healthy Selections: Yes.
Liquor: Beer and wine.
Serving: B (buffet,
  weekends only), L, D.
Credit Cards: AE, D, MC, V.
Handicap Access: Yes.
Reservations: No.

This place has become wildly popular with locals, although I can't explain why, except that it makes kids happy. The eight-page tabloid-sized menu covers 250 bases, not counting desserts — from a pageful of appetizers to sandwiches to seafood and pasta dinners. My son likes it here because of the Disney shows and cartoons that are continuously aired, although you can't hear them. That doesn't seem to bother children, of whom you'll find a lot at Hungry Heron. Don't go for quiet romance. The menu gives them 26 selections, another fact that makes it popular with parents. The roving magician act (a talented 15-year-old who

Special Features: TV monitors tuned to Disney Channel (but with no sound), and a roving magician.

works for tips) is another. I like it that the kids' menu has healthy selections — even if mine won't eat 'em. The kid's pizza is a good choice — homemade, not just popped from freezer to microwave. The macaroni and cheese is glumpy, however. I enjoyed my mustard-glazed tuna salad, one of the "Guiltless 'n Great" selections. It came perfectly medium-rare, to my specifications, on a platterful of crispy greens, red ripe tomato slices, and sweet melon chunks. We (two six-year-olds and I) gave the key lime pie thumbs up. Located in a little strip shopping center, the Heron doesn't kill with atmosphere, and the service can be a bit slow and the pace hectic. But if you're looking for a menu with extreme variety and affordable prices, this is the place on Sanibel.

LAZY FLAMINGO
941-472-5353.
6520-C Pine Ave., at Blind Pass.
Price: Moderate.
Early Dining Menu: No.
Children's Menu: Yes.
Cuisine: Seafood/American.
Liquor: Beer and wine.
Serving: L, D.
Credit Cards: AE, D, DC, MC, V.
Handicap Access: No.
Reservations: No.

This is the original Lazy Flamingo, which has spawned another on Sanibel's south end and others along the south coast. Look for a Pepto-Bismol-pink building at Blind Pass, just before the bridge to Captiva. Neighborhood and nautical are the concepts behind this first Flamingo, where you order and pick up your own food at the counter, eat off disposable plastic plates in the shape of scallop shells, and wipe your hands with paper towels on a roll at the table. The menu and ambiance have an essence of the Florida Keys; the owners even lifted the idea of a popular ring-and-hook game from a bar down there. Conch salad, conch fritters, clam pot, mesquite-grilled grouper sandwich, wings, prime rib sandwich, Caesar salad, and chocolate key lime cheesecake are some of the most popular menu items. Avoid the Dead Parrot Wings; they are inedible to all but the most calloused. Most of the meals come with fries, but you can substitute a small Caesar salad, which is usually tasty. The place is small: about a dozen counter seats and a few booths. For the same food, but more room, shrimp-boat decor, and table service, try the one at 1036 Periwinkle Way, 941-472-6939. Both are designated smoking areas in their entirety.

MATZALUNA
941-472-1998.
1200 Periwinkle Way.
Price: Moderate to Expensive.
Children's Menu: Yes.
Cuisine: Italian.
Liquor: Full.

This is one of those Italian restaurants with butcher paper on the table so the server can write his/her name in crayon and the kids can play artist or hangman, or whatever. The wood-fired oven pizza is terrific, even the kids' version. Adult pizzas are creative; try the Con Pollo Barbecue with wood-roasted chicken and pine nuts or the Cinque

Serving: D.
Credit Cards: AE, CB, D,
DC, MC, V.
Handicap Access: Yes.
Reservations: No.

Formaggi with five cheeses, spinach, and artichoke hearts. Plus there's a full array of Italian pasta, veal, chicken, and seafood dishes from which to choose, including design-your-own options. Pay special attention to the changing nightly specials for something creatively tasty. Dinner begins with complimentary roasted fresh garlic and olive oil and crusty bread. Nice touch. As is so chic these days, much of the decor consists of huge cans and jars of olives, marinara sauce, and other products. Big comfy booths are separated by giant wooden garlic cloves, bell peppers, tomatoes, and such. Black-and-white checkered tiles offset dark varnished wood for an interesting effect. Italian music plays in the background. Upstairs you may be able to spy the resident alligator from the back windows.

**McT's SHRIMP HOUSE &
TAVERN**
941-472-3161.
1523 Periwinkle Way.
Price: Moderate.
Early Dining Menu: Yes.
Children's Menu: Yes.
Cuisine: Seafood.
Healthy Selections: No.
Liquor: Full.
Serving: D.
Credit Cards: AE, CB, D,
DC, MC, V.
Handicap Access: Yes.
Reservations: No.

This place has been popular for years. My only problem with it is that it hasn't changed its approach to cuisine in all those years. What passed off as creative 15 years ago has become passé: huge portions, fat-laden dishes, canned products. But as they say, if it isn't broken . . . McT's made its reputation on all-you-can-eat shrimp, which is served steamed and in the shell. Fifteen other shrimp entrées range from classic fried shrimp to Zydeco Tous Pa Tous shrimp (Cajun style). Then there are other seafood and meat dishes and nightly specials for those less than fanatical about shrimp. The setting is nice — a lot of latticework and French doors, old island style. In the bar, where you're bound to wait for seating, upside-down trees support the roof. Mud pie for dessert is a tradition; at one time that was all the restaurant offered. Today it's supplemented with fresh-baked goodies.

**RIVIERA RESTAURANT
& LOUNGE**
941-472-1141.
2761 W. Gulf Dr.
Price: Expensive.
Early Dining Menu: No.
Children's Menu: No.
Cuisine: Mediterranean.
Liquor: Full.
Healthy Selections: No.
Serving: D.
Credit Cards: AE, MC, V.
Handicap Access: Yes.
Reservations: Yes.

This actually feels like going to the Riviera. The mood is set by tasteful mahogany, dark wood rafters, and a red barrel-tile "roof" over the bar. A single stem of sunflower brightens each table. The best surprise about the menu is that it reaches beyond the typical narrow definition of Mediterranean as strictly Italian and French, by using lamb, couscous, baba ganoush, and other North African contributions, and paella from Spain. It also reaches beyond the classic into the realm of cutting edge. The baba ganoush comes with the subtly spiced house bread. On the appetizer board, the baked oysters are the house's

Special Features: Live
piano.

rendition of oysters Rockefeller, but with ouzo instead of Pernod. Excellent! The beef carpaccio also improves upon the traditional, served with arugula, grilled portabella mushroom, and parmesan. Pasta, fish, poultry, and meat entrées get treated to exotic touches and side dishes. The yellowfin tuna, for instance, is crusted with hazelnut and served with polenta. Artichoke ratatouille accompanies the veal loin chop, which is grilled with roasted garlic and served with sage jus. Chicken Riviera is stuffed with Montrachet cheese, spinach, green peppercorns, and basmati rice. Sauces are exquisite. I ordered the day's surf-and-turf special, Florida lobster tail topped with a light orange sauce and a filet mignon with a full-flavored brown sauce. The roasted vegetables on the side complemented perfectly. The crisp duckling, in "cherry" condition, got thumbs up from my duck-loving husband. The only slight disappointment was the soufflé, which was light as light could be but too light on the orange and hazelnut flavors it promised. The key lime pie, with its layer of sliced strawberries between pie and real whipped cream, was a definite hit. The Riviera is quickly becoming the choice of island connoisseurs. If you enjoy a flawless martini, sit at the bar and revel in the ritual that precedes the final product.

TIMBERS RESTAURANT & FISH MARKET

941-472-3128.
703 Tarpon Bay Rd.
Price: Moderate.
Early Dining Menu: No.
Children's Menu: Yes.
Cuisine: Seafood and steaks.
Liquor: Full.
Serving: D.
Credit Cards: AE, CB, D, DC, MC, V.
Handicap Access: Yes.
Reservations: No.
Special Features: Sanibel Grill, an affordable, casual sports bar and grill.

For lovers of fine steaks and seafood, the Timbers' formula works well. Its regular menu spells out the classic in both. Nothing fancy, no surprises (with the exception of the slightly bizarre addition of Pepperidge Farm goldfish to the salad), only fresh product prepared just right. Each night the standards are complemented by a long list of fresh catches and daily specials that depend upon what comes into the fish market that day. These display a little more creativity but on the whole give fish lovers what they want most — pure, unadulterated seafood, simply broiled, fried, or char-grilled. The fish theme is taken to its extreme at The Timbers. You find them not only in your salad but on managers' ties and brocaded into the booths, and more subtly in the old fish-wharf motif of the newly renovated interior. Market umbrellas (inside!), tin roofs, crab crates, and bamboo set the mood for seafood that tastes as though it just flopped up on shore.

WINDOWS ON THE WATER

941-395-6014.
Sundial Beach Resort, 1451 Middle Gulf Dr.

Oddly enough, few restaurants in this town surrounded by water offer water views. Windows maximizes its location overlooking Sundial Resort's main swimming pool and the

Price: Very Expensive.
Children's Menu: Yes.
Cuisine: Seafood/
   Floribbean.
Healthy Selections: At
   lunch only.
Liquor: Full.
Serving: B, L, D, SB.
Credit Cards: AE, D, MC, V.
Handicap Access: Yes.
Reservations: Yes.
Special Features: Gulf view.

beach beyond by stepping the tables. The menu is always interesting at Windows, though overpriced on some items. Seafood and Floribbean style prevail. Bronzing is a trademark of sorts here, where blackening and Cajun methods were first introduced to the area. The bronzed grouper, for example, is prepared with a milder mix of spices and a lighter touch in the sauté pan than is used in traditional blackening. It comes with a garlic red wine sauce that is a bit heavier than it sounds but truly delightful. We also sampled a special shrimp appetizer, which was served on a potato pancake with Grand Marnier sauce, crisp-fried fresh spinach, and filets of yellow and red tomato. It was followed by a main course of rich lobster tart that was dreamy. Other regular menu offerings are salmon with a fruit glaze, seared snapper topped with carrot sauvignon blanc sauce, and shrimp, scallops, and lobster cream sauce tossed into lemon cilantro pasta. Meals start out with sourdough bread shipped from San Francisco and complemented with red pepper jelly. The house balsamic vinaigrette, thick like French dressing, is said to contain roasted shallots, but the balsamic overwhelms that subtle flavor. The changing lunch menu entices with roasted pork tenderloin taco salad, turkey focaccia, garlic rosemary grilled portabella mushroom, and other departures from the traditional club-and-burger selection. For dessert, we selected the chocolate bayou cake — a thin slice of chocolate cake wading in a pool of heavy cream sauce, topped with hot fudge — with no regrets.

FOOD PURVEYORS

BAKERIES

Andre's French Bakery (941-482-2011; Bridge Plaza, 12901 McGregor Blvd., Fort Myers) Small but chock-full of treats *francaises*: baguettes, great olive bread, cookies, sublime tortes, and custard-filled pastries.

Steve's Bagels (941-561-3009; 6900 Daniels Pkwy., Fort Myers) Declared the best by bagel aficionados, it sells 23 different varieties of New York-style, water-kettled bagels.

CANDY & ICE CREAM

Ben & Jerry's Ice Cream & Frozen Yogurt (941-936-4155; 12995 S. Cleveland Ave., Fort Myers)

Pinocchio's (941-472-6566; 362 Periwinkle Way, Sanibel Island) Homemade Italian ice cream and yogurt, cappuccino, espresso, and frozen coffee drinks.

The Purple Cow (941-992-3888; 4836 Bonita Beach Rd. SW, Bonita Springs)

More than 45 flavors of gourmet ice cream, yogurt, sorbet, and sugar-free and fat-free ice cream.

COFFEE

The Bean (941-395-1919; 2240 Periwinkle Way, Sanibel Island) Sanibel's wildly popular buzz shop, it serves the usual espresso, cappuccino, and latte selection, plus bagels, scones, frozen yogurt, Italian gelato, sandwiches, and eggs.

French Roast Cafe (941-936-2233; Outback Plaza, Fort Myers) Gourmet beans and blends, tasting tables, and a breakfast, lunch, and dinner menu.

DELI & SPECIALTY FOODS

Barney's Incredible Edibles (941-472-2555; 2330 Palm Ridge Rd., Sanibel Island) Bakery and deli specializing in croissants, stuffed croissants, and croissant-wiches. Also: muffins, cookies, cakes, pizza, and gourmet groceries.

C.W.'s Market & Deli (941-472-5111; South Seas Plantation Resort, Captiva) Small grocer with wine, deli meats, breads, coffee beans, and other gourmet items.

Jamaican Delites (941-337-5448; 3901 Dr. Martin Luther King Jr. Blvd., downtown Fort Myers) Island ingredients and specialties.

Mario's Italian Market (941-936-7275; 12377 Cleveland Ave., Fort Myers) Delicious homemade Italian cheeses, sauces, pastas, and prepared foods.

Oriental & Tai Grocery (941-936-0916; 3258 Cleveland Ave., Fort Myers) Fresh and packaged ingredients.

FRUIT & VEGETABLE STANDS

Roadside food stands sell local produce and fish at below supermarket prices and above supermarket freshness.

For the freshest produce, visit the plentiful roadside stands along the coast. Some feature U-Pick options, especially for tomatoes and strawberries.

Gladiolus Farm Market (941-489-0501; 8591 Gladiolus Dr., Fort Myers) Open-air fruit and vegetable stand in the middle of a tomato field. You can't help but trust the freshness of its products.

Mango Street Market (Estero Blvd. at Mango St., Fort Myers Beach) Roadside stand selling fresh produce.

Rodes Fresh & Fancy (941-992-4040; 3998 Bonita Beach Rd. SW, Bonita Beach) Fresh produce and local seafood stand.

Sunburst Tropical Fruit Company (941-283-1200; 7113 Howard Rd., Bokeelia, Pine Island) One of the oldest island groves, it specializes in mangoes, but also grows carambola, lychee, and other exotics, and sells fruit products and its own cookbook.

Sun Harvest Citrus (941-768-2686 or 800-743-1480; 14810 Metro Pkwy. S. at Six Mile Cypress, Fort Myers) Part tourist attraction, part citrus stand, it offers free samples, tours, demonstrations, a playground, and a gift shop.

Fruitful Islands

For those in the know, Pine Island is synonymous with exotic fruit. Guavas once grew wild throughout the island, brought to this subtropical land from the tropical Caribbean. Later, mangoes flourished. The only other place in Florida where tropical fruits grow in such abundance is Homestead, on the east coast, at a latitude some 90 miles south of Pine Island.

What makes Pine Island so nearly tropical? The warm waters of Charlotte Harbor run wide at the island's north end, around Bokeelia. They insulate the land, warming cold air before it reaches fragile fruit groves. Longans, sapodillas, carambolas, lychees, and other rare treats thrive as a result of this pocket of climate. Fructose freaks from miles around make a pilgrimage to roadside stands along Pine Island, Stringfellow, and Pineland roads throughout the summer and fall.

NATURAL FOODS

Ada's Natural Foods Market (941-936-4756; 3418 Fowler St., Fort Myers) Organic produce and other healthy foods. Licensed nutritionist on staff.

Healthy Habits (941-278-4442; 11763 S. Cleveland Ave., Fort Myers) Organic produce, dairy products, and other natural groceries.

Island Health Foods (941-472-3666; 1640 Periwinkle Way, Sanibel Island) Complete line of food and beauty products, plus sandwiches, frozen yogurt, and carrot juice.

PIZZA & TAKEOUT

Bullfeathers (941-395-1133; 2407 Periwinkle Way, Sanibel Island) Specializing in ribs and wings, with a wide range of other individual and family-pack selections.

Hickory Bar-B-Q (941-481-2626; 15400 McGregor Blvd., Fort Myers) Hickory smoking, a secret sauce, creamy cole slaw, and fresh coconut cream pie make this my favorite barbecue around.

Johnny's Pizza (941-472-3010; 2496 Palm Ridge Rd., Sanibel Island) Carryout and free delivery. Regular, gourmet, and deep-dish pizza, plus Italian subs and specialties.

Juicy Lucy's (941-454-0319; 17260 San Carlos Blvd., Fort Myers Beach) One of a local chain of burger joints.

Mama Rosa's Pizzeria (941-472-7672; Chadwick's Square, Captiva Island) Subs, pizza, stromboli, calzone, and salads.

Plaka I on the Beach (941-463-4707; 1001 Estero Blvd., Fort Myers Beach) Gyros, spinach pie, moussaka, and baklava in a screened-in dining room near the beach.

Taste of N.Y. Pizzeria & Subs (941-278-3222; 2215-B Winkler Ave., Fort Myers) Take-out or eat-in pizza — regular, vegetarian, gourmet, and white — and other New York-Italian specialties.

SEAFOOD

Beach Shrimp Packers (941-463-8777; 1100 Shrimp Boat Ln., San Carlos Island, Fort Myers Beach) Fresh seafood at its source, specializing in shrimp — fresh, steamed, and dinners.

Pine Bay Seafood Market (941-283-7100; 4330 Pine Island Rd., Matlacha, Pine Island) Fresh and smoked fish and shellfish from the area's major transshipment center.

Rodes Fresh & Fancy (941-992-4040; 3998 Bonita Beach Rd. SW, Bonita Beach) Fresh produce and local seafood stand.

Skip One Seafood (941-482-0433; 15820 S. Tamiami Trail, San Carlos Park) Fresh catches, sandwiches, and seafood for eat-in, takeout, or delivery.

CULTURE

For many years the Island Coast was considered a cultural limbo, void of any strong artistic or regional identity, except for a certain retiree/midwestern influence. Still lagging behind Sarasota and Naples in that department, the region nonetheless is making inroads toward "artsification." The population, furthermore, is beginning to diversify in terms of ethnicity and age.

The populations of Cape Coral and North Fort Myers include many nationalities — Italian, German, Jamaican, and Hispanic — that share their customs at social clubs, restaurants, festivals, and other places. Throughout Fort Myers, Afro-Americans, Asians, East Indians, Europeans, and other ethnic groups heighten the cosmopolitan flavor. Flashes of southern spirit and Cracker charm survive in the less resorty areas of North Fort Myers and Pine Island.

The islands along the coast have inspired their share of creativity. Singer Jimmy Buffett frequents Cabbage Key and Captiva Island. His brand of beachy folk song is the closest thing the Gulf Coast has to homegrown music.

One of the few arts that residents can truly call their own is shell art, a form that flourishes on Sanibel Island, Florida's ultimate shell island. In its highest form, shell art can be stunning and delicate; in its lowest, it can result in some pretty tacky shell animals.

Wealthy visitors to Sanibel and Captiva have exerted an influence on the fine arts through the years. The illustrious roll call began in the 1920s with Charles and Anne Morrow Lindbergh. Edna St. Vincent Millay's original manuscript for *Conversation at Midnight* burned in a hotel fire. Today Robert Rauschenberg, a maverick in the field of photographic lithography, is the Island Coast's impresario.

ARCHITECTURE

Fort Myers is home to some lovely architecture downtown and along McGregor Boulevard. Thomas Edison's home was, perhaps, Florida's first prefab structure. Because wood and materials were scarce (most newcomers made do with palmetto huts), Edison commissioned a Maine architect to draw up plans and construct sections of the home to be shipped down and pieced together on site. Downtown, the Richard Building, circa 1924, boasts an Italian influence, while the courthouse annex superbly represents Mediterranean Revival. So does the Miles Building, built in 1926 by Dr. Franklin Miles, the "father of Alka-Seltzer." The new Harborside Convention Center and other recent constructions echo the motif.

Pine Island possesses the best, most concentrated collection of preserved vernacular architecture, especially in Matlacha. Pineland's mound-squatting homes are also prime examples, occasionally dressed up with latticework and vivid paint jobs.

Indian mounds and Cracker houses make for a scenic, history-saturated drive through the community of Pineland on Pine Island.

Greg Wagner

In Bokeelia, the entire Main Street is designated a historic district. Notice especially the Captain's House, a fine example of slightly upscale folk housing of the early 1900s, with French Provincial elements. Nearby Turner Mansion represents a higher standard of living and is reminiscent of New England styles.

The club at Useppa Island, which nonguests can view only by boat, is a prime collection of Old Florida styles, both traditional and revival.

On Sanibel Island, side trips down shell-named streets such as Coquina Drive and King's Crown take you into residential areas, where styles range from renovated Cracker cottages to stately Victorian mansions. Even Art Deco dwellings are popping up, despite islanders' attempts to keep out what they call incompatible styles.

CINEMA

MOVIE THEATHERS

Bell Tower 20 (941-936-8680; Daniels Pkwy. and U.S. 41, Fort Myers) A modern megacomplex of theaters.

Coralwood 10 (941-936-8680; Coralwood Mall, Del Prado Blvd., Cape Coral)

Island Cinema (941-472-1701; Bailey's Shopping Center, 535 Tarpon Bay Rd., Sanibel) A two-screen theater showing first-run films.

Merchants Crossing 16 (941-995-1191; 15201 N. Cleveland Ave., North Fort Myers) State-of-the-art complex.

DANCE

Caloosa River Cloggers (941-542-2066; Fort Myers Activity Center, 2646 Cleveland Ave., Fort Myers) Perpetuators of a southern/mountain folk dance performed usually at festivals.

Dance Ensemble of Southwest Florida (941-768-1144; Accent on Dance, 12155 Metro Pkwy. #18) Classes and performance of tap, jazz, ballet, lyrical, clogging, and pointe dance for children.

Dance Theatre Academy (941-275-3131; 2084 Beacon Manor Dr., Fort Myers) Ballet and interpretative dance for adults and children.

Hall of Fifty States (941-334-7637; Harborside Complex, 2254 Edwards Dr., downtown Fort Myers) Hosts ballroom and country-and-western dancing.

GARDENS

FRAGRANCE GARDEN OF LEE COUNTY
941-432-2000.
Lakes Regional Park, 7330 Gladiolus Rd., Fort Myers.
Open: 8–6 daily.

Located at the park's west end, the garden was designed primarily for the disabled, although the general public also will enjoy this one-of-a-kind attraction. For the visually impaired there are pungent herbs, fragrant vines, and signs in braille. Paved paths with vegetation planted at wheel-

Parking: 75¢ per hour or $3 per day.

chair height accommodate the physically handicapped. Vined arbors are built wide enough for easy wheelchair access.

HISTORIC HOMES & SITES

BURROUGHS HOME
941-332-6125.
2505 First St., downtown
Fort Myers.
Open: Tours conducted
every hour on the hour
11–3 Tues.–Fri.
Admission: $3.18 adults,
$1.06 children 6–12.

Mona and Jettie Burroughs, in 1918 dress, host the living-history tour at Fort Myers' first luxury residence. Tour guides in period costume assume the playful characters of two sisters who once occupied the Georgian Revival-style mansion built in 1901. They'll invite you to add a few stitches to the afghan they're knitting for the war effort, then take you back in time to when cowboys drove cattle past their home and the Henry Fords hosted square dances. Authentically restored furniture and appointments provide a charming backdrop to this improv pageant on the banks of the Caloosahatchee River.

CHAPEL-BY-THE-SEA
941-472-1646.
11580 Chapin, Captiva
Island.

This quaint church is a popular spot for interdenominational Sunday services, weddings, and seaside meditation. Many of the island's early pioneers were laid to rest in a cemetery beside the chapel.

FISH SHACKS
Pine Island Sound at
Captiva Rocks, east of
North Captiva.

The last artifacts of the region's early commercial fishing enterprises have braved weather and bureaucracy to strut the shallows along the intracoastal waterway. The shack at the mouth of Safety Harbor on North Captiva is the most noticeable. It once served as an icehouse. If you look east you'll spot several others. Privately owned and maintained as weekend fishing homes for local enthusiasts, most are listed in the National Register of Historic Places and serve as a picturesque reminder of days gone by.

**KORESHAN STATE
HISTORIC SITE**
941-992-0311.
Tamiami Trail, Estero.
Hours: 8 am–sunset.
Admission: $3.25 per
vehicle with up to 8
passengers; $1 per cyclist,
pedestrian, or extra
passenger.

Contained within a state park, this site has restored the customs and ways of an early-1900s religious cult that settled on the banks of the Estero River. Under the leadership of Cyrus Teed, whose name in Hebrew is Koresh, members of Koreshan Unity were well versed in practical Christianity, speculative metaphysics, functional and aesthetic gardening, art, Koreshan Cosmogony, and occupational training. Their most unusual theory held that the earth lined the inside of a hollow globe and looked down into the solar system. Teed and his followers envisioned an academic and natural Utopia. They planted their settlement with exotic crops and vegetation. They built a theater, a communal mess hall, a store, and various workshops, all of which have been restored or reconstructed to tell the strange story of the Koreshans, who lost their momentum upon the death of their charismatic leader in 1908. Archives are kept at the Koreshan Unity Foundation and library across the road from the park (941-992-2184).

SANIBEL CEMETERY
Off bike path on Middle
  Gulf Dr., not accessible
  by car.

No signs direct you to it. Just follow the path and you'll come across a fenced plot with wooden headstones announcing the names of early settlers — a wonderful, quiet place to ponder times past.

SANIBEL LIGHTHOUSE
Southeast end of
  Periwinkle Way, Sanibel
  Island.

Built in 1884, the lighthouse was one of the island's first permanent structures. Once vital to cattle transports from the mainland, it still functions as a beacon of warning and welcome. The lighthouse and Old Florida-style light keeper's cottage were renovated in 1991.

Visitors walk through the roots of the nation's largest banyan tree at the Thomas Edison Home.

Karen T. Bartlett

**THOMAS EDISON
  WINTER ESTATE/
  FORD HOME**
941-334-3614.
2350-2400 McGregor Blvd.,
  Fort Myers.
Hours: Continuous tours

Nowhere in the U.S. will you find the homes of two such important historical figures sitting side by side. This site is so much more than just a couple of preserved houses, however. It is a slice of Floridiana, Americana, and Mr. Wizard, all rolled into 17 riverside acres. The 90-minute tour begins

9–3:30 Mon.–Sat., 12–3:30 Sun.; Edison Home only, 4. Tram tours of historical downtown Fort Myers, hourly 10–4 Tues.–Sat.
Admission: $10 adults; $5 children 6–12. Edison Home only: $8 adults; $4 children 6–12. Historical Tram tours: $5 adults; $2 children 6–12.

across the street under the nation's largest banyan tree, a gift from Harvey Firestone. The tree, 400 feet around, poses outside a museum that contains many of Edison's 1,000-plus patented inventions — the phonograph, the movie camera, the light bulb, children's furniture — as well as the 1907 proto-type Model T Ford his friend and wintertime neighbor, Henry Ford, gave him. Edison's late-1880s home hides in a jungle of tropical flora with which Edison experimented. Actually there are two homes, identically built and connected with an arcade. One contained the Edisons' living quarters; the other, guest quarters and the kitchen. His laboratory, full of dusty bottles and other ancient gizmos, sits in the backyard among reflecting pools and gardens. The Friendship Gate separated Edison's estate from Ford's. "The Mangoes," as it was called in honor of the fruit orchards the car manufacturer so loved, seems humble compared to its neighbor. Restoration in 1988 returned it to its turn-of-the-century heyday, with furnishings true to the era and the Fords' simple tastes.

KIDS' STUFF

THE CHILDREN'S SCIENCE CENTER
941-997-0012.
2915 NE Pine Island Rd., Cape Coral.
Open: 9:30–4:30 Mon.–Fri., 12–5 weekends.
Admission: $2 children 3–16, $4 adults.

Encourages visitors of all ages to touch and interact with the exhibits: mind-teaser puzzles, hands-on electrical gadgets, building blocks, Calusa Indian tools, wooden dinosaur skeleton puzzles, a whisper dish, and computer games. There is a nature trail and live snakes, iguanas, tarantulas, and scorpions.

IMAGINARIUM
941-337-3332.
Dr. Martin Luther King Jr. Blvd. and Cranford Ave., Fort Myers.
Open: 10–5 Tues.–Sat.
Closed: Sun., Mon.
Admission: $3 children 3–12 when accompanied by an adult, $6 age 13 and up, $5.50 seniors.

I have visited many of the new-wave interactive science museums that have hit Florida in the past decade, and I'm proud to say this is among my favorites. It is not overwhelmingly huge, like some, but is colorfully attractive and varied in its approach to teaching everything from the effects of chemical abuse to the world of finance. Emphasis is on weather and water (it occupies a former city water plant). The Hurricane Experience will, as they like to say there, "blow you away." You can feel a cloud, tape yourself on location broadcasting a tornado, and walk through a thunderstorm. Aquariums and a touch tank provide a window on local and reef water creatures. Other exhibits appeal to all ages with gadgets, toys, and computers.

Waltz through a thunderstorm at Fort Myers' Imaginarium.

Lee Island Coast Visitor and
Convention Bureau

THE SHELL FACTORY
941-995-2141 or
   800-282-5805.
2787 N. Tamiami Trail,
   North Fort Myers.
Admission: Shell Factory
   free; railroad museum $1;
   bumper boat rides $4.

A shell shop on steroids, this longtime attraction has grown into a megacomplex with bumper boats, historic railroad museum, "Waltzing Waters" lighted fountain shows, stuffed African animal collection, aquariums, and lots of souvenir shops carrying gifts from fine to tacky.

MUSEUMS

BAILEY-MATTHEWS
   SHELL MUSEUM
941-395-2233.
3075 Sanibel-Captiva Rd.,
   Sanibel Island.
Open: 10–4 Tues.–Sun.
Admission: $3 children
   8–17, $5 17 and up.

The only one of its kind in the U.S., this museum reinforces Sanibel's reputation as a top shell-collecting destination. Opened in 1995, it uses nature vignettes and artistically arranged displays to demonstrate the role of shells in ecology, history, art, economics, medicine, religion, and other fields. Centerpiece of the museum is a globe, six feet in diameter, surrounded by shells of the world. Outside is a memorial devoted to the late actor Raymond Burr, who helped establish the museum. New to the museum is the Children's Learning Lab, opened in 1997 for hands-on learning experiences in colorful reef-motif surroundings. The museum holds many shells — from the land and fresh water as well as from the sea.

CAPE CORAL
   HISTORICAL MUSEUM
941-772-7037.
544 Cultural Park Blvd.,
   Cape Coral.
Open: 1–4 Weds., Thurs.,
   Sun.

Burrowing owls, shells, fossils, and antiques comprise the headlining exhibits at this small facility. Also rotating collections on loan.

**CAPTIVA HISTORY
 HOUSE**
941-472-5111.
Entrance to South Seas
 Plantation resort, Captiva
 Island.
Hours: 10–4.
Closed: Mon., Sat.

This tiny museum occupies a 1920s cottage that originally served as a plantation worker's home back when key limes were farmed. Through photographs, memorabilia, and storyboards, the museum relates the history of Captiva Island, from prehistoric man through the farming and fishing eras of the early 1900s. A docent portrays C. W. Chadwick, plantation founder and inventor of the Checkwriter machine.

Greg Wagner

A classic example of a Cracker house in its most basic form can be viewed at the Fort Myers Historical Museum.

**FORT MYERS
 HISTORICAL
 MUSEUM**
941-332-5955.
2300 Peck St. (at Jackson
 St.), Fort Myers.
Open: 9–4 Tues.–Sat.
Closed: Sun., Mon.
Admission: $4 adults, $2
 children 3–12.

Housed in a handsome, restored railroad depot, the museum's displays take you back to the days of the Calusa Indians and through the eras of Spanish exploration, fish camps, gladiolus farming, and World War II training with well-arranged scale models, graphic depictions, and interactive historical games. Outdoors, tours examine an early-1900s replica of a local Cracker house and the world's last and longest Pullman private railcar, circa 1930.

**MUSEUM OF THE
 ISLANDS**
941-283-1525.
5728 Sesame Dr., Pine Island
 Center, Pine Island.
Open: 10–4.
Closed: Fri. in winter, more
 days in off-season.
Admission: Donations
 accepted.

Occupying the old Pine Island library at Phillips Park, the museum concentrates on the area's Calusa heritage. In 1992 it unveiled a shell mound replica modeled after one excavated on the island. Continue on to the settlement of Pineland to see time standing still upon intact native American mounds.

SANIBEL HISTORICAL VILLAGE & MUSEUM
941-472-4648.
850 Dunlop Rd., near City Hall, Sanibel Island.
Open: 10–4 Weds.–Sat.; also 1–4 Sun. mid-Dec.–Apr.
Closed: Mid-Aug.–mid-Oct.
Admission: $2 donation per adult requested.

The village began with a historical Cracker-style abode, once the home of an island pioneer. The museum focuses on Sanibel's modern history of homesteading, citrus farming, steamboating, and tourism, with photos and artifacts, and recalls the Calusa era with a dugout canoe and other relics of the times. The island's original Bailey's General Store, circa 1927, was moved to the site in 1993 as a kickoff to establishing a pioneer village on the grounds. Since then, a 1920s post office, a teahouse, and another vintage home have been added. The latter houses a lens that outfitted the Sanibel Lighthouse in the 1960s.

USEPPA MUSEUM
941-283-1061.
Useppa Island Club, Useppa Island.
Admission: $2.50 donation requested for visitors over age 18.

The wee island of Useppa is stuffed to the gills with history, a fact that calls for a historic museum. This one is exceptionally well presented for such a small place. (It helps that wealth out-measures square footage on the island.) Dioramas are interpreted via taped presentations you hear from small tape recorders and headsets. They describe the island's Calusa history, its fishing and resort eras, and its role in training revolutionaries for the Cuban Bay of Pigs confrontation in 1960. Since the island is owned by a private club, visitors must be island guests or guests aboard the *Lady Chadwick* luncheon cruise to the island (see Captiva Cruises under "Sightseeing & Entertainment Cruises" in this chapter).

MUSIC & NIGHTLIFE

Downtown Fort Myers is slowly metamorphosing into a hot new entertainment district, featuring jazz bars, bistros, night clubs, and Thursdays on First Street Sunset Celebration with free outdoor concerts from 5:30 to 8:30 pm. As for the islands, Fort Myers Beach is definitely the hoppingest. On Sanibel and Captiva, you'll find a quieter brand of partying; nightlife there is focused on theater and more highbrow forms of music. Friday's *Gulf Coasting* supplement to the *News-Press* covers the Island Coast's entertainment scene.

Captiva Island

Crow's Nest Lounge (941-472-5161; 'Tween Waters Inn, Captiva Rd.) Live contemporary dance bands Tuesday through Sunday. The islands' hottest spot.

Fort Myers

Casa Cabana (941-278-5533; Toys "R" Us Plaza, 2158 Colonial Blvd.) Salsa and merengue music and dancing lessons.

Cigar Bar (941-337-4662; 1502 Hendry St., downtown) Smokers' haven with air-filtering system, 100 brands of premium, humidored cigars, and specialty martinis and cocktails.

Jazz Alliance (941-939-2787; Lee County Alliance of the Arts headquarters, 10091 McGregor Blvd.) Sponsors a series of limited-attendance outdoor concerts featuring name artists, fine wine, and specialty foods.

Peter's La Cuisine (941-332-2228; 2224 Bay St., downtown) In a restored warehouse above a restaurant, it spotlights blues bands in a cozy setting.

Seminole Gulf Railway (800-SEM-GULF; Colonial Blvd. and Metro Pkwy.) Among its schedule of excursion, dinner, and themed train rides, it offers an evening Thursday Jazz Train, and Dinner and Murder Mystery Trains.

Shooter's Waterfront Cafe (941-334-2727; Holiday Inn Sunspree, 2220 W. First St.) A lively spot on the river with chickee bar, live and deejay music, and party boat cruises.

Southwest Florida Symphony (941-481-4849; Barbara B. Mann Performing Arts Center, Edison Community College campus, 8099 College Pkwy. SW) Performs classical and pops series November through April.

Fort Myers Beach

The Bridge Restaurant (941-765-0050; 708 Fisherman's Wharf) A popular spot with boat-in and drive-in barflies, featuring lively dance music outdoors on the docks.

Lani Kai Island Resort (941-463-3111; 1400 Estero Blvd.) The premier collegiate party spot on the beach, with live entertainment nightly and during the day on weekends, on the rooftop or on the beach.

Sanibel Island

Jacaranda (941-472-1771; 1223 Periwinkle Way) Top 40 hits, reggae, and island music performed live.

SPECIALTY LIBRARIES

Sanibel Public Library (941-472-2483; 770 Dunlop Rd., Sanibel Island) Contains an identification collection of seashells.

Talking Books Library (941-995-2665; 1324 N. Cleveland Ave., North Fort Myers) Library for the blind and physically handicapped, with books on tapes or records.

THEATER

The Arcade Theatre (941-338-2244; 2267 First St., downtown Fort Myers) The glory of the 1920s, this Victorian playhouse has been restored and advanced to the 21st century. Home to the **New Arts Festival, Gay and Lesbian Chorus, Gulf Coast Dance Company, Naples Philharmonic Chamber Orchestra, Palm Coast Youth Symphony,** and **Theatre Conspiracy.**

Barbara B. Mann Performing Arts Center (941-481-4849; Edison Community College campus, 8099 College Pkwy. SW, Fort Myers) Host to major Broadway shows, musical performers, and dance troupes. Season runs September to late April.

Broadway Palm Dinner Theatre (941-278-4422; Royal Palm Square, 1380 Colonial Blvd.) Lunch and dinner performances, primarily musicals, starring professional actors in a made-over grocery store that seats and serves 448. Its **Off-Broadway Palm Theatre** presents cabaret-style shows in an adjacent, intimate 125-seat playhouse.

Clairborne & Ned Foulds Theater (941-939-2787; Lee County Alliance of the Arts headquarters, 10091 McGregor Blvd., Fort Myers) An indoor and outdoor stage for recitals, concerts, and workshops. Theatre Conspiracy, a professional troupe, performs part of its season here, as does the **Gulf Coast Opera** and the **Edison Community College Theatre**.

Cultural Park Theatre (941-574-0465; 528 Cultural Park Blvd., Cape Coral) A 187-seat theater that hosts **Cape Coral Community Theatre** and **Cultural Park Theatre Project**.

Old Schoolhouse Theater (941-472-6862; 1905 Periwinkle Way, Sanibel Island) Installed in the charming setting of a historic schoolhouse circa 1896, this 96-seat theater-in-the-round has served for years as the island's cultural mainstay. In its current reincarnation it hosts **J. T. Smith Musical Productions,** a professional troupe, in season, and **Off-Beach Players,** a community theater group, during the summer.

Pirate Playhouse (941-472-0006; 2200 Periwinkle Way, Sanibel Island) Professional actors present mainstage comedies, musicals, and drama in two seasons on a stage adaptable to proscenium, theater-in-the-round, and thrust configurations.

VISUAL ART CENTERS

Flocks of wildlife and other eclectic galleries make a name for Sanibel Island in cultural circles, while smaller communities support their own offbeat galleries and art associations. The following entries introduce you to opportunities for experiencing art as either a viewer or a practicing artist. A listing of commercial galleries is included in the "Shopping" section.

Pirate Playhouse stages professional comedies and dramas in an intimate setting.

Karen T. Bartlett

BIG Arts (941-395-0900; 900 Dunlop Rd., Sanibel Island) Home of Barrier Island Group for the Arts, a multidisciplinary organization. Art shows and classes are scheduled regularly at the facility.

Cape Coral Arts Studio (941-574-0802; 4533 Coronado Pkwy.) Exhibitions and sales.

Cultural Park Theatre Fine Arts Gallery (941-574-0465; 516 Cultural Park Blvd., Cape Coral) Rotating exhibits of local art.

Fort Myers Beach Art Association (941-463-3909; Donora St. and Shell Mound Blvd., Fort Myers Beach)

Gallery of Fine Arts (941-489-9313; Edison Community College, 8099 College Pkwy., Fort Myers) Exhibits works of nationally and internationally renowned artists.

Lee County Alliance of the Arts (941-939-2787; William Frizzell Cultural Center, 10091 McGregor Blvd., Fort Myers) Operates a public gallery, theater, and outdoor stage, and conducts classes and workshops. Home to Theatre Conspiracy troupe and most local arts and cultural groups. It sponsors the First Friday Gallery Walk on the first Friday of each month.

RECREATION

Shelling, island-hopping, fishing, and warming chilled bones on hospitable beaches: These are a few of the favorite things to do along the Island Coast.

BEACHES

Local beaches are known for their natural state and their abundance of shells. Most charge for parking. Sanibel Island beach stickers can be purchased and allow you to park for free at most accesses. Along the gulf drives you will see signs at beach accesses designating sticker-only parking. Cyclists and walk-ins, however, can take advantage of these accesses without stickers. For more information about beach stickers, call 941-472-9075.

**BAREFOOT BEACH
PRESERVE**
941-353-0404.
Entrance at Hickory Blvd.
and Bonita Beach Rd.,
south end of Little
Hickory Island.
Facilities: Rest rooms,
showers, nature
interpretation stations,
snack bar.

The preserve holds 342 acres that contain a coastal hammock and 8,200 feet of beach and low dunes. Native vegetation landscapes the grounds. Good shelling.

Happy-go-lucky on Bonita Beach.

Karen T. Bartlett

BONITA PUBLIC BEACH
941-338-3300.
South end Hickory Blvd.,
Little Hickory Island.
Facilities: Picnic tables, new
rest rooms and snack
pavilion, lifeguard,
water-sports rentals,
nearby restaurants.
Parking: 75¢ per hour.

The only true public area on Bonita Beach, it becomes lively during high season and on weekends. Water sports and volleyball, plus a hamburger and bar joint, reflect a youthful spirit. Vegetation is sparse; there's nothing hidden about this beach. Parking fills up early in season and on weekends year-round. About 10 other accesses with free but limited parking line Hickory Boulevard to the north.

BOWDITCH BEACH
941-338-3300.

This pretty, green, 17-acre park fronts Estero Bay and the gulf. It's a nice, quiet beach, underuti-

North end of Estero Blvd.,
Fort Myers Beach.
Facilities: Picnic area, rest
rooms, showers, small
playground, hiking
paths.
Parking: Visitors must park
at a Park and Ride lot just
north of the Matanzas
Pass high bridge and
take a trolley to the
beach.

lized and unspoiled because of the parking situa-
tion. County, city, and private entities, however,
are working to change all that so the beach is more
accessible. Currently it's a favorite of boat-ins.

BOWMAN'S BEACH
Bowman's Beach Rd. off
Sanibel-Captiva Rd.,
Sanibel Island.
Facilities: Picnic area, rest
rooms.
Parking: 75¢ per hour.

Once known to naturalists as Sanibel's nude
beach, Bowman's reputation has been altered
by strict enforcement. Because it is county-owned,
it's the only Sanibel beach that forbids alcohol. It is
also Sanibel's most natural beach, long, coved, and
edged by an Australian pine forest, on a sort of
island all its own. It can be reached by footbridges
from the parking lot (a rather long walk, so go light
on the beach paraphernalia). Shells are plentiful here — in some places a foot
or more deep along the high-tide mark.

CAPTIVA BEACH
North end Captiva Rd.,
Captiva Island.

Only early arrivals get the parking spots for this
prime spread of deep, shelly sand. It's a good
place to watch a sunset.

CAYO COSTA ISLAND STATE PARK
941-964-0375.
La Costa Island, accessible
only by boat.
Facilities: Picnic ground,
rest rooms, showers, bike
rentals.
Admission: $2 per family.

The Island Coast is blessed with some true getaway beaches, untamed by connection to the
mainland. On these, one can actually realize that
romantic fantasy common to beach connoisseurs —
sands all your own. Cayo Costa stretches seven
miles long and is most secluded at its southern
extremes. A larger population of beachers congre-
gates at the north end, where docks and a picnic
and camping ground attract those who seek creature comforts with their sun and sand. Shelling is
superb in these parts.

LAKES PARK
941-432-2017.
7330 Gladiolus Dr., Fort
Myers.
Facilities: Picnic areas, rest
rooms, showers,

This land of freshwater lakes features a small
sand beach with a roped-off swimming area. A
great place for the family to spend the day, it offers
canoeing, paddleboating, fishing, nature and bike
trails, an exercise course, an observation tower, a

playgrounds, model railroad ride, fitness trail, bike path, water-sports rentals, restaurant.
Parking: 75¢ an hour or $3 a day.

LIGHTHOUSE BEACH
941-472-9075.
South end of Periwinkle Way, Sanibel Island.
Facilities: Picnic area, rest rooms, nature trail, fishing pier.

LOVER'S KEY/CARL JOHNSON STATE RECREATION AREA
941-463-4588.
Route 865 between Fort Myers Beach and Bonita Beach.
Facilities: Picnic area, rest rooms, showers, boat ramps, canoe and kayak rentals, concessions in season.
Parking: $4 per vehicle with up to 8 passengers, $2 for single passengers, and $1 for extra passengers, bicyclists, and pedestrians.

LYNN HALL MEMORIAL PARK
941-338-3300.
Times Square vicinity, Estero Blvd., Fort Myers Beach.
Facilities: Picnic areas, rest rooms, showers, playground, fishing pier, water-sports rentals, nearby restaurants and bars.
Admission: Fee for parking. (*Warning:* Park in designated areas or your car will be towed at great expense.)

miniature train ride (admission), and terrific playground facilities within 277 heavily vegetated acres. The quality of the water is questionable, since the lakes — erstwhile quarries — are stagnant.

S kirting Sanibel's historic lighthouse is an arc of natural beach fronting both the gulf and San Carlos Bay. One of Sanibel's most populated beaches, its highlights include a nature trail and a fishing pier. Strong currents forbid swimming off the point. The wide beach gives way to sea oats, sea grapes, and Australian pine edging. I like the neighborhood around it — more laid-back than other parts of the island.

R ide a tram through the natural mangrove environment to a beach very few visitors find. Or you can walk to it. The area between Estero and Little Hickory Island consists of natural island habitat populated by birds, dolphins, and crabs. On the barrier island of Lover's Key, Australian pines provide shaded picnicking along a narrow, natural stretch of sand. A gazebo provides a wedding and picnic venue.

M ost locals know this simply as Fort Myers Beach or "The Beach." Billed as a family destination, it attracts a youthful crowd, especially during spring break. A rocking, rollicking place, it appeals to beach bar-hoppers, crowd-watchers, and those interested in water sports — with loud music, volleyball, a fishing pier, beachside drinks, parties, parasailing, jet skiing, and action, action, action. The sand lends itself perfectly to sculpting and inspires an annual competition (see "Seasonal Events"). For thinner crowds, hit public accesses on the south end of Estero Boulevard.

Fort Myers Beach is known for its bar-hopping scene and sand castles.

Karen T. Bartlett

SANIBEL CAUSEWAY BEACH
941-472-9075.
Sanibel Causeway Rd.
Facilities: Picnic area, rest rooms.

Windsurfers especially favor this packed-sand, roadside beach. It's been dressed up with palms and pines, but it's still noisy, and typically jammed. Beach lovers in RVs and campers often pull up here to picnic and spend the day in the sun.

TARPON BEACH
941-472-9075.
Middle Gulf Dr. at Tarpon Bay Rd., Sanibel Island.
Facilities: Rest rooms, mobile food concession in season.
Parking: 75¢ per hour or $3 per day.

Another popular beach, this one is characterized by sugar sand and a nice spread of shells. It's a bit of a hike from the parking lot to the beach, and the area gets congested on busy days. RVs can park here.

TURNER BEACH
941-472-9075.
South end Captiva Rd., Captiva Island.
Facilities: Rest rooms, nearby restaurants, water sports, and store.

A pretty beach with wide, powdery sands, Turner tends to get crowded, and parking is limited. The entrance is also on a blind curve, which can be dangerous. More bad news: riptides coming through the pass make this taboo for swimming. Park your beach towel north or south of the pass for calmer, swimmable waters. We like to come here in the evening to watch the sunset and walk the beach. Surfers like the area to the north in certain weather. It's also a hot spot for fishermen, who line bayside shores and the bridge between Sanibel and Captiva.

UPPER CAPTIVA
Across Redfish Pass from South Seas Plantation

Like Cayo Costa, here's a place to go for private beaching. The sands are like gold dust, though

and Captiva Island; accessible only by boat.

narrow at the south end, which is state protected. You'll find no facilities unless you venture across the island to the bay, where restaurants and civilization inhabit the north end.

BICYCLING

L ocal officials are recognizing the potential of bicycle transportation in the cities of the future. In response to a growing, vocal segment of bike riders and environmentalists, they are looking at bikeways as one possible solution to pollution and congestion.

The bikeways of the Island Coast come in two varieties. Bicycle paths, the most common, are separated from traffic by distance and, ideally, a vegetation buffer. Bicycle lanes are a designated part of the roadway. Cyclists also take to the road in rural areas, where no bikeways exist but traffic is light. By law they must abide by the same rules as motor vehicles. Children under 16 are required to wear a helmet.

BEST BIKING

Sanibel's 23 miles of paved bike path take you past wildlife habitat and historic sites such as this playhouse, once a school for pioneer children.

Karen T. Bartlett

Bike trails run through Lakes Park, where bike rentals are also available. Long stretches of bike path in Fort Myers run along Daniels Parkway, Metro Parkway, and Summerlin Road. The Summerlin path leads to the Sanibel causeway (bikers cross for $1), to connect with island paths.

Many of Cape Coral's city streets designate bike lanes. Bikers favor Burnt Store Marina Road, which goes to Charlotte County from the northwest side of town.

Sanibel's 23-mile path covers most of the island and occasionally leaves the roadside to plunge you into serene backwoods scenery.

A short, sporadic bike path/route travels through Bokeelia and St. James City on Pine Island.

A bike path runs the length of Bonita Beach, nearly three miles long, and connects to another at its south end, which leads to Vanderbilt Beach.

RENTAL/SALES

A. J. Barnes Bicycle Emporium (941-772-2453; 1109 Del Prado Blvd., Cape Coral) Rentals and sales.

Bike Route (941-472-1955; 2330 Palm Ridge Rd., Sanibel Island) Rentals, repairs, and sales.

Bonita Beach Bike (941-947-6377; 4892 Bonita Beach Rd., Bonita Harbor Plaza, Bonita Beach) In-line skates and a variety of bikes.

Finnimore's Cycle Shop (941-472-5577; 2353 Periwinkle Way, Sanibel Island) Rents bikes and skates.

Scooters, Inc. (941-463-1007; 1698 Estero Blvd., Fort Myers Beach)

Sun Rentals (941-463-8844; 1901 Estero Blvd., Fort Myers Beach) Rentals and repairs.

BOATS & BOATING

With its sprinkling of unbridged islands and wide bay, the Island Coast begs for outdoor types to explore her waters. Island-hopping constitutes a favorite pastime of adventurers.

CANOEING & KAYAKING

Many resorts and parks rent canoes, in addition to those outlets listed below.

Gulf Coast Kayak Company (941-283-1125; Matlacha, Pine Island) Day or overnight trips in the Matlacha Aquatic Preserve and other local natural areas; full moon and new moon astronomy ventures.

Sea kayaking: the latest in environmentally correct recreation.

Karen T. Bartlett

Lakes Park (941-432-2017; 7330 Gladiolus Dr., Fort Myers) Canoe rentals for paddling on freshwater lakes.

Sea Kayak Wildlife Tours (941-472-9484; Sanibel Island) Instruction in kayak operation and guided tours in local waters.

Tarpon Bay Recreation (941-472-8900; 900 Tarpon Bay Rd., Sanibel Island) Rents canoes and kayaks for use in the bay and through "Ding" Darling Refuge's Commodore Creek Canoe Trail. Avoid doing the refuge trail at low tide, or you may have to do some portaging. Also guided canoe tours.

WildSide Adventures (941-395-2925; McCarthy's Marina, 15041 Captiva Dr., Captiva Island) Sea kayaking tours focus on natural history, sea life, sunrise, sunset, starlight, full moon, and children's adventures. Kayak and canoe rentals available; delivery and pickup.

DINING CRUISES

J. C. Cruises (941-334-7474; Fort Myers Yacht Basin, downtown Fort Myers) Lunch and dinner cruises aboard the *Capt. J.P.* three-deck paddlewheeler up the Caloosahatchee River. Not available in summer.

Sanibel Harbour *Princess* (941-466-2128; Sanibel Harbour Resort, off Summerlin Rd. before Sanibel Island causeway) Sunset dinner and champagne/hors d'oeuvre cruises aboard a 100-foot luxury yacht.

SeaKruz (941-463-5000 or 800-688-PLAY; Snug Harbor Restaurant, 645 San Carlos Blvd., Fort Myers Beach) Daytime brunch and evening dinner cruises include casino gambling, live entertainment, and dancing.

MARINE SUPPLIES

Boat/US Marine Center (941-481-7447; 12901 McGregor Blvd., Fort Myers) All boating, yachting, and fishing needs. Memberships available for discounts and emergency service.

PERSONAL WATERCRAFT RENTALS/TOURS

Holiday Water Sports (941-765-4386, Best Western Pink Shell Resort, 250 Estero Blvd. and 941-463-6778, Best Western Beach Resort, 684 Estero Blvd., Fort Myers Beach) Waverunner rentals, lessons, and dolphin-spotting tours.

Port Sanibel Marina (941-437-1660; 14341 Port Comfort Rd. off Summerlin Rd. near Sanibel) Dolphin sighting tours.

POWERBOAT RENTALS

Big Hickory Fishing Nook (941-992-3945; 26107 Hickory Blvd., Bonita Beach) Pontoon and powerboat rentals.

The Boat House (941-472-2531; Sanibel Marina, 634 N. Yachtsman Dr., Sanibel Island) Powerboats for trips into intracoastal waters only.

Bonita Beach Resort Motel (941-992-2137; 26395 Hickory Blvd., Bonita Beach) 20- to 22-foot pontoon boats.

Fish-Tale Marina (941-463-4448; 7225 Estero Blvd., Fort Myers Beach) Boston Whalers, Grady Whites, 24-foot pontoons, and other boats for rent.

Florida Houseboat Rentals (941-945-BOAT) 41-foot air-conditioned houseboats for three- to seven-day cruises. Full galley and fishing gear included.

Four Winds Marina (941-283-0250; 16501 Stringfellow Rd., Bokeelia, Pine Island) 17- to 19-foot powerboats.

Sweet Water Boat Rentals (941-472-6336; 'Tween Waters Inn Marina, Captiva Dr.) Rents 18^1/$_2$-foot center-console boats holding up to six passengers.

Waterway Boat Rentals, (941-997-0019; Marinatown Marina, 3446 Marinatown Ln., North Fort Myers) Pontoon boats and cabin cruisers.

PUBLIC BOAT RAMPS

Cape Coral Yacht Club (941-574-0809; 5819 Driftwood Pkwy., Cape Coral) Free public ramp on the Caloosahatchee River, with recreational facilities.

Lover's Key Recreation Area (Route 865 between Fort Myers Beach and Bonita Beach)

Matlacha Park (Matlacha, Pine Island) Playground and fishing pier.

Punta Rassa (Summerlin Rd., Fort Myers, before the Sanibel causeway) Picnic facilities and rest rooms.

Sanibel (Causeway Rd.) Two ramps at the west end of the Sanibel causeway.

SAILBOAT CHARTERS

Adventure Sailing Charters (941-472-7532; South Seas Plantation, Captiva Island) Two-hour, half- and full-day captained charters aboard a 30-foot sloop. Passengers are encouraged to participate.

Island Tall Ship Cruises (941-936-9300; Snug Harbor, Fort Myers Beach) Sunset and daytime cruises aboard a 72-foot schooner.

New Moon (941-395-1782; 'Tween Waters Marina, Captiva Island) Up to six passengers aboard a 35-foot sloop. Sailing classes and rentals available.

SAILBOAT RENTALS & INSTRUCTION

Offshore Sailing School (941-454-1700 or 800-221-4326; South Seas Plantation Marina, Captiva Island) Week-long instruction available, from beginning sailing courses to advanced racing and bareboat cruising preparation; operated by an Olympic and America's Cup veteran.

SIGHTSEEING & ENTERTAINMENT CRUISES

Calusa Coast Outfitters (941-463-4448; Fish Tale Marina, 7225 Estero Blvd., Fort Myers Beach) Tours of Mound Key, an uninhabited island that was once an important Calusa Indian center.

Captiva Cruises (941-472-5300; South Seas Plantation, Captiva Island) A complete menu of sightseeing and luncheon trips aboard the 150-passenger *Lady*

Chadwick. The only way, as a nonguest, to see private Useppa Island, where you can enjoy lunch at the Barron Collier Inn restaurant.

Island Water Tours (941-765-4354; Best Western Pink Shell Resort, 275 Estero Blvd., Fort Myers Beach) Ride aboard the *Pelican Queen*, a 40-foot pontoon, to Big Hickory Island, Mound Key, and other islands.

J. C. Cruises (941-334-7474 or 941-334-2743; Fort Myers Yacht Basin, Fort Myers) Sightseeing tours aboard a 600-passenger paddlewheeler into the Caloosahatchee River, Lake Okeechobee, and the gulf. Cruises last from three hours to all day.

Sea Kruz (941-463-5000 or 800-688-PLAY; Snug Harbor Restaurant, Fort Myers Beach) Daytime brunch and evening dinner cruises include casino gambling, live entertainment, and dancing.

Shooter's Paddle Wheel Cruiser (941-334-1200; Holiday Inn Sunspree, 2220 W. First St., downtown Fort Myers) A two-decker cruise boat departs for box lunch and margarita tours.

FISHING

Snook and tarpon are the prized catch of local anglers. Snook, which is a game fish and cannot be sold commercially, is valued for its sweet taste.

Redfish is another sought-after food fish. More common catches in back bays and waters close to shore include mangrove snapper, spotted sea trout, shark, sheepshead, pompano, and ladyfish. Deeper waters offshore yield grouper, red snapper, amberjack, mackerel, and dolphinfish. Most fish are released in these days of environmental consciousness. Check local regulations for season, size, and catch restrictions.

Nonresidents age 16 and over must obtain a license unless fishing from a vessel or pier covered by its own license. Inexpensive, temporary nonresident licenses are available at county tax collectors' offices and at most Kmarts and bait shops.

DEEP-SEA PARTY BOATS

Getaway Deep Sea Fishing (941-466-3600; Getaway Marina, 18400 San Carlos Blvd., Fort Myers Beach) Excursions are aboard a 90-foot craft for all day or half day.

FISHING CHARTERS/OUTFITTERS

Competent fishing guides work out of the region's major marinas. If it's your first time fishing these waters, I recommend hiring someone with local knowledge.

Captain Bill Cyzewski (941-283-0106; Pine Island)

Captain Mike Fuery (941-472-1015; 'Tween Waters Marina, Captiva Island) Has a good reputation for finding fish.

Captain Dave Gibson (941-466-4680; Fort Myers) Specializes in fly-casting, back-bay, and light tackle fishing.

Island Charters (941-283-1113; Pineland Marina, Pine Island)

Sanibel Marina (941-472-2723; 634 N. Yachtsman Dr., Sanibel Island) Several experienced fishing guides operate out of the marina. **Captain Dave Case** (941-472-2798) has been at it a long time.

FISHING PIERS

Cape Coral Yacht Club (941-574-0815; 5819 Driftwood Pkwy., Cape Coral) The 620-foot lighted fishing pier is part of a boating/recreational complex.
Centennial Park (Edwards Dr. near Yacht Basin, downtown Fort Myers)
Fort Myers Beach Pier (at Lynn Hall Memorial Park, Times Square) Holds a bait shop, hungry pelicans, and a lot of casting room.
Manatee Park (941-432-2004; 10901 Route 80, Fort Myers) On the Orange River.
Matlacha Park (Matlacha, Pine Island) Playground and boat ramps.
Sanibel Lighthouse Beach (southeast end of Periwinkle Way, Sanibel Island) A T-dock into San Carlos Bay.

GOLF

Home of such golfing greats as Patty Berg and Nolan Henke, the Island Coast keeps pace with the growing popularity of golf.

PUBLIC GOLF COURSES

Alden Pines (941-283-2179; 14261 Clubhouse Dr., Bokeelia) Semiprivate, 18 holes, par 71. Snack bar.
Bay Beach Golf Club (941-463-2064; 7401 Estero Blvd., Fort Myers Beach) 18 holes, par 62.
Cape Coral Golf and Tennis (941-542-7879; 4003 Palm Tree Blvd., Cape Coral) 18 holes, par 72. Restaurant and bar.
Dunes Golf & Tennis Club (941-472-2535; 949 Sandcastle Rd., Sanibel Island) Semiprivate 18-hole, par-70 course. Restaurant and bar.
Fort Myers Country Club (941-936-2457; 3591 McGregor Blvd., Fort Myers) Fort Myers' oldest. 18 holes, par 71. Restaurant and lounge.

GOLF CENTERS

Eagle Golf Center (941-481-3400; 15825 S. Tamiami Trail, South Fort Myers) Driving range with 30 hitting stations, free lessons.

HEALTH & FITNESS CLUBS

Gold's Gym (941-549-3354; 1013 Cape Coral Pkwy., Cape Coral) Jazzercise, step aerobics, slimnastics, sauna/steam, indoor pool, nutritional guidance, child care.

Sanibel Fitness Center (941-395-2639; 975 Rabbit Rd., Sanibel Island) Aerobics, free weights, cardiovascular and personal training, classes, dance, martial arts.

Sanibel Recreation Center (941-472-0345; Sanibel Elementary School, 3840 Sanibel-Captiva Rd., Sanibel Island) Lap pool, tennis courts, weight room, basketball courts. City owned and operated. No admission fees.

HIKING

Sanibel-Captiva Conservation Foundation (941-472-2329; 3333 Sanibel-Captiva Rd., Sanibel Island) Four miles through natural habitat along the Sanibel River.

KIDS' STUFF

Kids find the ultimate sandbox on Island Coast shorelines.

Karen T. Bartlett

BMX Park (1410 SW Sixth Place, Cape Coral) A Bicycle Moto-Cross track is provided for practice and racing, along with picnic grounds, a playground, a softball field, and a sand volleyball court.

Discovery Zone (941-277-1122; 7091 College Pky. at Hwy. 41, Fort Myers) A well-run indoor play land, with areas for toddlers to teens. Kids pay $5.95; adults enter free when accompanied by a child.

Greenwell's Bat-A-Ball and Family Fun Park (941-574-4386; 35 NE Pine Island Rd., Cape Coral) Named after the city's favorite sports son, Red Sox player Mike Greenwell, it contains batting cages, a miniature golf course (a bit shabby), a video arcade, and go-carts.

Kartworld (941-936-3233; 1915 Colonial Blvd. at Hwy. 41, Fort Myers) Miniature golf, batting cages, go-carts, bumper boats, and a video arcade with 70 games. Admission is free; charges per activity.

Periwinkle Park (472-1433; Periwinkle Way, Sanibel Island) The owner of this trailer park raises and breeds exotic birds and waterfowl. He daddies roughly 600 birds of 133 species, specializing in African and Asian hornbills and boasting the country's largest collection of the rare African touraco. Flamingos, parakeets, cockatiels, cockatoos, and others occupy the park and 15 aviaries. During the off-season, visitors can drive through; in season, biking is recommended. A few of the birds raised here can be seen more easily at **Jerry's Shopping Center** (1700 Periwinkle Way). Take the children in the evening, when the birds are most talkative.

Sun Splash Family Waterpark (941-574-0557; 400 Santa Barbara Blvd., Cape Coral) This spot offers wet fun in a dozen varieties, with pools, slides, a log roll, cable drops, a river ride, volleyball, and special events. Admission is $8.50 for guests 48 inches or taller, $6.50 for shorter children. The park is closed certain times of the year.

RACQUET SPORTS

Fort Myers Racquet Club (941-278-7277; 4900 DeLeon St., Fort Myers) Eight clay courts, two hard courts, lessons, and tournaments. Admission.

Sanibel Recreation Complex (941-472-0345; Sanibel Elementary School, 3840 Sanibel-Captiva Rd., Sanibel Island) Five lighted tennis courts.

Signal Inn Resort (941-472-4690; 1811 Olde Middle Gulf Dr., Sanibel Island) Two racquetball courts.

SHELLING

This is shelling heaven. Sanibel Island, in particular, is known for its great pickings. In 1995 the state of Florida passed a law prohibiting the collection of live shells on Sanibel Island, to preclude the possibility of dwindling populations. Elsewhere in the county, live collecting is limited to two species per person per day. Collecting live shells is also prohibited in state and national parks. Any shell with a creature still inside is considered a live shell. Shellers who find live shells washed up on the beach — a common occurrence after storms — are urged to gently (without flinging) return the shell to deep water.

HOT SHELLING SPOTS

Big Hickory Island (northwest of Little Hickory Island, accessible only by boat) An unhitched crook of beach favored by local boaters and shellers.

Bonita Beach (Little Hickory Island) Look north of the public beach.

La Costa Island (between North Captiva and Boca Grande, accessible only by boat) Because it takes a boat ride to get there, these sands hold caches of shells merely by virtue of their remoteness. North-end Johnson Shoals provides a thin strip of sandbar for good low-tide pickings.

The Sanibel Stoop: Everybody's doing it!

Karen T. Bartlett

Sanibel Island Known as the Shelling Capital of the Western Hemisphere, the island even has its own name for the peculiar, shell-bent stance of the beach collector: Sanibel Stoop. Unlike the other Gulf Coast barrier islands, Sanibel takes an east-west heading. Its perpendicular position and lack of offshore reefs allow it to intercept shells that arrive from southern seas. Its fame as a world-class shelling area has made Sanibel a prime destination for shell collectors for decades. With shell-named streets, store shelves awash in shells and shell crafts, an annual shell fair, and a shell museum, one risks suffering shell shock just by visiting there. Best gulfside shelling spot: Bowman's Beach, midisland, away from the paths leading to the parking lot.

SHELLING CHARTERS

Capt. Mike Fuery's Shelling Charters (941-472-1015; Captiva Island) A local shelling expert who authors how-to columns for the local paper takes you to Cayo Costa, Johnson Shoals, and other shell caches.

SPAS

Sanibel Harbour Resort & Spa (941-466-4000 or 800-767-7777; 17260 Harbour Pointe Dr., Fort Myers) Directly before the Sanibel causeway, Sanibel Harbour was a spa years before it became a resort. It began as Jimmy Connors's eponymous tennis center, complete with state-of-the-art fitness and spa facilities. Today there's a 300-plus-unit resort (see "Lodging"). Guests, members, and day visitors can take advantage of the swimming pool, whirlpools, training room, aerobics classes, saunas, hot steam, and racquetball courts. Special services include herbal wraps, aromatherapy massage, Swiss shower, spa luncheon, counseling, training, facials, and other salon treatments.

SPECTATOR SPORTS

CRAB RACES

'Tween Waters Inn (941-472-5161; Captiva Dr., Captiva Island) Held 7 to 10 every Monday night. Participate or watch.

PRO BASEBALL

City of Palms Park (941-334-4700; Edison Ave. at Jackson St., downtown Fort Myers) Home of the Boston Red Sox's spring exhibition games, starting in March and played into April.

A bit of classic Florida design in the Lee County Sports Complex, the Minnesota Twins' spring training camp.

Greg Wagner

Lee County Sports Complex (941-768-4270; 14100 Six Mile Cypress Rd., Fort Myers) Hosts the Minnesota Twins for spring training in March and early April. From April through August, the Miracle Professional Baseball team, member of the Florida State League, competes here (941-768-4210).

PRO FOOTBALL

Although the Island Coast claims no professional team of its own, professional and college football support runs high. Several local sports bars have designated themselves unofficial headquarters for fans from specific teams throughout the country.

WATER SPORTS

PARASAILING & WATERSKIING

Holiday Water Sports (941-472-5111, ext. 3433; South Seas Plantation, Captiva Island) Waterskiing, parasailing, and jet skiing.
Holiday Water Sports (941-765-4FUN; Best Western Pink Shell Resort, 250

Soaring views and elevated heart rates: the thrill of parasailing.

South Seas Plantation

Estero Blvd. and 941-463-6778, Best Western Beach Resort, 684 Estero Blvd., Fort Myers Beach) Sun Cat, kayak, aquacycle, and waverunner rentals available, with lessons.

Ranalli Parasail (941-542-5511; Fort Myers) Rides along the Caloosahatchee River from various dock locations.

Rebel Watersports (941-463-3351; 1028 Estero Blvd., Fort Myers Beach) Parasailing, waverunner rentals, dolphin tours, banana boat rides.

SAILBOARDING & SURFING

Summer storms bring the sort of waves surfers crave, but in general, gulf waves are too wimpy for serious wave-riders. Strong winds, however, provide excellent conditions for sailboarders in several locations throughout the region. Sanibel Causeway is the most popular windsurfing spot. On weekends, a mobile concession often does rentals.

SNORKELING & SCUBA

DIVE SHOPS & CHARTERS

Underwater Explorers (941-481-4733 or 941-481-5005; 12600 McGregor Blvd., Fort Myers) Certification courses and equipment, plus dive trips out of the region.

SHORE SNORKELING & DIVING

Cayo Costa State Park Nice ledges in two to five feet of water, alive with fish, sponges, and shells.

WILDERNESS CAMPING

Cayo Costa State Island Preserve (941-964-0375, LaCosta Island) You'll need boat transportation to reach this unbridged island, home to wild pigs and myriad birds. Bring your own fresh drinking water and lots of bug spray. And don't expect to plug in the camcorder. There are showers, picnic grounds, boat docks, nature trails, a tram that runs cross-island, tent sites, and some very primitive cabins. Call ahead to reserve the latter. Camping was once allowed anywhere on the 2,225-acre island, but today it's restricted to a certain area.

WILDLIFE SPOTTING

Baby loggerhead turtles scurry to the sea in an annual, age-old ritual. On beaches along the Gulf Coast, they get help from vigilant turtle patrols.

Karen T. Bartlett

L oggerhead turtles lumber up on local beaches each summer to lay their cache of eggs. (Only vigilant night owls actually see them, but you can find their tracks and see their nests, which patrols stake off.) Brown pelicans swarm fishing piers for handouts. Black skimmers nest on uninhabited sandy islands, while hundreds of other birds visit or stay in local habitats. The Island Coast is a vital area for wildlife, and many opportunities exist to spy on them in their natural setting.

ALLIGATORS

Once endangered, the alligator population has sprung back in recent years, thanks to organizations and laws that fought to protect the prehistoric reptiles. Sanibel Island paved the way by pioneering a no-feeding regulation that later became state law. (Hand-fed alligators lose their fear of man.)

Innate homebodies, alligators usually leave their home ponds only during spring and summer mating. Spotting them is easiest then. You will often hear the bellow of the bull gator in the night and see both males and females roaming from pond to pond in search of a midsummer night's romance. They can do serious damage to a car, so be alert. And never approach one on foot.

When it's cold, alligators stay submerged to keep warm. On sunny days throughout the year you can spot them catching some rays on banks of fresh-water rivers and streams. In the water you first spot their snout, then their prickly tire-tread profile. Once your eye becomes trained to distinguish them from logs and background, you'll notice them more readily.

Serious searchers should try Sanibel Island's J. N. "Ding" Darling National Wildlife Refuge.

BIRDS

Roseate spoonbills are the stars of the "Ding" Darling National Wildlife Refuge, but hundreds of others live among the sanctuary's wiry mangrove limbs and shallow estuarine waters.

DOLPHINS

The playful bottle-nosed dolphin cruises the sea performing impromptu acrobatic shows that it's hard to believe aren't staged. When the next perfor-mance will be is anybody's guess, but if you learn their feeding schedules you have a better chance of catching their act. They often like to leap out of the wake of large boats. Out in the gulf I've been surrounded by their antics to the point where I suffered minor whiplash from spinning around to keep track of them all. Don't expect them to get too close — take some binoculars — and for-get seeing them in captivity around here. Locals once staged a protest in Pine Island Sound when collectors tried to take some of their dolphins. When a swim-with-the-dolphins facility was proposed near Sanibel Island, citizens were again up in arms against animal exploitation.

MANATEES

In east Fort Myers, where warm waters discharged from the Florida Power & Light Company have always attracted the warm-blooded manatees in the winter months to so-called Yankee Canal, Manatee Park (941-432-2004; 10901 Route 80, Fort Myers) recently opened to provide a manatee viewing area, exhibits, and other recreational and educational assets on the wild and natural Orange River.

Pine Island's backwaters offer a good venue for manatee spotting. Check out the bay behind Island Shell & Gifts, a popular sea-watch site, just before the Matlacha bridge.

NATURE PRESERVES & ECO-ATTRACTIONS

CALUSA NATURE CENTER & PLANETARIUM
941-275-3435.
3450 Ortiz Ave., Fort Myers.

Offers a free two-mile wildlife trail with Seminole Amerindian village and native bird aviary. Indoors you can see live animal exhibits — snakes, tarantulas, alligators, and bees — and demon-

Open: 9–5 Mon.–Sat., 11–5
   Sun. Call for astronomy
   and laser show times.
Admission: Museum and
   trails, $4 adults, $2.50
   children under 12.
   Shows, $2–$5.

strations. The planetarium uses telescopes, laser lights, and astronomy lessons in its presentations.

**CAYO COSTA STATE
ISLAND PRESERVE**
941-964-0375.
LaCosta Island, accessible
   only by boat.
Admission: $2 per family.

A refuge occupies about 90 percent of this 2,225-acre island. Cayo Costa preserves the Florida that the native Americans tried to protect against European invasion. Besides the wild hogs that survive on the island, egrets, white pelicans, raccoons, ospreys, and black skimmers frequent the area. The path across the island's northern end features a side trip to a pioneer cemetery. Blooming cacti and other flora festoon the walk, which is sometimes a run when weather turns warm and uncontrolled mosquito populations remind us of the hardships of eras gone by.

C.R.O.W.
941-472-3644.
3883 Sanibel-Captiva Rd.,
   Sanibel Island.
Open: Tours at 11
   Mon.–Fri., also 1:00 Sun.
   Nov.–Apr. only.
Admission: $3 requested
   donation for adults.

C.R.O.W. is the acronym for Care and Rehabilitation of Wildlife. This hospital complex duplicates natural habitats and tends to sick and injured wildlife: birds, bobcats, raccoons, rabbits, and otters.

**J. N. "DING" DARLING
WILDLIFE REFUGE**
941-472-1100.
1 Wildlife Dr., off Sanibel-
   Captiva Rd., Sanibel
   Island.
Open: Refuge, sunrise to
   sunset. Visitors' center,
   9–4.
Closed: Fri.
Admission: $5 per car, $1
   per cyclist or walk-in.

More than 5,000 acres of pristine wetlands and wildlife are protected by the federal government, thanks to the efforts of Pulitzer Prize–winning cartoonist and politically active conservationist J. N "Ding" Darling, a regular Captiva visitor in the 1930s. A five-mile drive takes you through the refuge, but to really experience it, get out of the car. At the very least follow the easy trails into mangrove, bird, and alligator territory. Narrated tram and guided canoe tours are available (941-472-8900). The visitors' center holds wildlife displays and peeks into the world of the refuge's namesake.

MANATEE PARK
941-432-2004.
10901 Route 80, Fort Myers.
Open: 8–8 daily Apr.–Sept.;
   8–5 daily Oct.–Mar.

A 16-acre passive recreational park feeds our fascination with manatees. In addition to a manatee viewing area, it provides interpretative exhibits, a nature boardwalk, a canoe and kayak launch, a fishing pier, and picnic facilities. The park

Fort Myers' new Manatee Park overlooks the sea cow's favorite winter vacation spot.

Parking: 75¢ per hour, $3 per day.

MATANZAS PASS PRESERVE
End of Bay Rd., Fort Myers Beach.
Open: Dawn to dusk.
Admission: Free.

SANIBEL-CAPTIVA CONSERVATION FOUNDATION CENTER
941-472-2329.
3333 Sanibel-Captiva Rd., Sanibel Island.
Open: 8:30–3 Mon.–Fri. during summer; 8:30–4 Mon.–Sat. mid-Oct.–mid-May.
Admission: $2 for visitors 12 and older.

also serves as a rescue and release site for injured and rehabilitated manatees.

A quiet respite from vacation-land action, the preserve provides a short loop trail and board-walks through mangroves to out-of-the-way bay waters.

This research and preservation facility encom-passes more than 1,100 acres. A guided or self-guided tour introduces you to indigenous fauna and natural bird habitat. Indoor displays and dio-ramas further educate, and include a touch tank. Guest lecturers, seminars, and workshops address environmental issues during the winter season. The weekly beach walk is fun and informative; the foundation also sponsors a nature boat trip to nearby uninhabited Buck Key. Native plant nurs-ery and butterfly house also on the premises.

WILDLIFE TOURS & CHARTERS

Adventures in Paradise (941-472-8443 or 941-437-1660; Port Sanibel Marina, off Summerlin Rd. before the Sanibel causeway) Sea life encounter excursions led by marine biologist aboard a pontoon boat.

Canoe Adventures (941-472-6080; Sanibel Island) Guided tours with a noted island naturalist in "Ding" Darling National Wildlife Refuge, on the Sanibel River, and in other natural areas.

Manatee Tours (941-693-1434; Coastal Marine Mart, Route 80 at Interstate 75 exit 25, East Fort Myers) Specializes in tours up the Orange River to spot manatees. Educational video viewing.

Sanibel-Captiva Conservation Foundation Center (941-472-2329; 3333 Sanibel-Captiva Rd., Sanibel Island) Hosts guided nature trail, beach walk, and island boat tours.

Tarpon Bay Recreation (941-472-8900; 900 Tarpon Bay Rd., Sanibel Island) Guided canoe and tram tours through "Ding" Darling National Wildlife Refuge.

SHOPPING

ANTIQUES & COLLECTIBLES

Albert Meadow Antiques (941-472-8442; 15000 Captiva Dr., Captiva Island) Turn-of-the-century decorative arts by Tiffany, Gorham, and Steuben; antique jewelry, Navajo weavings, and Art Deco and Art Nouveau.

Centennial Park Antiques (941-479-6200; 1542 Carson St., downtown Fort Myers) An antique mall containing more than 20 dealers.

Fort Myers Antique Mall (941-693-0500; 924 Ortiz Ave., Fort Myers) Emporium of 15 dealers.

Judy's Antiques (941-481-9600; 12710 McGregor Blvd., Fort Myers) One of the oldest in the McGregor Antiques District, it sells a variety of merchandise: jewelry, clothes, and decorative items.

BOOKS

Barnes & Noble (941-437-0654; 13751 S. Tamiami Trail, Fort Myers.) Complete book dealer with extensive periodicals, local and travel section, children's books and activities, and coffee bar.

The Book Den South (941-332-2333; 2249 First St., downtown Fort Myers) Deals in used, rare, out-of-print, and first-edition books.

The Island Book Nook (941-472-6777; Palm Ridge Place, 2330 Palm Ridge Rd., Sanibel Island) Paperback exchange, hardbacks for sale and rent, complete collection of local books.

MacIntosh Books (941-472-1447; 2365 Periwinkle Way, Sanibel Island) A tiny shop packed full of books of local and general interest. A special room stocks children's books and provides toys to help out shopping parents.

Shakespeare Beethoven and Co. (941-939-1720; Royal Palm Square, 1400 Colonial Blvd., Fort Myers) Provides one of the area's best selections of magazines and periodicals, foreign and domestic. It also carries tapes, CDs, and a full line of books; well stocked in the children's section.

CLOTHING

Anna's Moroccan (941-482-5600; Bell Tower Shops, Fort Myers) Flowing, drapey, earthy women's fashions.

Candace's (941-472-3777; Chadwick's Square, Captiva Island) Stylish and casual women's resort fashions.

Chico's (941-472-3773; Palm Ridge Shopping Center, Palm Ridge Rd., Sanibel Island) I prefer this Chico's store to the original because it's more low-key, with less hustle and bustle.

H20 Outfitters (941-472-7507; Chadwick's Square, Captiva Island) Men's and women's beach and marina fashions.

Hurricane Bay (941-472-2251; Jerry's Shopping Center, 1700 Periwinkle Way, Sanibel Island) Women's swimwear.

Stanley & Livingston's (941-472-8485; The Village, 2340 Periwinkle Way, Sanibel Island) Travel clothes, books, and paraphernalia à la Banana Republic.

Trader Rick's (941-489-2240; Bell Tower Shops, Fort Myers) Casual cotton Florida wear for women, plus unusual and handmade jewelry and other accessories.

CONSIGNMENT

Buying secondhand on the Island Coast is not the embarrassment it is in some places. Because of the wealthy and transient nature of its residents, the area offers the possibility of great discoveries in its consignment shops.

Classy Exchange (941-278-1123; 12791 Kenwood Ln. #B1, Fort Myers) Designer women's fashions and housewares.

Coming Around Again (941-549-2922; 4635 Coronado Pkwy., Cape Coral) Specializes in wedding gowns, plus other women's clothing.

Designer Consigner (941-472-1266; Tarpon Bay Center, 2460 Palm Ridge Rd., Sanibel Island) Clothing, furniture, and household items.

The Encore Shop (941-936-6335; Columbus Square, 3563 Fowler St., Fort Myers) Household items and decor, men's and women's fashions.

Perenniels (941-275-8838; 7051 Crystal Dr., Fort Myers) Baby furniture, toys, and children's clothes.

Sarah's Consignments (941-283-3302; Stringfellow Rd. & Mackerel St., Pine Island) Housewares and decorative items, men's and women's clothing.

Solitary Consignment (941-332-5979; 2030 W. First St., downtown Fort Myers) Ladies' clothing and accessories.

FACTORY OUTLET CENTERS

Sanibel Factory Outlets (941-454-1616; McGregor Blvd. and Summerlin Rd., Fort Myers) Sitting at Sanibel's doorstep, outlets for Corning-Revere, Maidenform, Levi's, Bass Shoes, and American Tourister.

FLEA MARKETS & BAZAARS

Amtel Flea Market Mall (941-939-3132; Metro Blvd. and Colonial Blvd., Fort Myers) New indoor mall open daily Wednesday through Sunday.

Fleamasters Fleamarket (941-334-7001; 4135 Dr. Martin Luther King Jr. Blvd., Fort Myers) 300,000 indoor square feet of produce, souvenirs, and novelties, open Friday through Sunday.

McGregor Boulevard Garage Sales (Fort Myers) Drive the boulevard early — the earlier you go, the better the pickings — every Friday and Saturday morning and watch for the forest of garage sale signs directing you to private sales.

Ortiz Flea Market (941-694-5019; 1501 Ortiz Ave., Fort Myers) Every Friday, Saturday, and Sunday.

GALLERIES

Aboriginals Art of the First Person (941-395-2200; The Village, 2340 Periwinkle Way, Sanibel Island) More of a museum than a store, it focuses on the tribal art of Africa, Australia, and native Americans.

Crossed Palms Gallery (941-283-2283; 8315 Main St., Bokeelia, Pine Island) Original fine arts and crafts by local artists.

Griffin Gallery (941-283-0680; 4303 Pine Island Rd., Matlacha) New-wave Haitian art and showings of local and New York emerging artists and potters.

Jungle Drums (941-395-2266; 11532 Andy Rosse Rd., Captiva Island) On the outside, dolphins and birds are carved into the stair rail and floor studs. Inside, local and national artists depict wildlife themes in various media, much of it whimsical.

SyZyGy (941-275-8885; Royal Palm Square, Fort Myers) A well-respected repository of modern and other three-dimensional art.

Touch of Sanibel Pottery (941-472-4330; 1544 Periwinkle Way, Sanibel Island) Features utilitarian and decorative clayware, created both at the gallery and by guest artists. Its gladiolus vases, lighthouse lamps, and tropical designs make great souvenirs.

Sanibel Island's Tower Gallery occupies a restored 1920s beach cottage.

Karen T. Bartlett

Tower Gallery (941-472-4557; 751 Tarpon Bay Rd., Sanibel Island) In its charming Caribbean-motif old-beach-house digs, it specializes in fine tropical art by area artists: masterful black-and-white photography, Sanibel scenes, fish rubbings, giclée, pottery, and baskets.

GENERAL STORES

Bailey's General Store (941-472-1516; Periwinkle Way and Tarpon Bay Rd., Sanibel Island) An island fixture for ages, it stocks mostly hardware and fishing and kitchen supplies, with an attached grocery, bakery, and deli.

Island Store (941-472-2374; 11500 Andy Rosse Ln., Captiva Island) Here's where you can buy those necessities you forgot, but try not to forget too much because the prices reflect the location, here at the end of the earth.

GIFTS

A Swedish Affair (941-275-8004; Royal Palm Square, Fort Myers) Scandinavian gifts from funny to fine: Swedish joke books, lingonberry preserves, folk art, glassware, Christmas ornaments, and fine pewter serving pieces.

Captiva Island Pottery (941-395-1188; 14808 Captiva Dr., Captiva Island) Handmade utilitarian clayware, plus primitive Turkish antiques and East Indian clothing.

Jerry's Bazaar (941-472-5636; Jerry's Shopping Center, 1700 Periwinkle Way, Sanibel Island) Collection of T-shirt, beach toy, shell, and candy shops all under one roof, selling affordable mementos of the island.

Pandora's Box (941-472-6263; 2075 Periwinkle Way, Sanibel Island) A seashell motif in decorative items, creative jewelry, potpourri, specialty children's gifts, and art greeting cards.

Sanibel Five & Ten (941-472-8288; 2330 Palm Ridge Rd., Sanibel Island) Humor and gag gifts, cards, souvenirs, kids' stuff.

JEWELRY

Congress Jewelers (941-472-4177; Periwinkle Place, Sanibel Island) Dolphin, mermaid, and shell gold pendants, plus other fine jewelry.

Designs by J.R. (941-332-0440; 2105 First St., downtown Fort Myers) Custom designs and new life for old jewelry.

Kelly's Cocoons (941-472-8383; Chadwick's Square, Captiva Island) Specializes in jewelry made from shells and recovered treasure coins.

KITCHENWARE & HOME DECOR

Border Imports (941-437-8100; 15501-5 McGregor Blvd., Fort Myers) The emphasis is Mexican, but not the kitsch you might expect. Huge clay pots and ironware furniture.

Galloway's Clements & Assoc. (941-936-1231; Royal Palm Square, Fort Myers) Interior design elements with a tropical theme: beachscape watercolors, sea urchin sculptures, brass and enamel heron statues, shell-appliquéd pillows.

Going Home (941-432-9119; Bell Tower Shops, Fort Myers) Select original art, candles, and distinctive home decorative items.

Island Style (941-472-6657; Periwinkle Place, Sanibel Island) Whimsical, artistic, and one-of-a-kind decorative elements with a Sun Belt motif: hand-painted chairs, carved wooden mobiles and stabiles, Caribbean-inspired pieces.

Peel 'n Pare (941-433-3300; Bell Tower Shops, Fort Myers) Kitchen accents and implements.

Unpressured Cooker (941-472-2413; Olde Sanibel Shopping Center, Tarpon Bay Rd. and Periwinkle Way, Sanibel Island) Specialty Florida items: local cookbooks, alligator cutters, shell pie pans, sea-motif placemats.

SHELL SHOPS

Island Shells and Gifts (941-283-8080; 4204-4206 Pine Island Road, Matlacha) Huge facility carrying an unusual stock of shells, shell-craft materials, jewelry, and other novelties.

Neptune's Treasures (941-472-3132; Treetops Center, 1101 Periwinkle Way, Sanibel Island) Along with the usual line of shell specimens and jewelry, this shop carries fossils and arrowheads.

The Shell Factory (941-995-2141 or 800-282-5805; 2787 N. Tamiami Trail, North Ft. Myers) A palace of Florida funk and junk, the Shell Factory is built like a bazaar, with dozens of mini-shops within its 65,500 square feet. The main part displays specimen shells and shell-craft items of every variety. Jewelry, art, clothes, and knickknacks fill other nooks. Also at the complex (can't miss it; look for the giant conch shell on the sign), you will find restaurants, an arcade, a stuffed exotic animal collection, the Historic Railroad Museum, Waltzing Waters shows, and bumperboat rides.

Showcase Shells (941-472-1971; Heart of the Islands Center, 1614 Periwinkle Way, Sanibel Island) As elegant as a jewelry store, this boutique adds a touch of class to sifting through specimen shells by putting them under glass and into artistic displays.

SHOPPING CENTERS & MALLS

Fort Myers' tony Bell Tower shopping center is home to Saks Fifth Avenue.

Lee Island Coast Visitor & Convention Bureau

Bell Tower Shops (941-489-1221; Daniels Pkwy. and Tamiami Trail, Fort Myers) Jacobson's, a small and exclusive department store, and Saks Fifth Avenue anchor this alfresco, Mediterranean-style plaza of specialty shops, restaurants, and movie theaters.

Captiva Island Like Captiva in general, the shopping scene here is quirky and beach-oriented. Chadwick's Square, near the entrance to the South Seas Plantation Resort, provides the best (if somewhat pricey) concentration of gifts and fashion.

Coralwood Mall (941-574-1441; 2301 Del Prado Blvd., Cape Coral) An outdoor mall of restaurants and chain stores, including Bealls Department Store.

Downtown Fort Myers (First Street) Downtown is slowly looking up. More business and government-minded than commercial, it does harbor some interesting book and cigar stores and unusual antique and what-not shops. Emphasis for urban renewal is on entertainment and dining, so most shops are utilitarian.

Edison Mall (941-939-5464; 4125 Cleveland Ave., Fort Myers) An entirely commercial, enclosed mall with major department stores such as Burdines, J. C. Penneys, and Sears, plus about 150 smaller clothing and gift shops and a food court.

Matlacha (Pine Island) Sagging old fish houses, cracker-box shops, and fishing motels heavily salt the flavor of this island village. Knickknack historic structures painted in candy-store colors give the town an artistic, Hansel and Gretel feel. Sea-themed gifts, art, and jewelry comprise the majority of merchandise. Down the road at Pine Island Center are a few more artsy shops.

McGregor Antiques District (Fort Myers) A nucleus of 17 shops spread around five small strip centers at College Parkway.

Royal Palm Square (941-939-3900; Colonial Blvd. and Summerlin Rd., Fort Myers) This alfresco mall takes you down wooden walkways and past lush palms, exotic birds, fish ponds, and fountains.

Sanibel Island Periwinkle Way and Palm Ridge Road constitute the shopper's routes on Sanibel, which is known for its galleries (specializing in wildlife art), shell shops, and resort-wear stores. These are clustered in tastefully landscaped, nature-compatible, outdoor centers, the largest being Periwinkle Place on Periwinkle Way. One of the most interesting, both architecturally and in terms of merchandise, is The Village on Periwinkle Way.

Times Square (at the foot of Matanzas Pass Bridge, Fort Myers Beach) Shop in your bikini, if you wish, at this hub of ultracasual island activity. You'll find a profusion of swimsuit boutiques, surf shops, and fast food outlets. Plans are to create a pedestrian-only section in years to come.

SPORTS STORES

Note: This listing includes general sports outlets only. For supplies and equipment for specific sports, please refer to "Recreation."

Ken's Sports (941-936-7106; 4600 S. Cleveland Ave., Fort Myers) Specializes in scuba, archery, tennis, darts, and shuffleboard.

Sports Authority (941-418-0281; 2317 Colonial Blvd., Fort Myers) Full line of equipment, sportswear, and shoes.

CALENDAR OF EVENTS

JANUARY

Blizzard (941-338-3300; Lee County Sports Complex, Fort Myers) Two tons of snow bring back wintry memories: ice skating, entertainment, ice carving contest. One day in late January.

Lee Sidewalk Arts & Crafts Show (941-332-6813; First St., downtown Fort Myers) More than 250 artisans; two days midmonth.

FEBRUARY

Cape Coral Winter Festival (941-549-6900; Cape Coral) Ball, antique car show, parade, music, and art exhibits. Nine days in late February to early March.

Edison Festival of Light (941-334-2550; Fort Myers) Commemorates the birthday of Thomas Edison, culminating in a spectacular, lighted night parade. Two weeks early in the month.

Fort Myers Beach Shrimp Festival (941-334-0552; Lynn Hall Park, Fort Myers Beach) Blessing of the fleet, 5K run, parade, and shrimp boil. One week late in the month.

Greek Festival (941-481-2099; Greek Orthodox Church, 8210 Cypress Lake Dr., Fort Myers) Ethnic food and music. Two days late in the month.

Sanibel Music Festival (941-336-7999; Sanibel Island) Features concerts by classical artists from across the nation. Most events held at Sanibel Congregational Church, 2050 Periwinkle Way.

MARCH

Alliance Auxiliary Arts & Crafts Festival (941-939-2787; Lee County Alliance of the Arts, 10091 McGregor Blvd., Fort Myers) Two days of displays featuring more than 150 artisans.

India Festival (941-561-2496; Lee County Alliance of the Arts, 10091 McGregor Blvd., Fort Myers) Ethnic food and entertainment.

Irish Heritage Festival (941-939-2787; Lee County Alliance of the Arts, 10091 McGregor Blvd., Fort Myers) Irish music, food, and arts.

Sanibel Shell Fair and Show (941-472-2155; 2173 Periwinkle Way, Sanibel Island) Showcases sea life, specimen shells, and shell art. Four days in early March. Admission to show.

APRIL

Best Southwest Festival (941-574-0801; Cape Coral Yacht Club, Driftwood Pkwy., Cape Coral) Live music, western saloon, casino, dancing, and a taste fair. One day late in the month.

Koreshan Unity Lunar Festival (941-992-2184; Koreshan State Historic Site, Estero) Arts and crafts shows and tours of the site.

Taste of the Islands (941-472-3644; Sanibel Island) About 20 Captiva and Sanibel restaurants participate, with live music and competitions to benefit wildlife. One day.

MAY

Israel Family Independence Day Festival (941-481-4449; Lee County Alliance of the Arts, 10091 McGregor Blvd, Fort Myers) Jewish tradition prevails for one day. Ethnic dishes, entertainment, and children's Olympics.

JUNE

Caloosa Catch & Release Fishing Tournament (941-472-9484 or 800-223-5865, ext. 318; 'Tween Waters Inn, Captiva Island) Four-day event in June.

International Hemingway Festival (941-945-0308; various locations, Sanibel Island) Moved from Key West in 1997, the Hemingway Festival is held for three days over Father's Day weekend in honor of "Papa" Hemingway and his genius. Activities include a writers' conference, writing and art contests, and fishing and golf tournaments.

Juneteenth Celebration (941-334-2797; STARS Complex, 2980 Edison Ave., Fort Myers) A celebration of African-American freedom, highlighting dance, gospel music, martial arts, African fashion, drama, and ethnic food.

Southwest Florida Wine Fair (941-472-7572; South Seas Plantation, Captiva) Participation by leading California wineries. Early in the month.

JULY

Mangomania (941-283-7067; Pine Island) Celebrates Pine Island's favorite fruit with music, food, and fun. One day.

SEPTEMBER

Taste of the Cape (941-549-6900; German-American Club, 2101 SW Pine Island Rd., Cape Coral) Tastes from local restaurants, live entertainment. One day late in the month.

OCTOBER

Hispanic Heritage Festival (941-334-3190; Terry Park, downtown Fort Myers) A celebration of Hispanic culture, which centers in the North Fort Myers and Cape Coral areas, featuring ethnic food, music, dance, and crafts. One day.

Munich in Cape Coral (941-283-1400; German-American Club, Cape Coral) Cape Coral celebrates its strong German heritage with Oktoberfest activities. Two weekends.

NOVEMBER

All Things British International Festival (941-939-2787; Lee County Alliance of the Arts, 10091 McGregor Blvd., Fort Myers) The music, dance, food, arts, and theater of the Commonwealth. Two days early in the month.

BIG Arts Fair (941-395-0900; Sanibel Community Center, Sanibel Island) Juried arts and crafts exhibits. Thanksgiving weekend.

Sandsculpting Contest (941-454-7500; Fort Myers Beach) Amateur and masters divisions. One week in early November.

Taste of the Town (941-482-7377; Centennial Park, downtown Fort Myers)

About 50 restaurants sell their specialties; live entertainment and children's games. One day early in the month.

DECEMBER

Captiva Sea Kayak Classic (941-472-9484 or 800-223-5865, ext. 318; 'Tween Waters Inn, Captiva Island) Kayaking symposium and races for three days in December.

Christmas Boat-a-Long (941-574-0801; Four Freedoms Park, Cape Coral) Decorated boat parade with live entertainment, Santa, and other events.

Christmas Luminary Trail and Open House (941-472-1080; Sanibel and Captiva Islands) Luminary candles light the path down Sanibel's and Captiva's commercial areas, where businesses stay open and dole out free drinks and food. One weekend early in the month.

Edison/Ford Homes Holiday House (941-275-1088; Edison/Ford complex, Fort Myers) Period and seasonal exhibits and miles of light strings draw crowds to this popular attraction.

CHAPTER SIX
Precious Commodities
NAPLES & THE SOUTH COAST

Karen T. Bartlett

The architecture of the Village on Venetian Bay shopping district adds an Italian flavor to America's Naples.

Perched on alabaster sands at the edge of Florida's **Everglades**, meticulous **Naples** transcends its wild setting like a diamond in the rough. Settled by land developers late in its life, this cultural oasis historically has appealed to the rich and the sporting. Today the state's final frontier is known for its million-dollar homes, great golfing, art galleries, posh resorts, world-class shopping, and fine dining. In its northern reaches the town spreads into the quiet, residential district of **North Naples**, seaside **Vanderbilt Beach**, and the town of **Bonita Springs**.

The latter adheres to an early agricultural heritage with a reputation for tomatoes, citrus, and other cash crops. Citrus freeze-outs farther north, and the town's navigable Imperial River, created the community first called Survey in 1893. Here Henry Ford maintained a hunting lodge to which he and his Fort Myers friends traveled by horseback. Where the tomato fields end today,

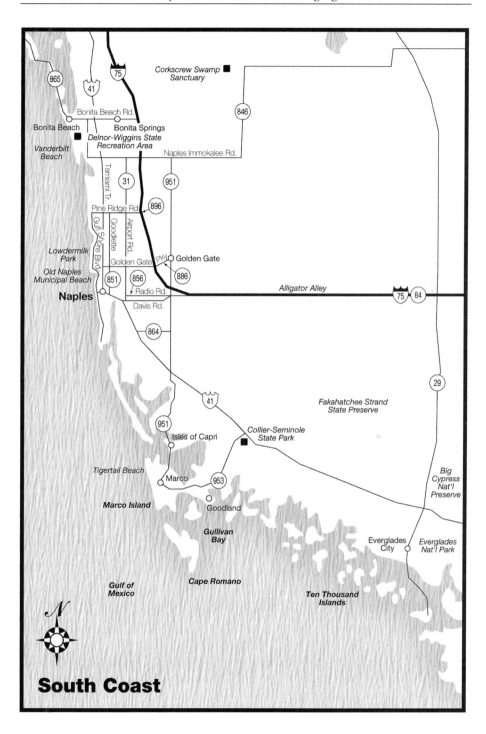

South Coast

upscale golfing communities begin, all surrounding a neighborly little town left frozen in time by dint of Tamiami Trail's rerouting.

At the south coast's southern and eastern extremes, the civility is balanced with swamp buggy mud races, agriculture, native American villages, fishing lodges, vanishing Florida panthers, and the unvarnished wilderness of the Everglades.

Neighboring **Marco Island** introduces the swampy, mysterious land of **Ten Thousand Islands**. Tempered in a rough-and-tumble history, the island, too, boasts contemporary upscale resorts and good manners. Ancient Indian mounds, clam canneries, and pineapple plantations color the past of its three communities: **Isles of Capri**, **Marco**, and **Goodland**. First settled by the William Collier clan in 1871, Marco Island has done most of its growing in the past few decades. Between 1960, when plans for a modern bridge were being formed, and 1980, the population increased by 755 percent. Goodland, so named because its land provided fertile soil for avocado farming, has purposely kept itself behind the times, giddily stuck in a good-time, catch-fish mode.

Karen T. Bartlett

An old fish shack in Ten Thousand Islands, remnant of a rougher, tougher era.

Everglades City, county seat until Naples took over, languishes in its wilderness setting at the doorstep to Big Cypress Swamp and Ten Thousand Islands. Its settlers have always kept a step ahead of the law, doing what they must to survive, whether it was fishing, alligator poaching, or pot smuggling. Today, commercial fishing restrictions have changed the town's orientation toward tourism. Across a long, narrow causeway, **Chokoloskee Island** remains relatively untouched by change. It's a haven for RV campers and fishermen.

LODGING

The south coast was once a place for roughing it and low-key vacationing. The old wooden Naples Hotel, built in the 1880s by town developers, was as posh as it got. In 1946 Naples became forerunner in the golf resort game when the 100-year-old Naples Hotel was bought and converted. In 1985, when the Ritz-Carlton came to town and set a new tone, Naples changed forever. The Registry and other smaller luxury hotels followed the Ritz. New properties continue to rise as Naples renovates its downtown. They tend toward intimacy and European style, giving Naples a well-rounded menu of options, from cottages and inns to golf meccas and grandes dames. Nearby Marco Island lines up high-rise after high-rise resort and condo community along its coveted beaches. Away from the metropolitan airs of Naples and Marco, lodging options reflect the simple, primitive nature of the Florida Everglades.

Privately owned second homes and condominiums provide another source of upscale accommodations along the south coast. Vacation brokers who match visitors with such properties are listed under "Home & Condo Rentals" at the end of this section.

The highlights of south coast hospitality listed here include the best and freshest in the local industry. Toll-free 800 or 888 reservation numbers, where available, are listed after local numbers.

A star after the pricing designation indicates that the rate includes at least a continental breakfast in the cost of lodging; a few follow the American Plan, including all meals in the rate charged, or the Modified American Plan, offering breakfast and dinner.

Pricing codes are explained below. They are normally per person/double occupancy for hotel rooms and per unit for efficiencies, apartments, cottages, suites, and villas. The range spans low- and high-season rates. Many resorts offer off-season packages at special rates. Prices do not include the 6 percent Florida sales tax. Some large resorts add service gratuities or maid charges. Collier County imposes a tourist bed tax as well, proceeds from which are applied to beach and environmental maintenance.

Rate Categories

Inexpensive	Up to $50
Moderate	$50 to $110
Expensive	$110 to $180
Very Expensive	$180 and up

The following abbreviations are used for credit card information:

AE - American Express	DC - Diners Club
CB - Carte Blanche	MC - MasterCard
D - Discover Card	V - Visa

Everglades City

PORT OF THE ISLANDS RESORT & MARINA
General Manager: Jocelyn Ting.
941-394-1010 or 800-237-4173.
25000 Tamiami Trail E., Naples 34114.
Price: Inexpensive to Expensive.
Credit Cards: AE, D, DC, MC, V.
Handicap Access: Yes.

A gateway to the Everglades, Port of the Islands plays both rough and genteel. The 500-acre resort is insulated by wilderness on all sides. From its harbor, Everglades tours and charters depart. Private planes can land on its 3,500-foot airstrip. Skeet and trap ranges give guests a taste of the days when visitors came to this region expressly for those and other sports. On the genteel side, the hotel puts on a pretty salmon-pink and green Mediterranean-style face. The lobby blends elements of the Riviera and an Everglades sporting lodge with a heavy wood-beamed cathedral ceiling, saltillo floors, stucco, rattan, red barrel-tile accents, and a grand fireplace. The dining room looks through French doors at the pool and its chickee bar. Another pool, a game room, a fitness room, a playground, volleyball, croquet, and tennis provide on-property recreation. The 185 rooms, efficiencies, and suites are plain in comparison to the grandeur of the lobby; some look as though they're ready for updating. Highlight of a stay is the two-hour narrated boat tour into Ten Thousand Islands aboard the *Island Princess*.

The lodge at Everglades City's Rod & Gun Club blends southern charm with wilderness sportsmanship.

Karen T. Bartlett

ROD & GUN CLUB
Innkeeper: Marcella Bowen.
941-695-2101.
200 Broadway, P.O. Box 190, Everglades City 34139.
Price: Moderate.

Steeped in both history and outdoorsmanship, this circa-1850 lodge crowns a modest town that serves as the south coast's gateway to the Everglades. The club's main building was built as luxury pioneer housing. The Old South-style mansion came under the ownership of the county's namesake, Barron Collier, who turned it into a fishermen's and hunters' haven during the 1920s. A

Credit Cards: No.
Handicap Access: No.

sportsman's lodge in the finest sense, its cypress walls are still decorated with mounted tarpon, a gator hide, and tools of the fishing trade. Seventeen rooms in tin-roofed cottages are scattered around the white clapboard lodge, which has a wraparound veranda and yellow trim. The rooms are furnished for function rather than pampering; TV and air-conditioning are the extent of the luxury. The club's restaurant has a screened porch, specializes in local delicacies, and will cook your catch for a nominal fee. The swimming pool lies off the dining room and is decorated with potted banana trees, lattice, and a coquina rock wall.

Marco Island

MARCO ISLAND RESORT MARRIOTT RESORT & GOLF CLUB
General Manager: Pete Hubschmitt.
941-394-2511 or 800-228-9290.
400 S. Collier Blvd., Marco Island 34145.
Price: Expensive to Very Expensive.
Credit Cards: AE, CB, D, DC, MC, V.

This vacation complex sprawls along the beach — a wide, shell-cluttered, sandbar-sheltered beach — to provide a fantasy playground for vacationers of all ages. For the kids, there's an 18-hole miniature golf course, three swimming pools, water-sports rentals, a pizza parlor, a game room, and a remarkable kids' program. Adults can shop in the marble-floored arcade, golf at an off-campus Marriott course, dine grandly or beach-style, and act like a kid when the mood strikes. The 735 rooms and suites provide a mini-fridge, coffee maker, hair dryer, and mini-bar, and are decorated to suit the tropics. Colorful beach art adorns the walls; blond wood furniture pieces are carved with palm fronds; curtains and spreads are jungle-themed.

RADISSON SUITE BEACH RESORT
General Manager: Brett Smith.
941-394-4100, 800-333-3333, or 800-814-0633.
600 S. Collier Blvd., Marco Island 34145.
Price: Expensive to Very Expensive.
Credit Cards: AE, CB, D, DC, MC, V.

Along the island's stretch of shell-strewn beach the Radisson accommodates guests in typical Marco high-rise style, with 269 roomy suites and hotel rooms. The suites come in the one- or two-bedroom variety and hold a completely equipped kitchen. All units have private balconies and comfortable furniture. Microwaves, refrigerators, and coffee makers provide all guests with in-room dining options. Off the impressive marble lobby you'll find a game room, gulfside dining room, grill, and tiki bar, for when cooking is out of the question. Active guests enjoy a heated free-form pool, two tennis courts, a Jacuzzi, waterskiing, kayaking, sailing, tubing, jet skiing, fishing, cruising, biking, and golf on three nearby courses. Families are attracted to this Radisson, where kids can enroll in a staffed recreational program or have fun in the splashy pool area or on the beach.

Naples

COTTAGES OF NAPLES
Innkeepers: Lori Raleigh
  and John McMorrow.
941-436-3915.
370 11th Ave. S., Naples
  34102.
Price: Moderate to Very
  Expensive (four-day to
  one-week minimum).
Credit Cards: No.
Handicap Access: No.

One of Naples' unique properties, the Cottages consist of a cluster of three cottages and a loft apartment that are most often rented out on a monthly or at least weekly basis, especially during the winter season. Accommodations range from an efficiency with a pull-out couch to one-bedroom apartments, all charmingly decorated in Florida-country style and outfitted with full kitchens and outdoor seating areas. This is personal — much more like staying with friends or having your own place than like renting a room in a cold high-rise hotel. Guests gather around the pool or keep busy exploring the nearby shopping and dining district and beach. They receive a "starter breakfast kit," but breakfast is not otherwise provided, and there is no daily housekeeping.

**THE EDGEWATER
  BEACH HOTEL**
General Manager: William
  Doyle.
941-262-6511 or
  800-821-0196.
1901 Gulf Shore Blvd. N.,
  Naples 34102.
Price: Expensive to Very
  Expensive.
Credit Cards: AE, CB, D,
  DC, MC, V.

Edgewater hints at New Orleans style with lacy white iron balustrades on two of its three buildings, all of which face the gulf-lapped beach. Its 124 one- and two-bedroom suites are spacious, convenient, and handsomely appointed with saltillo tile, rattan furnishings, and silk plants. The floor plan of each includes a full kitchen (with microwave), living/dining area, and private patio or balcony. Guests can dine in the award-winning Club Dining Room or poolside under stylish market umbrellas. There's an on-site exercise room and opportunities for other recreation nearby, including golf privileges at several local courses.

INN ON FIFTH
Owner: Philip McCabe.
941-403-8777 or
  888-403-8778.
699 Fifth Ave. S., Naples
  34102.
Price: Moderate to Very
  Expensive.
Credit Cards: AE, DC, MC,
  V.

Modeled after Europe's intimate city hotels, Inn on Fifth marks a crescendo in the burgeoning renaissance of Naples' historic downtown main street. It turned a staid, ugly bank building into an ocher-colored eye-opener with Mediterranean archways and flourishes. Smack dab in the middle of downtown's lively dining, shopping, and entertainment scene, it fronts Fifth Avenue South and edges a newly developed walking plaza and outdoor theater. Its greatest sensation is an Irish pub originally built near Dublin and reassembled on site here. It spills out into the plaza and serves guests and the local community alike. The inn's magnificent marble lobby foreshadows the rich European style carried out in the rooms. The 102 rooms and suites overlook the street, plaza, or hotel's court-

The new Inn on Fifth reflects the high fashion of Naples' downtown renaissance.

Karen T. Bartlett

yard. Thick-paned French doors and careful soundproofing ensure that the town's bustle does not interfere with privacy and relaxation. All rooms come with bathrobes, hair dryers, irons, and other deluxe amenities. Guests have access to a small pool located across the alley from the hotel, a small fitness room, and a spa with sauna, steam room, and massage services.

The Naples Beach Hotel: granddaddy of South Coast resorts, circa 1958.

Karen T. Bartlett

NAPLES BEACH HOTEL & GOLF CLUB
Owners: The Watkins Family.
General Manager: Jim Gunderson.
941-261-2222 or 800-237-7600.

The doyenne of Naples resorts, this combines the best of the area — its beaches and its golf — into a three-generation tradition in the heart of the town. The 18-hole golf course hosts the Florida State PGA Seniors Open. Har-Tru tennis courts, a heated pool, Beach Klub for Kids, and water-sports equipment rentals vie for off-the-course recre-

851 Gulf Shore Blvd. N.,
Naples 34102.
Price: Expensive to Very
Expensive.
Credit Cards: AE, CB, D,
DC, MC, V.

ational hours. The hotel's spacious lobby and Everglades Dining Room communicate Florida vacationing ease, and its 316 newly renovated guestrooms and suites are done in beach cabana decor, with some lingering classic trademarks of yesteryear. Accommodations overlook the wide, palm-studded beach or the lush golf course. In season there's a four-night minimum stay.

OLD NAPLES TRIANON
General Manager: Darren
Robertshaw.
941-435-9600 or
800-859-3939.
955 Seventh Ave. S., Naples
34102.
Price: Moderate to Very
Expensive.*
Credit Cards: AE, D, DC,
MC, V.

Another in a succession of intimate accommodations taking up residency in Old Naples, this one is close to downtown activity, yet tucked discreetly away in a residential neighborhood with a nearby park and its own swimming pool. The name implies "a special place," in the spirit of the Grand Trianon and Petit Trianon on the grounds of Versailles near Paris. It's heavy on European influence. The lobby displays both elegance and intimacy, the entry dramatic but segueing into a cozy lounge-breakfast nook where tropical iced tea and fruit are on hand to refresh guests. Attention to detail is a hallmark of the Trianon. In its 58 spacious guestrooms and suites you'll find such thoughtful considerations as a bathroom night-light, a shower in which the control knobs are located opposite the shower head, gourmet coffee service, and closets with heavy double doors. New (opened December 1997) and stylish, the rooms are decorated in European good taste, with French doors opening onto balconies or railing. The property's conversation piece is the Vila House, an old Florida cottage bought and refurbished by TV personality Bob Vila for his syndicated home-improvement series. Continental breakfast, served in the lounge and in Vila House, is included in the rates.

THE REGISTRY RESORT
General Manager: Jerry
Phirion.
941-597-3232 or
800-247-9810.
475 Seagate Dr., Naples
33940.
Price: Very Expensive.
Credit Cards: AE, CB, D,
DC, MC, V.

Luxury with beach casualness: The Registry fits Naples like a gold lamé wetsuit. Its distinctive red-capped tower, villas, and 15 Har-Tru tennis courts dominate north Naples' pristine, mangrove-fringed estuaries. The resort's style is impressive from the moment you walk in the front door into a marble and crystal lobby. Outside, on the second-floor level, is a boardwalk that leads around shops and restaurants, and downstairs there's a pool with a Flintstones feel and a long bridge to the beach. Tram service is available along the wooden walk that traverses tidal bays to Clam Pass Recreation Area, a three-mile stretch of plush sands with all manner of water-sports rentals. Fifty tennis villas edge the courts; another 424 rooms and suites overlook the gulf, each furnished with a wet bar, marble vanity, spaciousness, and class. The Registry owns a nearby 27-hole golf course and provides a golf concierge and shuttles to and fro. Three heated pools include Jacuzzis; the health club contains a sauna and steam baths and a fitness room with a view of mangrove wilderness. Seven restaurants and lounges range from casual to the world-class Lafite.

An entourage of royal palms hints at the regal, Old World elegance of the Ritz-Carlton in Naples.

The Ritz-Carlton, Naples

THE RITZ-CARLTON
General Manager: William Hall.
941-598-3300 or 800-241-3333.
280 Vanderbilt Beach Rd., Naples 34108.
Price: Very Expensive.
Credit Cards: AE, CB, D, DC, MC, V.

The gold standard for regal accommodations, Naples' Ritz molds Old World elegance to Old Florida environment. The hotel's façade looms majestically classic, with valets, sometimes in top hats, to park your car. Inside, oversized vases of fresh flowers, heavy chandeliers, cabinets filled with priceless china, 19th-century oil paintings, vaulted ceilings, and crystal lamps detail Ritz extravagance. Each of the 463 units in the U-shaped configuration faces the gulf. Guestrooms and suites are dressed in fine furniture, plush carpeting, and marble bath areas. Accommodations include honor bar, refrigerator, bathrobes, hypoallergenic pillows, telephones in the water closet, clothes steamers, and private balconies overlooking the hotel's unique backyard. In the courtyard, fountains and groomed gardens exude European character.

Classic arches, stone balustrades, and majestic palm-lined stairways lead to a boardwalk that takes you through a completely different world of Florida estuarine life via a self-guided flora and fauna tour. The tour ends at golden Vanderbilt Beach, where two beach restaurants serve refreshments. Other amenities and services that earn the Ritz its five stars and five diamonds include a formal dining room, afternoon tea service, grill, cafe, pool, lounge, ballroom, Jacuzzi, six tennis courts, off-property golf facilities, fitness center, beauty salon, masseuse, children's programs, bicycle rental, shops, transportation services, and twice-daily maid service.

Vanderbilt Beach

**LA PLAYA BEACH
   RESORT**
General Manager: Lee
   Weeks.
941-597-3123 or
   800-237-6883.
9891 Gulf Shore Dr., Naples
   FL 34108.
Price: Expensive to Very
   Expensive.
Credit Cards: AE, CB, D,
   DC, MC, V.

Recent renovations have elevated this old beach and tennis resort to among Naples' finest. The lobby makes an immediate statement of class and good taste with the tropical, neoclassic look of columns, wicker, tiles, paddle fans, white French doors, and grandeur. The 174 rooms and suites are situated in low- and high-rise buildings and feature modern tropical appointments, elegant white marble baths, and balconies or patios with rocking chairs. The tennis courts are gone, but the beach, recently widened, still beckons. A boutique swimming pool and water-sports rentals enhance the outdoor scene. A restaurant and a bar face the beach, with seating alfresco.

VANDERBILT INN
General Manager: Brian
   Schomacker.
941-597-3151 or
   800-643-8654.
11000 Gulf Shore Dr.,
   Naples 34108.
Price: Moderate to Very
   Expensive.
Credit Cards: AE, CB, D,
   DC, MC, V.

Informal and beachy, this long-time Vanderbilt Beach fixture focuses on poolside and water sports along a well-populated stretch of sand. Anyone who's been around for a while knows that its chickee bar is a place of vitality and fun, day or night. Its 147 rooms and efficiencies, like its lobby, restaurant, and grounds, let you know with cool, breezy lushness that you're in the tropics.

HOME & CONDO RENTALS

Bluebill Properties, Inc. (941-597-1102 or 800-237-2010; 9060 Gulf Shore Dr., Naples 34108) Rentals from Fort Myers Beach to Marco Island.

Naples Marco Accommodations and Travel (941-261-7577; 3401 Tamiami Trail, Naples 34103. Also 941-394-0589; 1081$^1/_2$ N. Collier Blvd., Marco Island 34145. 800-828-0042 outside Collier County) Homes, villas, and condos by the week, month, and season.

RV RESORTS

Chokoloskee Island Park (941-695-2414; P.O. Box 430, Chokoloskee 34138) Fisherman's paradise with easy access to the Everglades and the gulf. Full-service marina, tackle shop, guide service, boat rentals, ramps, and docks. Overnight or seasonal RV sites with complete hookups.

Outdoor Resorts of Chokoloskee Island (941-695-3788; P.O. Box 39, Chokoloskee 34138). Marina, boat rentals, a bait and tackle shop, and guide service for fishing and touring. Pull into one of 283 full-service sites or stay in the motel. Either way, you can take advantage of the resort's three pools, health spa, lighted tennis and shuffleboard courts, and restaurant .

Port of the Islands RV Resort (941-394-3101 or 800-237-4173; 20 miles south-east of Naples, 25000 Tamiami Trail E., Naples 34114) Location convenient to Ten Thousand Islands on the waterfront. Ninety-nine hookup sites, with laundry, boat ramp, and marina.

Rock Creek Campgrounds (941-643-3100; 3100 North Rd. at Airport Rd., Naples 34104) Full hookups for 221 RVs, pool, laundry, and shade trees. No pets.

DINING

Everglades City considers itself a fishing and stone crab capital, so figure you can expect some highly fresh seafood in these parts. Stone crab, in fact, was discovered as a food source in the Everglades; at least that's the way some of the old-timers tell it. Before a couple of locals began trapping them and selling them to a Miami restaurant, stone crabs' delicate, meaty flavor went unappreciated. Along with stone crab, alligator, frog legs, and other local delicacies make up the substance of Everglades cookery.

Stone crab claws: a truly authentic South Coast delicacy.

Karen T. Bartlett

Marco Island, too, is known as a good market for buying stone crab, which gets quite expensive farther from the source. With more than 100 restaurants on the island, Marco covers every genre of cuisine. Its trademark is its Old Florida style of no-nonsense, trend-resistant seafood preparation. German cuisine also surfaces frequently.

Naples' dining reputation is staked on hauteur and creativity. Even the old fish houses dress up their catches in the latest fashion, which ranges from redesigned home cooking and continental nouvelle to Floribbean and Pacific Rim styles. Naples is a dining-out kind of place. The renovation of downtown's Fifth Avenue South has brought restaurants out into the street and sparked the genesis of what has been termed a Naples "cafe society."

The following listings sample all the variety of south coast feasting in these price categories:

Inexpensive	Up to $15
Moderate	$15 to $25
Expensive	$25 to $35
Very Expensive	$35 or more

Cost is figured on a typical meal (at dinner, unless dinner is not served) that would include an appetizer or dessert, salad (if included with the meal), entrée, and coffee.

The following abbreviations are used for credit card information and meals:

AE - American Express	DC - Diners Club
CB - Carte Blanche	MC - MasterCard
D - Discover Card	V - Visa
B - Breakfast	D - Dinner
L - Lunch	SB - Sunday Brunch

Bonita Springs

THE SHIP
941-947-3333.
24080 N. Tamiami Trail.
Price: Moderate to
  Expensive.
Children's Menu: Yes.
Cuisine: Seafood and
  Steaks.
Healthy Selections: No.
Liquor: Full.
Serving: D.
Credit Cards: AE, D, MC, V.
Handicap Access: Yes.
Reservations: No.

This place is more than gimmick. Inside its replicated-ship structure, the seafood market, bakery, and kitchen hold a treasure of fresh products featured on its menu. The day's fish can be ordered broiled, grilled, fried, or blackened. The blackened grouper is especially good, neither too spicy nor charred. Prime rib, sirloin, filet mignon, and other cuts come from prime Angus beef. The pork à la Moby Dick is a tasty concoction of andouille sausage rolled in pork loin. Veal Grenobloise is lightly breaded, sautéed, and topped with a lemon capers butter sauce. For starters, try the blackened fish chowder or gator bites, Cajun-seasoned, seared,

Special Features: Ship-shaped building, on-site fish market and bakery.

and served with Cajun aioli sauce. The atmosphere is stateroom and tastefully seaworthy. Make sure to save room for a treat from the bakery.

Everglades City

ROD & GUN CLUB
941-695-2101.
200 Broadway.
Price: Moderate.
Early Dining Menu: No.
Children's Menu: Yes (dinner only).
Cuisine: Florida.
Healthy Selections: No.
Liquor: Full.
Serving: B, L, D.
Credit Cards: No.
Handicap Access: No.
Reservations: No.
Special Features: Historic, waterfront setting.

Dining here on a screened porch overlooking the Barron River and the mangroves on the other side always triggers the relaxation mechanism in my body, mind, and spirit. It goes deeper than the serenity of the scene, for there's a time-reversion effect here. Paddle fans twirl from pressed-tin ceilings. White columns, a rounded portico, a porch with wicker chairs, and yellow-and-white striped awnings at the lodge's entrance evoke plantation manors of the Old South. The inside dining room, the antithesis of the patio's lightness, is all dark, pecky cypress wood, polished wood floors, and mounted fish and fowl — remnants of the lodge's sporting past. From the 1890s to 1960 the club hosted presidents, stars, and other intrepid Everglades hunters and fishermen. Back then guests dined on frog legs, alligator tail, and fresh fish. They still do. Menus do offer more conventional fare — reubens, burgers, New York strip, and chicken marsala. But the ultimate Everglades City experience requires sitting back, taking in the view, enjoying local hospitality, and dining on Everglades specialties. The frog legs, by the way, are incredibly tasty; the gator nuggets, well tenderized but salty and a tad greasy; and the peanut butter pie, simply divine.

Goodland

LITTLE BAR RESTAURANT
941-394-5663.
205 Harbor Dr.
Price: Moderate.
Children's Menu: No.
Cuisine: Seafood/Florida.
Healthy Selections: No.
Liquor: Full.
Serving: L, D.
Credit Cards: D, MC, V.
Handicap Access: Yes.
Reservations: Yes, for dinner.
Special Features: Waterfront dining, historic "Boat Room."

Goodland is a town where a more modest pace of tourism has allowed folks to remain hometown and proud of it. A long-ingrained fishing tradition means you'll find the freshest catches and people who know how to prepare them. A friend had recommended Little Bar to me as friendly, and that it is. And then some. The hostess treated me like a regular as she led me through a forest of beautiful wood onto a screened porch overlooking Buzzard Bay harbor. Century-old stained-glass windows, hand-carved antique pieces, and a room divider made of wooden organ pipes bespoke the owner's passion for collectibles. One entire dining room, in fact, was created from the wreck of a 1927 boat, *Star of the Everglades*, which starred in movies and carried two presidents. From the porch I watched cruising boats bobbing alongside fishing scows as the waitress presented the menu board on a metal stand. The selections reflect the village's fishing reputation, with pleasant departures from standard fish-house fare — everything from Buffalo frog legs and grouper balls to frog legs, kielbasa and kraut, Cajun prime rib, and snapper almandine. On my first visit I ordered the softshell crab sandwich, a certain obsession of mine. It was the best I've had. More recently I sampled the day's special: blackened grouper cakes with black bean sauce. I had liked the way they do their tropical treatments, and this dish was a joy (could have been spicier, but that's another obsession of mine). If your obsession is desserts, you'll love it here. On the day's menu there were seven selections, including a special calamondin pie, making rare use of Florida's native sour orange. The wine list is surprisingly extensive, but beer — which arrived with the requisite frosty mug — seemed more appropriate here.

Marco Island (see also Goodland)

OLDE MARCO INN
941-394-3131.
100 Palm St., Old Marco.
Price: Expensive.
Cuisine: Continental.
Serving: D.
Credit Cards: AE, D, DC, MC, V.
Handicap Access: Yes.
Reservations: Accepted.
Special Features: Historic structure.

This Marco Island tradition was built in 1883 by pioneer Captain William D. Collier as a home, and later became his rustic inn. Restored to its original gracious southern style, it boasts a collection of Audubon originals and antique cranberry glass within its six rooms of varying motifs — from fully formal to airy, French-doored veranda. The international/seafood menu has a German accent, with such selections as Wienerschnitzel, sauerbraten with red cabbage and potato pancake, and German farmer's soup. Escargots à la bourguignonne, Florida grouper à la meunière, filet mignon au poivre vert, and veal Madagascar tour the culinary globe. Other dishes showcase local fresh seafood. On a recent visit my filet au poivre turned out to be an excellent choice, dressed in a subtle brandy peppercorn sauce and prepared to rare perfection. My husband's *jaeggerschnitzel* was equally well prepared — the veal pounded thin and lightly breaded, then skillfully finished with a light mushroom cream sauce. Our server was accommodating above and beyond the call, providing a child's portion of the excellent shrimp almondine for my son and substituting his salad with the day's clam chowder, a vegetable-rich version without all that gooey thickness restaurants often think they must add. Key lime critics all, the whole family enjoyed the wedge of pie, although it was suspiciously green. The caramel flan was well executed but too small for the price.

Karen T. Bartlett

When the Olde Marco Inn opened in the late 1800s, diners were required to provide their own meat.

SNOOK INN
941-642-6944.
1215 Bald Eagle Dr.
Price: Expensive.
Children's Menu: Yes (ages 5 and under).
Cuisine: Seafood.
Healthy Selections: No.
Liquor: Full.
Serving: L, D.
Credit Cards: V, MC, AE, DC.
Handicap Access: Yes.
Reservations: No.
Special Features: Chickee bar and outdoor waterfront seating.

Marco Island is known for its many restaurants, a great number of which serve fine, expensive food. To find something casual you have to travel to Goodland, a fishing village that shares the island, or head to Snook Inn, a long-standing tradition known equally for its congenial tiki bar (called in these parts by its Amerindian name, chickee bar) and its seafood. It still tips the scale on the overpriced side, and I found it perturbing that the children's menu was limited to preschoolers, but all in all it offers a nice taste of Marco's saltier, less exclusive side. You can sit in the fresh sea air dockside along the peaceful Marco River. If the day is hot, you may prefer the air-conditioned porch, where picture windows let you feel a little like you're alfresco. A huge aquarium is set into wood-paneled walls. Inside it's cool and dark, and there you'll find the salad bar, a strong drawing card for the restaurant. It's small, but the contents are crisp, fresh, and varied, including a big crock of fat dill pickle chunks for the taking. Salad bar is included in most lunch and dinner menu selections, which concentrate on fish, with some steak, chicken, and ribs exceptions. On Thursday and Friday nights the salad bar extends into a long seafood buffet that is highly acclaimed. Fried grouper is the house specialty, and worthy of the renown. The grouper sandwich is generous and smacks of just-caught flavor. Buttermilk shrimp, shrimp de jonghe, grouper in a bag, and softshell crab are some other favorites. The spicy tomato conch chowder is chockful of conch bits, with just the right touch of fire. Warning: Don't drink the water; even the slice of lemon doesn't disguise its off taste. Order a beer instead.

Naples

AMADOR'S BISTRO ITALIANO
941-775-7666.
3367 Bayshore Dr.
Price: Moderate to
  Expensive.
Early Dining Menu: No.
Children's Menu: No.
Cuisine: Italian.
Healthy Selections: No.
Liquor: Beer and wine.
Serving: D.
Credit Cards: AE, MC, V.
Handicap Access: Yes.
Reservations: Yes.

The lady at the next table informed us that Amador's serves "the best food in Naples." The tiny eatery instills that brand of loyalty. Amador's has lots of friends — more friends than room sometimes. In a remote corner of Naples, holding only about a dozen tables, Amador's at better moments could be called cozy, but in the winter months it feels more like cramped. Chef Richard Amador brings a just-made freshness and Greek accents to standard, usually prepped-ahead Italian sauces and dishes. We relished each bite of our meal, from the first herb-infused taste of stuffed mushrooms to the last crumbs of the moist and refreshing piña colada cake. The Caesar salad was flawless, a well-measured balance of tastes and crisp textures. The Amador salad was masterfully presented, a medley of colorful greens, fresh peeled orange slices, an artistically carved cucumber slice, Greek olives, and a tastebud-tingling balsamic vinaigrette. The selection of Italian entrées is all-encompassing, everything from baked lasagna and chicken cacciatore to scungilli fra diavolo and veal saltimbocca. To the classics Amador's adds a few of its own creations, such as fish of the day in a Dijon white wine cream sauce with capers, sun-dried tomatoes, and fresh basil. We were intrigued by the day's specials. I ordered the yellowtail snapper broiled with fresh spinach, sambucco, portabella mushrooms, and orange juice — well prepared but too sweet for my palate. My husband's lamb chops were served in a reduction brown sauce with portabella and shiitake mushrooms, fresh-tasting and simple. A side of perfectly al dente pasta and vivacious marinara sauce accompanied our meals. The cake and a foamy cappuccino with a rock-candy stick ended the meal on a high note, just in time to escape the press of the waiting hungry at the door.

BACKSTAGE TAP & GRILL
941-598-1300.
Waterside Shops, 5535
  Tamiami Trail N.
Price: Inexpensive.
Cuisine: American.
Healthy Selections: No.
Liquor: Beer and wine.
Serving: B, L, D.
Credit Cards: AE, D, MC, V.
Handicap Access: Yes.
Reservations: No.
Special Features: Patio
  seating.

Have fun here, especially if you're a stage buff or wanna-be actor. Nostalgia theater props hang from the walls and ceiling, are served under glass at tables, and even decorate the ladies' room, which is made up to look like an actor's dressing room, roses and all. Wood-floored and black-walled, the Backstage offers seating at tables, at the U-shaped bar, or on the patio under green market umbrellas. The bar, with its fat jars of pickles and fake fancy chandelier converted to hold stemware, is a favorite with lunching locals. The combination lunch and dinner menu presents a nice mix of selections. I was tempted by the portabella bruschetta (with tomato and Havarti dill cheese) and the meatloaf sandwich (again Havarti dill, with black olives and mushrooms, served cold), but opted for the peppered tuna steak. I replaced the fries with red beans and rice, which turned out to be my best decision. They were fabulously flavored, with just a touch of sweetness. The rhubarb pie posed another temptation; to this one I succumbed. Not bad, but it left me wondering how yummy the jazzy caramel walnut brownie or triple chocolate cheesecake with raspberry sauce must be. The Backstage — which, incidentally, gets its name and theme from its proximity to the Philharmonic Performing Arts Hall — also features a great lineup of beverages, despite the fact that its liquor license allows only beer and wine sales. It serves nine beers on tap, including Guinness Stout, Sam Adams, Bass Ale, and Newcastle Brown Ale. Or try an espresso or cappuccino. On the breakfast menu, Phantom of the Omelette fits in nicely with the theme, with country ham, red onions, bell peppers, and Jack cheese.

BAYSIDE

941-649-5552.
4270 Gulfshore Blvd. N.
Price: Very Expensive.
Early Dining Menu: No.
Children's Menu: Yes.
Cuisine: Seafood/Grill.
Healthy Selections: No.
Liquor: Full.
Serving: L, D.
Credit Cards: AE, D, DC, MC, V.
Handicap Access: Yes.
Reservations: Recommended.
Special Features: Waterfront view, piano downstairs.

Stylish heather-blue wicker and watercolor fish prints counterbalance classic columns and arches. The restaurant is divided into two levels, both overlooking bay waters — which, unfortunately, tend to be floating too much garbage to be totally scenic. Part of an upscale, Mediterranean-style shopping village, it, too, affects the architectural airs of an Italian canal community. More casual fare is served downstairs: barbecued shrimp, pizzetas (small pizzas), and smoked turkey BLT. Upstairs is upscale and upbeat. The menu presents a finer choice of dishes, inspired by Florida's fresh seafood, global styles, and inventive preparation that doesn't go overboard to impress. The shrimp bisque is classic, with chunks of shrimp commingling with a light, tomatoey, sherry-tinged creaminess. The spinach salad marvelously blended textures and tastes — mildly biting Gorgonzola with sweet currants, crunchy walnuts with sautéed red onions, all treated with port vinaigrette. A fan of Caribbean spice, I was enchanted by the oak-grilled mahi mahi with its Barbados honey pepper glaze — piquant as it should be — but disappointed that the kitchen didn't deliver the promised fried plantains. A rice pilaf (flavorful, yes) was substituted without consultation. The dressing in the crab-stuffed shrimp was a tad light on crab, but wore a champion herb beurre blanc. We sealed the meal with a fragilely crusted crème brûlée, port, and cappuccino.

BHA! BHA!

941-594-5557.

An Iranian chef and an American artist partner in this new, deliciously exotic enterprise. The

Bha! Bha! fuses culinary and artistic elements from old Persia and new continental.

Chelle Koster Walton

The Pavilion, 847
    Vanderbilt Rd.
Price: Moderate.
Early Dining Menu: No.
Children's Menu: No.
Cuisine: Persian.
Healthy Selections: No.
Liquor: Beer and wine.
Serving: L, D.
Closed: Monday.
Credit Cards: AE, MC, V.
Handicap Access: Yes.
Reservations: Yes, for
    dinner.

merger of creativities results in a sleek, bright, and sunny setting of ocher and key-lime-green walls, ottomans, fountain, and Turkish tapestries. They call it a Persian bistro. In an Iranian dialect the name means "Yum! Yum!" And that's where chef Michael Mir comes in. He fuses his native background with his experience in fine American kitchens to present an intriguing menu that maintains the authenticity and boldness of Middle Eastern cuisine while employing a few tricks of classic continental and experimental new American styles. Prepare your palate for a magic carpet ride. Flavors tick, tantalize, then burst in a medley of unusual seasonings and combinations. *Aash*, a peasant-style bean soup, starts out simple but, as you nibble into the center garnish of pickled Persian noodles, becomes more and more complex and extraordinary. In the appetizer of eggplant and artichoke we could discern an orchestra of flavors: distinctive Bulgarian feta, dill and a hint of sweetness in the mustard sauce, and the peanut oil in which the eggplant was sautéed. Yum, yum. The dinner menu is divided between classic and innovative Persian cuisine and *khoreshes* (specialties). Persian couscous accompanies a host of seafood — clams, mussels, calamari, shrimp, scallops, and fish, plus chicken — under "Innovative." The almond-crusted turmeric fish is a tempting choice. Classics range from kabobs to char-broiled lamb (incredibly beautiful and tasty), and specialties include garlic eggplant chicken, dried plum lamb, and duck *fesenjune* — braised in orange saffron stock and served with pomegranate walnut sauce (a bit heavy-sweet). Persian coffee comes served in delicate espresso service with an ornamental wood box full of rock candy, raw sugar cubes, and sugar substitute.

MESON OLÉ
941-649-6616.
Oaks Plaza, 2212 N.
  Tamiami Trail.
Price: Moderate.
Children's Menu: Yes.
Cuisine: Mexican/Spanish.
Healthy Selections: No.
Liquor: Full.
Serving: L, D.
Credit Cards: AE, MC, V.
Handicap Access: Yes.
Reservations: Yes.

It seems Meson Olé has descended to Florida from a New York State chain, but it has no regional counterparts and stands decidedly apart from conventional chain Mexican restaurants. Its menus do carry the typical tostados and chimichangas, but I suggest you be more daring here. The menu is certainly daring, as it enters into more genuinely Spanish territory. Take, for instance, *sopa de ajo* Casera, a traditional Castilian soup that floats a crouton and a poached egg. The latter added richness to the untimid garlic broth, which suffered only from too much salt. *Los mejillones en salsa verde* — mussels in green sauce — was a totally unexpected pleasure, the sauce not spicy, peppery hot as I anticipated, but buttery and garlicky, with green peas wading in it. The mussels were the most tender I've tasted in a long while. Lobster tail and seafood come in the same rich bath on the entrées portion of the menu. Other enticements: Spanish shrimp in champagne sauce; chicken in creamy whiskey sauce; mignon of veal sautéed with mushrooms, asparagus, and ham; and two varieties of paella. The atmosphere is more typical of the Mexican genre — the requisite serapes and pounded-metal plates — all tucked into a strip mall. This place was recommended to me by a Texan connoisseur who assured me the margaritas were the real thing — not all puckery or sugary. They are indeed.

**THE DINING ROOM AT
  THE RITZ-CARLTON**
941-598-3300.
280 Vanderbilt Beach Rd.
Price: Very Expensive.
Early Dining Menu: No.
Children's Menu: No.
Cuisine: Nouvelle
  Continental.
Healthy Selections: No.
Liquor: Full.
Serving: D.
Credit Cards: AE, CB, D,
  DC, MC, V.
Handicap Access: Yes.
Reservations: Yes.
Special Features: Piano and
  cello music.

An evening out at The Ritz-Carlton's Dining Room constitutes an occasion. Something you mark down on your calendar. In gold ink. The Dining Room sinks back into the Gilded Age as one sinks back into a plush, overstuffed chair. Old World art, newly renovated baroque surroundings, piano and cello music, and polished silver set the stage for an experience that far transcends putting food in mouth. For our occasion we selected an appetizer of ravioli of langostino and salmon dressed in a prosciutto sauce with roasted asparagus; cocktail of stone crab and avocado, served martini style; ballotine of foie gras with pear and roasted hazelnuts; and terrine of duck with sweet apple and sauterne confit. All came artistically presented and in the proper proportions so as to whet, not weigh. The entrées arrived with dramatic fanfare. The Ritz-Carlton's trademark silver domes topped each plate set before us, then in perfect unison were lifted. My dish revealed a creative arrangement of lobster roasted subtly with mango and served with nuggets of deep-fried gnocchi and pineapple sauce. We passed around samples. The roasted mahi mahi was superb, seasoned with turmeric and in orchestra with rice noodles and frizzle-fried julienne of spring onions. The roasted filet of Angus beef with sweet potatoes and corn salsa was executed to perfection. The most delightful surprise was the *pastilla* of rabbit. Roasted with almonds and complemented with citrus sauce, it gave the palate something amazingly mild, juicy, and tender. As the sun sank behind the mangroves beyond the parapet outside our window, we savored our last bites and listened to the musicians perform "Putting on the Ritz" (a bit too loudly; I suggest asking for a back table if you're in a talking mood). Portions being reasonable as they are in the Dining Room, we were left with enough appetite and red wine to want something chocolaty for dessert. Two of us ordered the chocolate raspberry selection, sort of a fresh raspberry and shingle-thin-chocolate sandwich that was beautifully assembled and efficiently curative of chocolate fixations. One order of warm chocolate cake with melted caramel center, an unusual and tasty strawberry consommé with slightly sweet coconut ravioli, and rich coffee brought our evening at the Dining Room to a soft, soothing close.

RIVERWALK FISH & ALE HOUSE
941-263-2734.
Tin City, 1200 Fifth Ave. S.
Price: Moderate.
Children's Menu: Yes.
Cuisine: Seafood.
Liquor: Full.
Serving: L, D.
Credit Cards: AE, D, MC, V.
Handicap Access: Yes, but some manipulation required.
Reservations: No.
Special Features: View of bay, open-air dining.

This is Naples' spirited side, where things can get a little noisy and everything isn't always polished. I like it. Ambiance is provided by splintered wood, with only clear plastic sheets separating you from the sea air in inclement weather. Last time we visited, a summer shower forced them to roll down the plastic. We watched as a fisherman — very authentic-looking in his yellow slicker — cleaned fish on the dock right outside. Seafood preparations transcend the standard. Shrimp and andouille pasta with a Cajun flair is a filling and pleasantly spicy lunch or dinner option. Other interesting choices: jalapeño crab fritters appetizer, perfectly piquant; grilled seafood salad, a complex medley of greens; English shrimp and crab melt sandwich; chili garlic scallops; grouper Rockefeller; shrimp and scallops Raveneaux, with fettuccine, shallots, mushrooms, and lobster cream.

TERRA
941-262-5500.
1300 Third St.
Price: Expensive.
Children's Menu: No.
Cuisine: Mediterranean.
Liquor: Full.

Formerly Chef's Garden, a long-standing Naples culinary tradition, Terra represents a makeover in menu and style. Like many restaurants today, it has gone Mediterranean. This means a shift from classic good looks to tile flooring, French doors and walls painted yellow, and bright-print shirts on the

Serving: L, D, SB.
Credit Cards: AE, D, DC, MC, V.
Handicap Access: Yes.
Reservations: Recommended.
Special Features: Alfresco porch seating.

servers. The green and off-white wicker chairs remain, questionable in taste. Decor aside, the menu triumphs as a masterpiece of modern Mediterranean cuisine and the gastronomic gallantry for which Chef's Garden was known. For lunch, the soup, salad, focaccia bread pizza, risotto, and quiche change daily. We made our selections from this, and were thrilled. The tomato, bacon, and spinach soup was creamy and well balanced. My dining companion pronounced the featured salad "maybe the best salad I've ever had." The mixture of greens was interesting and fresh, with just the right touches of chopped pepperoncini, feta cheese, tomato, cucumber, and red onion. A mound of sliced grilled chicken breast and a creamy balsamic vinaigrette topped it all off in a way equally pleasing to the eye and the palate. The risotto dish smacked of folk tradition in a stewlike blend of pan-seared shrimp, prosciutto, portabella mushroom, peas, basil, and plum tomato sauce. The regular menu offers a choice of salads, pizza, pasta, sandwiches, meats, and seafood. These demonstrate a blend of old and new in such delights as the veal-prosciutto meatball and cornmeal-fried oysters (with spicy garlic sauce) appetizers, wild mushroom lasagna, Moroccan chicken over penne, pulled lamb shank with ratatouille, Mediterranean seafood stew, and herb-encrusted tuna. Fine desserts and a well-planned wine list conspire to create a near-perfect meal in a setting less than marvelous.

TRUFFLES
941-597-8119.
8920 N. Tamiami Trail, North Naples.
Price: Moderate to expensive.
Children's Menu: Yes.
Cuisine: American/ Continental.
Liquor: Full.
Serving: L, D.
Credit Cards: AE, D, DC, MC, V.
Handicap Access: Yes.
Reservations: No.

In 1996 the owners of Truffles made a daring move. They closed their popular eatery in swanky Old Naples. Neapolitans would not have it, however. They demanded their Truffles back. And so it is, but moved to North Naples as the casual, fun adjunct to the Italian-style Villa Pescatore. Known above all for its fresh and impossible-to-resist desserts, Truffles also serves a simple, all-day menu with something to please everyone. Black bean chili, gazpacho, the signature tuna Caesar, hamburgers, a sandwich of avocado, Muenster, tomato, and sprouts, and a wide selection of soups, salads, and appetizers feed light appetites. The gazpacho demonstrates Truffles' philosophy of bold flavors, with cracked black pepper and chili pepper liberally applied to the slightly thick tomato base afloat with crunchy vegetables. Full entrées include the popular crispy fish — fried grouper with an Oriental flair — chicken carbonara, vegetable lasagna, sirloin steak, and jerk pork tenderloin. The dessert menu lists more than 20 selections.

I can personally recommend the key lime pie, chocolate truffle tart, and raspberry Grand Marnier cake. Truffles makes sure every detail adds to the enjoyment of the experience. The by-the-glass wine list offers a well-rounded selection, heavy on the Italians. The basket of fennel bread chunks and bruschetta and the well-flavored baby Caesar make pleasant accompaniments. The atmosphere is rather plain. Nonsmokers have a view of the kitchen and the vegetation outside; smokers cluster around a cozy bar.

ZOE'S
941-261-1221.
720 Fifth Ave. S.
Price: Expensive to Very
    Expensive.
Children's Menu: No.
Cuisine: New
    American/Fusion.
Liquor: Full.
Serving: D.
Credit Cards: AE, MC, V.
Handicap Access: Yes.
Reservations:
    Recommended.

The latest sensation by one of Naples' foremost restaurateurs, Zoe's presents a diverse menu that features multidimensional dishes but doesn't strain under the weight of Naples cutting-edge one-upmanship. With such comfort dishes as macaroni 'n cheese and meatloaf (of course considerably dressier than you'd find at the local diner), Zoe's menu is relatively conservative. Yet Mom is not the only influence here. The paella is a bow to Spanish cuisine; the honey and tamarind grilled pork chop to Caribbean. Sesame-crusted yellowfin tuna with Asian noodles, smoked Thai barbecued chicken with coconut ginger rice, and appetizers of spicy pork potstickers, vegetarian summer roll, and other dishes pay homage to Asian flavors. Swordfish with calamari stew, orzo with gulf shrimp, and bucatini with grilled chicken breast demonstrate Mediterranean influences. My husband chose his entrée from the latter persuasion, a juicy, well-seasoned veal chop grilled with garlic, rosemary, and lemon. The side dish of penne Putanesca — Greek and Spanish olives, tomato, and capers — harmonized in the key of Aegean. My grouper had been wrapped in fresh parsley, oregano, and other herbs, and was outstanding in its well-balanced flavors, but on the dry side, as grilled fish tends to be. Again, the side dish rivaled the main dish. Pickled Napa cabbage and saffron vinaigrette enlivened a julienne of vegetables in a way that tickled each tastebud individually. Our pre- and post-entrée selections displayed what emerged as Zoe's modus operandi — simply described dishes made extraordinary by evenhanded seasoning. Fennel, thyme, and Pernod enhanced the escargots without overwhelming. The spinach salad was dressed elegantly in an uncomplicated, light, sweet-sour-salty offering of bacon and maple. The country carrot cake, a rustic version, transcended peasantry with the lightest cream-cheese layers, caramelized pineapple sauce, and a shard of white chocolate slashing stylishly into the top. Our coffees arrived in generous, funnel-shaped mugs that embellished upon Zoe's style, a style defined by angles, curves, blues, and *haute simplicité* — from the sealike sweep of the corner booth backs to the understated design of the flatware.

FOOD PURVEYORS

BAKERIES

Bakeries today are often combined with delis, grocery stores, and even wine shops.

Great Harvest Bread Company (941-262-1887; 3099 Ninth St. N., Naples) Specialty breads.

Island Bakery (941-394-4508; 287 N. Collier Blvd., Marco Island) Specializes in cakes. Also: key lime pie, tortes, croissants, Danish, breads.

Naples Cheesecake Co. (941-598-9070 or 800-325-6554; 8050 Trail Blvd., Naples) Eight to 12 different flavors, including key lime, amaretto, and peanut butter.

Tony's Off Third (941-262-7999; 1300 Third St. S., Old Naples) European bakery featuring legendary desserts, pastries, and breads, and a well-respected selection of wine and coffee.

CANDY & ICE CREAM

Breakfast & Cream (941-591-4060; 881 103rd Ave. N., Naples) Homemade ice cream and yogurt.

The Chocolate Strawberry (941-394-5999; Shops of Marco, San Marco Rd. and Barfield Dr., Marco Island) Hand-dipped chocolates, seahorse lollipops, ice cream, gelato, yogurt, sorbet, chocolate turtles, shells, pelicans, fish, other local critters, and coffee.

Olde Marco Fudge Factory (941-642-5200; 20 Marco Lake Dr., Marco Island) Homemade fudge in key lime, rum raisin, and other flavors, plus gourmet jelly beans, chocolate-covered pretzels, and gourmet preserves.

Regina's Ice Cream Pavilion (941-434-8181; 824 Fifth Ave. S., Old Naples) An old-fashioned soda fountain with modern frozen yogurts, sorbets, and sugar-free and name-brand ice cream.

COFFEE

Espresso Andiamo (941-514-1700; The Pavilion, 815 Vanderbilt Beach Rd., Naples) Espresso, cappuccino, specialty coffees, croissants, muffins, bagels, magazines to read while you sip.

P.J.'s Coffee & Tea Co. Cafe (941-261-5757; 599 Fifth Ave. S., Naples) Coffee, tea, cappuccino, cafe latte, cafe granita, bakery goods. Seating indoors and out.

Roberto's Complete Coffee House and Ice Cream Parlor (941-394-8388; Marco Town Center Mall, 1031 N. Collier Blvd., Marco Island) Espresso bar, fresh bagels and other bakery goods, light lunches. Seating indoors and out.

DELI & SPECIALTY FOODS

Artichoke & Company (941-263-6979; The Village on Venetian Bay, Naples) Gourmet takeout, soups, breads, cheeses, pastries, and wines.

Pelicatessen Fine Foods (941-597-3003; Waterside Shops, 5435 Tamiami Trail N., Naples) Huge selection of prepared gourmet dishes, beers, and wines. Coffee and espresso.

Wynn's Family Market (941-261-7157; 745 Fifth Ave. S., Old Naples) Since 1945 the Wynn family has operated this Fifth Avenue landmark, most famous for its fine selection of wine, fresh bakery goodies, and hot and cold prepared deli foods.

FRUIT & VEGETABLE STANDS

European-style market convenes Saturdays during the winter in Old Naples.

Karen T. Bartlett

Naples Farmers' Market (Parking lot at Third St. S. and 13th Ave., Old Naples) Every Saturday, November through March, 7 to 11 am.

Stallings Farm (941-263-1028; 2600 Pine Ridge Rd., Naples) U-Pick, We Pick, and shipping. Citrus and vegetables.

NATURAL FOODS

General Nutrition Center (941-597-8909; The Pavilion, Naples) Full-service chain health food store.

Martha's Natural Food Market (941-992-5838; Sunshine Plaza, 9118 Bonita Beach Rd. E., Bonita Springs) Natural baby food and diapers, pet care products, sports nutrition, vitamins and supplements, organic coffee, beer, and wine.

PIZZA & TAKEOUT

Cracker's Grill (941-643-7400; 493 Airport Rd. N., Naples) Burgers and over-sized sandwiches, eat-in or takeout; breakfast and lunch.

J.T.'s Island Grill 'N Grocery (941-695-3633; 238 Mamie St., Chokoloskee Island) An island-style grocery store with sandwich and grill takeout.

SEAFOOD

Captain Jerry's Seafood (941-262-7337; 995 Central Ave., Naples) Shrimp, stone crab, and fish.

Ernest Hamilton's Stone Crabs (941-695-2771; 100 Hamilton Ln., Chokoloskee Island) A longtime wholesaler that caters to individual buyers as well.

Kirk's Fresh Seafood Market (941-394-8616; 417 Papaya Dr., Goodland) Right on the fish docks, with crab traps piled around it, selling wholesale and retail.

CULTURE

The affluent residents of Naples — many of them transplanted CEOs and captains of industry from lands to the north — share their county with impoverished migrants who work in Immokalee, the nearby agricultural center. The influences of Haitian, Puerto Rican, Jamaican, and other Caribbean peoples are finding their way into the mainstream. Flashes of southern spirit and Cracker charm surface in Goodland, Everglades City, and Chokoloskee.

The Miccosukee and Big Cypress Seminole Indians inhabit reservations in the Everglades. They celebrate their culture each year at the Green Corn Ceremony, during the first new moon in June. They contribute the south coast's only authentic, indigenous art — colorful weaving, stitching, jewelry, and other age-old handicrafts. Highbrow art has become a trademark of Naples and its long roll of galleries and performance spaces. Artist Jonathan Green, who portrays Gullah childhood scenes, and Paul Arsenault, a transplant from up East, are a couple of Naples' best-known resident artists.

ARCHITECTURE

In Naples, commercial architecture is marked by style and panache, not to mention the architectural beauty of the homes and resorts. Banks and insurance companies seem to compete for virtuosity. It's truly a land of visual allure. Pelican Bay developments provide examples of a new residential style and provide a contrast with old-money Port Royal.

Old Naples, that neighborhood in the vicinity of the pier and Fifth Avenue South, has held on to some real treasures, including the tabby-mortar Palm Cottage, the old Mercantile, and the Old Naples building at Broad and Third. In the same neighborhood, on Gordon Drive, pay attention to the charming board-and-batten Cracker survivors.

In Everglades City and Chokoloskee Island, recreational vehicles and cement-block boxes typify the fishing-oriented community's style. The Rod & Gun Club, built in 1850, stands out and dresses the town in southern flair. The style of thatch housing known as chickee (pronounced cheeky), perfected by the Indians, prevails in the Everglades and serves as a trendy beach-bar motif at the ritziest resorts throughout the coastal region.

The humble and lavish extremes of South Coast architecture.

Karen T. Bartlett

Karen T. Bartlett

CINEMA

Movie Theaters

Marco Movie Theater (941-642-1111; Mission Plaza, 599 S. Collier Blvd., Marco Island) Four screens with beer and wine service.

Pavilion Cinema 10 (941-598-1211; Pavilion Shopping Center, N. Tamiami Trail, Naples)

Towne Center 6 Theatres (941-793-0006; 3855 Tamiami Trail, Naples)

GARDENS

CARIBBEAN GARDENS
941-262-5409.
1590 Goodlette Rd., Naples.
Open: 9:30–5:30 daily (last ticket sold at 4:30).
Admission: $13.95 adults; $8.95 children 4–15.

These tropical gardens, today the setting for a nicely proportioned zoo (see "Kids' Stuff" in this section), were planted in 1919 by Dr. Henry Nehrling, a botanist who brought his private collection to Naples. After he died, Julius Fleischmann, a developer, restored and expanded upon the doctor's 3,000-plus specimens and opened the gardens to the public in 1954. Besides native vegetation, exotics such as magnificent laurel figs, monkey puzzle trees, white birds of paradise, poincianas, orchids, and sausage trees flourish in wetlands and on hammocks. Signs identify more than 40 species.

HISTORIC HOMES & SITES

INDIAN HILL
Scott Drive, Goodland.

Though rich in natural and historic heritage, Marco Island hides it well among 20th-century trappings. Witness Indian Hill. On your own you'll have to search to find it, and when you do, only a barely noticeable plaque marks the spot. (Or take a trolley tour; Marco Island Trolley, 941-394-1600, to get there.) Southwest Florida's highest elevation at 58 feet above sea level, built up by ancient Caloosa Indian shell mounds, it now holds a ritzy neighborhood called The Heights, which feels a little like San Francisco.

PALM COTTAGE
941-261-8164.
137 12th Ave. S., Old
  Naples.
Open: 8:30–11; 12:30–4 or
  by appointment.
Closed: Weekends.

Land was selling for $10 a lot when Naples founder Walter N. Haldeman (no relation to H. R. Haldeman of Watergate fame) built a winter home for fellow worker Henry Watterson. Haldeman, publisher of the *Louisville Courier Journal,* had discovered the exotic beaches and jungles of Naples in 1887 and proceeded to buy up land and sing its praises. His enthusiasm persuaded winter escapees from Kentucky and Ohio to visit, including Watterson, his star editorial writer. The cottage Haldeman built for his friend was made of Florida pine, tidewater cypress, and a certain type of tabby mortar made by burning seashells over a buttonwood fire. It was one of the first buildings in southwest Florida to be constructed of local materials. Before reaching its present museum status, the cottage — rather spartan by modern standards — knew many lives. If the walls could speak at Palm Cottage, as it eventually came to be known, they would tell of wild parties with the likes of Gary Cooper and Hedy Lamarr in attendance. The Collier County Historical Society now has its headquarters here. The cottage recently underwent a $400,000 renovation.

SMALLWOOD STORE
941-695-2989.
360 Mamie St.,
  Chokoloskee Island,
  south of Everglades City.
Open: 10–5 Dec.–Apr.; 10–4
  May–Nov.
Admission: $2.50 adults, $2
  seniors, children under
  12 free.

A historic throwback to frontier days in the 'Glades, this museum preserves a native American trading post of the early 1900s. Splintery shelves hold ointment containers, FlyDed insect killer, livestock spray, and hordes of memorabilia. Rooms recall life in the pioneer days. The best feature is the view from the back porch. This was the site of a Jesse James-era murder immortalized in Peter Matthiessen's novel *Killing Mr. Watson.*

KIDS' STUFF

**THE ZOO AT
  CARIBBEAN
  GARDENS**
941-262-5409.
1590 Goodlette Rd., Naples.
Open: 9:30–5:30 daily (last
  ticket sold at 4:30).
Admission: $13.95 adults,
  $8.95 children 4–15 (plus
  tax).

Big cats are the specialty of this newly renovated zoo. Not just your lions and Bengal tigers, but such rarities as the serval and caracal. They are the stars of "Meet the Keeper" programs and the multimedia Safari Canyon, where predators take the stage and video footage enhances live demonstrations of dingos, monitor lizards, and leaping lemurs. Different shows concentrate on alligators,

David Tetzlaff, co-owner of the Caribbean Gardens, with his kitty cat.

Karen T. Bartlett

other reptiles, and mammals. A free boat ride takes a close-up look at the zoo's primate population, which is sequestered on nine islands. Favorite spots for the kids include the "Cub Corral" playground and the petting zoo, where they can feed Sicilian donkeys, Barbados lambs, potbellied pigs, and pygmy goats. Shaded, meandering, chirp-orchestrated paths take you past other fenced animals. For $2 you can purchase a zoo key, which allows you audio access at the exhibits. The 52-acre grounds are attractively maintained with the lush vegetation of the zoo's so-called Caribbean Gardens (see "Gardens" in this section).

TEDDY BEAR MUSEUM OF NAPLES
941-598-2711.
2511 Pine Ridge Rd., Naples.
Open: 10–5 Weds.–Sat. (also Mon. in season), 1–5 Sun.
Admission: $6 adults, $4 seniors, $2 children 4–12.

On its own, this attraction begs for children. (See listing under "Museums" in this section.) Volunteers host a Saturday morning story hour at 10:30 and 11.

MUSEUMS

COLLIER COUNTY MUSEUM
941-774-8476.
3301 Tamiami Trail E., Naples.
Open: 9–5.
Closed: Weekends.
Admission: Donations accepted.

The unique aspects at this village of history include typical Seminole chickee huts, a vintage swamp buggy, the skeleton of an Ice Age giant ground sloth, a working archaeological lab, a collection of antique stuffed local animals, and a steam locomotive from the county's cypress logging era. Exhibits of prehistoric fossils and native American artifacts, housed in pretty, vintage structures, take you back 10,000 years. More recent historical reminders include a recreated 19th-century trading post, 1920s furnishings, and a native plant garden.

**MUSEUM OF THE
    EVERGLADES**
941-695-0008.
Downtown Everglades
    City.
Hours: 10–3.
Closed: Weekends.
Admission: $2.

Newly opened in April 1998, the museum takes over a renovated historic dry cleaning facility started by Barron Collier to serve the community of road builders during the construction of the Tamiami Trail in the 1920s. The museum, still developing, concentrates on the tremendous feat of blazing a trail through the swampy, buggy Everglades, with an emphasis on the human side of the story.

**TEDDY BEAR MUSEUM
    OF NAPLES**
941-598-2711.
2511 Pine Ridge Rd.,
    Naples.
Open: 10–5 Weds.–Sat. (also
    Mon. in season), 1–5 Sun.
Closed: Tues. (also Mon. in
    off-season).
Admission: $6 adults, $4
    seniors, $2 children 4–12.

Home to more than 3,500 teddies, this cuddly museum showcases collector, antique, and limited-edition bears, and includes a signed first edition of A.A. Milne's *Winnie the Pooh*. The collection began as one woman's penchant for the stuffed animals and is whimsically displayed: bored bears at a board meeting, bears on parade, etc. A gift shop sells bears and fine gifts.

MUSIC AND NIGHTLIFE

The Club at The Ritz-Carlton (941-598-3300; 280 Vanderbilt Beach Rd., Naples) Live contemporary music Thursday through Saturday.

Club Zanzibar (941-514-3777; The Registry Resort, 475 Seagate Dr., Naples) Music and dancing in one of Naples' most fashionable locales.

McCabe's Irish Pub (941-403-7170; 699 Fifth Ave. S., Naples) Authentic Irish music in a Dublin-built pub, most weekends.

Snook Inn (941-394-3313; 1215 Bald Eagle Dr., Marco Island) Live local bands, contemporary and island music.

Terra (941-262-5500; 1300 Third St. S., Naples) Music and humor Tuesday through Sunday.

Vanderbilt Inn (941-597-3151; 11000 Gulf Shore Dr. N., Naples) Live music and karaoke indoors and at the chickee bar on the beach.

THEATER

Marco Players (941-642-7270; Marco Town Center Mall, 1083 N. Collier Blvd., Marco Island) Nonprofit community theater that produces comedies, musicals, dance performances, and children's theater.

Philharmonic Center for the Arts (941-597-1900 or 800-597-1900; 5833 Pelican Bay Blvd., Pelican Bay, North Naples) "The Phil," as locals call it, is home to the 77-piece **Naples Philharmonic.** It hosts audiences of up to 1,222 for Broadway shows, touring orchestras, chamber music, children's productions, and the Miami City Ballet.

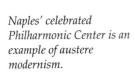

Naples' celebrated Philharmonic Center is an example of austere modernism.

Karen T. Bartlett

Sugden Community Theatre (941-263-7990; 701 Fifth Ave. S., Old Naples) The new home of the **Naples Players**, a community theater troupe that has been entertaining year-round for 40 years. Completed in fall 1998, the $5.3 million complex features a main theater, studio theater, and outdoor stage.

VISUAL ART CENTERS & RESOURCES

Like its Italian namesake, Naples serves as the region's aesthetic trendsetter. Gallery-lined streets host artists of local, national, and international stature. The following entries introduce you to opportunities for experiencing art as either a viewer or a practicing artist. A listing for commercial galleries is included in the "Shopping" section.

Art League of Marco Island (941-394-4221; 1010 Winterberry Dr., Marco Island) Workshops, lectures, gallery, and gift shop.

Naples Art Association (941-262-6517; 643 Fifth Ave. S., Naples) Workshops, classes, and gallery for local artists.

Naples Artcrafters (941-947-9095; Naples) Artisan group that sponsors arts and crafts shows and demonstrations.

Philharmonic Galleries (941-597-1111; Philharmonic Center for the Arts, 5833 Pelican Bay Blvd., Pelican Bay, Naples) Exhibitions of well-known works; guided tours. Admission: $3 adults, $1.50 students.

RECREATION

The Ten Thousand Islands are the meat of the south coast's recreational banquet. Here, the old-fashioned sports — fishing, canoeing, hiking — are most in style. The beaches of Naples and Marco Island serve up the fancified side dishes — everything from parasailing to jet skiing.

BEACHES

Naples area beaches were recently widened with several yards of sand. Parking fees are levied at most beaches; county residents can purchase stickers that allow them to park free.

CLAM PASS RECREATION AREA
941-353-0404.
Registry Resort of Seagate Dr., North Naples.
Facilities: Rest rooms, showers, food and beach concessions.
Parking: $3 per day.

Open to the public, but not widely known, this beach is reached by a tram that follows a boardwalk over a tidal bay and through mangroves. Boat and cabana rentals are available. It's crowded at the entrance, but the park comprises 35 acres, which get more sparsely populated as you walk north. The sand is fine, fluffy, and newly widened. You can kayak or sail into the sea, or canoe among the mangroves, which are frequented by ospreys, hawks, and a variety of other creatures.

Turtle talks educate visitors about the plight of the endangered loggerhead at the Delnor-Wiggins State Recreation Area.

Karen T. Bartlett

DELNOR-WIGGINS PASS STATE RECREATION AREA
941-597-6196.
11100 Gulf Shore Dr. N. at Route 846, Vanderbilt Beach.
Facilities: Picnic areas, pavilion, rest rooms,

This is a highly natural, low-key beach that extends for one mile south from the mouth of the Cocohatchee River. The lush white sands are protected during loggerhead nesting season (summer) and support stands of natural vegetation such as cactus, sea grapes, nickerbean, and yucca. A nature trail leads to an observation tower at the

showers, boat ramp, lifeguard.

Admission: $4 per car, up to 8 passengers; $2 per car, single occupant; $1 walk-ins, bike-ins, or extra passengers.

beach's north end. Restrict your swimming to south of the pass's fast-moving waters, which are a boon to fishermen.

Lowdermilk Park draws an active beach crowd.

Karen T. Bartlett

LOWDERMILK PARK
941-434-4698.
Gulf Shore Blvd. at Banyan Blvd., Naples.
Facilities: Picnic area, rest rooms, showers, volleyball, playground, concessions, special handicap access, and wheeled surf chairs.
Parking: Metered.

Beach headquarters for the south coast. Lots of special activities at this gulfside party spot with its 1,000 feet of sandy beach.

NAPLES MUNICIPAL BEACHES
Gulf Shore Blvd. south of Doctors Pass, Naples.
Facilities: Rest rooms, shower, concessions, fishing pier.
Parking: Metered.

Stretches of natural beach are anchored by the historic pier on 12th Avenue South, where facilities and a parking lot are located.

TIGERTAIL BEACH
941-353-0404.
Hernando Dr., north end of Marco Island.

The only public beach on Marco, this is a good place for shelling and sunning. In season, arrive early to find a parking spot. Wooden ramps cross dunes to 31 acres of wide, marvelous beach.

Facilities: Picnic area, rest rooms, showers, water-sports rentals, restaurant, playground volleyball.
Parking: $3 per vehicle.

VANDERBILT BEACH
941-353-0404.
End of Vanderbilt Dr., Vanderbilt Beach, north of Naples.
Facilities: Rest rooms, showers, food; water-sports rentals available at nearby resorts.
Parking: $3 per vehicle at nearby lot on Vanderbilt Dr.; metered on the street.

The south end fronts high-rises, but the north end stretches into wilderness. The playground is fun and divided for two different age groups. At low tide, tidal pools attract feeding birds and shellers.

This recently refurbished stretch runs alongside resorts and is well suited to those who like sharing the beach with a lot of people and bar- and restaurant-hopping along the beach.

BICYCLING

City and country biking are available to those who prefer this slow, intimate mode of exploration. Sidewalks, bike paths, and roadsides accommodate cyclists. By state law, cyclists must conduct themselves as pedestrians when using sidewalks. Where they share the road with other vehicles, they must follow all the rules of the road. Children under 16 must wear a helmet.

BEST BIKING

Naples has laid out a sporadic system of metropolitan bike paths. A favorite route of local cyclists loops through 10 miles of pathway in the north-end Pelican Bay development. Within it, a 580-acre nature preserve provides a change of scenery from upscale suburbia.

Bike paths traverse Everglades City and cross the causeway to Chokoloskee Island. Backroad bikers take to the 12-mile W. J. Janes Memorial Scenic Drive through Fakahatchee Strand State Preserve, off Highway 29 north of Everglades City. Royal palms, cypress trees, and air plants provide pristine scenery and bird habitat. Morning or sunset riders may spot wild turkeys, alligators, raccoons, snakes, otters, bobcats, or deer.

RENTALS/SALES

Beach Sports Surf & Tackle (941-642-4282; 571 S. Collier Blvd., Marco Island) Rents a wide variety of bikes and in-line skates. Delivers equipment free of charge.
Bicycle Shoppe of Naples (941-566-3646; 813 Vanderbilt Beach Rd., Naples)
Ivey House B&B (941-695-3299; Everglades City) Rents bikes to the public.

BOATS & BOATING

Setting sail through the maze of Ten Thousand Islands.

Karen T. Bartlett

CANOEING & KAYAKING

In addition to the outlets listed below, many resorts and parks rent canoes and kayaks.

Collier-Seminole State Park (941-394-3397; 20200 E. Tamiami Trail, between Naples and Everglades City) Rents canoes for use on the park's 13-mile canoe trail into wilderness preserve.

Estero River Tackle and Canoe Outfitters (941-992-4050; opposite Koreshan Park, 20991 S. Tamiami Trail, Estero) Rents and outfits canoes for a four-mile adventure down the natural Estero River to Estero Bay.

Everglades National Park Boat Tours (941-695-2591 or 800-445-7724 in Florida; Everglades Ranger Station, Everglades City) Canoe rentals and shuttle service.

Get Wet Sports (941-394-9557; Port of Marco Shopping Village, 240 Royal Palm Dr., Marco Island) Sales, rentals, and tours.

G.R. Boating (941-947-4889; near the public beach at 4892 Bonita Beach Rd., Bonita Beach) Rents canoes and kayaks.

North American Canoe Tours/Everglades Canoe & Kayak Outpost (941- 695-4666; Everglades City) Rents 17- to 19-foot aluminum canoes and kayaks, equipment. Complete outfitting and shuttle service. Tours range from one-day guided adventures to seven-day Everglades paddles.

DINING CRUISES

The Naples Princess (941-649-2275; 1001 10th Ave. S., Naples) Excursions include a Conservancy-narrated nature cruise with continental breakfast, island buffet lunch, sunset hors d'oeuvres, sunset dinner, or Sunday brunch.

MARINE SUPPLIES

Boat/US Marine Center (941-774-3233; 3808 Tamiami Trail E., Naples) All boating, yachting, and fishing needs. Discounts and emergency service available with membership.

PERSONAL WATERCRAFT RENTALS/TOURS

Marco Island Jet Ski & Water Sports (941-394-6589; Marriott's Marco Island Resort, 400 S. Collier Blvd., Marco Island) Rents waverunners for and conducts one-hour waverunner excursions through Ten Thousand Islands.
Moran's Barge Marina (941-642-1920; at the Goodland Bridge on San Marco Rd., Marco Island) Rents waverunners.

POWERBOAT RENTALS

Factory Bay Marina (941-642-6717; 1079 Bald Eagle Dr., Marco Island) Rents pontoons, center consoles, and Grady Whites.
Moran's Barge Marina (941-642-1920; at the Goodland Bridge on San Marco Rd., Marco Island) Rents 18-foot consoles and 22-foot pontoons.

Marco Island's marinas cater to watery whims.

Karen T. Bartlett

Port-o-Call Marina (941-774-0479; off Hwy. 41 E., Naples) Rents deck boats and powerboats 17 to 23 feet in length, to accommodate 6 to 12 persons.

PUBLIC BOAT RAMPS

Caxambas Park (S. Collier Ct., Marco Island) Rest rooms, bait, fuel, and access to Roberts Bay.
Cocohatchee River Park (Vanderbilt Dr., Vanderbilt Beach) Park with three ramps onto the river (which runs to the gulf), rest rooms, picnic tables, and a playground. Parking fee.

Delnor-Wiggins Pass State Recreation Area (11100 Gulf Shore Dr. N., Naples) Admission.

Marco Island approach (one mile before the bridge on Route 951)

Naples Landing (off Ninth St. S.)

SAILBOAT CHARTERS

Sweet Liberty (941-793-3525; the Boat Haven off Hwy. 41, Naples) Daily shelling, sightseeing, and sunset trips aboard a 53-foot catamaran.

SIGHTSEEING & ENTERTAINMENT CRUISES

Everglades Private Airboat Tours (941-695-4637 or 800-368-0065; one mile west of Route 29 on Hwy. 41, Everglades City) Two-passenger vessel zips through Florida's backyard.

Odyssey Boat Tours (941-566-6557; City Dock, Naples) Shelling, sightseeing, and sunset trips daily by powerboat for up to six passengers.

Wooten's Everglades Tours (800-282-2781; 32330 Tamiami Trail, Ochopee, 35 miles south of Naples) Follow ancient native American trails through the mysterious "River of Grass" via airboat or swamp buggy, the trademark vessels of the Everglades. The loud airboat is designed for the area's shallow waters; the swamp buggy is an all-terrain bus. Touristy, but an easy introduction to this complex wilderness.

FISHING

A forest of masts at the Naples City Dock.

Greg Wagner

Many visiting sportsfolk arrive at the south coast eager to fight the big fish and brave the deep waters of the Gulf of Mexico. They come equipped with their 50-pound test line, heavy tackle, and tall fish tales. Yet closer to home, in the back bays and shallow waters of Ten Thousand Islands, experienced fishermen find what's best about the region. Sea trout, snook, redfish, sheepshead, mangrove snapper, and pompano abound in the brackish creeks, grass flats, and channels.

Nonresidents age 16 and over must obtain a license unless fishing from a vessel or pier covered by its own license. You can buy inexpensive, temporary nonresident licenses at county tax collectors' offices and most Kmarts and bait shops. Check local regulations for season, size, and catch restrictions.

DEEP-SEA PARTY BOATS

Lady Brett (941-263-4949; Tin City, 1200 Fifth Ave. S., Naples) Half-day trips aboard a 34-foot powerboat.

Sunshine Tours (941-642-5415; Marco River Marina, Marco Island) Takes small parties aboard a 32-foot boat with bathroom for offshore excursions, full and half day.

FISHING CHARTERS/OUTFITTERS

Check the large marinas for fishing guides. Experienced guides can take the intimidation and guesswork out of open-water fishing.

Captains John and Pam Stop (941-394-8000; Stop's Marine, Calusa Island Marina, Goodland) Backwater fishing.

Captain Max Miller (941-695-2420; Everglades City) Specializes in light-tackle back-bay fishing.

Mangrove Outfitters (941-793-3370; 4111 E. Tamiami Trail, Naples) Guides charters and, in season, teaches classes on fly tying.

Sunny Daze (941-775-8292; Turner's Marine, 10th St. S., Naples) Charters for up to six persons for half- to full-day trips.

FISHING PIERS

Naples Fishing Pier (12th Ave. S., Naples) Extends into the gulf 1,000 feet, with bait shop, snack bar, rest rooms, and showers.

GOLF

Naples earns its title as Golf Capital of the World with more golf holes per capita than any other statistically tracked metropolitan area.

PUBLIC GOLF COURSES

Embassy Woods (941-353-3699; 6680 Weston Way, Naples) Semiprivate course with 18 holes, par 70.

Lely Resort's Flamingo Island Club (941-793-2223; 8004 Lely Resort Blvd.

off Route 951, east Naples) Public course designed by Robert Trent Jones, Sr. Offers 18 holes, par 72, and a golf school.

Marco Shores Country Club (941-394-2581; 1450 Mainsail Dr. off Route 951, east of Marco Island) Public, 18 holes, par 72. Restaurant and bar.

Naples Beach Golf Club (941-434-7007; 851 Gulf Shore Blvd. N., Naples) 18-hole, par 72 resort course. Restaurant and lounge.

Pelican's Nest Golf Club (941-947-4600 or 800-952-6378; 4450 Bay Creek Dr. SW, Bonita Springs) 18-hole course, par 72, and 9-hole course, par 36.

GOLF CENTERS

Gulf Coast Golf (941-597-8868; 6700 N. Airport Rd., Naples) Full-service driving range with chipping and putting greens, and lessons.

Naples Golf Center (941-775-3337; 7700 E. Davis Blvd., Naples) Lighted driving range with putting and chipping greens and sand traps. Video, single, series, and group lessons.

HEALTH & FITNESS CLUBS

Body Quest (941-643-7546; 2975 S. Horseshoe Dr., Naples) Complete fitness center, aerobics, karate, heart-healthy cafe, nursery.

Golden Gate Fitness Center (941-353-7128; Golden Gate Community Park, 3300 Santa Barbara Blvd., east of Naples) Full range of modern equipment and free weights. Personal training and assessment available.

Marco Fitness Club (941-394-3705; 871 E. Elkcam Circle, Marco Island) Cardiovascular and weight machines, free weights.

HIKING

Collier-Seminole State Park (941-394-3397; 20200 E. Tamiami Trail, south of Naples) A 6.5-mile trail winds through pine flatwoods and cypress swamp, and a self-guided boardwalk leads into a salt marsh.

Conservancy of Southwest Florida (941-262-0304; Merrihue Dr. at 14th Ave. N.) Guided and unguided nature hikes through a subtropical hammock.

Corkscrew Marsh (941-332-7771; Corkscrew Rd., North Naples) Five miles of hiking trails through pine flatwoods and oak and palm hammock. Free guided tours the second Saturday of every month.

HUNTING

The Everglades provide some of Florida's best shots at hunting. You must obtain a state license and a Wildlife Management Area stamp. Permits are required for early-season hunting and special types of hunting. For information on seasons and bag limits, request a copy of the *Florida Hunting Handbook & Regulations Summary* when you buy your license.

Big Cypress National Preserve (941-695-4111) 564,320 acres adjacent to the Everglades.

KIDS' STUFF

Coral Cay Adventure Golf (941-793-4999; 2205 E. Tamiami Trail, Naples) Two 18-hole courses with a tropical island theme. Admission.

Golden Gate Aquatic Complex (941-353-7128; Golden Gate Community Park, 3300 Santa Barbara Blvd., east of Naples) Swimming fun for all ages with water slides, wading pool and fountain, and low and high dives. Admission.

Golf Safari (941-947-1377; 3775 Bonita Beach Rd., Bonita Springs) Jungle-themed miniature golf.

King Richard's Amusement Park (941-598-1666; 6780 N. Airport Rd., Naples) Water bumper boats, batting cages, a castle full of video and other electronic games, go-carts, a kiddie train, and two 18-hole miniature golf courses. No admission; you buy tickets per attraction.

Naples Go-Cart Center (941-774-7776; 11402 Tamiami Trail E., Naples) Video games, pinball, and a snack center. Rides cost $3 each, less for multiple rides.

RACQUET SPORTS

Beach and Tennis Health Club (941-992-1121; 5700 Bonita Beach Rd., Bonita Beach) Public club with 10 Har-Tru courts, three lighted, plus health club and instruction. Admission.

Collier County Racquet Center (941-394-5454; 1275 San Marco Rd., Marco Island) County facility with five deco-turf courts, two racquetball courts, pro shop, and lessons.

Naples Park Elementary (111th Ave. N., Naples) Two lighted courts.

Tommie Barfield Elementary (Goodland, Marco Island) Two lighted courts.

SHELLING

It is illegal to collect live shells in state and national parks. Collier County discourages the collection of live shells.

HOT SHELLING SPOTS

Coconut Island (north of Marco Island) A destination for most Marco Island shelling expeditions.

Key Island (south of Naples, accessible only by boat) A partly private, partly state-owned, unbridged island, it holds a great many shell prizes that are not as picked over as on beaches that are accessible by car.

Ten Thousand Islands Shell Island, Kingston Key, and Mormon Key provide lots of empty shells to collect.

SHELLING CHARTERS

Captains John and Pam Stop (941-394-8000; Stop's Marine, Calusa Island Marina, Goodland) Go via pontoon or luxury vessel.

Odyssey Boat Tours (941-566-6557; Crayton Cove City Dock, Naples) Power-boat shelling excursions.

SPECTATOR SPORTS

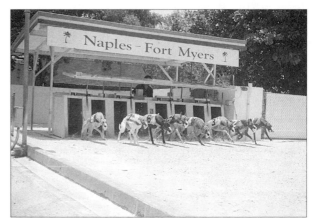

And they're off! "Going to the dogs" is a favorite pastime in Bonita Springs.

Karen T. Bartlett

RACING

Naples-Fort Myers Greyhound Track (941-992-2411; 10601 Bonita Beach Rd. SE; Bonita Springs) Matinees, night races, and trackside dining. Admission.

WATERSKIING

South Coast (941-732-0570; Lake Avalon, Outer Drive, Naples) Gulf Coast Skimmers stage live shows every Sunday at 3 pm.

WATER SPORTS

PARASAILING & WATERSKIING

Marco Island Ski Water Sports (941-394-6589; Marriott's Marco Beach Resort, Marco Island) Parasailing, towed tube rides, and waverunner and other water-sport rentals.

Naples & Bonita Beach Watersports (941-591-2839; Vanderbilt Beach Inn, 11000 Gulf Shore Dr. N., Vanderbilt Beach) Go parasailing, kayaking, waverunning, windsurfing, sailing, or paddleboating with a tour or rental.

SNORKELING & SCUBA

Murky waters here send most divers to Florida's east coast and the Keys, although some charters take you out in deep local waters.

Beach Sports Surf & Tackle (941-642-4282; 571 S. Collier Blvd., Marco Island) Instructs PADI scuba courses and has the island's only compression facility.

Scubadventures (941-434-7477; Seabreeze Plaza, 971 Creech Rd. at Hwy. 41 N., Naples) Supplies and diving arrangements.

WILDERNESS CAMPING

Big Cypress Trail Lakes Campground (941-695-2275; Highway 41, 5 miles east of Route 29) Tent or RV camping in Big Cypress National Preserve, a 721,000-acre sanctuary adjacent to Everglades National Park.

Collier-Seminole State Park (941-642-8898; 20200 E. Tamiami Trail, 17 miles south of Naples) This 6,470-acre park straddles Big Cypress Swamp and Ten Thousand Islands Mangrove Wilderness and provides the least primitive camping in Everglades Country. There are RV hookups and tent sites. The park is full of possibilities for exploring nature and history, but no swimming.

Everglades National Park (941-695-2591) Backcountry camping along the Everglades canoe trails requires a permit, available from the Everglades City Ranger Station on Route 29. Most sites provide chickee huts on pilings, with chemical toilets. Take mosquito repellent.

Koreshan State Historic Site (941-992-0311; Tamiami Trail, Estero) There's a lot to do within these 130 acres, for tenters and RVers. Historic buildings recall the property's past as a cult settlement. Canoeing, playgrounds, trails, and fishing are available. The park has 60 tent and RV sites with or without electricity.

WILDLIFE SPOTTING

The Florida Everglades and Ten Thousand Islands are home to the reclusive golden Florida panther, along with bobcats, manatees, wood storks, brown pelicans, black skimmers, roseate spoonbills, and ibises. Some creatures, such as the panther and bobcat, are rarely seen out of captivity. Others, especially the brown pelican, live side by side with residents.

ALLIGATORS

The Everglades are the New York City of Florida's alligator population. They thrive in the freshwater ponds and brackish creeks of the River of Grass. Along Alligator Alley (Interstate 75) and Tamiami Trail, in certain weather (sunshine helps), you can see hundreds on the banks sunning themselves.

Birds

Karen T. Bartlett

Pelicans gather on a "Florida snow cap," otherwise known as a sandbar.

Southwest Florida is a bird-watcher's haven, especially in winter when migrating species add to the vast variety of the coast's residential avifauna. Rare visitors and locals include the roseate spoonbill, black skimmer, yellow-crowned night heron, wood stork, and bald eagle. More commonly seen are frigates, ospreys, Louisiana herons, great blue herons, ibises, snowy egrets, pelicans, anhingas, cormorants, terns, seagulls, plovers, oystercatchers, doves, pileated woodpeckers, owls, and hawks.

For the best bird-watching on the south coast, try Naples' Corkscrew Swamp, home to the largest nesting colony of wood storks in the U.S., Rookery Bay Sanctuary near Marco Island, and Ten Thousand Islands, a haven for birds of all sorts. Marco Island is a proclaimed sanctuary for bald eagles. Barfield Bay in Goodland is one of their favorite locales.

Nature Preserves & Eco-Attractions

BIG CYPRESS PRESERVE
941-695-4111.
West of Everglades City on Hwy. 41.

At the Visitors' Center you can stroll the short boardwalk (less than a mile long) to sample the preserve's 716,000 acres of Everglades environment. You'll see the royal palms and bald cypress stands for which Big Cypress is known, and also birds and an alligator nursery. The preserve boasts the state's major population of the reclusive, endangered Florida panther. Primitive camping, picnic tables, and hiking trails are available.

THE CONSERVANCY
941-263-0119.
Merrihue Dr. at 14th Ave.
  N., one block east of
  Goodlette Rd., Naples.
Open: 9–4:30 Mon.-Sat.;
  also 1–5 Sun., Jan.–Mar.
  only.
Admission: Nature Center,
  $5 adults and $1 children
  5–17 (good for same-day
  admission to Briggs).
  Admission to nature
  trails and rehab facility is
  free.

This tucked-away nature complex on the Gordon River was built to educate the public about the environment. Within its 13.5 acres it encompasses a nature store; trail walks; free boat tours of the river; a rehabilitation center for birds, deer, turtles, and other injured animals; and a beautiful nature center with live Florida snakes, an offshore tank (where you'll often find a loggerhead turtle swimming), fascinating touch tables, interactive games, and habitat vignettes. Guides are friendly and chattily informative; they conduct special programs throughout the day as they feed their live critters. The Conservancy also hosts interpretative nature field trips in conjunction with its Briggs Nature Center south of Naples (see "Rookery Bay Estuarine Reserve," below). Canoes and kayak rentals are available for use on the Gordon River.

CORKSCREW SWAMP
  SANCTUARY
941-348-9151.
Off Naples-Immokalee Rd.,
  21 miles east of N.
  Tamiami Trail, Naples.
Open: 9–5 daily.
Admission: $6.50 adults, $5
  college students, $3
  children 6–18.

The 11,000-acre sanctuary, operated by the National Audubon Society, protects one of the largest stands of mature bald cypress trees in the country. Some of the towering specimens date back nearly 500 years. The threatened wood stork once came to nest here in great numbers. Diminished populations still do, at which time the nesting area is roped off to protect them. A boardwalk 1.75 miles long takes you over swampland inhabited by rich plant and marine life. You can usually spot an alligator or two. Winter adult education programs teach about astronomy, birds, nature drawing, and such.

DELNOR-WIGGINS
  PASS STATE
  RECREATION AREA
941-597-6196.
11100 Gulf Shore Dr. N.,
  Vanderbilt Beach.
Admission: $4 per car, up
  to 8 passengers; $2 per
  car, single occupant; $1
  bikers or walk-ins.

Prehistoric loggerhead turtles lumber ashore to lay and bury their eggs every summer, away from the lights and crowds of other area beaches. Fifty-six days later the baby turtles emerge and scurry to the sea before birds can snatch them up. Beach turtle talks are available during the loggerhead season.

**EVERGLADES
   NATIONAL PARK**
941-695-2591.
Tamiami Trail south of
   Naples; Welcome Center
   at intersection of Rt. 29 or
   Ranger Station on Rt. 29,
   Everglades City.

This massive wetlands — home to the endangered Florida panther and other rare animals — covers 2,100 square miles and shelters more than 600 types of fish and 300 bird species. It also contains the largest mangrove forest in the world. So what's the best way to see this seemingly overwhelming expanse of wildlife? Take your pick. Driving through is quickest but least satisfying. Make sure to veer off the Tamiami Trail on at least one side road, to the park's interior. Closest to Naples is Route 29 to Everglades City. Canoe trips from 8 to 99 miles long put you in closer range of birds, manatees, dolphins, and alligators. There's also a variety of other options: pontoon boating (if you're good at reading charts), sightseeing cruises, bike rentals, and foot trails. Get advice at the Welcome Center or Ranger Station, or see "Wildlife Tours & Charters," below.

**FAKAHATCHEE
   STRAND STATE
   PRESERVE**
941-695-4593.
W. J. Janes Scenic Dr. in
   Copeland, off Hwy. 29
   north of Hwy. 41.

Rangers lead swamp walks one Saturday each month during the winter. You can also access the strand (a slow-moving river without defined shorelines) at the Big Cypress Preserve boardwalk (see above).

NAPLES AQUARIUM
941-403-7300.
Old Naples Seaport, 1001
   10th Ave. S., Naples.

Opened in January 1998, this ecology-conscious attraction doesn't try to compete with the new and magnificent in aquariums. As a working lab, it stays focused on what's local and how it can improve marine habitat. Aquariums and touch tanks display starfish, sea urchins, nurse sharks, stone crabs, and snook. Tours and a film educate visitors about the adverse effects of construction and agriculture on marine life. The aquarium was built by the Marine Habitat Foundation, which uses rope and recycled plastic to construct new underwater habitat for homeless fish and shellfish.

**ROOKERY BAY
   ESTUARINE RESERVE
   & BRIGGS NATURE
   CENTER**
941-775-8569.
Shell Road off Rt. 951 on
   way to Marco Island.
Open: 9–5 Mon.–Sat.
Closed: Sunday.
Admission: Boardwalk only,
   $3 adults, $1 children.

The Gulf Coast's largest and most pristine wildlife sanctuary occupies more than 8,000 acres at the gateway to Ten Thousand Islands. It's "Ding" Darling without the crowds. A favorite for fishermen and bird-watchers. Visitors can enjoy the mysteries of mangrove ecology from a 2,500-foot boardwalk. You can stroll through the butterfly garden and walk Monument Trail around the bay for free. A visitors' center, also free, introduces you to the estuarine world, including a touch table kids will like. I recommend taking one of the center's boat, canoe, birding, or off-site beach trips if you want to get close up and personal with nature. Manatees and alligators populate bay waters. Boat ramp for small craft.

WILDLIFE TOURS & CHARTERS

Conservancy of Southwest Florida (941-262-0304; Merrihue Dr. at 14th Ave. N., Naples) Boat tours of the mangrove waterway. Hosts other interpretative hiking, beach, and canoeing nature ventures.

Double Sunshine (941-263-4949; Tin City on Hwy. 41, Naples) Departs five times daily for 1-$^1/_2$-hour narrated nature and dolphin-sighting cruises.

Estero Bay Boat Tours (941-992-2200; Weeks Fish Camp, Coconut Rd., Bonita Springs) The best sightseeing tour of Mound Key's Calusa history and Big Hickory Island's wildlife is conducted by a local native and his staff, who know these islands and waters like family.

Everglades National Park Boat Tours (941-695-2591 or 800-445-7724; Ranger Station on Chokoloskee Island) Naturalist-narrated tours through the maze of Ten Thousand Islands and its teeming bird and water life.

Majestic Tours (941-695-2777; Route 29, Everglades City) Excursions designed specifically for the eco-tourist into Ten Thousand Islands aboard a small pontoon. This is southwest Florida's best opportunity to see and learn about birds, dolphins, alligators, and other wildlife with intimate, entertaining, and educational narrative from a husband-and-wife team. Light lunch or wine and cheese provided.

Naples Sea Kayaking Adventures (941-353-4878) Half-day, full-day, and overnight trips into local wilderness. Kayaking lessons available.

SHOPPING

Custom-designed jewelry, exclusive top-designer fashion lines, original masterpiece art, and the world's first street concierge make the experience of browsing, buying, and window-yearning in Naples entirely unique. Naples ranks among Florida's most chic arenas for spending, including Palm Beach's Worth Avenue and Sarasota's St. Armands Circle. Downtown's recent renaissance concentrates the shopping frenzy in the Old Naples districts of Fifth Avenue South and Third Street Plaza, but a number of other fashionable shopping centers are found throughout town. Downtown shops are known for their individually owned, one-of-a-kind, and designer outlets.

ANTIQUES & COLLECTIBLES

Antiques & Things (941-262-7333; 975 Central Ave., Naples) Furniture, clocks, decorative statues and accessories, china, crystal, and Christmas collectibles.

La Rocco Antiques (941-262-7357; 28 Tenth St. S., Naples) Fine collection of rare and original antiques, including glass, bronze, and Art Deco, and 20th-century pieces.

Tried-'N-True (941-948-0266; 3634 Bonita Beach Rd. SW, Bonita Springs) Specializes in country cottage style; antiques and collectibles.

BOOKS

The Bookstore at The Pavilion (941-598-2220; Vanderbilt Beach Rd. and Tamiami Trail N., Naples) Old-fashioned bookstore that's crowded with the printed word; the antithesis of the new generation of megabookstores. Wide selection of specialty periodicals, new and used books.

Dunn & Dunn Booksellers (941-435-1911; 1300 Third St. S., Old Naples) Smart new bookstore with great local-interest section.

Your Local Bookie (941-261-3608; Park Shore Plaza, 4139 N. Tamiami Trail, Naples) Large selection of local books, mainstream books, magazines, newspapers, and greeting cards.

CLOTHING

Back of the Bay (941-649-8622; 555 Fifth Ave. S., Old Naples) Comfortable, unusual designer wear in bright colors and feel-good fabrics.

Beth Mone Children's Shoppe (941-394-3600; Shops of Marco, Marco Island)

Casablanca (941-394-2511; Marco Island Marriott Resort, 400 S. Collier Blvd., Marco Island) Fashionable women's resort apparel.

Island Woman (941-642-6116; 1 Harbor Pl., Goodland) Imported batik fashions and handcrafted jewelry, tropical art, and crafts.

Kangaroo Klub (941-434-9510; 1170 Third St. S., Old Naples) Precious children's clothes, tennis outfits, toys, and other Florida-style wear.

Kirsten's Boutique (941-598-3233; Waterside Shops, Naples) Subheaded "A Gallery of Fine Art to Wear," this unique shop sells African and African-inspired clothes, jewelry, and art.

Marissa Collections (941-263-4333; 1167 Third St. S., Old Naples) Exclusive local carrier of the Donna Karan New York Collection; also Gianni Versace, Gucci, Krizia, Jill Sanders, Manolo Blahnik, and other prestige designers.

McFarland's of Marco (941-394-6464 for men's, 941-742-7277 for women's; Shops of Marco, Marco Island) A stretch of three shops specializing in menswear — casual, golf, suits, and resort — women's dressy and bright fashions, and shoes.

Mettlers (941-434-2700; 1258 Third St. S., Old Naples) Active men's and women's designer wear for boating, golfing, and Florida living.

Mondo Uomo (941-434-9484; The Village on Venetian Bay, Naples) Fine fashion and European styles for men: tropical wool and linen, bright colors, and distinctive casual and dress wear for Gulf Coast climes.

Outback T-Shirts (941-261-7869; Tin City, Naples) The best in souvenir T-shirts, with wildlife and local themes.

CONSIGNMENT

Naples is a secondhand shopper's paradise. In many of the clothing consignment shops you can find designer fashions with the price tags still attached. Oh, the joys of hunting down the castoffs of the well-to-do!

Act II (941-495-6647; Springs Plaza, Hwy. 41 & Bonita Beach Rd., Bonita Springs) Women's clothing and accessories.

Classy Collections (941-649-0344; 888 First Ave. S., Naples) Quality ladies' clothing and accessories, from casual to designer wear.

Encore Shop (941-262-5558; 308 Fifth Ave. S., Old Naples) Designer furniture, paintings, decorative items, and collectibles.

Kid's Consignment (941-596-1764; 4444 N. Tamiami Trail, Naples) Children's clothing, toys, furniture, and equipment.

New to You Consignments (941-262-6869; 933 Creech Rd., at Hwy. 41, Naples) Women's designer clothing, furniture, and decorative items.

FACTORY OUTLET CENTERS

Coral Isle Factory Stores (941-775-8083; Route 951 on the way to Marco Island) Factory outlets for Bass shoes, Nordic kitchenware, Izod and Van Heusen clothing, and other name brands.

FLEA MARKETS & BAZAARS

Naples Drive-In Flea Market (941-774-2900; 7700 Davis Blvd., Naples) Open Friday through Sunday.

GALLERIES

Arsenault-Arno Gallery (941-430-2331; 680 Fifth Ave. S., Old Naples) Featuring the works of four artists, it also holds a working artist's studio that visitors can see. Featured artist Paul Arsenault paints Naples scenes. Other artists depict Italian locations, social scene pop art, and moody landscapes.

The Darvish Collection (941-261-7581; 1199 Third St. S., Old Naples) Features the work of North American and European masters.

Harmon-Meek Gallery (941-261-2637; 601 Fifth Ave. S., Old Naples) A respected name in fine art, it hosts exhibitions of American master artists of the 20th century and local artists.

Koucky Gallery (941-261-8988; 1300 Third St. S., Old Naples) I like this gallery because it doesn't take itself quite as seriously as the others. It shows its sense of humor with a variety of whimsical carvings, cartoonish sculptures, and bright sea-life paintings. Look for the sculptures of Sarasotan Jack Dowd.

Mangroves Wildlife Gallery (941-394-0103; Marco Town Center Mall, Marco Island) Original art, sculpture, and wood carvings, limited-edition prints.

Naples Art Gallery (941-262-4551; 275 Broad Ave. S., Naples) This 30-year-old facility specializes in glass, representing 30 internationally known American studio glass artists. The spacious, stylish gallery also exhibits paintings and sculptures with specially scheduled showings.

Rick Moore Fine Art (941-592-5455; Waterside Shops, Naples) Glass and wood animal sculptures, paintings, ceramics, and stunning acrylic sculptures by Frederic Hart.

United Arts Council (941-263-8242; 1051 Fifth Ave. S., Old Naples) Paintings and sculpture of local artists.

GENERAL STORES

J.T.'s Island Grill 'N Grocery (941-695-3633; 238 Mamie St., Chokoloskee Island) An island-style grocery store with souvenirs and other bric-a-brac.

GIFTS

Some of Naples' best souvenirs are found in the gift shops at nature and other attractions.

Born to Be Wild (941-261-0560; Dockside Boardwalk, 1100 Sixth Ave. S., Naples) Stuffed toys, books, T-shirts, and gifts dedicated to promoting environmental awareness.

Coconuts Children's Shop (941-642-2645; Marco Island Marriott Resort, 400 S. Collier Blvd., Marco Island) Beanie babies, books, games, T-shirts, and Sesame Street and Rugrats toys.

Conch Shelf (941-394-2511; Marco Island Marriott Resort, 400 S. Collier Blvd., Marco Island) Fine sea-themed gifts.

Holiday House Gifts (941-642-7113; Shops of Marco, Marco Island) Yankee Candles, country-style items, Christmas ornaments and decorations.

Island Treasures (941-394-6264; Shops of Marco, Marco Island) *Atocha* and treasure fleet jewelry, sea-themed gifts, shells, and T-shirts.

La Casita (941-642-7600; Shops of Marco, Marco Island) Handcrafted fabric angels and dolls, Mexican serapes, and other decorative items.

Things from the Sea (941-261-3820; Tin City, Naples) Quality souvenirs: scrimshaw, metal sculptures, brass, and other nautical gifts.

The Village Place (941-394-1990; 213 Harbor Place, Goodland) Nonprofit shop that benefits the town's schoolchildren. Handcrafts and homemade local preserves (sea grape, cocoplum, etc.) in a quaint cottage setting.

JEWELRY

Images (941-394-3456; Port of Marco Shopping Village, Marco Island) Gold jewelry appropriate for Florida: bird-of-paradise pins, tennis pendants, starfish earrings; also wood-sculptured fish and Swarovski crystal.

Port Royal Antique Jewelry (941-263-3071; 706 Fifth Ave. S., Old Naples) 18th-century royal jewels, custom-designed, estate, Diamond Deco, and other rare jewelry. So exclusive you have to ring a doorbell to get in.

Schilling Jewelers (941-642-3001; Shops of Marco, Marco Island) Custom design and manufacturing; cloisonné turtles and fish jewelry.

Thalheimer's Fine Jewelers (941-261-8422 or 800-998-8423; 255 13th Ave. S., Old Naples) The most respected name in jewelers, carrying quality watches, diamond jewelry, gems, crystal, and porcelain. Watchmaker, designer, and appraiser on premises.

William Phelps, Custom Jeweler (941-434-2233; Village on Venetian Bay, Naples) Fine crafted pendants, rings, earrings, and pins on display, plus colored stones and diamonds for customizing.

Yamron Jewelers (941-592-7707; Waterside Shops, Tamiami Trail, Naples) A ladies' Columbia cabochon emerald and diamond ring valued at $121,000 is for sale here, along with a select stock of other exquisite jewelry.

KITCHENWARE & HOME DECOR

El Condor Marketplace (941-591-2833; 2021 Pine Ridge Rd., Naples) Rooms filled with colorful tropical imports: furniture, pottery, wall hangings, glassware, cookware, and other gifts.

Gattle's (941-262-4791 or 800-344-4552; 1250 Third St. S., Old Naples) Linens for bed, bath, and table; fine home accessories and nursery items.

The Good Life (941-262-4355 or 800-846-2540; 1170 Third St. S., Old Naples) Gourmet cookware, tabletops, serving pieces, imported Povtmeiron tableware, quality implements, and paper and silk floral arrangements.

A Horse of a Different Color (941-261-1252; 1300 Third St. S., Old Naples) One-of-a-kind, pricey, highly contemporary gifts, lamps, clocks, and accessories, featuring imports from Scandinavia and other European regions.

Lady from Haiti (941-649-8607; 476 Fifth Ave. S., Old Naples) Steel drum sculptures, hand-painted wood items, fine Haitian art. Enjoy the sand on the floor and Caribbean music while you shop.

Simply Natural Home (941-403-4799; Village on Venetian Bay, Naples) Hand-painted floor cloths, Mexican metal cabinets, frames, huge pots, vases, and other rustic furniture and items.

SHELL SHOPS

Blue Mussel (941-262-4814; 478 Fifth Ave. S., Naples) Rare showpiece shells, jewelry, custom-designed mirrors, and other shell crafts.

Shells by Emily (941-394-5575; 651 S. Collier Blvd., Marco Island) Shells from around the world, shell craft accessories, and classes.

SHOPPING CENTERS & MALLS

Coastland Center (Tamiami Trail N. and Golden Gate Pkwy., Naples) Recently expanded to more than 950,000 square feet, it is Naples' largest and only enclosed, climate-controlled shopping center. The mall's 150 stores include a full array of shopping options, from major department stores to small specialty shops.

Coconut Grove Marketplace & Marina (1001 10th Ave. S., Naples) A pleasant contrast to the touristy character of Tin City and the expensive merchandise of Old Naples' plazas, Coconut Grove exudes a tropical temperament with its light wood interior, stylish wood signs fashioned by local artists, and a focus on things wild and islandy.

Blossomy, lush Fifth Avenue South is making a comeback as Naples' chic shop-and-dine district.

Karen T. Bartlett

Fifth Avenue South (Naples) Once upon a time, members of the Seminole Indian tribe sold their crafts from a stand on Fifth Avenue. Today it's one of Naples' most fashionable addresses. In 1996 there was a movement to update the historic district, which had begun to look run-down. Famed Florida architect Andre Duany was hired to breathe new life into the district. Besides cosmetic improvements, he brought a new bustle to the street. A tony hotel, new shops, and almost 20 restaurants and sidewalk cafes attract Naples' new "cafe society."

Marco Town Center Mall (Collier Blvd. and Bald Eagle Dr., Marco Island) A popular cluster of more than 10 distinctive eateries and 40 shopperies.

Mission de San Marco Plaza (599 S. Collier Blvd., Marco Island) A modified strip mall, done in an interesting interpretation of Spanish style, holding specialty stores of all sorts.

Old Marine Marketplace (Tin City, Naples) I love the structure of this mall, which resurrected old tin-roofed docks. You'll most commonly hear it called Tin City because of its rustic demeanor. Its 40 shops tend to be ultratouristy, selling mainly nautical gifts and resort wear, but it has enjoyable waterfront restaurants, and it's a good place to catch a fishing or sightseeing tour.

The Pavilion (Vanderbilt Beach Rd. and Tamiami Trail N., Naples) Strip mall with movie theater complex and anchor supermarket.

Port of Marco Shopping Village (Royal Palm Dr., Marco Island) A small, comfortable, Old Florida-style center in the historical heart of Marco Island. Gifts, clothes, and souvenirs on a midrange scale.

Shops of Marco (San Marco Rd. and Barfield Dr., Marco Island) One-of-a-kind clothing and gift shops.

Third Street South Plaza and the Avenues (Naples) Visit this upscale shopping quarter in Old Naples, the heart of the arts scene, and view fine outdoor sculptures on loan from local galleries. This is window-shopping (on my budget, anyway) at its best: exquisite clothes, art, jewelry, and home decorations and furnishings. This shopping district is so posh it has its own street concierge, who advises shoppers, assists with package delivery, lends umbrellas, and so on.

The Village on Venetian Bay (Gulfshore Blvd. N. at Park Shore Dr., Naples) Upscale, Mediterranean-style domain of fashion, jewelry, and art, located on the waterfront.

Waterside Shops at Pelican Bay (941-598-1605; Seagate Dr. and Tamiami Trail N., Pelican Bay, Naples) This shopping enclave features Saks Fifth Avenue, located amidst cascading waters and lush foliage. It hosts a summer concert series May through September.

SPORTS STORES

Note: This listing includes general sports outlets only. For supplies and equipment for specific sports, please refer to "Recreation" in this chapter.

Beach Sports of Marco (941-642-4282; 571 S. Collier Blvd., Marco Island) Bikes, in-line skates, tackle, bait, surfboards, swimwear, fishing licenses.

Play It Again Sports (941-263-6679; 2204 Tamiami Trail, Naples) New and used sports gear; in-line skates and exercise equipment rentals.

Sports Authority (941-598-5054; 2505 Pine Ridge Rd., Naples) Complete line of sports and outdoor equipment and clothing.

CALENDAR OF EVENTS

FEBRUARY

Black Cultural Arts Festival (941-774-8476; Collier County Museum, Naples) Black dance troupes and musicians perform on an outdoor stage. Two weekend days midmonth.

Everglades Seafood Festival (941-695-4100; Everglades City) Three days of music, arts and crafts, and fresh seafood.

Grecian Festival (941-591-3430; St. Katherine's Greek Orthodox Church, Airport-Pulling Rd., Naples) Greek food specialties, music, costumed dancers, and exhibits. First weekend.

LG Championship (941-403-1030; Bay Colony Golf Club, Pelican Marsh, Naples) Senior PGA golf tournament.

Naples National Art Festival (941-592-9530; Cambier Park, Naples) More than 200 artists from around the world meet to display and sell their work. Two days late February.

MARCH

Bonita Springs Tomato Seafood Festival (941-992-2556; Bonita Recreational Center, Lee Blvd., Bonita Springs) Honors the town's two culinary trademarks. Two days at the end of the month.

Chalk Art (941-649-6077; Eighth St., Naples) Artists create sidewalk masterpieces and sell souvenirs. Two days.

Conservancy Fish Fry (941-262-0304; Southwest Florida Conservancy's Naples Nature Center) Fried grouper, live music, and dancing. One day late in the month.

Festival of the Arts (Naples) Costumed Mardi Gras Gala, street music, open houses, art exhibits, and an international food court. Three days.

Naples Seafood Festival (Naples Airport, Naples) Local delicacies, entertainment, arts and crafts fair, and a boat raffle. Three days midmonth.

Nuveen Masters Tennis Tournament (941-435-1300; Kensington Golf and Country Club, Pine Ridge Rd., Naples) Competition among the top eight players on the Nuveen professional tennis tour. One week.

Swamp Buggy Races (941-774-2701 or 800-897-2701; Florida Sports Park, Route 951, east Naples) Nationally televised event; the Everglades' equivalent of tractor pulls or monster truck racing.

Watermelon Festival (941-992-2110; Bonita Springs) Summertime celebration of the town's juicy bounty. Free watermelon, games, and entertainment.

APRIL

A Taste of Collier (Fifth Ave. S., Naples) Naples' renowned restaurants serve samples of their culinary specialties. Live music. One day.

MAY

Great Dock Canoe Race (941-263-9940; The Dock at Crayton Cove restaurant, 12th Ave. S., Naples) More than 200 teams, many in festive costumes, paddle across Naples Bay in good-spirited competition one Saturday.

SummerJazz (941-261-2222; Naples Beach Hotel & Golf Club, Naples) A series of sunset concerts under the stars on the third Saturday of every month, May through September.

Swamp Buggy Races See above, under MARCH.

JUNE

South Florida PGA Open (941-261-2222, ext. 2350; Naples Beach Hotel & Golf Club, 851 Gulf Shore Blvd. N., Naples) Golf enthusiasts can qualify to play side-by-side with PGA pros in the six-day competition.

OCTOBER

Swamp Buggy Races See above, under MARCH.

NOVEMBER

Festival of Lights (941-649-6707; Third Street Plaza and Fifth Avenue South, Naples) Holiday street- and tree-lighting festivities. Late in the month.

Old Florida Festival (941-774-8476; Collier County Museum, Naples) Music, Seminole War reenactments, history camps, and traditional arts and crafts remember Florida as it was. First weekend.

CHAPTER SEVEN
Practical Matters
INFORMATION

A comment on crime and humor on Anna Maria Island.

Greg Wagner

We hope you never need a hospital or a policeman, but in case you should, we offer that information here, as well as information on other topics:

AMBULANCE/FIRE/POLICE

A ll four west coast counties have adopted the 911 emergency phone number system. Dial it for ambulance, fire, sheriff, and police. Listed below are nonemergency numbers for individual communities.

Town	Ambulance	Fire	Police/Sheriff
FOR EMERGENCY	911	911	911
Anywhere in the region			
CHARLOTTE COUNTY			
Boca Grande			941-964-0863
Punta Gorda			941-639-4111
Charlotte County Sheriff			941-639-2101
Florida Highway Patrol (Venice)			941-483-5911
COLLIER COUNTY			
Everglades City			941-695-2902
Naples	941-434-4853		941-434-4844
Collier County Sheriff			941-793-9300
Florida Highway Patrol			941-455-3133
LEE COUNTY			
Bonita Springs			941-992-3320
Cape Coral	941-574-3223		941-574-3223
Captiva			941-472-9494
Fort Myers	941-334-6222		941-334-4155
Fort Myers Beach			941-463-6163
Pine Island (Matlacha)			941-283-0030
Sanibel	941-472-5525		941-472-3111
Lee County Sheriff			941-477-1200
Florida Highway Patrol			941-278-7100
SARASOTA BAY COAST			
Anna Maria			941-741-3900
Bradenton		941-747-1161	941-746-4111
Bradenton Beach		941-741-3900	941-778-6311
Cortez		941-778-6621	
Holmes Beach		941-741-3900	941-741-3900
Longboat (Manatee County)		941-383-5666	941-383-3738
Longboat (Sarasota County)		941-316-1944	941-316-1977

Town	Ambulance	Fire	Police/Sheriff
Sarasota		941-951-4211	941-316-1199
Siesta Key			941-365-1616
Venice		941-492-3196	941-488-6711
Manatee County Sheriff			941-747-3011
Sarasota County Sheriff			941-951-5800
Florida Highway Patrol (Venice)			941-483-5911

AREA CODE/TOWN GOVERNMENT & ZIP CODES

AREA CODE

The area code for the section of the Gulf Coast covered in this guide is 941. You must dial the area code for all long-distance calls within the region.

GOVERNMENT

All incorporated cities within the region are self-governing, with councilmen, commissioners, mayors, and city managers in various roles. The unincorporated towns and communities are county-ruled.

The incorporated cities of the Sarasota Bay coast include Bradenton, Anna Maria, Holmes Beach, Bradenton Beach, Sarasota, Longboat Key, and Venice. On the Charlotte Harbor coast, North Port and Punta Gorda are incorporated. Bradenton is the county seat for Manatee County; Sarasota for Sarasota County.

Cape Coral, Fort Myers (county seat), Fort Myers Beach, and Sanibel make up the Island Coast's incorporated cities. Naples is Collier County's seat; Naples, Marco Island, and Everglades City are incorporated.

ZIP CODES

Town	Government Center	Zip
CHARLOTTE HARBOR COAST		
North Port	941-426-8484	34287
Punta Gorda	941-575-3302	33950
ISLAND COAST		
Cape Coral	941-574-0401	33990
Fort Myers	941-332-6700	33902-2217
Sanibel	941-472-3700	33957

Town	Government Center	Zip
SARASOTA BAY COAST		
Anna Maria	941-778-0781	34216
Bradenton	941-748-0800	34206
Bradenton Beach	941-778-1005	34217
Holmes Beach		34217
Longboat Key (Manatee)	941-383-3721	34228
Longboat Key (Sarasota)	941-316-1999	34228
Sarasota	941-365-2200	34236
Venice	941-486-2626	34285
SOUTH COAST		
Everglades City	941-695-3781	34139
Marco Island	941-389-5000	34145
Naples	941-434-4601	34102

BANKS

Several old and established banks have branches located throughout Florida's Gulf Coast. Some are listed below, with toll-free information numbers where available.

Bank	Number(s)
Barnett	
Bradenton	941-755-0050
Charlotte County	941-743-1000
Englewood	941-474-9504
Fort Myers	941-337-7770
Naples	941-643-2265
Sarasota	941-953-6009
Venice	941-474-9504
SunTrust	800-732-9487

BIBLIOGRAPHY

LITERARY SOUVENIRS

BIOGRAPHY & REMINISCENCE

Brown, Loren G. "Totch." *Totch: A Life in the Everglades.* Gainesville: University Press of Florida, 1993. 269 pp., photos. A folksy, firsthand adventure tour of Ten Thousand Islands through the words of a former native.

Lindbergh, Anne Morrow. *Gift from the Sea.* New York: Pantheon, 1955. 142 pp., illus. Hardcover $16. New York: Vintage Books, 1955. 138 pp., illus. Paper, $7. A small book packed with sea-inspired wisdom. Strong evidence points to Captiva as its inspiration.

Newton, James. *Uncommon Friends.* New York: Harcourt, Brace, Jovanovich, 1987. 368 pp. $10.95. Local man's memories of his friendships with Fort Myers' illustrious winterers: Thomas Edison, Henry Ford, Harvey Firestone, and Charles Lindbergh.

Weeks, David C. *Ringling: The Florida Years, 1911-1936.* Gainesville: University Press of Florida, 1993. 350 pp., photos, annot., index. $24.95.

Workman, Joe. *Darn the Torpedoes, I Have a Boo-Boo.* Fort Myers Beach, FL: Island Press Publishers, 1994. 143 pp. Collection of Fort Myers *News-Press* columns from one of the area's most humorous newspapermen.

COOKBOOKS

Armitage, Kate, et al. *For Citrus Only.* Sanibel Island, FL, 1994. 159 pp., illus., index. $9.95.

Junior League of Fort Myers. *Gulfshore Delights.* Fort Myers, FL, 1984. 286 pp., illus., index. $14.95.

_____. *Tropical Settings.* Fort Myers, FL, 1995. 254 pp., illus., index. $19.95.

Reynolds, Doris. *When Peacocks Were Roasted and Mullet Was Fried.* Naples, FL: Enterprise Publishing, 1993. 175 pp., photos. $23.95. Naples history flavored with recipes.

FICTION

Dever, Sean Michael. *Blind Pass.* Kearney, NE: Morris Publishing, 1996. 244 pp. $7.99. Mystery set in Sanibel and Captiva.

MacDonald, John D. Many of his Travis McGee and other mysteries take place in a Sarasota Bay coast setting, where he had a home.

Matthiessen, Peter. *Killing Mr. Watson.* New York: Random House, 1990. The parents of this award-winning author live on Sanibel Island. The subject of his historical novel is the posse killing of a murderer who hid out in the frontier of Ten Thousand Islands.

White, Randy. *Captiva.* New York: Berkley Publishing Company, 1996. 319 pp. $5.99.

_____. *The Heat Islands*. New York: St. Martin's Press, 1992. 276 pp. $4.99. Mystery by a local fishing guide/journalist in local setting.

_____. *Sanibel Flats*. New York: St. Martin's Press, 1990. 307 pp. $3.95. His first Doc Ford mystery; set on Sanibel Island.

HISTORY

Beater, Jack. *Pirates & Buried Treasure*. St. Petersburg: Great Outdoors Publishing, 1959. 118 pp., illus. $2.95. Somewhat factual, ever-colorful account of Jose Gaspar and his cohorts, by the area's foremost legendaire.

Board, Prudy Taylor, and Esther B. Colcord. *Historic Fort Myers*. Virginia Beach, VA: The Donning Publishers, 1992. 96 pp., photos, index. $15.95. Largely photographic treatment, written by two of the area's leading historians today.

_____. *Pages From the Past*. Virginia Beach, VA: The Donning Publishers, 1990. 192 pp., photos, index. $29.95. Largely photographic treatment of Fort Myers' history.

Dormer, Elinore M. *The Sea Shell Islands: A History of Sanibel and Captiva*. Tallahassee, FL: Rose Printing Co., 1987. 274 pp., illus., index. $16. The definitive work on island and regional history.

Jordan, Elaine Blohm. *Pine Island, the Forgotten Island*. Pine Island, FL: 1982. 186 pp., photos.

_____. *Tales of Pine Island*. Ellijay, GA: Jordan Ink Publishing, 1985. 142 pp. $12.

Matthews, Janet Snyder. *Edge of Wilderness: A Settlement History of Manatee River and Sarasota Bay*. Sarasota, FL: Coastal Press, 1983. 464 pp., photos, index. $21.50.

_____. *Journey to Centennial Sarasota*. Sarasota, FL: Pine Level Press, 1989. 224 pp., photos, index. $29.95.

_____. *Venice: Journey to Horse and Chaise*. Sarasota, FL: Pine Level Press, 1989. 394 pp., photos, index.

Zeiss, Betsy. *The Other Side of the River: Historical Cape Coral*. Cape Coral, FL, 1986. 215 pp., photos, index. $8.95.

NATURAL HISTORY

Campbell, George R. *The Nature of Things on Sanibel*. Fort Myers, FL: Press Printing, 1978. 174 pp., illus., index. $14.95. Factual yet entertaining background on native fauna and flora.

Douglas, Marjory Stoneman. *The Everglades: River of Grass*. St. Simons, GA: Mockingbird Books, 1947. 308 pp., $4.95. The book that focused the nation's attention on the developing plight of the pristine Everglades.

PICTORIAL

Butcher, Clyde. *Clyde Butcher: Portfolio I*. Fort Myers, FL: Shade Tree Press, 1994. 64 plates. The master of natural landscape photography collects his haunting black-and-white large-format images in a coffee-table edition.

Campen, Richard N. *Images of Sanibel, Captiva, Fort Myers*. Cape Coral, FL: Direct Impressions, 1995. 84 pp., photos, index.

Capes, Richard. *Richard Capes' Drawings Capture Siesta Key*. Sarasota, FL, 1992. 175 pp. An artistic tour of the island in pen and ink, with handwritten descriptions.

Stone, Lynn. *Sanibel Island*. Stillwater, MN: Voyageur Press, Inc., 1991. 96 pp., photos. $15.95. Sanibel's natural treasures in words and striking pictures.

RECREATION

Fuery, Captain Mike. *Florida Shelling Guide*. Captiva, FL: Sanibel Sandollar Publications, 1987. Written by a Sanibel charter captain. Features Sanibel, Captiva, and other Gulf Coast barrier islands.

_____. *South Florida Bay and Coastal Fishing*. Captiva, FL: Sanibel Sandollar Publications, 1987.

TRAVEL

MacPerry, I. *Indian Mounds You Can Visit*. St. Petersburg, FL: Great Outdoors Publishing, 1993. 319 pp., photos, index. $12.95. Covers the entire west coast of Florida, arranged by county.

Marquis, Darcy Lee, and Paul Roat. *The Insiders' Guide to Sarasota & Bradenton*. Manteo, NC: Insiders' Guides, Inc., 1996. 369 pp., photos, index. Copublished by the *Bradenton Herald*. Lots of information that would be especially helpful to anyone relocating to the area.

Walton, Chelle Koster. *Adventure Guide to Florida's West Coast*. Edison, NJ: Hunter Publishing, Inc., 1998. Covers Tampa to the western Everglades.

_____. *Florida Island Hopping: The West Coast*. Sarasota, FL: Pineapple Press, 1995. 324 pp., illus., index. $14.95. Focuses on outdoor recreation, adventure, and culture.

CHECK IT OUT

HISTORY & REMINISCENCE

Bickel, Karl A. *The Mangrove Coast: The Story of the West Coast of Florida*. 4th ed. New York: Coward-McCann, 1989. 332 pp., photos, index. Vintage regional history of the area from Tampa Bay to Ten Thousand Islands, from the time of Ponce de León to 1885, spiced with romantic embellishments.

Briggs, Mildred. *Pioneers of Bonita Springs (Facts and Folklore)*. Florida, 1976. 100 pp., photos. Pirates, Indian healers, outlaws, and more.

Fritz, Florence. *Unknown Florida*. Coral Gables, FL: University of Miami Press, 1963. 213 pp., photos, index. Focuses on southernmost Gulf Coast.

Gonzales, Thomas A. *The Caloosahatchee: History of the Caloosahatchee River and the City of Fort Myers, Florida*. Fort Myers Beach: Island Press Publishers, 1982. 134 pp. Memories of a native son, descendant of city's first settler.

Grismer, Karl H. *The Story of Fort Myers*. Fort Myers Beach, FL: Island Press Publishers, 1982. 348 pp., photos, index.

_____. *The Story of Sarasota*. Tampa, FL: The Florida G Press, 1946. 376 pp., photos, index.

Hann, John H., ed. *Missions to the Calusa*. Gainesville: University of Florida Press, 1991. 460 pp., historic documents, index.

Marth, Del. *Yesterday's Sarasota*. Miami, FL: E. A. Seemann Publishing, 1977. Updated. 160 pp., photos. Primarily pictorial history.

Matthews, Kenneth, and Robert McDevitt. *The Unlikely Legacy*. Sarasota, FL: Aaron Publishers, 1980. 64 pp., illus. The story of John Ringling, the circus, and Sarasota.

Peeples, Vernon. *Punta Gorda and the Charlotte Harbor Area*. Norfolk: Donning Co., 1986. 208 pp., photos, index. Pictorial history authored by local politician.

Romans, Bernard. *A Concise Natural History of East and West Florida*. Gainesville, FL: University of Florida Press, 1962. 342 pp., index. A facsimile reproduction of the 1775 edition.

Schell, Rolfe F. *De Soto Didn't Land at Tampa*. Fort Myers Beach, FL: Island Press, 1966. 96 pp., illus.

_____. *History of Fort Myers Beach*. Fort Myers Beach, FL: Island Press, 1980. 96 pp., photos, index.

Tebeau, Charlton W. *Florida's Last Frontier: The History of Collier County*. Coral Gables, FL: University of Miami Press, 1966. 278 pp., photos, index.

Widmer, Randolph J. *The Evolution of the Calusa*. Tuscaloosa: University of Alabama Press, 1988. 334 pp., index. Very technical discussion of the "nonagricultural chiefdom on the Southwest Florida Coast."

CLIMATE, SEASONS, AND WHAT TO WEAR

"The tropics brush the Mangrove Coast but do not overwhelm it."

— Karl Bickel, *The Mangrove Coast*, 1942

Florida's nickname, the Sunshine State, was once as fresh as it was apt. Although overuse has tended to cloud the once-perfect image, Florida still remains the ultimate state of sunshine through the sheer power of statistics. The sun beams down on the Gulf Coast for nearly 75 percent of all daylight hours and constitutes the one asset that locals can bank on. Businesses along the coast are known to promise free wares or substantial discounts on sunless days.

To residents, the sun's smile can seem more like a sneer as they await fall's begrudging permission to turn off air conditioners and open windows. They suffer their own brand of cabin fever during the summer months, which often seem to go on as long as a Canadian winter. Although visitors revel in the warmth and sunlight, they often wonder how residents endure the monotony of seasonal sameness.

The seasons do change along the southern Gulf Coast, although more subtly than "up north." Weather patterns vary within the region. The Sarasota Bay and Charlotte Harbor areas often get more rain. However, weather can be very localized — it may rain on the southern end of 12-mile-long Sanibel Island while the north end remains dry. Islands generally stay cooler than the mainland in summer and warmer in winter, thanks to their insulating jacket of water. This is especially true where Charlotte Harbor runs wide and deep, creating a small pocket of tropical climate.

Winter is everyone's favorite time of year weatherwise, with temperatures along the coast reaching generally into the 70s during the day and dropping into the 50s at night. Visitors find green, balmy relief from snow blindness and frostbite. Floridians enjoy the relative coolness that brings with it a reprieve from sweltering days, steamy nights, and bloodthirsty insects. The fragrance of oranges, grapefruits, and key limes fill the air. It's a time for activity; one can safely schedule a tee time past noon. Resort areas fill up and migratory house guests from the north arrive.

Greg Wagner

An afternoon summer shower descends upon Sanibel Island.

Spring comes on tiptoe to the coast. No thaw-and-puddle barometer alerts us; the sense of spring giddiness affects only longtime residents. Floridians emerge from hibernation raring to leap and frolic, and perhaps do a little mischief. Gardenias and jasmine bloom, and everything that already looks green and alive bursts forth with an extra reserve of color. It's a time to celebrate the end of another season and to enjoy greedily the domain that's been shared with visitors during the winter months.

Summers used to be reserved for die-hard Floridians. All but the most devoted residents boarded up their homes and businesses and headed somewhere — anywhere — cooler. Now there's a summer trade, composed of Floridians, Europeans, and northern families — enough to keep alive the resort communities through temperatures that snuggle up to 100 degrees. Although technically classified as subtropical, starting in June the region feels the bristles of that tropical brush. The pace of life slows, and late-afternoon rains suddenly and unpredictably revolt against the sun's constancy. Mangoes and guavas blush sweet temptation. Moonlit nights bring magic to the vining cereus, with its white starburst blooms the size of a Frisbee.

Fall appears in October, as a sharpening of vision after a blur of humidity. Residents don't exactly go out and buy wool plaids, but they do break out sweatshirts. Many build fires in hearths that have held dried floral arrangements for eight months. The leathery leaves of the sea grape tree turn as red as the northern oak, and the gumbo-limbo coaxes out rakes. The best part about a Gulf Coast fall, for those residents who once endured northern winters, is that they bode not of rubber boots and long underwear.

Winter temperatures dip, albeit rarely, into the freezing range, so be prepared for just about any weather between December and February. Fortunately swimsuits take up little room, so pack more than one (Florida's high humidity often prevents anything from ever really drying out). Loose-fitting togs and cotton work best in any season. Long sleeves are welcome in the evenings during the winter. Summer showers require rain gear, especially if you plan on boating or playing outdoors.

Don't worry about dress codes in most restaurants. Ties and pantyhose are strictly for the office and, possibly, the theater. Worry more about comfort, especially if your skin burns easily. Pack hats and lots of sunscreen. Bring insect repellent, too, especially if you plan on venturing into the jungle — or watching an island sunset, for that matter. Counties do spray for mosquitoes, but it has little effect on the tiny but prolific no-see-um (sand flea). Any DEET product repels mosquitoes. The best protection against both pests is sitting under a ceiling fan — practically standard equipment in homes and hotels.

On the cloudier side, Florida weather includes a high incidence of lightning, summer squalls, tornadoes, waterspouts, and the dreaded H-word. Hurricane season begins in June, but activity concentrates toward season's end in October. Watches and warnings alert you in plenty of time to head inland or north; to be safest, do so at first mention, especially if you are staying on an island.

Florida's celebrated sunshine is at its best on the Gulf Coast. Ol' Sol visits practically every day, and it's also where he slips into bed. Gulf Coast Florida boasts the most spectacular sunsets in the continental United States.

Green Flash

The sun is setting, melting, golden, into the sea like a round pat of butter balanced on its edge. Just as the final crescent of light disappears, it sends up on the horizon a final green farewell flare.

What you've just witnessed is a tropical phenomenon called a "green flash." It occurs infrequently, and most people miss it — or only realize what they've seen after the fact.

Skeptics will tell you that green flashes are just a good excuse to sit on the beach at sunset, perhaps with a celebratory glass of champagne or rum punch. The drinking part of the sunset ritual, they further theorize, may be more responsible for green flash sightings than reality.

Physics, however, backs up the notion that the sun emits a split-second green explosion as it winks below the sea's surface. It all has to do with spectrum, wavelengths, refraction, and other terms you may remember from school science experiments.

In short, it takes conditions such as those we enjoy on the Gulf Coast — sunsets over the sea and near-tropical climes — to make the green flash happen. Cloudless evening skies are also required, which occur more regularly during the cool months. Binoculars or a small telescope will help widen the band of refracted green light so it lasts longer. Patience and persistence are crucial. Once you've seen a green flash, some say, your trained eye is apt to spot more. With or without rum.

AVERAGE GULF COAST AIR TEMPERATURES

Month	Avg. Max.	Avg. Min.
Jan.	72.8°	52.8°
Feb.	73.8°	53.8°
Mar.	78.3°	57.8°
Apr.	82.5°	61.6°
May	87.7°	67.1°
June	89.7°	72.1°
July	90.5°	73.7°
Aug.	90.9°	73.8°
Sept.	89.1°	72.7°
Oct.	84.9°	66.8°
Nov.	77.9°	59.4°
Dec.	74.1°	53.8°

GULF COAST WATER TEMPERATURES

Annual average	77.5°
Fall/winter average	70.8°
Spring/summer average	84.1°
Winter low	66.0°
Summer high	87.0°

SERVICES FOR THE PHYSICALLY IMPAIRED

Regulations concerning disabled access vary, depending on locale. In general, most restaurants, parks, attractions, and resorts provide physically impaired visitors with special ramps, bathroom stalls, and hotel rooms.

HOSPITALS

CHARLOTTE HARBOR COAST

Englewood

Englewood Community Hospital, 700 Medical Blvd., Englewood 34223; 941-475-6571. Emergency room open 24 hours.

Port Charlotte

Columbia Fawcett Memorial Hospital, 21298 Olean Blvd., Port Charlotte 33949; 941-629-1181. Emergency room open 24 hours.

Bon Secours-St. Joseph Hospital, 2500 Harbor Blvd., Port Charlotte 33952; 941-625-4122. Emergency room open 24 hours.

Punta Gorda

Charlotte Regional Medical Center, 809 E. Marion Ave., Punta Gorda 33950; 941-639-3131. Emergency room open 24 hours.

ISLAND COAST

Cape Coral

Cape Memorial Hospital, 636 Del Prado Blvd, Cape Coral 33990; 941-574-2323. Emergency room open 24 hours.

Fort Myers

Fort Myers' new and stylish HealthPark Hospital.

Karen T. Bartlett

HealthPark Medical Center, 9981 HealthPark Circle, Fort Myers 33908; 941-433-7799. Emergency room open 24 hours.

Lee Memorial Hospital, 2776 Cleveland Ave., Fort Myers 33901; 941-332-1111. Emergency room open 24 hours.

Columbia Regional Medical Center, 2727 Winkler Ave., Fort Myers 33901; 941-939-1147. Emergency room open 24 hours.

SARASOTA BAY COAST

Bradenton

HCA L.W. Blake Hospital, 2020 59th St. W., Bradenton 34209; 941-792-6611. Emergency room open 24 hours.

Manatee Memorial Hospital, 206 Second St. E., Bradenton 34208; 941-746-5111. Emergency room open 24 hours.

Sarasota

Columbia Doctors Hospital of Sarasota, 5731 Bee Ridge Rd., Sarasota 34232; 941-342-1100. Emergency room open 24 hours.

Sarasota Memorial Hospital, 1700 S. Tamiami Trail, Sarasota 34239-3555; 941-917-9000. Emergency room open 24 hours.

Venice

Bon Secours Venice Hospital, 540 The Rialto, Venice 34285; 941-485-7711. Emergency room open 24 hours.

SOUTH COAST

Naples

Naples Community Hospital, 350 Seventh St. N., Naples 34102; 941-262-3131. Emergency room open 24 hours.

North Collier Hospital, 11190 Healthpark Blvd., Naples 34101; 941-597-1417. Emergency room open 24 hours.

LATE-NIGHT FOOD AND FUEL

Certain categories of Florida liquor licensing require bars to serve food, which provides a good source for late-night eating. Many chain restaurants located along major thoroughfares stay open late or all night, such as Grandma's Kitchen, Denny's, and Perkins.

Chain convenience stores, gas stations, and fuel/food marts also are open around the clock. These include 7-Eleven, Starvin' Marvin, Mobil Mart, and Circle K.

MEDIA

Media flood the Gulf Coast like high tide. Many publications are directed toward tourists, and some are only as permanent as the shoreline during a tidal surge. Magazines come and go, and radio stations often shift format.

Four daily newspapers stand out for their endurance and dependability: the *Bradenton Herald*, the *Sarasota Herald-Tribune*, the Fort Myers *News-Press*, and the *Naples Daily News*. Weeklies are also firmly established in their respective communities, primarily because many are owned collectively by one corporation. Specialty tabloids address seniors, shoppers, fishermen, women, and other groups.

Magazines show the most fluctuation. Traditionally they were created to appeal to the region's upscale, mature population, which is concentrated in Sarasota and Naples. *Sarasota Magazine* and *Gulfshore Life* have been the stalwarts of regional lifestyle glossies, but even they shift focus to address changing populations and economic trends.

Fort Myers carries the majority of the region's broadcast media, which reach to the Charlotte Harbor and south coasts. Much of the Sarasota Bay coast's TV comes from Tampa.

Charlotte Harbor Coast

NEWSPAPERS

Boca Beacon, P.O. Box 313, Boca Grande 33921; 941-964-2995, 800-749-2995. Weekly.

Charlotte Sun-Herald, P.O. Box 2390, Port Charlotte 33949; 941-629-2855.

Englewood Sun Herald, 167 W. Dearborn St., Englewood 34223; 941-474-5521. Weekly.

Gasparilla Gazette, P.O. Box 929, 301 Park Ave., Boca Grande 33921; 941-964-2728.

RADIO

WCCF-AM 1580; Punta Gorda. Talk.
WCVU-FM 104.9; Port Charlotte. Easy listening.
WENG-AM 1530; Englewood. Talk.
WIKX-FM 92.9; Punta Gorda. Country.
WKII-AM 1070; Punta Gorda. Adult.
WVIA-FM 91.7; Port Charlotte. Christian.

Island Coast

NEWSPAPERS

Cape Coral Breeze, 2510 Del Prado Blvd., Cape Coral 33910; 941-574-1110. Daily.

Captiva Current, P.O. Box 549, Captiva 33924; 941-472-1580.

Fort Myers Beach Bulletin, P.O. Box 2867, 19260 San Carlos Blvd., Fort Myers Beach 33932; 941-463-4421.

Island Reporter, P.O. Box 809, 2340 Periwinkle Way, Sanibel 33957; 941-472-1587. Weekly.

News-Press, P.O. Box 10, 2442 Dr. Martin Luther King Jr. Blvd., Fort Myers 33902; 941-335-0200. Publishes editions for Charlotte County and Bonita Springs.

Observer Papers, 17274 San Carlos Blvd., Fort Myers Beach 33931; 941-482-7111. Publishes weekly editions for Fort Myers Beach and other neighborhoods.

Pine Island Eagle, 10700 Stringfellow Rd., Suite 60, Bokeelia 33922; 941-283-2022. Weekly.

Sanibel-Captiva Islander, P.O. Box 56, 395 Tarpon Bay Rd., Sanibel 33957; 941-472-5185. Weekly; free subscription.

MAGAZINES

Florida Journal, 6238 Presidential Ct., Fort Myers 33919; 941-481-7511. German publication.

Get Up & Go, 4575 Via Royale, Suite 102, Fort Myers 33919; 941-931-9191. Florida editions of a national seniors magazine.

Times of the Islands, P.O. Box 1227, Sanibel Island 33957; 941-472-0205.

RADIO

WAYJ-FM 88.7; Fort Myers. Easy listening.
WAVV-FM 101.1; Fort Myers. Adult contemporary.
WAYG-FM 89.1; Fort Myers. Christian contemporary.
WCKT-FM 107; Fort Myers. Country.
WCRM-AM 1350; Fort Myers. Spanish Christian.
WDRR-FM 98.5; Fort Myers. Adult contemporary.
WFSN-FM 100.1; Fort Myers.
WINK-AM 1240; Fort Myers. News/talk.
WINK-FM 96.9; Fort Myers. Adult contemporary.
WJBX-FM 99.3; Fort Myers. Adult alternative.
WJST-FM 106.3; Fort Myers. Big band.
WMYR-AM 1410; Fort Myers. Country.
WOLZ-FM 95.3; Fort Myers. Oldies.
WRXK-FM 96.1; Estero. Adult rock.
WGCU-FM 90.1; Fort Myers. Classical/jazz/news.
WSOR-FM 90.9; Fort Myers. Christian.
WSRX-FM 89.5; Fort Myers. Contemporary Christian.
WXKB-FM 103.9; North Fort Myers. Contemporary.
WWCL-AM 1440; Fort Myers. Spanish.
WWCN-AM 770; Estero. CNN/talk.
WWGR-FM 101.9; Fort Myers. Country.

TELEVISION

WBBH-TV Channel 20; Fort Myers. NBC.
WFTX-TV Channel 36; Cape Coral. Fox.
WINK-TV Channel 11; Fort Myers. CBS.
WZVN-TV Channel 26; Fort Myers. ABC.

Sarasota Bay Coast

NEWSPAPERS

Bradenton Herald, P.O. Box 921, Bradenton 34206; 941-748-0411. Daily.
Bulletin, P.O Box 2560, Sarasota 34230; 941-953-3990. Black community weekly.

Islander Bystander, 5408 Marina Dr., Holmes Beach 34217; 941-778-7978. Covers all of Anna Maria Island. Weekly.

Longboat Observer, P.O. Box 8100, Longboat Key 34228; 941-383-5509. Weekly.

Pelican Press, 230 Avenida Madera, Sarasota 34242; 941-349-4949. Weekly covering Siesta Key and Sarasota.

Sarasota Herald-Tribune, 801 S. Tamiami Trail, P.O. Box 1719, Sarasota FL 33577; 941-953-7755.

Venice Gondolier, 200 E. Venice Ave., Venice 34285; 941-484-2611. Published semiweekly.

Weekly, 3755 S. Tuttle Ave., Sarasota, 34239; 941-923-2544. Heavy on entertainment.

MAGAZINES

Sarasota Arts Review, 1269 First St., Suite 211, Sarasota 34236; 941-364-5825. Monthly coverage of the area's lively arts scene.

Sarasota Magazine, 601 S. Osprey Ave., Sarasota 34236; 941-366-8225. Lifestyle for upscale Sarasotans.

Sarasota Scene, 2015 S. Tuttle Ave., Sarasota 34239; 941-365-1119. Weekly covering the Sarasota-Bradenton area.

West Coast Woman, P.O. Box 819, Sarasota 34230; 941-954-3300. Monthly free publication.

RADIO

WAMR-AM 1320; Venice. Oldies.

WBRD-AM 1420; Bradenton. News/talk.

WCTQ-FM 92.1; Venice. Country.

WDUV-FM 103.5; Bradenton. Easy listening.

WJIS-FM 88.1; Bradenton. Christian jazz.

WKZM-FM 105; Sarasota. Christian.

WSPB-AM 1450; Sarasota. Classical.

WSRZ-FM 106.3; Sarasota. Oldies.

TELEVISION

WBSV-TV Channel 62; Sarasota. Independent.

WEDU-TV Channel 3; Sarasota. PBS.

WSB-TV Channel 40; Sarasota. ABC.

South Coast

NEWSPAPERS

Bonita Banner, 9102 Bonita Beach Rd., Bonita Springs 34135; 941-765-0110. Semiweekly.
Naples Daily News, P.O. Box 7009, Naples 33941; 941-262-3161.

MAGAZINES

Gulfshore Life, 2975 S. Horseshoe Dr., Suite 100, Naples 34104; 941-643-3933. Longtime, slick lifestyle and news guide to the southwest coast.
Home & Condo, 2975 S. Horseshoe Dr., Suite 100, Naples 34104; 941-643-3933. Specifically addresses relocators.
N, The Magazine of Naples, 4500 Executive Dr., Suite 1, Naples 34119; 941-594-0100. Fashion and society oriented.
Naples Illustrated, 274 Monterey Dr., Naples 34119; 941-352-2946. New lifestyles glossy.

RADIO

WARO-FM 94.5, Naples. Rock-and-roll oldies.
WGUF-FM 98.9; Naples. Smooth jazz.
WNOG-AM 1270; Naples. Oldies.
WNOG-FM 93.5; Naples. Talk.
WSGL-FM 103.1; Naples. Adult contemporary.
WSRM-FM 105.5; Naples. Easy listening.

TELEVISION

WGCU-TV Channel 30; Naples. PBS.
WTVK-TV Channel 46; Bonita Springs. UPN.

REAL ESTATE

Real estate prices run the gamut from reasonable to ultra-expensive. In parts of Bradenton, Sarasota, and Fort Myers, planned communities cater to young families. Exclusive areas such as Longboat Key, Casey Key, Manasota Key, Sanibel Island, Captiva Island, and Naples are known for their pricey waterfront homes and golfing developments. Florida's $25,000 homestead exemption gives residents a break on primary home purchases.

Real estate publications can be found on the newsstands, or check local newspapers. Otherwise, contact the agencies listed below.

Florida Association of Realtors, P.O. Box 725025, Orlando 32872-5025; 407-438-1400.

Sarasota Association of Realtors, 3590 Tuttle Ave. S., Sarasota 34239; 941-923-2315.

Fort Myers Association of Realtors, Inc., 2840 Winkler Ave., Fort Myers 33916; 941-936-3537.

Sanibel & Captiva Islands Association of Realtors, Inc., 695 Tarpon Bay Rd., Suite #10, Sanibel 33957; 941-472-9353.

Naples Area Board of Realtors, Inc., 1455 Pine Ridge Rd., Naples; 941-597-1666.

ROAD SERVICE

AAA Auto Club
>   3844 Bee Ridge Rd., Sarasota; 941-362-2220
>   24-Hour Emergency Road Service 941-362-2222

>   258 Ringling Shopping Center, Sarasota; 941-362-2500

>   2516 Colonial Blvd., Fort Myers; 941-939-6500
>   24-Hour Emergency Road Service, 800-365-0933

>   4910 North Tamiami Trail, Suite 120, Naples; 941-594-5006
>   24-Hour Emergency Road Service, 800-365-0933

TOURIST INFORMATION

Visit Florida , 661 E. Jefferson St., Suite 300, Tallahasee, FL 32301; 800-7FLA-USA

Charlotte Harbor Coast

Boca Grande Chamber of Commerce, P.O. Box 704, Boca Grande 33921; 941-964-0568. Information center located in Courtyard Plaza at the island's north end.

Charlotte County Chamber of Commerce, 2702 Tamiami Trail, Port Charlotte 33952; 941-627-2222.

Englewood Area Chamber of Commerce, 601 S. Indiana Ave., Englewood 34223; 941-474-5511.

Island Coast

Cape Coral Chamber of Commerce, P.O. Box 747, Cape Coral 33910; 941-549-6900 or 800-226-9609. Information center at 1625 Cape Coral Pkwy. East.

Fort Myers Beach Chamber of Commerce, 17200 San Carlos Blvd., Fort Myers Beach 33931; 941-454-7500 or 800-782-9283.

Greater Fort Myers Chamber of Commerce, P.O. Box 9289, Fort Myers 33902; 941-332-3624. Welcome center located downtown at 2310 Edwards Dr.

Greater Pine Island Chamber of Commerce, P.O. Box 525, Matlacha 33909; 941-283-0888. Information center located before the bridge to Matlacha on Pine Island Road.

Lee Island Coast Visitor & Convention Bureau, 2180 W. First St., Suite 100, Fort Myers 33901; 941-335-2631 or 800-237-6444.

North Fort Myers Chamber of Commerce, Shell Factory, 2787 N. Tamiami Trail, North Fort Myers 33903; 941-997-9111.

Sanibel-Captiva Islands Chamber of Commerce, 1159 Causeway Rd., Sanibel Island 33957; 941-472-1080. Information center located shortly after the causeway approach to Sanibel.

Southwest Florida Hispanic Chamber of Commerce, 3422 Willard St., Fort Myers 33916; 941-561-0090, ext. 229.

Sarasota Bay Coast

Anna Maria Island Chamber of Commerce, 501 Manatee Ave., Suite D, Holmes Beach 34217-1991; 941-778-1541.

Bradenton Area Convention & Visitors Bureau, P.O Box 1000, Bradenton 34206; 941-729-9177 or 800-4-MANATEE. Welcome center located off Interstate 75, exit 43.

Longboat Key Chamber of Commerce, Whitney Beach Plaza, 6854 Gulf of Mexico Dr., Longboat Key 34228; 941-383-2466.

Manatee Chamber of Commerce, 222 Tenth St. W., Bradenton 34205; 941-748-3411.

Sarasota Convention & Visitors Bureau, 655 N. Tamiami Trail, Sarasota 34236; 941-957-1877 or 800-522-9799.

Siesta Key Chamber of Commerce, 5100 Ocean Blvd., Unit B, Sarasota 34242; 941-349-3800.

Venice Area Chamber of Commerce, 257 N. Tamiami Trail, Venice 34285-1534; 941-488-2236.

South Coast

Bonita Springs Area Chamber of Commerce, P.O. Box 1240, Bonita Springs 34133; 941-992-2943 or 800-226-2943. Welcome center located just off Tamiami Trail across from entrance to Pelican Landing development.

Everglades Area Chamber of Commerce, P.O. Box 130, 32016 E. Tamiami Trail, Everglades City 33929; 941-695-3941.

Marco Island Area Chamber of Commerce, 1102 North Collier Blvd., P.O. Box 913, Marco Island 33937; 941-394-7549.

Marco Island & The Everglades Escape Line, 800-788-MARCO (6272).

Visit Naples, 895 5th Ave. S., Naples 34102-6605; 941-262-6141 or 800-605-7878.

IF TIME IS SHORT

Not enough time to do it all on this trip to southwest Florida? Here are some highlights I suggest to weekenders and short-term vacationers who wonder how they can best spend their precious time. Beach time, of course, is a high priority for those with only a few days to spend in the sun. I list must-see beaches as well as other attractions, adventures, restaurants, and lodgings you should not miss.

Sarasota Bay Coast

Siesta Key County Beach (941-346-3310; Midnight Pass Rd. at Beach Way Dr., Siesta Key), despite its weekend and high-season crowds, is the area's ultimate beach, with sands whiter and fluffier than anywhere else in southwest Florida. While on the island, spend a night or two at the eclectic **Banana Bay Club** (941-346-0113 or 888-6BAN-BAY; 8254 Midnight Pass Rd., Siesta Key 34242), off the beach but on a quiet birding lagoon, and have dinner at **The Summerhouse** (941-349-1100; 6101 Midnight Pass Rd.), purely Florida in atmosphere and very haute in the cuisine department.

Downtown Sarasota is a happening place. Take in a play and circle the galleries of the Theatre and Arts District. Don't miss the shops of **Palm Avenue** and the galleries of **Towles Court Artist Colony** (941-365-9146; 1945 Morrill St.).

The **John and Mabel Ringling Museum of Art**, the **Ringling Estate**, and its various circus and Gilded Age attractions (941-359-5725; 5401 Bay Shore Rd.) crown in glory Sarasota's famed cultural scene. **Longboat Key** provides a drive on the coast's wealthy side. Depending on your budget, dine in high style at **Euphemia Haye** (941-383-3633; 5540 Gulf of Mexico Dr.) or in the spirit of maritime fun at **Mar-Vista Dockside Restaurant & Pub** (941-383-2391; 760 Broadway St.).

Charlotte Harbor Coast

The best of Charlotte Harbor lies in its hidden-from-the-spotlight barrier islands. **Manasota Key** and **Englewood Beach** boast sunny beaches flecked with sharks' teeth. For a unique and nature-intensive lodging experience, book at **Manasota Key Club** (941-383-8821 or 800-237-8821; 301 Gulf of Mexico Dr., P.O. Box 15000, Longboat Key 34228), a long-standing beach resort with accommodations from rustic to lavish.

On Gasparilla Island, **Boca Grande** supplies a full day of beaching, shopping, and dining. Have lunch or dinner at **Harper's** at Miller's Marina (941-964-0232; Harbor Dr.), and watch the luxury yachts while you savor something from the sea, inventive and well crafted. For a different flavor of island life, take a room at the old, gracious **Gasparilla Inn** (941-964-2201; 5th St. & Palm St., Boca Grande 33921), as the Vanderbilts and Du Ponts have since 1912.

Explore the extensive aquatic preserves of Charlotte Harbor aboard a catamaran or kayak with **Grand Tours** (941-697-8825 or 941-964-0000 from Boca Grande; 11 Fishery Rd., Placida). For an island wilderness adventure that returns you to the days of Florida cow-hunting, ride the bouncy swamp buggy through a modern-day cattle and alligator ranch at **Babcock Wilderness Adventures** (941-489-3911 or 800-500-5583; Rte. 31, Punta Gorda).

Island Coast

Fort Myers' finest attraction, the **Thomas Edison Winter Estate and Ford Home** (941-334-3614; 2350-2400 McGregor Blvd.), peeks into the times and genius of America's greatest inventors, who lived side by side in winter months. Dine Victorian in the two historic homes that make up **The Veranda** (941-332-2065; 2122 Second St.), which specializes in southern charm and fine cuisine.

Much of what's special about the Island Coast has to do with what's wild. Half of Sanibel Island is devoted to the **J.N. "Ding" Darling National Wildlife Refuge** (941-472-1100; 1 Wildlife Dr., off Sanibel-Captiva Rd.), home to alligators, roseate spoonbills, manatees, river otters, and bobcats. The best way to see it is by canoe or kayak from **Tarpon Bay Recreation** (941-472-8900; 900 Tarpon Bay Rd.). For sea kayaking instruction and a guided tour of local waters, see **Wild Side Adventures** (941-395-2925; McCarthy's Marina, 15041 Captiva Dr., Captiva Island).

Sanibel's beaches are renowned for their bountiful shells and minimal impact on nature's primeval beauty. Most natural and secluded is **Bowman's Beach** (Bowman's Beach Rd. off Sanibel-Captiva Rd.). To find the utmost in remote beaches, rent a boat or hop a charter to unbridged **LaCosta Island** and **Upper Captiva Island**, where state parks preserve slices of Old Florida.

For lively beaching, follow **Route 865** through Estero Island's Fort Myers Beach and down along lovely, undeveloped Lover's Key en route to Bonita Beach. On the way you'll pass bustling resort scenes and quiet island vistas.

South Coast

To explore the highbrow face of Naples and its environs, stop for after-noon tea at **The Ritz-Carlton** (941-598-3300 or 800-241-3333; 2 Vanderbilt Beach Rd., Naples 34108) and take in a concert and gallery stroll at the

Naples Philharmonic (941-597-1900 or 800-597-1900; 5833 Pelican Bay Blvd.). Downtown's **Fifth Avenue South** evolves magnificently into a fashionable shopping and sidewalk dining district. Try **Zoe's** (941-261-1221; 720 Fifth Ave. S.) for an example of the latest in Naples' cutting-edge chic.

To really have experienced Naples, you must do sunset at the **Naples Pier** (12th. Ave. S.). It's a nightly ritual for fishermen, strollers, lovers, and pelicans. By day the pier is the center of activity along a beach that stretches for miles.

My favorite part of Marco Island is **Goodland**. A little fishing village on pause, it serves fresh seafood and country fun in its restaurants and introduces the unruly flavor of **Ten Thousand Islands** and the **Florida Everglades.**

Everglades City is headquarters for tours that explore this labyrinthine land down under. **Everglades National Park** (941-695-2591 or FL 800-445-7724; Everglades Ranger Station, Everglades City) has a base here, conducts boat tours, and rents canoes for launching into the 98-mile **Wilderness Trail**. For the equally curious but less adventurous, **Majestic Tours** (941-695-2777; Everglades City) leads intimate, highly informative forays into the mangrove world of alligators, panthers, dolphins, and ospreys.

Index

LODGING BY PRICE CODE

RESTAURANTS BY PRICE CODE

RESTAURANTS BY CUISINE

About the Author

Karen T. Bartlett

Chelle Koster Walton came to visit a friend on Sanibel Island in 1981. She's still there. As a writer, she specializes in Florida and Caribbean travel, food, and culture. She is author of *Florida*, a Fodor Compass America guide; *Fun for the Family in Florida*; Frommer's *Best Beach Vacations: Florida*; *Adventure Guide to Florida's West Coast*; and *Florida Island Hopping: The West Coast*. Her *Caribbean Ways: A Cultural Guide* and *Hidden Florida* have both won awards in Lowell Thomas Travel Journalism competitions for Best Guidebook. She has coauthored *Florida*, Frommer's America on Wheels series guide, and Reader's Digest's *Wild Kingdoms*. A member of the Society of American Travel Writers, Walton is contributing editor for *Caribbean Travel and Life*. Her work has appeared in, among other publications, Disney Online's *Family.Com*, the *Miami Herald*, *Endless Vacation*, and the *New York Post*.